Praise for SELF-PRINTED:
The Sane Person's Guide to Self-Publishing

"An exceptional breath of realism, real knowledge and hard experience — don't dream of self-publishing your book without it. This is the self-publishing guide to read if you actually care about the quality of your writing and your readers." — *Nicola Morgan, award-winning author of 90 books — including the Carnegie-nominated* Wasted *and* Write to be Published — *and the blog Help! I Need a Publisher!*

"The best thing about Catherine is that she not only lives the dream, but offers you a stepladder up to join her. The advice she gives is utterly practical — because she's done what she describes — and the whole [book] is suffused with humour. I am a fan." — *Alison Baverstock, author of* Is There a Book in You…? *and senior lecturer on the Publishing MA at Kingston University (UK)*

"It's authoritative, engaging, and, like [Catherine's] blog, caffeinated. If you're thinking of self-publishing and you want to give your book a great start in life, get *Self-Printed*." — *Roz Morris, author of* Nail Your Novel: Why Writers Abandon Books and How You Can Draft, Fix and Finish With Confidence

"Catherine explains clearly and concisely how to make self-publishing work for you. Laugh-out-loud funny in places, this book covers everything you need to know to make your book a success."
— *Vanessa O'Loughlin, founder of Writing.ie*

"This book is almost frighteningly readable. Catherine's writing style … is so captivating and comical I literally had a hard time putting the book down. [If] you are tired of the "How to Make Millions Publishing Your Own Books While Sticking It To the Big 6 Publishers" manuals, and are ready for some real-world, real-life advice that will leave you chuckling, you definitely should read this book."
— *Michael Harling, author of* Postcards from Across the Pond

"The BEST book on self-publishing … Seriously, GET THIS NOW!"
— *David Wright, co-author of the bestselling* Yesterday's Gone *series*

ISBN-10: 1478385545
ISBN-13: 978-1478385547

Catherine Ryan Howard © 2010–2012
This second edition published September 2012.

DISCLAIMER:
This book's aim is to serve as a guide for authors intending to make work available for sale through the Print-On-Demand service CreateSpace, Amazon's Kindle Direct Platform and the e-book publishing website Smashwords. It is not intended to be a comprehensive guide to self-publishing, a guide to self-publishing in any other form or a replacement for legal or other expert advice. While every effort has been made to ensure that the information in this book is accurate and up to date, mistakes or inaccuracies may well exist. The author accepts no liability or responsibility for any loss or damage caused, or thought to be caused, by following the advice in this book and recommends that you use it only in conjunction with other trusted sources and information. All foreign currency exchange calculations are approximate and were conducted in July 2012.

Follow Catherine on Twitter
@cathryanhoward
www.catherineryanhoward.com

SELF-PRINTED

The Sane Person's Guide to Self-Publishing

*How to Use Digital Self-Publishing, Social Media and Common Sense
to Start Earning A Living as a Writer Through
E-Books and POD Paperbacks
(And Do It Without Ever Saying "Gatekeepers"
or Shouting "Down With The Big Six!")*

Also by Catherine Ryan Howard:

Mousetrapped:
A Year and A Bit in Orlando, Florida

More Mousetrapped:
A Little Bit More From That Year and A Bit*

Backpacked:
A Reluctant Trip Across Central America

The Best of Catherine, Caffeinated:
Caffeine-Infused Self-Publishing Advice*

Travelled:
10 Tales About Not Staying at Home
(coming soon)

*e-book edition only

SELF-PRINTED
The Sane Person's Guide to Self-Publishing

PART 3: Publishing An E-book

PART 4: Publishing Your Paperback

PART 5: Selling Self-Published Books

Part 6: Being A Self-Published Author

SELF-PRINTED
The Sane Person's Guide to Self-Publishing

INTRODUCTION
The Whose Guide To What Now?

Welcome to *Self-Printed: The Sane Person's Guide to Self-Publishing.*

Perhaps I should start by explaining the thinking behind that title, and to do that I need to explain how and why I came to write this book.

My favourite piece of writing advice has always been "write the book you want to read" but in this case it was more like "write the book you *need* to read", or "write the book you'd need to read if you could find a quantum physicist to build you a time machine that would allow you to go back three years, to *before* you self-published, and thus instead of having to figure all of this out for yourself—and figure out some of it by making *very* costly mistakes—you could have read this book and got it right first time."

Writing things I could've done with reading once upon a time has become a bit of a theme with me. My first book, *Mousetrapped: A Year and A Bit in Orlando, Florida*, started life as the travel memoir I wish I'd read *before* I moved to Florida without a driver's licence, anywhere to live or indeed the first clue of what lay in store for me on the other side of the Atlantic.

It was back in early 2010 that I found myself and *Mousetrapped* at a crossroads. It had got the same rejection everywhere it went: we like it, but there's no market for it. Publishing is a business, and it would be bad business to spend money editing, designing, printing, distributing and promoting a book no one thought would sell in significant amounts. Only a publisher who didn't quite know what they were doing would disagree and so I realised that continuing to submit it would be just like repeatedly hitting my head off a wall, only more painful.

It was time to take the hint. But what to do next, if anything?
As I saw it, my options were these:

- Never mention it again, despite having told every *single* person I'd ever met that I was writing it
- Recycle the 400 sheets of paper it was printed on (double-spaced 12 point Courier, of course) and try to forget about it

- Have it bound in leather, leave it on the coffee table and tell guests — whether they asked about it or not — that it was my travel memoir, saying it in a French accent so that it sounded all posh, i.e. *mem-wah*
- Use a Print-On-Demand (POD) service to, um, print a few copies on demand, so that I could attempt to sell it to the small group of people I knew would be at least *mildly* interested in buying it: my parents, my friends who were in it, my friends who'd think they were going to be in it, a handful of Disney fans, a handful of NASA fans and the 30 or so people I'd squeeze into the acknowledgements.

I couldn't face having to tell everyone that a summer locked in my bedroom and a credit card melted by a new computer had come to nothing. And since I didn't particularly care about the planet and my French wasn't great, that left just one option: using a POD service to print and sell copies of *Mousetrapped*.

(E-books, I should say at this point, were not yet on my radar. They would be soon enough.)

But that would be *self-publishing*, and for years I had been a certifiable self-publishing snob. I mean, who in their right mind would publish their *own book*? Only losers who knew nothing at all about getting published, the publishing industry or writing books, in my pre-2010 opinion. Every week the local newspaper would highlight the latest delusional scribe to bind together a few copies of their book ("It's called *The Loxatocki Protocol*," the author would be quoted as saying. "It's historical lesbian romance meets dystopian science fiction meets *P.S. I Love You*. I wrote it last Friday afternoon and my little brother made the cover on his Etch A Sketch. I've just sent a review copy of it to Janet Maslin at *The New York Times*...") and my insides would contract at the sheer mortification of it all.

So how could I, the girl who by now had spent ten years of her life reading books like *500 Pages About How The Publishing Industry Works Even Though You'll Never Need to Know Unless You Stop Reading Books Like This and Write Your Own Instead*, resort to self-publishing? And if I did, how could I differentiate myself from the likes of *The Loxatocki Protocol*?

Well, since I'd recklessly quit my job six months before to devote myself full-time to writing and my drug of choice was Nespresso coffee capsules (nearly €5 for a pack of 10!), I came around to the idea of self-publishing pretty *quick*, let me tell you. As for differentiating myself, I decided the only way was to be unfailingly, unforgivingly, *brutally* realistic.

I would acknowledge that none of the following things were going to happen to me as a result of self-publishing: getting rich, getting famous, getting "properly" published, getting skinny, getting to meet Josh Groban, getting a condo with pool access somewhere in or near the town of

Celebration, Florida, where I could live out my days drinking mojitos and reading Apollo astronaut biographies on my iPad.

Or, it being the *Sunshine* State, perhaps on my Kindle.

If anything, my Realistic Self reasoned, this endeavour was going to *cost* me money, not make it. But I soon discovered that being realistic made me a rare creature in the dark and murky world of POD publishing — or so it seemed as I trawled through the information on Lulu and CreateSpace, two of the most popular POD sites. I ventured into their community forums, where the decorative scheme was five shades of Crazy, the distinct scent of *eau de delusional* hung in the air and everyone seemed to be complaining, confused, or both.

One guy was particularly agitated because his 350,000-word novel about the adventures of Rafellius the Great, a talking purple unicorn who lives between this world and the next and has a penchant for Bird's Eye fish fingers, had only sold one copy in six months, which was a shock to him even though all he'd done was upload his files and click "Publish". He was upset that, first of all, Lulu, the *distributor*, wasn't doing anything to sell his book (!) and second of all, that they'd as yet failed to pay him the $2.87 that was rightfully his.

Then there was this:

"I am very apprehensive. I am frightened. I wrote my first children's book five years ago and I still haven't figured out how to publish it. I hope this works. I don't have illustrations. My book is one of the best books I have ever read. I have read over 3,000 children's books."

Indeed.

In the midst of all this there appeared to be one or two sane people helpfully and patiently dispensing advice to the likes of Miss Apprehensive, but other than them I felt quite alone, what with my realistic expectations and, dare I say, modesty. I was embarrassed, almost apologetic, about self-publishing my book. How did I fit in with these people who clearly thought that the one thing the world was waiting for was a bound copy of their copyright-infringing *LOST* fan fiction complete with a cover that looked like several small house-pets had enthusiastically vomited on it?

The answer was that I didn't.

I had yet to learn anything significant about the whole POD world, but thanks to *500 Pages About How The Publishing Industry Works Even Though You'll Never Need to Know Unless You Stop Reading Books Like This and Write Your Own Instead*, I knew enough about the book and publishing worlds to know that all clicking the "Publish" button would do for me was bind a copy of the PDF document I'd submitted to the POD service, slap the cover I'd designed on it (mistakes and all), list the book for sale in the darkest corner of Amazon.com and deduct $14.49 from my credit card for the privilege. It wouldn't benefit from the work of a graphic designer, an editor or a typesetter. Heck, the page numbers might not even be in sequence. And while it would be available on Amazon, it wouldn't grace the shelves of any bookstore, chain or independent — it *couldn't* because the wholesale cost per unit of it was way too high for anyone to consider stocking it. I thought my book was certainly a better read than the back of a cereal box but I didn't expect to sell more copies than I could find people easily bribed with offers of chocolate. Without the backing of a marketing department or money to spend on advertising, very few people might end up even knowing my book *existed*, let alone handing over money in exchange for a copy of it. And it was about me, Disney World, Florida, NASA, the Space Shuttle, Bruce Willis, humidity-challenged hair and the Ebola virus — there wasn't a talking purple unicorn in sight.

In short, I wasn't publishing at all. I was just getting copies printed and from there, we'd have to see where it could go, if it could go anywhere.

So I wasn't self-publishing. I was self-*printing*.

Now I just had to figure out *how*.

Beyond the community forums, I struggled to find self-publishing advice that didn't come served with a generous helping of "Traditional publishing is dead!" propaganda, or that wasn't seemingly written by someone with a literary agent-shaped chip on their shoulder who could clearly benefit from attending some kind of Resolving Your Bitterness self-improvement course.

It just all seemed so *angry*. There was talk of evil "gatekeepers" and a shadowy group known only as "The Big Six." (I was surprised to learn that these weren't in fact horned demons but merely literary agents and major US publishing houses.) These people weren't just self-publishing their novels or trying to sell e-books; they were sticking it to The Man, man! They were going to prove that their book was as good as anything Stephen King could produce. They were gonna show 'em all, just you wait and see. As soon as their novella, *Complicated Stuff That Happens in Space During a Bleak Time in the Future*, hit No. 1 on the *Sunday Times* bestseller list, they were going to send a reply to every one of the 1,532 rejection letters the book had received, along with a photocopy of the bestseller list and a crayon drawing of a middle finger.

Yeah. Take *that*, Big Publishing. Take THAT.

In the section of the self-publishing world I'd stumbled into, it seemed that reality was as rare a commodity as it is in so-called reality TV. One website advised would-be self-publishers that writing a book actually wasn't all that hard — if you could *say* it, they claimed, then you could *write* it. Another said that agents, as a rule, never responded to unsolicited submissions and only used their slush piles for kindling. And don't bother pursuing your dreams of traditional publication—publishing is like a business class lounge us civilians aren't allowed into, and anyway all publishers want to do to aspiring writers is point and laugh. *Hard*. A parade of the usual Bad Writing, Big Selling suspects (Dan Brown, James Patterson, Stephanie Meyer) were regularly dragged out to prove the point that Big Publishing wouldn't know good writing if it set up camp on their desk, as were famous stories of missed opportunities, such as J.K. Rowling repeatedly being told there was no money to be made in children's books while she and Harry Potter were getting rejected up the wazoo. (These days, they'd be citing E.L. James.) And everyone seemed to think that by uploading a file to a website today, their book was going to be stacked in a pile just inside the door of every bookstore in the world no later than Tuesday.

I just wanted to self-publish. (Or rather, self-*print*.) I wasn't angry, or bitter, or on a list of Persons Unwelcome at the security desk of a major publishing house. Yes, my book had been rejected, but I wasn't taking it personally. I was also brutally realistic and knew that by self-publishing a paperback with a Print-On-Demand site like CreateSpace and e-books with Amazon and Smashwords, I was *not* going to get rich, famous, or rich *and* famous. In all likelihood, I'd be lucky just to recoup the cost of the coffee I'd have to drink to get me through the formatting process. And I knew that despite what the Self-Publishing Evangelists claimed with their James Patterson arguments and the like, most self-published books were just not up to scratch. This was just a fact, and a fact that could be easily proven with a quick trip to the store on any self-publishing service's website. While I would try to ensure that mine was as not-rubbish as it could possibly be, I wasn't under any illusions that it wouldn't get picked out as the impostor amongst a line-up of "properly" published books.

Where was the information for people like *me*?

I couldn't find it. So just as I had written *Mousetrapped*, the travel memoir I'd needed to read before I moved to Florida, I started posting about self-publishing on my blog, making it the blog I'd needed to read before I started this whole self-publishing adventure. Whenever I collected some information, I'd run it through a Delusions of Grandeur filter, spray it with common sense, and then post it under the heading "self-printing." The posts became popular, and soon I was getting e-mails from other would-be self-publishers—or self-*printers*—asking for the answers to questions I hadn't covered, or that they couldn't find in the ever-growing collection of posts I'd written on the subject.

Mousetrapped was out a year in March 2011 and my thoughts turned to writing its sequel. Before I got started on *that* though, I wanted to do something for the new visitors to my blog who perhaps didn't have the time or inclination to trawl through what was now more than a year's worth of posts. Maybe I could consolidate them into a downloadable document, and copy and paste them in chronological order. A PDF maybe? A little e-book? I sat down one weekend to start doing just that, but soon realised that there was so much more about this whole self-printing business than just the stuff I'd blogged about.

So I started writing a guide, from scratch. That guide became this book, the guide that—yes, you've guessed it—I wished I could have read three years ago, back when I didn't know what POD meant, or what a Kindle was, or anything about the migraine-inducing horror that is formatting your manuscript for e-book conversion.

Self-Printed became my best-reviewed book and if I'm honest, it's also my personal favourite of the books I've released. Let's not dwell on what this says about my *other* books, okay? Moving quickly along... Now, a little over a year later, I'm releasing a second edition, fully updated (thanks, self-publishing world, for changing something every damn day of the week), fully revised (because with an added year of experience, I've actually changed my mind about what works and what doesn't; controversial!) and even expanded by a few thousand words (because things like KDP Select didn't even *exist* a year ago).

I hope you find it useful. Or at least, don't feel the need to request a refund.

Before we proceed, there are a few things I need to tell you, some things about me and some things about this guide.

The first thing about me is that in the self-publishing world, I'm small fry. Yes, I sold 4,000 copies in a year (and another 7,000 copies or so since) of a non-fiction book about a strange collection of things, a book that agents and publishers assured me had no market—and I did it without spending any money on marketing or promotion—but if you've been within spitting distance of the internet lately, you'll know that there are self-published e-book authors selling 4,000 copies of their book every *weekend*. So why would you want a self-publishing guide written by someone like me, if there are thousands of other writers out there selling a lot more books?

Perhaps you've heard of Amanda Hocking, a writer who made a few million dollars from her self-published books and subsequently signed a seven-figure deal with a major publishing house. Her success has been truly amazing, and utterly deserved. But there's only one Amanda Hocking and if there's ever another one, the odds are you *won't* be it. On the other hand, you have *every* chance of being the next me or someone like me: a writer who has used self-publishing to build an author platform, find a readership and start to earn a living from their writing, maybe even enough to enable them to do it full-time. It's not impossible. It's *achievable.* So instead of reading this book and thinking, "That's great for her, but this couldn't happen for *me*", you can read it and think, "What am I going to spend my first royalty cheque on?"

(Tip: I could do with some Nespresso capsules.)

The second thing about me is that I have very strong views on self-publishing, namely that we *shouldn't* have very strong views on self-publishing. You know when you're watching *Dragon's Den* and you see someone pitch an idea for a problem that doesn't exist, like the guy who wanted to change the traffic light system even though (a) the existing system works fine and (b) the Road Safety Authority had told him it was the most dangerous thing they'd ever seen? And you know how, watching it, you marvel at the mind-boggling *pointlessness* of it? Well, that's how I feel whenever someone brings up the so-called self-publishing versus traditional publishing "debate." Or when an author paints Amazon as the Big, Mean Capitalist Machine while, at the same time, happily collecting royalty cheques from them. Or when self-publishing evangelists use things like Stockholm Syndrome or the Irish potato famine as analogies for the publishing industry.

It makes me want to scream, "It's just books, people. BOOKS!"

If you think self-publishing is the first step in some sort of anti-establishment uprising, you are, of course, entitled to your opinion. And you might want to take a Xanax. But you should stop reading this right now, because this isn't the book for you. This book is for people who know that we're just talking about *books,* and *writing,* and *being authors.* (And coffee and Josh Groban, occasionally.) We're not interested in sticking it to The Man, proving something to the people who rejected us or coming up with new and even more inappropriate ways to describe the publishing industry.

Now needless to say, selling a million copies of a book that got rejected all over town would certainly bring on a case of the Warm and Fuzzies, but that's not our goal. Our goal is to self-publish our book well, build an audience for our work and, potentially, make a living (or at least, coffee money) from this endeavour.

The final thing about me is that I'm a *little* bit bossy. Well, okay, I'm a *lot* bossy. And if the people who sign up for new Gmail accounts just so they can send me abusive e-mail anonymously are anything to go by, chances are that there will come a time when you and I do not agree, and you may feel a ripple of anger, bitterness or resentment (or all three) when I tell you things like "don't put Comic Sans within three feet of your book" or "Amazon Customer Reviews only matter in *volume.*"

But the fact of the matter is that I'm not here to make suggestions. This book isn't called *If You're Going to Self-Publish, Here are Some Things I*

Think You Should Potentially Maybe Do, You Know, If You Want To, Or Whatever. I've seen what works and what doesn't. I'm a self-published author, but I'm also a reader who buys a frightening amount of books on a weekly basis, so I also know what sells books to readers and what makes their eyes glaze over with disinterest and boredom.

"But," you'll cry, "what about that guy who not only put Comic Sans on his cover, but put the *entire text* into it as well? He sold ten million copies of his book *yesterday*. What do you know, Miss Four Thousand in a Year, eh?!" There are exceptions to *every single rule*, yes, but it's not helpful to dwell on them, or worse yet, model yourself on them. For instance, if you knew a writer who had just signed a six-figure deal after accidentally wrapping her son's ham sandwich in a page from her synopsis, a ham sandwich that her son then left in his desk at school over the Easter holidays, a desk that started to smell so much that the caretaker came to investigate, a caretaker who happened to read the synopsis page and think it might be something important, the synopsis page that he subsequently showed to his daughter, his daughter who was interning for a major literary agency and was desperate to prove herself, a major literary agency where they took things like synopsis sandwich wrappers seriously, from where an agent called your writer friend a week later to give her the good news: a six-figure, three-book deal, foreign rights sold in ten countries and a potential movie deal, what would you do? Would you continue to send out query letters, or would you start wrapping your children's sandwiches in Chapter Ones?

We shouldn't aspire to be an exception to the rule when, chances are, *we won't be it.* We should do what *works*. And I'm going to tell you what works, and works with little other than common sense, time and imagination. (Rest assured, *Self-Printed* is Jedi mindtrick, cerebral sales strategy and spamtastic tactics free. Also, I'm going to share with you all *my* ideas so you don't even have to use the imagination bit, if you like.) I may come off as a little bossy while I'm doing it, but you're just going to have to deal with it. Because yes, I'm here to hold your hand through this process, but that leaves my other hand free to slap you should I catch you putting Comic Sans anywhere near your book.

Now, on to things about this *guide*.

I can't stand it when I pick up a reference book and there's a section called "How to Use This Book" that takes the time to explain to me that I should read the book, from start to finish, without skipping bits. (Um... oh-*kay*. And should I also, like, read from left to right? Because I wasn't sure.) One time I opened a "how to" book that warned me against highlighting text because, according to the author, there was *so* much useful information in it I'd just end up highlighting the whole thing.

Cue me deciding not to bother even *reading* it.

My point is, I don't need to tell you how to use this book. You had the good sense to buy it—or borrow it, at least—so my confidence in your ability to figure out how to use it is high.

But I will say this: find out about *every*thing before you do *any*thing. The information in this book isn't presented in the exact order you'll need it because if it was, the sections would be all over the place. For example, how we'll sell our books comes after the bit about how we publish them, even though a good chunk of our promotional efforts will take place *before* the book comes out. But it makes more sense to keep all the publishing bits together, rather than dividing them into two and separating them with a chapter about getting reviews.

Successful self-publishing is all about seeing the big picture, and you won't get to see that until you've read the whole book. So please don't be tempted to publish your paperback when you get halfway down page 142 of this book, or drop everything to create your blog somewhere around page 213. Just *wait*. Wait. Things will be *so* much easier then. Trust me.

So that was the first thing about this guide. On to the second:

One of my favourite "how to write books" books is *Wannabe a Writer?* by Jane Wenham-Jones. I *love* that book. It makes me laugh, it motivates me to write and it's full of practical advice too. (It also makes me want to drink wine, even though I hate the stuff.) It's essentially the wine-soaked tale of how Jane became a writer herself, spiced with plenty of hilarious anecdotes and insider tips about living the writing life. That's what makes it great.

Which is why I was a tad confused to read a review of it that lambasted (oooh, good word!) Jane for repeatedly mentioning her own books. "It's all about *her*," the reviewer spat, "and what *she* did with *her* books." And I was practically nauseous to read a review of the first edition of *this* book that said—and I quote/copy and paste—"Good information, but you really have to wade through a lot of stories ... about what the author did or did not do on her book ... to get to it."

Um, *yeah*. That's, like, the whole idea?

I have only self-published my own books. (The clue there is in the term *self-publishing*.) Therefore I'll be mentioning them and what I did with them throughout this book. The stories about what I did—or did not do—with them *is* "it." Apologies in advance, but I'm not quite sure how else I would do this, especially since I can only presume that you'd like to read a self-publishing guide by someone who has actually *done* it. Right?

The third and final thing about this guide—and the final point of this introduction—is that when I say "self-publishing" I mean:

- publishing an e-book with Amazon Kindle Direct Publishing
- publishing an e-book with Smashwords

- publishing a Print-on-Demand paperback book* with CreateSpace
- selling copies of them.

And I'll be saying "self-publishing" because that's the term we're all familiar with, but you'll know I mean "self-*printing*."

I won't be telling you anything about other types of self-publishing or how to use the other services, because this book is about how *I* did it, and how I did it was the cheapest and simplest way possible to get a book out into the world without said book being a total embarrassment, but in fact with said book looking pretty good, if I do say so myself.

And *doing* pretty good as well.

And what I *will* be telling you is everything you need to know to do just that.

A book that consists mainly of text. Illustrated books or other books that require interior pages in colour are not best produced by a POD service as the expense is prohibitive.

PART 1:
Preparing To Self-Publish

A Whole New World

Let's start with the good news: now is a *great* time to self-publish a book.

It wasn't that long ago that the self-published author cut a lonely figure on the outskirts of the publishing world, forced to drink juice from a plastic cup at the kids' table while the real writers sipped champagne from crystal flutes at the adults' one. He had self-published, most likely, for one of two reasons: either his writing room's ceiling was resting on columns of stacked rejection letters, or he had decided to circumvent the entire try-to-get-published process completely. Maybe he was even unaware that there was one. He'd paid thousands for hundreds of copies of his book, most of which were now gathering dust in boxes beneath his stairs because, even if he'd managed to avoid the pitfalls of bad cover design, lazy editing and prohibitively expensive unit costs, he *still* found himself with a major credibility problem. The term *self-published* was synonymous with *not good enough to get published,* and so convincing anyone of his book's merit, beyond his circle of obligated family and friends, had proved near impossible.

But it was the *logistics* of selling books that had ultimately doomed him to fail.

He might have managed to convince his local bookshops to stock a few copies — the independent ones, anyway; the chains rarely empowered their store managers to make stock decisions — but getting his book on the shelves of stores anywhere else would require the help of a distributor. If by some miracle a distribution company agreed to take his book on, they'd require thousands of copies of it and, as they'd sell them to bookshops on a sale-or-return basis, our self-publisher could end up getting them all back. *If* they sold them to bookshops, because with limited shelf space, a high unit price and competition from the world's bestselling and most lauded authors, it would be unlikely that any stores would bother to stock self-published works by writers unknown and, as yet, unproved. They'd know that there wouldn't be any marketing campaign or publicity push gently nudging customers into the store to buy it and that, in fact, the book was sure to be ignored by all print media, book reviewers and literary prize judging panels.

But let's pretend our self-publisher caught a break and won a few sales in store. Out of the retail price comes the bookshop's cut, the distributor's cut *and* the cost of the book to the self-publisher himself, i.e. the manufacturing cost, leaving just a few pennies to serve as profit. With the amount of time and effort it's taken to organise the book's distribution — the research, the paperwork, delivering the books to the warehouse, etc. — our self-published author isn't sure if it's all worth it.

Especially since he won't receive payment until *months* after the sales of his book have taken place.

And what of the rest of the world? What of the readers who don't live within driving distance of our self-published author or one of the stores stocking his book? What of readers in other countries? Well, our self-published author could, theoretically, sell his books directly from a website or blog, but that would bring about a whole new headache of processing credit card payments, packing and shipping books, and always keeping enough copies in stock to fulfil orders even when you've no guarantee that any will come in at all. And how are people going to find out that the book is for sale on his website? How is he going to convince them to buy it if and when they do? He could sell his book on Amazon, but with his choices being either to set himself up as a "Marketplace Seller" or getting his distributor to sell his book there on his behalf, it's a pain not too dissimilar to the one brought on by his bookshop experience. And again, how does he tell the world about it in the first place? How does he convince strangers to shell out more on his book than they would on a traditionally published book of the same length? How does he persuade them to take a chance on *The Loxatocki Protocol*?

The short answer is that he *doesn't*. And so, a few months or maybe a year in, our self-published author is left with no choice but to accept the failure of his book, to write off the thousands he invested in publishing it and to flog all the copies he has left at Sunday morning car boot sales for a fraction of what it cost him to print them.

I mean, *really*. Who'd have self-published?

Today—that is a whole, um, five years later—the landscape is completely different. Unrecognisable, even. And in this new world of digital self-publishing, *The Loxatocki Protocol* could have every chance of finding a readership and *earning* our self-published author friend some money, instead of just costing him lots of it.

(Although probably not with *that* title...).

In this new world, our self-published author begins by spending a lot less. Two things require investment: editing, which is relatively expensive, and a cover design, which doesn't have to be. (A survey of self-publishers in 2012 found that on average, they spend around $500 getting a book to market. I think this is a bit low, and that $1,000 would be more like it. We'll talk money matters later.) He finds a professional editor and cover designer online and while they get to work, he starts building anticipation about the release of his book on social networks, his blog, forums, etc. Once both book and cover are ready, he registers for free accounts on sites like Amazon Kindle Direct Publishing (KDP) and CreateSpace, and uploads his files. Within twelve hours, a Kindle edition of his book is for sale in most parts of the Western World. Within a week, a paperback is too. (And whenever one of these paperbacks is sold, it's not from any stock he's had to provide; CreateSpace only print a copy when a copy is ordered, Amazon ship it, both companies take their cut and our self-published author friend gets the rest—he can sell paperback editions of his book on a global scale without ever holding a copy in his hands, if he likes.) On Amazon, his book virtually sits next to work by the world's bestselling authors, and gets treated no differently. Having no manufacturing costs to cover with his e-book price tag means he can use low prices to entice new readers to try his work, and programs like KDP Select enable him to promote it as free for limited periods, bringing him thousands of downloads and among them, hopefully, new fans as well. Eventually the Amazon Customer Reviews start rolling in, backed up by reviews from book bloggers he's sent digital copies to. Along with the blog posts, tweets and Facebook updates that serve as the coal in the steam engine of his promotion train (and with each purchase making his book more visible on sites like Amazon), sales begin to trickle in, then they pick up, and then they start to steadily *pour* in. All our self-published author friend need do is lodge the royalty cheques he receives once a month and start working on his next book.

Now yes, that is a *very* rosy picture of self-publishing that I've painted there. But then I did say I'd start with the good news, didn't I?

Self-publishing is breaking into the mainstream. Readers who would never in a million years have considered trying a self-published book are now enticed to do so by cheap e-books, free promotions or online connections such as reading and liking the author's blog. Self-publishers can make their books available to readers all over the world, and do it without spending thousands or even leaving their house. Self-published titles sit atop bestseller lists, and some of the authors of them have gone on to sign six- and seven-figure traditional deals. Going it alone is now a badge of honour in some circles when, not long ago, it was evidence of stubborn delusion in all of them.

Self-publishing, dare I say it, has become *cool*.

(Gasp!)

We've pulled up a chair to the adults' table and we're holding out our own flute for some champagne. But it's not *all* good news. Some of our tablemates are eyeing us suspiciously, and the waiter is hesitating as he tries to work out whether or not we're gatecrashers who need to be asked to leave. It's not their fault; we can't blame them. Because the last self-publisher they invited to join them got messy drunk, threw food and accused the literary agent sitting next to him of moving all unsolicited submissions directly to the recycle bin and not being able to identify good writing if it smacked him across the face.

And then, he smacked him across the face.

My point is, this new self-publishing world is amazing. It's wonderful. It's practically *glistening* with opportunity for authors at all stages of their careers. But not all of us are treating it with the respect it deserves. Not all of us are behaving ourselves. And whenever one of us behaves badly — be it by releasing a book they only started a week ago, or attempting their own Microsoft Paint cover design, or spamming other authors with "Buy my book!" tweets and e-mails — it affects *all* of us.

To quote Voltaire — and *Spiderman* — with great power comes great responsibility. And so before you attempt to self-publish, you should ask yourself if you're *ready* for this responsibility, and if you're willing to act in accordance with it. Because I'm not here to help you bang out 100,000 words of typing over the weekend only to throw it up on the Kindle store by Monday afternoon. If that's your plan, I'd really rather you didn't bother.

My advice is intended for what I call *The New Self-Publisher*.

The New Self-Publisher is dedicated to the craft of writing. They know that books are not written, but re-written. They take their time. They wouldn't *dream* of putting anything out into the world that hadn't been at least professionally proofread, and ideally copy-edited too. They didn't decide to be a writer yesterday; they've wanted to do this for years. Perhaps they can't remember a time when they *didn't* want to be a writer. Self-publishing is something they've come to after getting tantalisingly close to realising their publication dreams, only to be stopped by a niche market, an overcrowded genre or bad timing. Maybe they even have an agent, or had one. Or perhaps they're a mid-list author with an extensive backlist and no new contract visible on the horizon who wants to take the future of their career into their own hands. Maybe they're a bestselling author who wants to cut out the middle man from here on in.

For them, this isn't an experiment or a project, but a step towards the realisation of their lifelong writerly dreams. They aren't fuelled by bitterness or resentment. They've got professional feedback on their book and so they don't just believe it's good, they *know* it is because unbiased experts have told them so. (And they recognise industry professionals with years of experience in the book world as *experts*.) They're realistic about what they can achieve and professional in their approach. They ensure that their book doesn't look out of place side by side with traditionally published books. They're not just out to get-rich-quick, but their goal is to make a living from their writing. They're in this for the long run. They know that the only way to succeed is to assume the role of an entrepreneur as soon as they've typed "The End", and to treat their book like the product it is. They're willing to get out there and sell their book. They know what that'll take. They appreciate the opportunities this new world brings, and they never take it for granted or abuse it.

They don't get into long, rambling arguments about the future of publishing, use the word *gatekeepers* or publicly attack reviewers who didn't like their book with four-letter words. They don't do anything to bring the side down. On the contrary, the self-publishing world is delighted to have them.

The New Self-Publisher can be summed up with one of my favourite quotes about self-publishing, which comes from my blogging friend Roz Morris, author of *Nail Your Novel: Why Writers Abandon Books and How To Draft, Fix and Finish with Confidence* and *My Memories of a Future Life*:

"Self-publishing isn't for authors who couldn't get published. It's for authors who *could*."

In other words, self-publishing is for:

- Books that under different circumstances would've *got* published
- Authors that any publishing house or agent would be happy to have.

Roz herself has an example of a book that under different circumstances would've got published. *Nail Your Novel* is a fantastically useful book, but it's short—too short to be worth the investment a publishing house would have to cough up in order to print and distribute it. So Roz released it in e-book and POD paperback herself. My own book, *Mousetrapped*, got positive feedback from each of the agents and editors I sent it to, but ultimately they all concluded the same thing: that there just wasn't a market for a book like that. I agreed with them, and I still do. If *Mousetrapped* had got a traditional deal, it would've been published, most likely, in Ireland and the UK. I've only sold the amount I have because I was able to sell it all over world, and so reach all the little pockets of potential readers instead of just the few who live near me on my side of the Atlantic. Talli Roland self-published after finding that her first book, *The Hating Game*, released by a small, independent publisher, sold best in e-book—and sold mainly because of her own promotional efforts. Realising that she could do just as good a job herself, she self-published her follow-up, *Watching Willow Watts*, and has since become a bestselling self-published author. Crime writer Mel Sherratt was represented by a top UK literary agent, but no deal ever materialised. Thinking impressive sales figures might help things along, she self-published *Taunting the Dead*, and only a few months later can say she's sold over 50,000 copies of her book— *herself*. Her self-publishing adventures have been so successful that she's left her agent and self-published a second title, *Somewhere to Hide*. J.A. Konrath famously began to self-publish after traditional publishing success, and today we have everyone from Jackie Collins to J.K. Rowling doing the same.

These writers — and these books — were all *good enough to get published*. They just couldn't make it over hurdles that were unconnected to their quality: a non-standard length, a niche market, an overcrowded market. Self-publishing was an option that enabled the authors themselves to overcome these hurdles and so was a great solution, the perfect Plan B.

From what I've seen, almost all successful self-published authors are great at being authors. I don't mean the writing bit, although they're good at that too. I mean the bits of being an author where you have to *get out there and convince people to buy your book*. Imagine for a minute that you're the publicity director at a major publishing house. You have a debut novel to promote and you're brainstorming ways to get the word out about it. You can try to get the book reviewed in the press, place advertisements, supply bookstores with special displays, but you know that's all a bit hit and miss and it costs a small fortune. What you *really* need is an author who can sail through a radio interview, or give a sparkling performance on a TV talk show; who gives great writing workshops, or is an entertaining public speaker; who is active on social media and motivated to find her own fans; who always carries business cards with her book's cover on them; who gets a bunch of friends together to make a fun book trailer; who sends daily e-mails to the publicity department outlining plans for new (cost-free) ways to promote her book; who is always professional and pleasant, someone you *like* to work with; who doesn't make diva demands, or have unrealistic expectations, or expect everyone else to sell her book while she sits back and relaxes because after all, she *wrote* the bloody thing, didn't she?

Now I'm not saying you can't successfully self-publish without also being able to confidently speak in public. Most writers don't like to, what with us generally being shy, retiring types more comfy in our sweat pants than in our diamonds (or, this being *writers* we're talking about, our cubic-zirconias more like), and most of us won't get the opportunity anyway. Focus on my bigger picture, which is that the self-publisher destined for success is not only one the *self-publishing* world is happy to have, but one any *publishing house* would be happy to have too. (And possibly will be sorry they *don't* have when the self-publisher goes on to sell a gazillion books. Let's hope, anyway.)

Is this you? Are *you* a member of The New Self-Publishing Club? Are you willing to do everything you must to make your book the best it can be, to become an entrepreneur, to devote as much time, energy and imagination as you can spare to get that book selling?

If you are, read on.

If you're not, all this will be is an exercise in losing money, wasting your time and maybe even being humiliated in public about the quality of your work. And there are easy ways. For instance, you could drop this book right now, throw all your cash out the window, watch a few episodes of *I Didn't Know I Was Pregnant* and then run naked down your street, and you'd have basically achieved the same thing.

Don't say you weren't warned.

Why You Need A Good Book—And How To Tell If You Have One

You've probably already formulated the thought, while you were reading the heading.

I need a good book? Why? Just look at 50 Shades of Grey...

As I write this, *50 Shades* has had its third print run in a week, all three instalments are sitting pretty atop every bestseller list and, at last count, E.L. James is banking over a million dollars every seven days. But according to all sources, they're not good books. They aren't written particularly well. And yet they've sold something in the region of ten million copies and look like they're going to be made into movies by the same team that produced the Oscar-winning *The Social Network*. So what am I on about when I say that you need to self-publish a *good* book, when surely the success of *50 Shades* puts paid to that?

We can all name a few authors who have sold millions and millions of copies of their books even though we don't think their books are very good. We can also probably name a few mega-selling authors whose books *no one* thinks are any good. But they're the exceptions to the rule, the *outliers*, and as I said in the introduction, they're not ideal for modelling ourselves on because the odds of the same thing happening to us are one in a million or more. Meanwhile, *most* successful authors write *good* books. I can name maybe three or four very successful self-publishers with "bad" books, but I can name four times as many with books that would easily have been good enough to *get* published. Why not increase your chances of success by making sure that *you've* written a good book too?

And what is the point of releasing a bad book, pray tell? There isn't a single one. Just because you *can* do something doesn't mean that you *should*. The point of books is not just that they were written. And going back to the being an entrepreneur principle, don't forget that your book is your product. Wouldn't you make sure if instead of selling books you were selling, say, light bulbs, that those light bulbs *worked* before you put them on the shelves? Wouldn't you make sure they were good ones? Of course you would, unless you were a chucking-money-down-toilets enthusiast with an advanced degree in shamelessness. And how would you feel if someone else released their crappy book and duped you into paying money for it? I know the first thing *I'd* do is leave an Amazon Customer Review warning everyone else off doing the same and, just like that, your self-publishing career is dead in the water.

There's also the issue of harsh feedback. Everyone gets both good and bad reviews, but for some reason unclear to me, some readers need to leave *baaaad* reviews. These are the kind so filled with spite and hate that you wonder if you wrote a book they didn't like or killed their puppy. If you've never read a *baaaad* review of your work, I can't adequately explain to you how deep inside those words can go. *Eviscerating* is probably the only word that comes close. The worst lines will be forever tattooed on your brain.

And trust me when I say that the only thing worse than reading an acidic, spiteful, hate-filled review of your book that's been posted in public is reading an acidic, spiteful, hate-filled review of your book that's been posted in public and suspecting, deep down, that the reviewer might have a point.

Being a self-published author can be a lonely business, and some days you'll feel like the world is trying to convince you that you just don't have what it takes to be a writer. If you've never had anyone but friends, family and your inner voice telling you that you *do*, you might start to believe them. Soon paranoia begins to seep in; anxiety levels rise. *What if the book really is rubbish? What if all those good reviews are from people I know, just being nice? What if out there in the darkness, everyone who read the book is pointing and laughing at me?* If you have the quiet confidence that your book *is* good, then you can at least lean on it for comfort.

It's also infinitely easier to sell a good book. There'll be glowing reviews and enthusiastic word-of-mouth recommendations, and you can send out copies of your book to bloggers and book reviewers with the confidence that they're likely to like it.

If you dream of writing becoming your career then you should take that into consideration as well; once you release the book, you can't take it back. (You can unpublish it, of course, but you can't scrub the magical interweb of its existence, or take it back from the people who bought it.) You never know: a future interested agent or publisher might be on the verge of offering you a deal, only to google your name and find out about *The Loxatocki Protocol*, and read about how the general consensus was that it was less entertaining than the instruction manual for a microwave oven.

There's also the issue of your self-published author responsibility, of not letting side down. Do you know how hard it is to get someone to read a self-published book? I think self-publishers lose their perspective when it comes to the answer to this question, because of course we're encountering scores of people every day who do read self-published books—*ours*. But in fact, most people don't read them. Most people *won't*.

But let's say that one of us manages to break through and gets someone who never, ever, *ever* wanted to read a self-published book to read a self-published book. Maybe accidentally. If it's a good book then our new convert might buy another one. Maybe mine. But what if it's a terrible book that reads like a Google Translate malfunction? Now this self-publishing toe-dipper has just confirmed what they thought about self-published books all along—that they're not worth it—and you can guarantee that they won't be buying any more. Maybe the book they would've bought next would've been mine.

If the bad one was yours, *you've* cost *me* a sale. You haven't treated this opportunity with the respect it deserves and you've messed it up for more people than just yourself.

Hang on a minute though. What do I mean by a "good" book? Do I mean well written? Because *The Da Vinci Code* isn't exactly Hemingway, but it's still a good book. (Well, *I* think it is.) Some books read well, but the story bores me. Are *they* "good"? What about the fact that trying to get through some Booker Prize nominees is like trawling through muddy sludge, and doing it in the *dark*? And isn't "good" just a matter of opinion? We don't all like the same things. So who's to say whether or not mine is—

Let me stop you there.

We could take up every page in this book debating over what constitutes a good book. But for the purposes of self-publishing, I mean a book that *deserves* to be published, that has earned its price tag and that, going back to the entrepreneur/product analogy, delivers on its promise as a product.

In other words, something that isn't a big stinking pile of poo. Something that isn't 890 pages about your unremarkable life in which nothing exciting ever happened. Something that hasn't just been written for the sake of it, or because the writer has plans to get-rich-quick from flogging 99c copies of it.

When I say "a good book", I simply mean:

- A book written by someone who is proficient in the English language
- A book that other people will likely want to read.

I think we can all agree that *every* book intended for publication should be both those things, can't we?

How To Tell If Your Book Is Good

I don't believe that friends, family or even—tad controversial—fellow members of your writers' group can be trusted to tell you whether or not your book is good. This is because (a) they know you and so are biased, regardless of how much they protest that they're not, (b) they have to deliver the feedback to your face so unless they're horrible people, they'll hold something back and (c) they don't know what they're talking about.

I know. I just said that your friends, family members and writing buddies don't know what they're talking about. How *very* dare I. But they don't. At least not when it comes to the question of whether or not your book is good. Because all they can say is whether or not *they* liked it, whether or not *they* think it's good. They can only offer their *personal opinions*, which is made up of what kinds of books they like, what kind of books they've read and what kind of writing they consider to be worthwhile, and that is all pretty much useless to you. What you need is someone who has learned to set aside their personal preferences and, thanks to training, experience and specialist knowledge, can tell you whether or not your book is good in an objective way. Someone whose *job* it is to do just that.

Someone like, say, a literary agent or an editor.

I think the easiest way to find out whether or not the book you want to self-publish is good is to try to get it published first.

If you've come to self-publishing because trying to get published hasn't worked out, then you'll have already done this. Hooray! If, however, you've written a book that was always intended for self-publication, then you might think this is a bit strange. But I really think it's the only way to get unbiased, informed and reliable feedback, and to get it for *free*.

(Or at least for stamp money.)

Write a query letter, send it out. If you don't know how to write a query letter, go online and find out how. Approach agents and publishers who you know have clients like you or have already published books in the same genre as yours. Your aim is to get a full manuscript request and then see what the agent or editor has to say.

I wouldn't self-publish unless I was at *least* getting full script requests. The first three chapters and a synopsis of *Mousetrapped* went to one agent and five or six Irish publishing houses, and all but two of them requested the full book. (The ones who didn't said they were small publishing houses who had to be certain of sales before releasing a title, and that based on my synopsis, my book's subject matter didn't inspire confidence that it would bring those sales.) The agent and two of the editors sent me detailed e-mail replies, and one editor called me on the phone to discuss it.

They all said the same thing: they enjoyed reading it, they thought it was well written, they thought it was funny (in some places, anyway) but ultimately there was just no market in Ireland for a book like it. If *Mousetrapped* had got nothing but faint photocopied rejection slips addressed to "Author", I wouldn't have self-published it. I would have left it to gather dust in a drawer, or chucked it in the recycle bin.

What happens if someone says "Yes, we'll publish this"? Um, are you kidding me? YOU say yes to THEM! Then you can avoid this whole self-publishing thing altogether and get the money up front. Or maybe reinvest some of your advance in another self-publishing project. Or, if you're hell bent on self-publishing, just say no. Querying agents and editors doesn't tie you to any contractual obligations.

I said this to an author in the self-publishing process once, and his response was along the lines of, "That's a good idea, but there's no point in *me* doing it. I sent out a query letter about my novel to ten agents, and none of them asked to even see some chapters. They all said no. They wouldn't even give it a *chance*. So I'm just going to go ahead and self-publish it."

Hmm.

You know when you watch *American Idol* or *X-Factor* or whatever, and some vocally-challenged warbler squeaks out a bad rendition of Lady Gaga, gets rejected and then cries out, "But you didn't even give me a *chance*!"?

Those two stories are not entirely unrelated.

The thing is, if you can write a good book, you can write a good query letter to advertise that book. If you can't write a good query letter, well, maybe your book is still good, but you're not going to be able to do many of the things you'll need to do if you self-publish (like write your own blurb, write a press release, sell your own book, etc.). The moral of the story: you need to be getting full manuscript requests, or at least have got them of other work in the past.

There are exceptions to this, as there are to every rule. Certain genres — like romance and erotica, for instance — may actually have a better chance of success getting self-published and sold as a 99c e-book than they ever would if they were traditionally published, and sometimes publishers say no to a book simply because there is no precedent, and therefore they can't figure out whether or not it'll make money. A good example of this is the (ultimately self-published) *Chicken Soup for the Soul* series, which was rejected by umpteen publishers. You also need to ensure that you are sending your query letters or opening chapters to *suitable* agents and publishers; all you're going to get is no if you've written science fiction and you're targeting an editor who only deals in chick-lit.

This process takes time—I submitted *Mousetrapped* for over a year—and you may not have that time to spare. Since I released the first edition of this book, I've also come to understand that querying agents and editors in the United States is a much more difficult process than it is on this side of the pond. It may be impossible to get any sort of answer that isn't either a form rejection letter or a yes.

There is a shortcut, but it's not ideal because it costs money and *because* it costs money, this person is never going to say, "This book makes [air-headed soap actress who has turned to novel-writing] look like Shakespeare. It should never see the light of day again." I'm talking about a *manuscript critique service.* You find one, send your book off to them and a professional reads it, assesses it and writes a report. There are a couple of services recommended at the end of this book which you can contact by e-mail, but you should easily be able to find one in your area if you prefer. Just make sure you go with one that isn't connected in ANY way to a self-publishing company, as some are, and that has previous clients' testimonials or other recommendations you can rely upon.

One important note here: *listen to what they say.* I know of a self-published author who did this and was told that he had to cut his 450,000-word novel (!) down to at least 180,000, which is about the length of a Stephen King (i.e. a longish book), because it was fatally overwritten. He was using 37 words where one would have done. He decided not to (because it would have "interfered" with the story) and self-published it as it was. I've read the first chapter of this book, and all that happens in the first 1,500 words is that someone gets out of a car. All you'd need to count how many copies he's sold are the fingers on one of your hands.

Now maybe you've been skimming this entire section because you've either already decided that (a) you're not going to bother with this bit—your book is amazing and you're self-publishing and that's that, or (b) despite never receiving anything but a faint photocopied rejection letter in return for a manuscript submission, you're forging ahead anyway—hey, what do they know? You should never let someone else's "no" be anything other than the start of your next beginning. And who's to say these publishing types are such experts, eh? Didn't *The Help* get rejected like, 50 times? Didn't J.K. Rowling get rejected loads of times too? Didn't Stephen King—

Look, I can't stop you from self-publishing your book. But if you haven't self-published yet, you have *no idea* of the work that lies ahead of you, of the effort it will take just to get people to stop and spend a second finding out more about your book—not to read it, or to buy it, or even to download the free sample, but just to pause for a moment, on Amazon or on Twitter on or a blog post, and look at your book's cover, or read its blurb.

But I *do* know, and that's why I'm encouraging you to *collect as much evidence of your talent as possible*, because that's what'll get people to stop. If you had to read—or could only read—works by one of the authors described below, which one do you think is more likely to be "good"?

"John Smith always wanted to be a writer, but with his 9–5 job in banking more like a 7–8, he struggled to find the time to finish his novel, The Loxatocki Protocol. *He did, however, manage to squeeze in a writing workshop run by the renowned IMPAC winning novelist, Jonathan Smithson, who having read a sample of Smith's work, encouraged him to apply for a grant from the Arts Council of Ireland. Despite fierce competition Smith was awarded enough to write full-time for a year, and rewarded for his efforts with the representation of one of the UK's most respected literary agents. Smith's dreams of publication were now tantalisingly close but unfortunately it was not to be. Despite glowing feedback from numerous editors, none felt confident enough in the market to publish the first title in what Smith planned to be a six-part series. One suggested he try self-publishing it in e-book himself and after doing some research, Smith decided that that's exactly what he'd do. He also took another piece of the same editor's advice: to change the title.* The First Protocol *is available now."*

or

"John Smith always want to be a writer. The Loxatocki Protocol *is his first novel."*

(If you picked the second one, oh puh-*leese*. Give me a break! And what are you still doing here? Didn't I tell you to stop reading back at *I Didn't Know I Was Pregnant*?)

And here's the thing about *50 Shades*, before we go any further. Yes, it began life as self-published fan fiction. Yes, it was its self-publishing success that caught the eye of a traditional publisher. But I read a lot of self-publishing blogs, industry news, etc. and I heard not a peep about *50 Shades* until *after* it'd been traditionally (re-)published. It couldn't have sold the numbers it has without being available in paperback, and without that paperback being widely available in stores. The reason it's currently mentioned in every newspaper and magazine you pick up and on every talk show you turn on is because "self-published book gets traditional deal" is a story, as is "book about bondage a bestseller" and "[any book] selling so well it had to be reprinted three times in a week." As you'll soon discover for yourself, "self-published book sells a few copies" isn't considered a newsworthy story. *50 Shades* may have begun life as a self-published book, but it is a *traditional publishing* success story and, therefore, irrelevant to us. So don't worry about it.

You're So Vain, You Probably Think This Bit Is About You

Maybe you know your book isn't that good, or someone told you it wasn't good and you chose not to believe them, and yet you're dead set on going ahead with self-publishing anyway. Maybe you just want to see your book in book form, and that's allowed. Of course it is. But that's called *vanity* publishing (for a reason), and that's not what *this* book is about. You're more of a *hobbyist*, and this book—and my approach—is aimed at *entrepreneurs.*

Anecdotal evidence suggests that the most successful self-publishers are the ones who treat it like a business, just like starting up a new company or opening a restaurant or producing a new product. If you just want to see your name on a paperback spine, there are easier ways. Upload your files to CreateSpace, order a proof copy and—ta-daa!—there's your book. Save yourself the time, effort, blood, sweat and tears (and us from your potentially bad book), and let's leave it at that. Because no entrepreneur sinks time, money and energy into a bad product, at least not knowingly.

So don't bother. Just get yourself a copy of your book and be done with it instead.

You should also take that advice if you and your book are in what I call the *Selling Houses* category. *Selling Houses* was a property TV programme where a suave estate agent with floppy Nineties hair went round to houses that had been on the market for ages without as much as a nibble, to see what he could do to make them sell. (In a similar vein: *The House Doctor.*) Typically, Floppy Hair would walk into a house where the paint was peeling off the front door, cardboard boxes were stacked in the hallway, the living room was painted Barbie pink, the playroom was home to sixteen cats (and their litter trays), the kitchen had no room for a fridge, the fridge was in fact in the dining room, the master bedroom had a stripper pole and there were no doors on any of the bathrooms. It would be painfully obvious to Floppy Hair and to the viewer that no one was *ever* going to walk around that house and then say, "I'll take it!" But the owners would disagree. They'd look around at their cardboard boxes and their stripper pole and their doorless bathrooms and say to themselves, "Well, *I* like this house, so there must be someone else out there who will too."

Just because *you* liked reading your book doesn't mean everybody—or *anybody*—else will.

Not until you move those boxes and repaint the living room walls, anyway.

Sales Goals: What's Realistic?

I don't believe you should set out to do anything without having some goals in mind, but when it comes to self-publishing it can be hard to find the cold, hard numbers of success. It also depends on what *you* want for yourself. The vast majority of self-published books on a POD site like Lulu or CreateSpace only sell one or two copies, so if you sold 10 you'd be considered a success. But would selling 10 copies of your book make you happy? I know it wouldn't do it for me.

When I was setting my own goals, I searched for as many examples of sales figures as I could find and then tried to find a spot somewhere in the middle of them for me and *Mousetrapped*. I read on one publishing blog that very few POD books sell more than 200 copies, so I set that as my embarrassment level, i.e. I could avoid humiliation if I managed to sell that much, but would have to dig a hole and hide in it if I sold any fewer.

But of course I wanted to sell more than *that*.

A pretty level-headed self-publishing book told me that a well-produced POD title could expect to sell between 50–200 copies per month, but would likely only achieve those sales after being on sale for a year, as it seemed to take that long for POD books to reach their full potential. So I took that into consideration as well, and finally decided on 100 copies in the first month, 500 copies by six months and 1,000 copies in the first year. If I managed to reach those targets, then I'd think up some new ones.

Two years later, I've sold around 18,000 books. My goals were *way* off and there's a specific reason why: *e-books*. I didn't factor e-book sales into my goals because when I was getting ready to self-publish and deciding on things like my goals, I didn't even know I was going to release e-book editions. E-books are easier to sell than paperbacks (mainly because they're priced much lower), but how *well* your e-books will sell is anyone's guess.

There seems to be absolutely no way to tell in advance if sales will trickle through in dribs and drabs, or if they'll take off like a rocket, catapulting you and your book right to the top of the charts. For nearly a year after *Mousetrapped* was released, it only sold about 100 copies a month. That was two years ago, in 2010. But when a blogging friend of mine released a 99c novel earlier this year, she promptly shifted 30,000 copies of it within a few weeks.

Luck plays a part, as does the nature of your book. Fiction, from what I've seen, sells in much larger quantities than non-fiction, and genres like romance and thrillers are some of the biggest sellers of all. Success in this arena certainly isn't one size fits all.

But if you *really* need some hard numbers, I'd go with a scale of success that looks a lil' something like this:

Copies sold per month*

100+	Your book is selling
300+	Your book is selling well
500+	Your book is selling very well
1,000+	Your book is selling amazingly well
2,500+	Your book is selling, like, ridiculously well
5,000+	Your book is selling better than most traditionally published books
10,000+	HOW ARE YOU DOING THIS?! Tell us now!

(*Copies sold a month would either be your actual copies sold each month if you manage to keep it at a consistent level, or your first year's sales divided by 12 if they tend to fluctuate.)

So what should we do in terms of setting ourselves goals? Well, starting out, I think you should have three different sets of them.

The first should be the number you'll have to sell in order to recoup all of your costs. Let's say you spend $1,000 on editing and a cover design for your book that you then sell for $2.99. If you sell that on the Kindle store, you'll earn about $2.09 from each sale. That means you'll have to sell 479 copies in order to break even. Let's call that figure our We'll Cry If We Don't Sell This Amount Goal. It doesn't need a time scale, but of course we'd like to reach it as soon as possible.

The second should be a number that is reasonable with a touch of aspiration, an amount that's within our grasp, but that would also make us really happy if we got there. An achievable goal, in other words, but not one that's *too easily* achievable. The parameters of this goal will depend on what kind of book you're self-publishing—you might want to find a similar self-published book and see if you can find out how well it's selling. It should be a nice, round figure, like 1,000, 10,000 or even 50,000 if you're feeling particularly lucky. This should also be the focus of your first year, i.e. the amount of books you're aiming to sell within the first twelve months. We'll call this our We'll Crack Open the Champagne When We Sell This Amount Goal.

The third should be your Pinch Me, I'm Dreaming Goal, and I think this should be something *other* than cold, hard sales figures. We need something to daydream about, something to focus on *just in case* we reach that champagne moment and keep on going. What, if it happened to you, would make you feel like all your writing dreams had come true? If we were talking traditional publishing here, this would be the cherry on top of the book deal cake. For me, it would probably be something like hitting #1 in the Irish charts, or appearing on *The Late Late Show* (a long-running talk show here in Ireland; if you're on it, you're deemed to have "made it"!), or having my book optioned for a movie. (We can also call this the Let's Not Admit To Anyone That We've Ever Even *Thought* About These Things, Okay? Goal.)

Here are some ideas for your Pinch Me, I'm Dreaming Goal:

- Get an e-mail from a fan (a *fan*!)
- See your book in a bookstore
- Hit #1 overall in the Kindle bestseller charts
- Catch the attention of a publishing house
- Earn enough from self-publishing to quit the day job.

Think about it, pick one and then tuck it away somewhere safe.

Readers of the first edition might be wondering who I am and what I've done with Catherine, the girl who loved to warn self-publishers off daydreams of success. Well, the whole idea of *Self-Printed* is to help you do better than the average self-publisher, and a year ago, when the first edition of this book came out, the numbers that equalled self-publishing success were smaller than they seem to be today. (I suspect this has a lot to do with the KDP Select programme and the increased professionalism of self-publishers, both of which we'll get into later.) The idea of a successful self-published book being one that sells 200 copies in total is about as relevant today as floppy disks; from what I've seen, many self-publishers who release good books and treat their promotion professionally sell more than that in their first month.

So I'm encouraging a *little* dreaming.

Having said all that, I still think a good base line for all books is 100 books a month to begin with, or 1,200 books in the first year. If you managed that you would have something to be very proud of, but those sales are still achievable (with time and hard work) so you're not setting yourself up for disappointment. If you do sell more, well then, *great*! And if you think 100 books a month would be a failure, then please come back out of the Forest of Self-Publishing Delusion. It *would* be a success, and no small achievement. That's 6,000 books in five years, more than most traditionally published books shift in their lifetime.

And remember: we're only talking about the beginning. Your sales may start to grow — they might even take off — and if they do then you can readjust your figures.

But let's stick to being (mostly!) realistic for now.

How Does All This Work?

If you know nothing about how self-published e-books and POD (Print-On-Demand, if you've forgotten already) paperbacks work, let's get a little overview out of the way now. Hold your questions; there'll be more technical information later, when we're actually producing the books. This is just to give you an idea of what will happen.

E-books

For our e-books, we're going to use two services simultaneously, **Amazon's Kindle Direct Publishing** (KDP) and **Smashwords**.

You will need:

- A cover image (just the front and with text big enough to be read in a thumbnail size)
- The book in a MS Word document, formatted to optimise e-book conversion (I'll tell you how).

How it works:

1. You sign up for a free account at both sites
2. You set up a new title, i.e. enter description, price, etc.
3. You format your MS Word interior as per guidelines OR pay someone else to convert it
4. You upload your interior and cover files
5. The site's conversion software converts them into e-books for you if need be
6. You check everything looks okay, and if it does:
7. Your book appears for sale on e-book stores (keep reading for specifics).

What does my e-book look like?

Different on every single e-reading device but fine, if you've done the formatting correctly. But more on *that* migraine later.

What happens when someone buys my e-book?

Nothing happens to you unless you're obsessively tracking your Amazon sales, in which case you'll probably experience a momentary high. Amazon or Smashwords will take care of everything. They collect the money, allow the customer to download the book to their e-reading device and set aside your profit to pay you later.

At any time you can log on to KDP or Smashwords and see how many copies you've sold. Amazon tends to update these in near enough real time but Smashwords can take months to do it.

How do I get paid?

Amazon KDP pays out royalties once a month by cheque or electronic transfer, depending on where you live. In this payment will be your earnings for the month that ended 60 days previously. Smashwords pay once a quarter by automatically transferring your profits into a PayPal account. You can then either spend them immediately on other people's books at The Book Depository, like I do (damn them for accepting PayPal!), or transfer them into a bank account.

Print-On-Demand (POD) Paperbacks

Paperbacks are a tad more complicated, but still relatively easy to produce. For them, we're going to use CreateSpace, a POD service owned by Amazon which, because I'm lazy, I'm going to call CS a lot from here on in.

You'll need:

- The interior of your book in a PDF file
- The cover of your book in a PDF file
- A credit card with which to pay for the proof copy, usually less than $20 including the cost of shipping it to you.

How it works:

1. You register for a free CS account at www.createspace.com
2. You set up a new title, i.e. enter the description, decide on a size, number of pages, price, etc.
3. You take a note of the free International Standard Book Number (ISBN) CS have assigned you
4. You enter the ISBN into your interior file's copyright notice
5. You upload your PDF files
6. You submit your files for review (CS will check the cover is the right size, ISBN is correct, etc.)
7. You order and pay for a proof copy
8. You check the proof copy when it arrives

9. If everything is okay, you approve the proof and the book becomes "Published"
10. If everything isn't okay, you repeat the process until it is
11. Within a few days, the book appears on Amazon.com, Amazon.co.uk, etc.
12. If you want it to appear on additional online retailers like Barnes and Noble, you pay $25 for Expanded Distribution.

What does my book look like?

Good, if you do it right. CS has a number of different trim sizes you can choose from and paper that's available in cream or white. I've found both their interior and cover printing to be of very high quality and I have to say I'm extremely pleased, overall, with the appearance of the end product. It is not, however, the same as a "properly" printed book and it doesn't wear as well, probably because the cover card is not as thick as it would be on a non-POD book. I've noticed, for example, that POD books that are handled a lot end up with a front cover that is slightly curling back. But I was very happy with my CS-made books and would even go so far as to say I was surprised at how good they turned out. Trust me, when it comes to what your book will look like, it isn't CS you have to worry about it. It's *you*.

Your book will not say "CreateSpace" anywhere unless you put it in there, and CS will automatically add a barcode for you.

FYI: If you're holding a paperback right now, it's one that CreateSpace made. So *this* is what it looks like.

What happens when someone buys a copy of my book?

Nothing happens to *you*; you can sit back and relax. Amazon and CS take care of everything for you. If I go online and order a copy of your book, it arrives, brand new and freshly printed, in my mailbox a few days later. Someone else has printed it, packaged it, shipped it and collected the cost. Amazon will then take their cut and give CS the rest, and CS will then take *their* cut (the manufacturing cost) and give *you* the rest. Whenever a sale is made, you'll also see your sales jump up one on your CS dashboard, the screen you see whenever you log in to the site.

If you want to order some copies of your book, either to, say, sell at a book launch or just to put on a shelf and gaze at adoringly (the best part of this whole thing, I've found) then you can order them yourself at cost price direct from CS.

I should also say here that whenever you publish a book on CS, you automatically get your own 'eStore,' which is basically a page where anyone can go and buy your book directly from CS. But I'll be explaining later why we don't want *anyone* to do that.

How do I get paid?

Similar to KDP, CreateSpace pays once a month by cheque or electronic transfer, depending on where you live. In this payment will be your profits — or "royalties" as they call them, even though strictly-speaking they're not — for the calendar month that ended 30 days previously.

Why are you pushing CreateSpace? Aren't there loads of other POD sites?

Yes, there are. Lulu is probably the most popular one. But I'm only talking about using CS for *two* reasons: firstly, this book, as I've already said, is about doing it the way I did; secondly, I looked at both Lulu and CS and even ordered proof copies from both sites so I could compare the quality and, for me, CS won hands down. Then I compared the cost per unit. Again, CS won hands down. In fact, CS was so much cheaper than Lulu that even when I factored in CS's then astronomical shipping charges (they've improved since), CS was still *half the price* of Lulu. Did you digest that? Lulu's cost per unit was 50% more expensive than CS's cost per unit multiplied by two. (I e-mailed Lulu about this huge discrepancy and they told me it was due to the "cost of doing business in the Euro zone.") So I went with CS.

So that's great and all, but what about brick-and-mortar bookstores, eh?

Have a skim back over that section again and tell me, where do you see the phrase "Your book will appear in bookstores"? And the phrase "Your book can be ordered by wholesalers"? And "You should be on the *New York Times* list by Friday"?

I'll save you the bother: *they're not there.*

Your book will not be in bookstores unless you put it there. This will involve you ordering copies of your own book at cost price, getting them shipped to you and then persuading individual stores to take on your book, buying it from you at a discounted price. You will then have to invoice them, wait ages for them to pay you and take back at no cost any books they don't sell, even if they've been completely wrecked by careless browsers. And that's only if you can persuade the stores to take them; most bookstores, especially the larger ones, don't deal with authors on an individual basis because it messes up their accounting. They prefer just to deal with distributors, the link between publishing houses and bookshops. You could try to get a distributor to take on your book, but you'd have to provide them with a significant amount of stock, maybe a couple of thousand copies (which you'd have to pay CS for outright and you can't return *them*), and again, you'd have to be prepared to take them back if they didn't sell. You would also end up losing money because the POD cost per unit price isn't low enough to accommodate both a distributor discount *and* a bookshop discount. Bookstores may be able to *theoretically* order your book into stock directly, but they won't; the wholesale price won't be cheap enough for them and some chain stores don't order in POD books as a rule.

If you do what I describe in this book, you will end up with a paperback for sale on Amazon.com and all the Amazon European sites (Amazon.co.uk, which also covers Ireland, and the sites for Germany, Italy, France and Spain.) If you spring for Expanded Distribution your book will also — eventually — appear for sale on sites like Barnes and Noble and The Book Depository. If you publish e-books with Amazon KDP and Smashwords, you will have e-books for sale on all Kindle stores, the Smashwords website and, if you pass Smashwords's Premium Catalogue test, the Sony store, Apple's iBooks, Barnes and Noble's e-book store, Kobo and Diesel.

If your eyes are glazing over about now, let me put it like this: by default, **your book will only be for sale online**. So if you harbour notions of seeing your book in the display at your local Waterstones or Barnes and Noble, or even that kooky independent bookstore with the great coffee and comfy armchairs, you're going to have to sneak it in there yourself.

Do I need to do both an e-book and a paperback?

You certainly don't need to publish both an e-book and a paperback, although in this new digital publishing world it seems pointless to publish a paperback but not an e-book. Producing only an e-book makes your life as a self-publisher a lot easier, and saves you some money as you won't have to fork out for a proof copy or a full cover design, but then you might lose sales because many readers — myself, ironically, included — still haven't embraced e-books.

For all my books to date, I have released both editions simultaneously, but I think there's something to be said for releasing the e-book *ahead* of the paperback, making the e-book the equivalent of traditional publishing's hardback. I plan to release the e-book of my next title, *Travelled*, in November 2012, but will leave the paperback until January or February of 2013. This not only spreads my workload out into a more manageable schedule, but it also means that by the time I have to pay for proof copies and larger, more expensive jacket designs, I'll have already earned something from the book that I can reinvest. Most importantly, it provides me with *two* online launch opportunities instead of just one.

However if this is your first book, I'd recommend going the whole hog, e-book *and* POD paperback, right out of the gate, if only because seeing your name on the grey screen of a Kindle is nowhere *near* as exciting as seeing it on the spine of a book.

A word of warning before you pay a visit to CreateSpace. All the major POD sites and self-publishing services offer additional "author services" and bundle them into packages. The idea is that you hand over a wad of cash and in return they'll take care of things like editing, cover design and making flimsy postcards and bookmarks with a picture of your book on it, which will look terrible because they'll have designed the cover for you. They are, without exception, overpriced. From what I've seen other authors pay thousands and thousands of dollars for, they are also terrible. One self-published author had a cover he'd paid a POD service a thousand dollars for that my cover designer would use as an example of what *not* to do, and my cover designer charges a tenth of that. My advice: steer well clear of them.

And watch out, because some of the more sinister self-publishing sites arrange advertisements of these packages and services in such a way that you may believe you *have* to pay for them. You don't. The only thing you *have* to pay for to get your paperback for sale online is the price of your proof copy, which generally is less than $20.

This book is not about paying through the nose to get someone else to project manage your book. It's about producing a high quality self-published book for the least amount of money possible. This means finding your own editor and cover designer, and paying CreateSpace no money other than the price of your proof copy and your extended distribution plan, if you need it. In this book, we'll be keeping as much *self* in our self-publishing as possible.

International Standard Book Numbers (ISBNs)

In order for your paperback book to be distributed and sold through retail channels, it has to have an International Standard Book Number or ISBN. CreateSpace will give you one for free. Smashwords also require ISBNs to be attached to all e-books sold through their Premium Catalogue, e.g. retailers such as Apple's iBooks, Barnes and Noble, etc. They will also give you one for free.

(Amazon KDP don't require ISBNs; they give you one of their own unique identification numbers instead. Also for free.)

My advice: **take the free ISBNs**. In fact, I'm *telling* you to take them. Self-publishing authors shunning freebies is fine, but when it comes to a free ISBN they always seem to be doing it for the wrong reason.

And it drives me a tad insane.

What Is An ISBN?

ISBN stands for International Standard Book Number. This 10- or 13-digit numerical identifier helps catalogue, track and, um, identify various editions of books. Although not legally required, in order for your book to be distributed and sold through the same channels as a 'properly' published book, you need to have one.

The ISBN appears above and below the barcode in this image.

It will be on the copyright page (because we're going to put it there, and we have to) and above the barcode on the back of your paperback book which CreateSpace will add for you.

We don't have to put our ISBN anywhere in our e-books, but it will appear on our e-book's eventual listing on sites like iBooks.

Peter Paranoia

An ISBN normally appears alongside the copyright notice, but it has *nothing* to do with ownership. The main purpose of an ISBN is to *identify*, whereas copyright serves to *protect*.

As long as the self-publishing service you use operates a non-exclusive agreement (and it should; all the ones I talk about in this book do), you have nothing to worry about with regards to ownership or your rights. If you take a free ISBN from CreateSpace, they own the ISBN — you can't use it with anyone else — but they do *not* own your work. Same goes for Smashwords.

You can buy your own ISBN, of course, but it *costs money* and is kind of a pain in the arse. And since we're trying to do this for as little money as possible, why spend it on something we can get for free?

I have seen countless self-publishers get their independent knickers in a *right* twist over ISBNs, and while some concern (however unfounded) over the ownership of your work is perfectly natural, being wildly paranoid about scenarios that have about as much chance of transpiring as I do of getting an urge to run a marathon (or anything, or anywhere) is just plain crazy. For example, I recently encountered online an author who is considering self-publishing asking what would happen if she got a movie deal for her novel. Would taking the free ISBN affect that?

[Pause while I take a very deep breath and you brace yourself for the tirade that you suspect is coming.]

Okay, I won't resort to a tirade. (*This* time.) But can we take a minute here to have a glass of sanity juice? I mean, seriously. *Movie deals?* How about we take things one step at a time, sunshine?

Stop worrying about whether or not taking a free ISBN will affect your future Universal Studios movie rights/NBC sitcom development deal contract negotiations and come back and join the rest of us here in the real world, where *we're* selling books.

And again, it's just *a number that identifies your book.*

I can only assume that this ISBN confusion stems from shady vanity publishing houses who get you to sign stuff and then claim that you can't publish your book with anyone else or in any other formats because they own the publishing rights to it now. But CreateSpace and the other services we'll be using are not like that. When we take their free ISBN, all we're doing is publishing with them.

We're not giving them the rights to *anything.*

(And no, it wouldn't affect it, if you were wondering about your own future movie deal.)

The Publisher Of Record

Not all self-publishers who don't want to take the free ISBN are crazy. (Just most of them.) Some of them don't want to take the ISBN from CreateSpace, for example, because if they do, CreateSpace will be the publisher of record. I have no problem with CS being my publisher of record; my only concern is selling books, and one doesn't affect the other one bit.

The term "CreateSpace" appeared nowhere on *Mousetrapped* without me putting it there, inside or out. On the very last page was a barcode, the phrase "Made in the USA, Charleston, S.C." and the date on which that particular copy was printed. That was the only evidence of its POD beginnings, and even then you'd have to know what you were looking at to understand what it meant.

CreateSpace is listed as the publisher on *Mousetrapped*'s Amazon listing and other online retailer listings, but so what? When was the last time you looked up a book on Amazon and noticed who'd published it? And "CreateSpace" may be a term that's familiar to you and me, but what portion of the book-buying public have heard of it? Not a lot. And even fewer of them know what it is.

The Dishonest Self-Publisher

Maybe you don't want to take the free ISBN because you don't want anyone to know that you've self-published, or at least you don't want to advertise the fact. When I talk about making our book look like a traditionally published book and not like a self-published one, I'm talking about *quality* or the perception of it. We want to fit in with the big boys because they do it right, and because we want to be taken as seriously as they are. We also want to separate our book from the generally held opinion about self-published books, which is that they're bad. I'm not talking about *pretending we haven't self-published*, which is a completely different thing and utterly idiotic, because you'd have to be seriously *stoopid* to fall for it.

Scenario #1 (the most common): the writer buys their own ISBN, registers it to a publisher (themselves) with a name that almost always includes the word "books" or "press." They set up a website and go ahead with the self-publishing process, all the while pretending that they and the publisher are not one and the same, or attempting to give that impression.

Scenario #2 (the half truth): the writer buys their own ISBN, registers it to a publisher (themselves) and sets off self-publishing. If questioned, they'll say that they've started a new publishing house that wants to specialise in publishing [insert group of writers perceived to be slighted by Evil Big Publishing]. Oh, and it just so happens that the first title they're going to produce is their own book.

Scenario #3 (illegal): the writer claims they're being published with a major publishing house and attempts (miserably) to make their self-published book look like something that house would produce. I encountered a writer once who had copied the logo of a very well-known publishing house and pasted it onto the spine of her POD book.

Um... *really?*

If you are ashamed or embarrassed about self-publishing your book, if you're convinced people won't want to buy it when they find out it's self-published or you are considering any of the above scenarios, then don't bother self-publishing. Simples.

So what have we learned here? Say it with me: TAKE THE FREE ISBN!

Money Matters

Ah, money. Of all the questions I'm asked about self-publishing, *how much do you have to spend?* and *how much do you make?* are always sitting pretty in the top two spots. You've probably been speed-reading everything else up to now, wondering when I was going to get to this bit, or perhaps you've even skipped straight here from the table of contents. Either way, let's put you out of your misery.

And into a new one, because **self-publishing — or writing of any kind — is *not* a get-rich-quick scheme**. It's not even a get-slightly-less-poor-slowly scheme. I know it *seems* like it is, as we're presented almost daily with what seems like evidence to the contrary. J.A. Konrath gets monthly royalty cheques with lots of numbers on them; Amanda Hocking made millions on her own and then signed a seven-figure traditional deal; E.L. James will soon be earning more in interest on her bank balance than most people earn in a lifetime of full-time work.

That's *three* people we can name who got rich from self-publishing. Can you name any more? I think I can name three more, four if we count one duo as two individual writers (John Locke, Stephen Leather, Mark Edwards and Louise Voss). I also know a few people who aren't exactly millionaires but have still got some hefty royalty cheques, so I'll throw them in too. There's about twenty of them. What are we up to now — twenty-seven? Let's say thirty just to round it up. And let's pretend that you know thirty *different* writers who got rich by self-publishing. That makes it sixty. And just to make it really fair, to make sure we're not rounding down at all, let's call it one hundred. Between the two of us, we know of one hundred writers who have either got stinking rich or made a lot of money from this self-publishing lark.

One hundred writers.

Smashwords.com has published around 150,000 self-published books. Amazon don't release numbers, but there's over 1,000,000 books in the Kindle store, and anywhere from ten to fifty percent of them could be self-published. Maybe even more. And that's not including e-books self-published through other services, like Barnes and Noble's Pubit or Kobo's Writing Life, or authors who've only self-published in paperback. My point is that even though it seems like every day there's a new "WRITER SELF-PUBLISHES, BECOMES SICKENINGLY RICH" headline, the number of self-published authors getting sickeningly rich is a very, *very* tiny fraction of the number of self-published authors. *Tiny*, I tell you! Like, not visible to the naked eye. Maybe even only visible to the type of electron microscopes top-secret government laboratories have.

The self-published millionaires are the exceptions to the rule and, as I've said already, it's not helpful to think that you'll be one too when the odds are against you. And just because you're not earning millions doesn't mean that you're not earning *money*. I, for example, sell a very moderate amount of books, but in a few days Amazon will send me a cheque worth around $2,500. That's just what I made from my Kindle sales in May of this year.

My biggest selling Kindle book, *Mousetrapped*, is about the year and a half I spent working full-time in a hotel in Walt Disney World for $9.25 an hour, or $1,600 a month.

Before taxes.

(Sidenote: don't move to Florida if you like being able to buy things and eat and stuff.)

While it's fine, within reason, to *hope* that you're going to strike it rich, *believing* that you will is only going to pave a path to bitter disappointment. Somebody buying your book is a wonderful thing, and you should be able to celebrate each purchase.

And it's actually better if you only make a handful of sales to begin with, because then you can frame your first royalty cheque, like Amanda Hocking did. Hers was for $15.72.

As for the question *how much do you have to spend?*, it's really more a case of **how much should I spend?**

Sadly, the vast majority of would-be self-publishers I encounter do not want to spend any money at all. They have various reasons for this— they don't *have* any money, they don't want to spend money when they're only going to be charging 99c for the book, the whole point of doing this self-publishing thing is to make money so by not spending any, they'll be in the green as soon as they make their first sale—but they all have one thing in common: *they shouldn't self-publish.*

Remember when I said that The New Self-Publisher treated self-publishing like a business, and assumed the role of a dedicated entrepreneur? Well let's pretend for a second that instead of releasing a book you've written, you're opening a coffee shop. Would you attempt to open a coffee shop if you didn't have any money? Would you say you didn't want to spend money on it because the coffees were only going to be $3.50? Would you say you *weren't* going to spend any money on it because the whole point of opening a coffee shop was to make money and by not spending any, you'll be in the green just as soon as you sell your first latte?

And even if you *would* say all that (God help us all...), do you think *I* would pay *you* anything at all for a cup of coffee served to me in a chipped mug you brought from home and brewed in lukewarm water from half a spoon of the cheapest instant blend, that I was then expected to drink without milk or sugar and in a space with no chairs, tables or countertops?

Because I wouldn't. No sane person would. And yet this is what self-publishers expect people to do every minute of every day. Just replace coffee with books, and a coffee shop with the Kindle store.

Your book will soon be a product with a price tag on it, and you'll have a duty to deliver on the promises that product makes. If I was going to spend $3.50 on a latte, I'd expect the shop to be a pleasant place to be, with comfy chairs, nice cups and well-trained, friendly staff, and I'd want the coffee to come from good quality, freshly ground beans and to be made in a suitable machine. When I spend $15 on a paperback, I want text that's big enough to read, tightly bound pages and an attractive cover. I want it to look like a real book, to match my expectations of what a book should look like. I want to see what I'm used to seeing when I open a book: title pages, page numbers, a standard font. When I spent $5 or $3 or even $1 on an e-book, I want the formatting to be perfect and I want to be able to navigate it like I do all my other e-books. In both cases, I want to be reading text in correct English, with no grammar or spelling mistakes.

You *have* to bring your book up to a minimum standard—the standard that's expected of it if you put a price tag on it and sell it as a book. If you don't, asking people to pay $2.99, $1.99 or even a handful of sofa change on your book is just *dishonest*. And the reality is that in almost all cases, you'll need someone else's help to make this happen. Someone who's a professional, which by definition means that they won't be helping you for free.

Some self-publishers release a book in which they haven't invested any money in the hope that once sales pick up, they'll be able to use the profits to hire an editor or get a professional cover design or whatever. "I want to see if it'll sell," they say, "before I spend any money on it." This sort of thinking makes my head hurt and my wallet recoil in horror. The counter-arguments are all obvious ones—you have only one chance to make a first impression, so the first release of your book has to be the best version possible; whether or not your book sells in a crappy DIY version is no indication of how well it would sell in a professionally produced great version; you don't deserve to have people spending their hard-earned money on your book when you aren't even willing to invest in it yourself—but the main problem with it is that this book will be a *prototype*. It's an inferior version of the real thing. And would you sell people a prototype of something *other* than a book—a car, for example—in order to fund the finished product, when the prototype doesn't work as well and looks terrible? Of *course* you wouldn't. It's just books' bad luck that you can get your product to market for free. Have a conscience and don't make it your *readers'* bad luck that they fell for it.

At the same time, we don't want to spend a fortune. You could sink thousands into a book if you liked. You could commission an original illustration for the cover, hire a typesetter to make the pages of your paperback dazzle and pay someone to convert your e-book for you instead of learning how to format it yourself.

But it wouldn't make any business sense. Going back to the coffee shop, yes, I have to have tables and chairs, but having the chairs upholstered by Laura Ashley and the tabletops under white Egyptian cotton cloths is overkill.

When it comes to our self-publishing budget, we need to achieve two things:

- Spending what we need to in order to bring our book up to the minimum standard required of it
- Spending as little as possible.

I think you need to have a budget of **$1,000.** We may not have to spend that much or we may require a few dollars more, but that's a good ballpark, in my opinion. It's also a *fraction* of what traditional publishing houses — the people producing the books that will compete directly with ours — spend getting a title to market, so if you think that's too much, you can probably guess what I'm going to say to you.

(*Don't self-publish*, if it wasn't clear.)

What are we going to spend it on? We'll get to that.

The Price Is Right

There's one other money-related question self-publishers need to ask: *how much should I charge for my book?*

Now, chances are you're not going to like what I have to say about this, but then chances are you're already annoyed with me after the whole "if you can't afford to self-publish, don't" so I'm just going to power through. Think of this like Dr. Phil does Self-Publishing Prices: you may not want to hear it, but you know I'm right. (Or at least *I* know I'm right.) There are only two places in this book where if you ignore what I say, you definitely *won't* be a successful self-publisher. *Pricing* is one of them.

Before we go any further I want you to read these next three sentences aloud: *I cannot expect each individual reader to compensate me for the years of blood, sweat and tears that went into writing this book. The price tag on my book is not a reflection of how much work went into it. I have to look at the big picture and acknowledge that if I insist on being greedy and overcharging people, then I won't sell any copies at all.*

Pricing Your Paperback

Let's start with our paperbacks, because pricing our paperbacks is not entirely within our control; we have to cover the manufacturing costs. When it comes to deciding on your price, the most important thing you need to take into consideration is how much similar books that have been traditionally published cost. People will not buy your book if it's significantly more expensive than all the other books in the world. Keep in mind I'm talking about their *recommended retail price*, not how much Tescos (the UK and Ireland equivalent of WalMart) is selling them for, which could be half-price. You'll find this printed on the back of the book, near the barcode, but not necessarily on the price tag. (In Ireland, this is about €9.99.) Obviously it will cost you more to produce a book than, say, Random House, and so some leeway is inevitable. However I'd always try to stay within at least a euro—or a dollar or a pound—of the standard recommended retail price of similar sized books. Remember that doing this will also help you fit in with your traditionally published counterparts; the fewer "I'm a self-published book!" signals we can give off, the better.

The next thing you need to consider is that in all likelihood, paperbacks will not be your main source of income. When I started out on this process I concentrated on my paperback and thought that any e-book sales would just be a bonus, but it's proved to be the other way around. I doubt there's a self-published author in the world making more from POD paperbacks than they are from e-books. If you're going to make money from this, you'll make it from your e-books. So don't fret too much about how much you're getting from paperbacks.

Lastly, think about what your aim is here—and then douse it with reality. *Lots* of it. What would be the worst case scenario? Selling a book that costs *us* money. CS won't let you do that (they have a minimum list price) so that's not going to happen, and hopefully we'll manage to offset any money we spend pre-publication with our e-book sales. What's the best case scenario? Turning a profit, making some money. In order to do that, we have to price our books reasonably. And what's in the middle? Making more off our books than a traditionally published author would, which we will, as you'll soon see. So if we've satisfied all those requirements, we're doing good.

(Some of you may be thinking, *but what about my time? Isn't that a cost?* No, not at the moment. Just like any entrepreneur starting up a business, you are going to be working for free for a while.)

So let's see first how much it's going to cost you to create your paperback book. CS has a royalty calculator on their website that anyone can access (click on the "Distribution and Royalties" tab in the "Book" section on the homepage) and it allows you to get a rough cost estimate for your book based on the size and the number of pages. You may not yet know what size you want or how many pages it will be, so let's just use a generic example of a 5.5 x 8.5 trim size (the size of *Mousetrapped*), 300 pages (an average paperback) and a list price of $14.95 which is about the cost of the traditionally printed equivalent, give or take a buck or two.

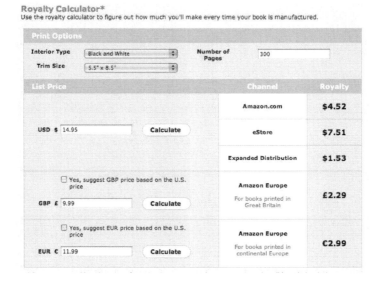

CreateSpace's royalty calculator.

If you did that, you'd get:

- $7.51 from every book sold from your eStore (CS takes $7.44)
- $4.52 from every book sold from Amazon.com (CS and Amazon take $10.43)
- $1.53 from every book sold on other online retailers under Expanded Distribution (CS, the distributor and the retailer take $13.42).

If you charged the British pound equivalent of £9.99 for your book on Amazon.co.uk, you'd earn around £2.29 per sale, and if you charged the Euro equivalent of €11.99 for your book on other European Amazon sites, each sale would earn you around €2.99.

Now if you're thinking that earning over a third of the list price off every paperback you sell is a bad deal, then clearly you've never had a publishing contract. And you're wrong. It's *great*. If you were traditionally published, the best you could hope for on a paperback is 10% and even the smallest amount we can possibly earn, $1.53 from an Expanded Distribution sale, is more than that. What you need to focus on here is (i) the fact that other than your single proof copy and potentially the Expanded Distribution charge of $25, you don't need to hand over any money upfront, and (ii) the percentage of the list price you're earning rather than just the amount itself. What you're paying for here is the convenience of not having to spend a few thousand bucks on a print run of a few hundred copies that you may or may not sell, and organising things like a printer and a typesetter. Going to a printer yourself might bring the cost per unit down, but it's a far more complicated process and then you'll have the added headache of getting the book for sale on Amazon. Why bother, when in all likelihood your paperback sales will only account for a fraction of your sales overall? Trust me: it's a good deal.

You can buy as many copies of your own book from CreateSpace as you like. In our 300-page, 5.5 x 8.5 example, each book would cost us $4.45. There's no volume discount; buy one copy for $4.45 or buy a hundred for $445. And then there's shipping on top of that.

Continuing to use the same example, CreateSpace would charge us $43.00 to send us 100 copies of our $4.45-per-unit book. If we were selling those copies on to family and friends at $15 — I've added 5c to the list price because who is going to be bothered giving us back that amount of change? — we'd be collecting a profit of $10.12 on each book. *($43 to ship 100 books equals 0.43 per book, plus unit price of $4.45 equals a total cost of $4.88; $15 minus $4.88 equals $10.12.)*

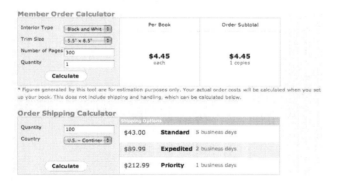

CreateSpace's member order and shipping calculator, shipping to continental US

Unfortunately things don't look as good for those of us on the other side of the Atlantic. If you're living in the UK or Ireland, for example, CreateSpace will charge you $112.99 to ship 100 copies of your book, and then take up to 31 business days to get them to you. But it's still workable. If family and friends paid us $15 for a copy, we'd collect $9.42 worth of profit each time. (*$112.99 to ship 100 books equals $1.13 per book, plus unit price of $4.45 equals a total cost of $5.58; $15 minus $5.58 equals $9.42.*)

Order Shipping Calculator

Quantity	100	**Shipping Options**		
Country	United Kingdor ⬍	$112.99	**Standard**	31 business days
		$130.99	**Expedited**	8 business days
Calculate		$145.99	**Priority**	2 business days

CreateSpace's member order shipping calculator (shipping to the UK).

I suspect better news for non-US-based CreateSpacers is on the horizon though. When the first edition of this book came out, your book was only guaranteed to appear on Amazon.com, and you had to pay $39 for the chance for it to possibly appear on other sites, including other Amazons. If it did and you managed to sell a copy, you'd be making less than a couple of dollars off it, because everything but Amazon.com came under Expanded Distribution. But recently, CreateSpace began printing in the UK and Europe as well, guaranteeing free listing on European Amazon sites and increasing the amount of money you earn off sales there. Yet, if you place a personal stock order, it still ships from CreateSpace in South Carolina, which is why the shipping costs are so high and the times so lengthy. The next logical step is to begin printing stock orders in Europe and the UK as well, so fingers crossed.

The cost of shipping copies of your book to yourself is something I see a lot of self-publishers get their knickers in a twist over, and their knicker-twisting perplexes me. How many times are you planning on shipping books to yourself, eh? You'll be sending yourself one proof copy, maybe two if you fail to find all the mistakes first time round, and then you might want to order a box of them for family, friends and a prominent bookshelf. If you decide that you don't like having money all that much and throw yourself a book launch, you might have to order another box for stock. But that's pretty much it and even in the worst case scenario, we're *still* landing on a profit margin cushion thicker than the one we have on Amazon.com. So why the fuss about shipping costs? They're not that big of a deal.

And what if Amazon discounts your book? I got an irate e-mail a while back from a blog reader spitting bullets because Amazon had started selling her book at 25% off "without her permission." How much a retailer pays for a book *never changes*. No matter what they charge for it, you still get the agreed amount. Discounts or even price hikes won't affect you one way or the other, except for bringing you more or less sales.

Pricing Your E-book

Now onto **e-books**, where the news is better but perhaps harder to take.

E-book royalties vary but the important ones—Amazon's Kindle store, Smashwords and the majority of Smashwords's sales channels—offer you around 70% of the list price.

There is some small print to go along with this, i.e. the Amazon 70% royalty rate is only awarded if a US or UK customer purchases from the US or UK Kindle store; if they live somewhere else, the rate is only 35%. But honestly, you'll barely notice this, as most of your sales will be US- and UK-based. (They have been in my experience, and from what I hear from other e-book self-publishers, most of their sales are in the 70% bracket too.) So we're not going to worry too much about the 70%/35% thing and likewise, we're not going to worry too much about Smashwords, because most of your sales will be from Amazon's Kindle Direct Platform, or KDP from now on. They just *will*, because Amazon has a much bigger share of the e-book market than anyone else. Eventually B&N and iBooks might catch up but right now even people who have iPads seem to be using Kindle's Mac application to read their e-books on them.

(Yes, we'll upload to *both* services, but when we make decisions about our e-books, we'll focus on their consequences on KDP.)

In order to qualify for that 70% royalty rate, your book has to be priced at *least* $2.99. Basically:

- Charge less than $2.99 or more than $9.99, earn 35% of the price
- Charge between $2.99 and $9.99, earn 70% of the price.

My recommendation is that every self-publisher releases their book at $2.99.

You know all those mega-selling e-book authors you've been hearing about, the ones who are having to store cash under their mattresses because they've made so damn much of it from selling their self-published work in electronic format? They're all writing fiction and they're all charging less than $5. Most are charging 99c. You might bristle at selling your book for an amount of money you could probably raise in change that's fallen down the back of your sofa cushions, but this again is where we need to concentrate on The Big Picture. Charging 99c for a book encourages people to take a chance on it because, hey, even if it's the computer code equivalent of soiled toilet paper, the most they're down is 99c, and that's *exactly* the kind of thinking you want to take advantage of.

(But hopefully your book will be better than that!)

However if you're reading the e-book edition of this, you didn't pay 99c for it (unless I've had a few too many mojitos and logged onto Amazon KDP, or you bought it in a promotion period, or you stole it, you naughty thing) and *Mousetrapped* and its sequel, *Backpacked*, are both priced $2.99 or more. So how come *I'm* not charging 99c?

Well, there's a couple of factors in there. One is that if you've only one book to sell, charging 99c for it isn't exactly going to make a dent in your credit card bill. All those big selling e-book self-publishers have multiple titles for sale, so unless you do too, I'd aim a little higher, like at $1.99 or $2.99. The second factor is that I don't *need* to charge 99c.

When I brought out *Mousetrapped* as an e-book, I didn't have a clue how much to charge for it. I also didn't particularly care about how much money I'd make, because I didn't think I'd make any. Remember, I was (stupidly) focused on my paperbacks as my main earner. So I set it at $4.99. But as luck would have it, I released it right before Read an E-Book Week, when Smashwords encourages its authors to enrol their books in discount promotions, e.g. 25% off for the duration of the week. I enrolled *Mousetrapped* at 50% off, and so it became about $2.50. Then, it started to sell. I hadn't sold a single copy at $4.99 but at half that, it was selling steadily. So when the promotion was over, I changed it to $2.99 all over e-book town and it's been selling well ever since. So I don't *need* to lower the price, not at the moment anyway. If sales stopped or slowed, I might drop it down to $1.99, and if and when I release another e-book, I might make *Mousetrapped* 99c after six months or so. But I don't want to because I don't get 70% unless I price it at $2.99 or more, and I quite like getting $2 every time someone buys my e-book.

My recommendation to you is that you start off at $2.99 and see what happens. If it sells, up it to $3.99 or even $4.99 and see if it's *still* selling at a rate you like. Chances are it won't be, but you never know. If you aren't shifting many copies at $2.99, drop it to 99c for a while. Call it a special promotion or something. I should say here that I do *not* recommend you have your book priced at $2.99 on Monday, $4.99 on Tuesday and 56c on Wednesday. That would be Grade A Stoopid, which is my least favourite kind. To really test how well a book is selling at a certain price, you'd want to give it *at least* six weeks and up to three months, ideally.

Another factor is that although you're setting your price in dollars (because both KDP and Smashwords are based in the US), not everyone is buying it in them. For example, *Mousetrapped* is $2.99 but if you see it on Amazon.com's Kindle store and you live in, say, Ireland, it's actually $3.41. Why? Because in Ireland we pay Value Added Tax (VAT) on e-books (but not print books) at a rate of 21% and Amazon charges [exaggerated eye roll] "international delivery" when you purchase Kindle books outside of the US. (Even though they're delivered by way of the internet. Go figure.) Conversely, €4.99 might sound reasonable for an e-book to you but when you convert it into dollars you get nearly $7, or way too much for a self-published e-book.

I will say this, though: I wouldn't be as quick to charge 99c for my book as I would've been when the first edition of this book came out. In the past year, while self-publishing has been shedding its stigma, 99c books have been collecting it.

Once upon a time, 99c was the go-to price for self-published authors—especially authors of fiction—but the tide appears to be turning against such low-priced books. Setting your book to such a low price no longer guarantees sales, if it ever did. Whether or not it's true, having the lowest price tag possible attached to your work sends a message to potential readers that it may only be worth a sum they could make up in change found beneath their sofa cushions. I know it's extremely difficult for us self-published authors to get perspective when we are surrounded by other self-published authors all the live long internet day, but you have to remember that the vast majority of readers do not read self-published books. You're kidding yourself if you think they do. So our next task, as self-publishers, is to show this group that our books can be as good as the ones they're used to. We must show them that our books are worth their attention. And I don't think 99c is the way to do that.

Sometimes we also have to consider the other books in our category. This happened to me with *Self-Printed*. I was charging $2.99 for it until I went looking for a reference guide myself about another subject, and noticed that the #1 bestseller was $9.99, while the #2 was only $1.99. I thought two things: the #1 must be a fantastic book if it's so expensive and it's still #1, and the #2 must be pretty rubbish if it's so cheap and still can't manage to overtake the #1. When a book promises to contain valuable information, the price has to go some way to conveying that.

I personally believe that the less you charge for a book, the less time people spend humming and haahing over their decision whether or not to click "Buy". Therefore if your price tag is 99c, you're likely to experience what I call the "I'll Give It a Go, I Suppose—And Then Hate It and Shred Your Insides With a Spiteful Amazon Review" factor. They didn't take the time to read the synopsis, or even the other reviews, because what's the worst that could happen? They're only down 99c.

It drives me mad to read one-star reviews that complain about things that either have been a) covered in the product description, or b) already highlighted by another reviewer. Why didn't they read that before they bought it?! Because we were charging so little for our work that we encouraged them not to.

$2.99 avoids all the bad associations of 99c, while still being low enough to encourage readers to give it a chance, and earns you 70% of the price. So stick with $2.99.

But Catherine, I'm sure at least one of you is saying now, and perhaps in a small voice because you've grown a bit scared of me and my "Make Your E-book Cheap!" ways, *why do I have to charge $2.99 for my e-book when Harper Collins or Little, Brown or Simon and Schuster or whoever is charging $9.99 for theirs? Are you telling me that my book isn't worth as much as theirs is? You won't allow me to stick it to traditional publishing, and yet you seem to be allowing traditional publishing to stick it to me. What's up with that?*

All over the traditional publishing world right now, a fight is going on about how much an e-book should cost. This is partly because readers — and authors, to some extent — have a perception that because there's no manufacturing costs involved in e-books (such as paper, printing, etc.), they should cost a lot less than their print equivalents, while publishers, knowing that things like paper and printing only ever represented a tiny percentage of what books were sold for, want to charge a similar price for both e-books and print books. E-book rights were also written into contracts before e-books made anyone any money, and so were put on a par with say, serialisation rights. Now with their market share growing more and more every day, authors are, understandably, thinking they should be paid more for them. Add in the perception that something you can hold in your hands is worth a lot more than something that comes from the internet and in computer code, an industry already in crisis and traditionally published authors turning to Amazon KDP to release their latest work because Amazon will give them seven times what their publisher would, and you have one fine mess on your hands.

As self-publishers this doesn't really concern us, except for the fact that the longer it goes on, the better it is for us and the more books we'll sell. Why? Because the only opinion that really matters is that of our potential readers and they have shown without question that they think e-books should be cheaper than print books. So if *Eat, Pray, Love* is $9.99 and its paperback is $12, they're not going to buy the e-book. But they've bought a Kindle or a Nook or an iPad, and so they still need something to read on it, something they can buy without feeling swindled. Enter *your* book, priced at $2.99. I'm not suggesting your writing is worth less than Elizabeth Gilbert's. I'm saying that the fact that her work is currently overpriced in the eyes and wallets of most e-book readers is a situation you can take advantage of.

To summarise, when you decide on an e-book price, it should be:

- Focused on getting readers, not making pots of cash (although getting the first greatly increases your chances of getting the second)

- Low enough to encourage people to take a chance on your book
- Not so low that people subconsciously get the impression your book is worthless or fail to research before they buy
- Not lower than it needs to be (test the waters first, then raise or lower accordingly)
- Either $1.99, $2.99, $3.99 or $4.99 (although I'd recommend starting at $2.99)
- The same price on BOTH Amazon KDP and Smashwords (them's the rules).

The good news for you is that if you can be reasonable with your price, and so see the big picture and not just the price tag, you are already head and shoulders above most of your competition, who *can't*. A self-publishing author I met recently told me he was about to charge the equivalent of €20/$27/£17 for his 300-page paperback, or *double* the norm. I mentally rolled my eyes and asked how much his e-book was going to be, thinking that maybe he'd save himself there. But no: his e-book was going to be €9.99/$14/£9. I'd bet money that the reason he was doing this was because he was thinking how much he was going to make off these books on an individual basis, i.e. *if Mary buys a paperback, I get x amount. X? Really? For all that work? I don't think so. Let's double it...* instead of, *if 1,000 Marys buy that paperback, which they are more likely to do if the price bears some relation to, you know, the price of all the other books in the world, then I'll make X, which is actually quite a nice bit of compensation for all that work.* Best of all, he was telling me this with a condescending tone and a smirk that said, "I'm not silly enough to practically give my book away like you did." Indeed. When I told him to drop the e-book to 99c, he actually *laughed* at me, like I was a little child explaining my theory that babies come from storks. What's he doing now? I don't know, but I know what he's *not* doing, and that's selling books.

(Ooh, burn!)

NB: Sales from Smashwords.com earn you on average 85% of the list price, and their retail partner sales a minimum of 65%.

Why You (Yes, YOU!) Need An Editor

I've been blogging about self-publishing for almost three years (three *years*?! Whaa...?) and I can tell you that the number one thing self-publishers don't like to be told is that every *single* self-published book needs a professional polish before its release. It's also the thing they need to be told the *most*.

Why does this matter? Because *writing* matters. Don't stick any old crap out there just because you can. Make your mistakes in private. Don't ask your readers to be the assessors *and* editors *and* spell-checkers of your work; they shouldn't have to be. By the time their eyes hit your pages, all of that should've been done already. And with another nod to our self-publishing-as-a-business idea, you are not merely self-publishing a book. You are *selling a product.* As unromantic as this may sound, it's the truth. It's reality. And just like you couldn't sell an apple pie that was in fact filled with thumb-tacks, you can't sell a book that just isn't up to scratch. You are taking people's money and in exchange you must deliver the goods.

I don't care what excuses you're forming in your mind right now, or what your story is, or how you're different to everyone else, or your long list of reasons for why this doesn't apply to you. Unless your book has no words in it, there is absolutely *nothing* you can tell me that will make the next sentence untrue.

You need an editor.

Yes, you. No, really. You. It *does* includes *you*.

Why self-publishers get so angry at being told this is a bit of mystery to me, but they *do* get angry. Whenever I mention this on my blog or at a talk or something, I get virtual sacks of bitchy e-mails accusing me of everything from forcing self-publishers into debt to insulting their intelligence. Maybe it's because they think that someone telling them "you have to get your book edited" is the same as someone telling them "your book isn't good." That's not the case *at all*. Giving our book a professional polish before it gets released is *exactly* the same thing as ensuring that it has a cover or sequential page numbers, or that it reads from left to right. It's about *standards*.

I think this lack of understanding accounts for most of the Anti-Editing Syndrome I come across. These, for example, are typical responses from a self-publisher after being told that they absolutely *have* to get their book edited:

- "Who is an 'editor' to say that a book is good or bad for everyone? Just because one person doesn't like a particular turn of phrase does not mean the other six billion of us won't like it."
- "I'd love to hire an editor, but I can't afford it. I use spell-check and get my friend who, like, reads books all the time to read over it for me."
- "Most people will overlook a couple of typos if they like the story. I find typos in traditional books all the time and no one says anything about them."

- "I am perfectly capable of doing my own editing. I mean, I *am* a writer, aren't I?"

Now maybe you can see their points, or have even said some similar things yourself. But if we took them out of the book world, would you still agree with these statements?

- "Who is a 'mathematician' to say that two plus two equals four? Just because one person gets that answer doesn't the mean the other six billion of us will get the same one."
- "I'd love to hire a translator, but I can't afford it. I put all my text through Google Translate and then get my friend who, like, goes to France for her holidays every year to read over it for me."
- "Sometimes you order a salad in a restaurant and it comes out with a hair on it, and it's no big deal. So in my restaurant, there'll be no washing of hands, wearing of hair nets or cleaning the kitchen."
- "I am perfectly capable of doing my own brain surgery. I mean, I *have* a brain, don't I?"

What Is Editing?

So what *is* editing? Let's talk about that first, because the term "editing" actually covers a lot of different things, not all of which are relevant to self-publishers.

The first stage of the editing process is **structural editing**, where an editor looks at the book as a whole and notes any "big picture" problems like a slow pace, a confusing plot or someone being pregnant for eleven months. If you paid for a manuscript critique, the report you got will be the problems flagged or suggestions raised after a structural edit of your book. This is the one stage where the only goal is to make the book better, and it's the only stage I'd allow a self-publisher to skip. This is because it's the most expensive, takes the most time and doesn't make much business sense if (i) we're charging very little for our book and (ii) we've already got positive feedback from an agent or paid for a manuscript critique. To go back to our coffee shop analogy, paying for a structural edit is like putting Egyptian cotton tablecloths on our tables: we would if we could afford it, but it's unlikely we'd recoup the cost. Instead, I think you should assemble a trusted group of beta readers: fellow writers or readers who are very familiar with your genre and who are willing to give you the constructive criticism you need.

The next stage is **copy-editing** or line-editing, where an editor goes through your book line by line looking for typos, sentences that could be changed for clarity or correctness, misuse of words, missing words, misspellings, consistency (e.g. *e-mail* and *email*) and anything else that isn't correct use of the English language. This is where the bulk of a self-publisher's budget should go, and I would strongly advise against skipping this. If you've written fiction, I would urge you not to skip it.

The final stage is **proofreading**, where a proofreader (or your editor; they usually do both) goes through the text with a fine toothcomb one last time to make sure that everything is perfect, and it is the absolute *minimum* a self-publisher should do before they release their book.

So, to recap:

- Getting your book proofread will meet the basic requirement for books with price-tags on them
- Getting your book proofread and copy-edited will produce a professionally put-together, polished product that meets accepted standards
- Getting your book proofread, copy-edited and structurally edited will make your book the best it can be, but at a substantial cost.

You *cannot* do it yourself, or get a friend who, like, reads all the time to do it for you. Because:

1. *You can't edit your own work.* This isn't my opinion, but a universal truth. You are too close to the work, and have read over it too many times to ever be able to look at it with fresh eyes. Even editors can't edit their own work, just like psychiatrists can't treat themselves.
2. *You don't know what you don't know.* You may be convinced that with enough go-throughs, you'll find every last mistake there is to find in your book. But how can you find something you aren't looking for? How can you weed out the mistakes that you don't know you've made?
3. *This isn't about spell-checking and typos.* A copy editor is someone who has a special skill that they've acquired through study, training and experience. They cannot be replaced by your friend who reads all the time, even if your friend is so pedantic about the English language that they drop friends for using "your" instead of "you're."

Hiring Professional Help

Freelance editors are easy to find online, but beware: there are plenty of people *saying* they're qualified editors, especially now that they know plenty of self-published authors are looking for them. I would make sure I got a personal recommendation from another author, and/or that the editor in question was a member of a professional association like Ireland's Association of Freelance Editors, Proofreaders and Indexers (AFEPI) or the UK's Society for Editors and Proofreaders (SfEP).

You can also go to companies who offer a one-stop shop for editing services, like Bubblecow.co.uk, again based in the UK.

Everything is done by e-mail so as long as both author and editor is proficient in the same *type* of English, i.e. British or American, location isn't really an issue.

I'd be wary of "bargain" editing offers, because like building a house, this isn't exactly the kind of job where you want everything to go to the lowest bidder. SfEP has suggested minimum hourly rates and while they won't apply all over the world, they are a good reference point for self-published authors:

- Proofreading: $33/€26/£20
- Copy-editing: $40/€31/£24
- Developmental (structural) editing: $44/€35/£27

Why an hourly rate and not a per 1,000 words one? Because my 1,000 words might need a lot more work than yours does. To find out how much your project is going to cost, send your prospective editor a few pages and let them be the judge.

You might also ask two or three of them—your shortlist—to edit the pages for you, so you can see what working with them is going to be like.

Payment is usually half before the job and the rest afterwards, or in full once the work has been delivered. Make sure you both agree on exactly what you're paying for. For example, is the proofread a once through the book, or will the proofreader go through it one more time after that to ensure it's perfect?

If you're writing science fiction with unusually spelled names or places, or have, say, a non-fiction book full of technical terms, it's helpful to make a definitive list of the correct spellings and send them to the editor along with your book. Then he or she can check them against your text to make you're spelling them right each time.

It goes without saying—but I'm going to say it anyway—that while it might be prudent to employ the services of an up-and-coming book cover designer, web designer or video trailer-maker to save money, it is certainly NOT a good idea to hire someone who's "just starting out in editing".

Preparing Your Manuscript

It's difficult for self-publishers to re-create what happens at a publishing house, where an entire staff is dedicated to bringing books to market, and nowhere is this more evident than in the editing and proofreading stages. I myself have struggled to find a way to get all my books perfect right out of the gate, even though I do pay for professional help. I think though that if you follow these steps and resist the temptation to rush your book out into the world, you'll have no trouble with typos.

1. Re-write, re-write, re-write.
2. Recruit a group of beta-writers and ask them for their feedback on your book. At this stage, it's "big picture" questions like *does the plot make sense? Is the ending satisfying? Is the main character likeable?* Take their criticisms and suggestions and re-write some more. OR hire a structural editor if you can afford it.
3. Get your book copy-edited. Once the copyedit is complete, go through your manuscript again to see if you can eliminate any more errors.
4. Enlist the help of some reader friends and have them read through the manuscript. Ideally these will not be the same people we got to read it back in step 2; we want as many different eyes on our book as possible, and we want them fresh. Make sure they understand they're looking for mistakes like spelling errors or missing words, and that the time for suggestions on the language used, plot, etc. has passed. Update your manuscript to eliminate any errors they find.
5. Hire a proofreader (or your editor again) to go through the manuscript.
6. Remember that friend who drops people for using "you're" instead of "your"? Well get her to go through your book, now that it's perfect. When she comes back to you having failed to find any mistakes, you'll know you're good to go.

If you've got to this point and you're still thinking, *my book's in pretty good shape; I think I'm good to go,* then please, reconsider. Let me tell you that as a writer, there is no worse feeling in the world than reading a bad review. I don't mean a negative review, because we don't all like the same things and negative reviews are just par for the course, but a *baaaaad* review, one that rips your book (and your confidence) into tiny shreds. If you've had your book professionally edited, you can console yourself with the fact that you know your book is good, and that that reviewer must have a bee in their bitchy bonnet for some reason unrelated to you. If your book hasn't been professionally edited, you don't have this comfort.

Furthermore, the bitchy reviewer will undoubtedly point out any errors they've found in your book—and if you don't have an outsider look at it, there will be at least a couple—which will lead other potential readers looking to your reviews to help them decide whether or not to buy it to believe that, since this is clearly a fact, everything else in the review must be true too. And then they'll cease to be a potential reader of yours.

I wasn't going to get *Mousetrapped* looked at at all, mainly because I'd already written several drafts of it and was sick of the sight of it. But then I started reading a blog by Jane Smith called The Self-Publishing Review (SPR). Jane has worked as an editor for over twenty years and she also writes a hugely popular blog called How Publishing Really Works. On the SPR, she invites authors to send in their self-published books and then she reviews them, honestly and as she would a traditionally published book. If she likes a book, she'll recommend it but if she doesn't, she'll explain why. It's not only a fantastic blog and riveting reading, but it's the best reality check for self-publishing authors I've ever come across. I recommend you read through as many entries as you can before you release your book, and read through them all if you still think you don't need to get your book assessed and edited by a professional.

And here's the thing about *Mousetrapped*. I worked on it for two years. I had feedback from an agent and editors that I considered during re-writes. I had it copy-edited and proofread. I had friends read it before publication. I've lost count of how many times I'd read the book myself. And still, in the finished product there were errors: an "if" that should've been an "it" and inconsistent spelling of a person's unusual last name. And it wasn't like the manuscript came back clean from either the editor or the proofreader; during each round, there was barely a paragraph free of a red mark. If you're wondering how that could have possibly happened, you clearly have never attempted to make 70,000 words completely error-free. It's extremely difficult, even *with* professional help. So what kind of state would your book end up in without it?

It's a sad fact that most self-published books have errors in them, and that most people read self-published books *looking* for them. So while my eyes might skip over a typo in a Michael Connolly novel—not that, to my knowledge, they've ever had to—a reader *will* remember the errors in your book. And then in all likelihood, mention them in her review.

Finally, this isn't just about you. You'll benefit hugely from having your book edited, yes, because you'll be able to carry everything you'll learn forward with you into your self-published career, but it's not you that you have to think about. It's your readers. When they buy a book, they want to *read* it. Not keep their eyes peeled for errors you couldn't be bothered to catch.

A few months back, I was reading an interview with a self-published author when I came across this quote: "Unfortunately I don't have the luxury of an editor." An editor is not a luxury, it's a necessity. And it's the *readers of her books* who'll have to do without it, along with the money they've spent on her badly produced book.

Please don't do the same to yours.

The Minefield That Is Cover Design— And How To Cross It

Remember how I said that there were only two places in this book where, if you didn't listen to me, you definitely wouldn't be a successful self-publisher? Well, pricing was one of them, and this, *cover design*, is the other.

You can write a bad book. You can write a truly *terrible* book, that's also a little offensive. You can publish it chock full of grammar and spelling mistakes, lay it out sideways and do the whole thing in super large print and upside down. You can call it something boring, do no promotion and claim in your book description that you're the next J.K. Rowling or something equally pompous and annoying. ("My book is the best book I've ever read", for instance.) You can do all these things and *still* sell books. It's unlikely, but it can happen. But charge too much money for it or wrap it in a stinky cover and you *will not sell books*. Those two mistakes *cannot* be overcome, partly because they are so obvious and the tell-tale signs of a badly self-published book. Hopefully I've already convinced you that you need to be reasonable in your pricing, so now let me clatter you over the head with my arguments for why you need to have a good cover and why this may make or break your entire self-publishing career. The good news is that covers are by far the trickiest thing in this whole process, so if you can do this right, you're more than halfway to a successful self-publishing adventure.

We are now entering what I like to call The Bermuda Triangle of self-published cover design, because chances are everything you know about books is about to mysteriously disappear. Self-publishing is indeed a strange world: there are purple unicorns that talk, plastic toys that come to life and hundreds of thousands, if not *millions*, of writers who've (hopefully) been reading books all their lives who then go on to make their own and instantly *forget every single thing they know about them*. It amazes me on a daily basis how self-published authors create books that look absolutely *nothing* like the books they've been buying, borrowing, reading, stacking, stroking (or is that just me?) and gazing at adoringly and then, even more amazingly, don't see that they've done anything wrong.

Why does that happen? Behold, the five biggest mines in the minefield of self-published cover design:

Mine #1: Laziness

The antidote to successful self-publishing, laziness gets in between many self-publishers and properly self-published books. You just don't want to be *bothered* finding, hiring and working with a cover designer. Where do you even *find* those people? And you'd rather lie on the sofa and watch *The Biggest Loser* than think up something to go on the cover of you book. Ugh. BOR-ing. Haven't you done enough already by *writing* the bloody thing? You need some Me Time. So you're just going to watch TV and then spend a few minutes knocking up a cover on the POD website with their cover creator wizard thingy. I mean, they wouldn't call it a wizard if it didn't work, right? So get off my back. *Gawd.*

How to avoid this? Hire a cover designer.

Mine #2: Lack of skills and/or imagination

You either have a very good idea of what might go on your book's cover, or none at all. Having spent all of your creative energy on writing the thing, it's not unusual to have little or no clue of what might work well on the jacket. This is okay, but it's *not* okay for you to do nothing about it. Similarly, you might not want to get involved in doing anything "too fancy" for your cover because you don't know how to use Photoshop or any of those design programs—which, again, is okay. I don't know how to use them either. But I didn't let that stop me from getting a good cover for my book.

How to avoid this? Hire a cover designer.

Mine #3: Delusion

This is my favourite one, and I'd hazard a guess, the most common problem. Self-publishers (the ones destined to do it badly, anyway) can be so damn defensive, and they are especially defensive when it comes to choosing a cover design, in particular *why* they need to choose a good one. "But Catherine," they're saying now, if they enjoy talking aloud to books, "I *never* choose books because of their covers. I read books because the blurb is interesting, or because I like the author. Whatever picture is on the cover doesn't sway me in the slightest. Why, just last week I bought the new Harlan Coben and I'll tell you, I didn't care for the cover on it *at all*. So I think you going on for pages and pages about how my cover is the most important part of my book is occasionally amusing — mildly — but ultimately utterly irrelevant. My book is, like, the best book I or anyone else has ever read and when people see the thousands of five-star reviews I'm going to get on Amazon, they won't even *glance* at the cover before clicking 'Add to Cart.' It just doesn't matter."

How to avoid this? Don't be a moron. And hire a cover designer.

Mine #4: Distorted perspective/ "My Name is on the Spine!" Syndrome

It is *very* exciting to see your name on the spine of a book, and words you wrote in between its covers. Very exciting indeed. In fact it's *so* exciting that I recommend you go straight to CS right now, upload any old PDF you can find, run through the Cover Creator wizard thingy and send yourself a proof copy just so you can get it out of your system. Then you won't be so overwhelmed by the sight of your name on anything that looks like a printed book that you'll fail to notice the book your name is on looks like a pile of self-published poo. It is not enough to produce something that feels like a book in your hands, that has pages inside of it and that has those pages bound together at one end to form a spine. You need to produce a great looking book, and if your eyes are filled with tears at the sight of your newborn book baby, you won't be able to see it clearly enough to tell whether you have or not.

How to avoid this? Take a book with a white spine and write your name on it with a Sharpie. Look at it for while, and then hire a cover designer.

Mine #5: Lack of money

Maybe you already knew how important a cover was, but you just don't have the money to hire a cover designer and get them to make a good one for you. If you are planning on releasing both a paperback and an e-book, then I'd bring out my standard "no money" response, which is don't self-publish. Would you build a house if you didn't have enough money for a roof? Hardly. If, however, you're only planning on releasing an e-book, there might a way around your budgetary issue. We'll talk about it in a minute.

How to avoid this? Keep reading.

You may have got the sense by now, if you're *very* astute, that I don't recommend you use any "cover creation" software available on POD sites, such as CreateSpace's Cover Creator. This is because the only creation involved is deciding between one bad template and the next, and even if you push it to the max and do the *very* best you can with it, you will *still* end up with a cover that screams "self-published!" They look bad because they don't look like real, proper books, and all of them are on my Top 3 list of Stinky Self-Published Front Covers:

- A rectangular photograph centred on the front cover that takes up a large portion of it, is against a plain colour background and has text above (the title) and below (the author's name)
- A patterned or plain background with no photographs at all, just text
- Almost anything generated by a cover creation wizard installed on a POD site.

If you insist on using the Cover Creator, then you'll do it after you upload your interior files and CS will automatically size it for your book's page count and trim, and then add the barcode for you. As I've said already, do not pay for any packages or services offered by the POD site, and that includes cover design. (I'd even go so far as to say *especially* cover design.) All you are doing here is paying through the nose for a cover that is almost completely indiscernible from one you could have made yourself — and for *free* — using the cover creation software. So DON'T do it.

Getting A Cover For Your Book

So I've told you what *not* to do. (Repeatedly.) But what *should* you do to ensure that your cover is worthy of your book and of rubbing shoulders with anything produced by the Big Boys, and won't stand out as a self-published POD book when it does?

The most useful thing you can do is *study real books*. It doesn't cost any money to do this and you can learn a lot. It is especially useful to study books that are similar to yours. If you've written a travel guide, look at some travel guides. If you've written a romance novel, look at some romance novels. If you've written science fiction involving My Little Ponies, well... good luck with that. Get some ideas from these books. If you already have an idea, compare it to what's out there already and see if it works. Would it stand on its own two feet, or would it make a holy show of itself?

Another good source of inspiration are *stock photo websites*. These are libraries of photographs, just like the ones that professional cover designers use, and although you have to pay to use them, you can browse for free. The easiest book cover you can make that will still look good is a full bleed single photograph (i.e. a photograph that takes up the whole front cover, right out to all the edges) with a large title on top and the author's name towards the bottom. Pick out something in your book — an object, a character or a location — and then find a suitable photo of it on one of the stock image sites. You never know: deciding what to put on your cover might be as simple as that. There are some stock photo sites listed at the back of this book.

You need to *hire a cover designer*. Don't baulk; I initially didn't want to do this either. I thought that, first of all, finding a cover designer would be a right pain in the arse. And if I did find one, I assumed that getting a cover professionally designed would cost thousands and eat into any profit I might make from selling the book. Luckily I was *totally* wrong on both counts.

Cover designers are easier to find than you think. The best way to find them is to look on successful self-published authors' blogs or in their books (if you like the look of their covers, of course!) and find out who did it for them. Then contact them for a quote. This is ideal because you know they've worked with self-published authors before and you can see actual examples of their work. (If you like *my* covers and want to use my cover designer, his contact details are at the back of this book.)

Get several quotes before deciding on who to go with and don't tell any of them what the others have offered you. Make sure that a specific number of design rounds is included in the price. This is how many times the design can go back and forth between the designer and the author before incurring extra charges; if this isn't specified, you could end up making the designer do 10 different designs or, conversely, he or she could refuse to give you anything but one go. You should also agree in advance whether or not any stock images that have to be purchased are included in the price, or if they're extra.

A *good* cover designer will then prepare a design brief based on questions they've asked you about your book, or you might even prepare one yourself with all your ideas, book covers you like, a synopsis of the subject matter, etc. Have a browse around the internet — Pinterest.com would be a great starting point — for any images that take your fancy, and copy and paste them into a Word document. They don't have to be literal interpretations of your book. It might just be a picture that reminds you of your book, or reminds you of how you feel when you read it. If I was doing this for *Mousetrapped*, for example, there'd be loads of pictures of beaches, sunshine and fireworks, even though only one of those things appears on the actual cover. Think of it less like instructions and more like your book's mood board.

How do either of you know what shape and size the cover needs to be? Thankfully, you don't need to worry. Once you've decided on your trim size and page count, you can plug the details into CS and they will generate a cover template for you that's already perfectly sized. You send this to your cover designer and they build your cover inside it. CS will automatically add a barcode; make sure your designer knows this so they don't put anything in that area. But we'll talk more about the specifics of this when we come to actually making our POD paperback.

And please, self-publishing people—*pretty please*—step away from the easel and put down the water-colours. While you're at it, lose the oils, the crayons and the magic markers. *Please*. I get why you think that creating your own cover image is a good idea—it'll be unique and you own the rights to it—but do you get that it's really, *really* not (unless it's for a children's book or a book about water-colours)? The goal here is to produce a POD book that looks like a real book, one that will be at home on your bookshelves amongst the traditionally published books, and to date every self-published book I've seen with a water-colour picture on the front has no hope of doing that. Also, look at your shelves! Look at the books on them. What's on their front covers? They're called *photographs*.

(There are, of course, exceptions. Some books on my shelves have illustrations or cartoons on their covers, and they work really well. But they have been done by professional illustrators, cartoonists or graphic designers. Not by you and a paint-by-numbers set.)

Now I promised I would have a solution for you if you don't have cash to spend. A year ago if *I* didn't have any money to spend—and I practically didn't—I would've released my e-book first and then after two or three months, when I'd raised enough money to pay for a decent cover, got working on the paperback. Yes, you need a cover for an e-book too, but a much simpler one and one you can make yourself. I'll show you how in the how to produce an e-book section later on. (Sadly this same method doesn't work for paperbacks because the resolution isn't high enough, and you'd end up with a cover that looks like you're viewing it through the bottom of a jam jar.)

Alternatively, you can do the bulk of the work yourself. Mock up a cover using MS Word and then find someone really, *really* nice to convert it into the format it needs to be in for CS to accept and okay it, for either no money or a very small amount of it. Remember too that you are about to put a product out into the universe, of which there may ultimately be thousands and thousands of copies. And if you take my advice in the promotion section, you might be blogging about it too. So why not do a little skills exchange? Maybe there's a graphic designer just getting started, or a college student studying design, and they need something to add to their portfolio. In exchange for their work, you can offer to advertise their website or e-mail in your finished book, as well as on the cover itself.

Covers are important to books, but they are the *most important thing* about self-published books. If I walk into a Waterstones and see the latest Michael Connelly novel, I'm going to buy it because I know he's a bestselling author (so lots of other people think he's good), he's traditionally published (so an agent and an editor think he's good) and because he's my favourite author (so *I* think he's good). His covers don't really matter to me. And even if you walked in there and you had no idea who he was or what he'd written previously, you wouldn't have to rely on the cover as evidence that the book is likely to be of good quality. But what if the same book was self-published? What if it had *just* been self-published, and hadn't yet sold many copies or got too many reviews? What if you're looking at it on a shelf, and so you can't see the blurb? What is the *one thing* that is available to you to help you decide whether or not that book is any good? If you haven't guessed by now, it's *the cover*. So even if you're the next Jonathan Franzen and your book is better than *The Corrections* and *Freedom* combined, no one is going to buy it if your cover looks like a pile of (water-coloured?) poo.

Whatever You Do, Don't Mention The War

I don't want to devote time or space to the whole traditional publishing versus self-publishing, us versus them, The People versus The Man "debate", so I'll just say this: it is all *completely irrelevant*.

When it was announced that J.K. Rowling was going to sell Harry Potter e-books through her own site, Pottermore, self-publishing evangelists couldn't get their "NOW EVEN J.K. ROWLING IS SELF-PUBLISHING!" flags printed fast enough, completely missing the point that Rowling became the world's only billionaire author through a *traditional* publishing deal, and that if she sets up a lemonade stand outside her house and sells handwritten stories on Post-It notes, it doesn't matter to us — it has *no relevance* whatsoever to the average self-published author.

You don't need to "pick a side" in order to self-publish, and you'll be a better self-publisher if, instead of shouting your mouth off about how publishing companies are wrong about everything, you spend your time, say, writing better books.

And despite the sensationalist headlines, let's not forget that right now, most books sold in the world are:

- Print books
- Purchased from bookstores
- Published by mainstream, traditional publishing houses.

Even when we hear things like "e-book sales overtake hardback sales for the first time", that's not a win for self-publishing; it's a win for *e-books*. I think sometimes we self-publishers forget that the two aren't one and the same.

In this book — and in my life and hopefully in yours too — there will be no "Down with Big Publishing!" chants, literary agent-shaped voodoo dolls or rants about nobody even giving my novel about My Little Ponies come to life a proper chance. Yes, sometimes the traditional publishing industry prints a few million copies of a book that isn't as entertaining as the instructions for our microwave oven, but clinging on to that as evidence of the beginning of their end is like being a lunar-landing conspiracy theorist who goes on about the shadows in the photos taken on the moon, and ignores the 400,000-plus people employed by the Apollo program who would have had to keep the world's largest secret for going on sixty years.

Another popular anti-traditional publishing argument is that they're only interested in making money. *What?* A business is only interested in making the money it needs to keep paying its rent, its employees and the factories that print its products? Surely you're not serious! Of *course* they're interested in making money. So am I. And if *you're* not, then what is this all about? Because self-publishing is a business too, and if you just want to go chuck money down a toilet, go chuck money down a toilet.

And if you insist on calling yourself an "indie author", then I presume you'll be pressing your own paper, binding your books together with thread and selling them door-to-door? Because the only other option is to rely on one of the largest corporations in the world — Amazon — to publish and sell your books, and some of the largest banks in the world to process your royalty payments. Sorry, but that doesn't sound very *independent* to me.

I'm not self-publishing because I want to beat some kind of revolutionary drum, and I hope you're not either. Because what does it have to do with books? What does it have to do with wanting to be an author? If you really love writing and want it to be your career, then you need to be *making* connections, not burning them away with an ill-informed acid tongue. And do you really think anyone who buys a copy of your book even thinks about what "side" of the so-called war you're on? Do you really think they even *know* there's such a thing? Do you think they *care*?

I'm not a self-publishing evangelist and I don't think you should waste your time being one either. Even if you disagree with everything I've just said, I'm sure you *can* agree that debating the issue is, at this point, a massive waste of time. And that· with an already busy self-publishing schedule, we don't have any time to spare.

* * *

And so concludes the bit where I try to prepare you for your new career as a successful self-published author, replace any fanciful ideas you may have had about what lies ahead with cold, hard realistic ones and — hopefully — convince you that the only way to do this is to do it *right*.

Now it's time to lay the foundations of our online homes, the blog, Twitter account and Facebook page from where, later on, we'll do almost all of our promotional activities and through which we'll meet the people who'll — again, hopefully! — be among the first to buy it.

If you already *have* a functioning blog, Twitter account and Facebook fan page or public profile (as opposed to your personal one where you post drunk photos of yourself) then most of Part 2 will not be news to you, but you never know, you might pick up a few new tips or tricks.

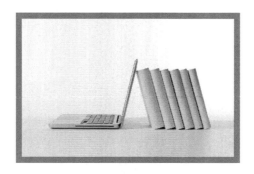

PART 2:
Building An Online Platform

Here Comes The Science Bit

(Is "the science bit" too outdated a reference? You know I'm talking about those old L'Oreal hair ads, right? Where some gorgeous girl swings her hair while talking about shiny and glossy and weightlessness, and then she frowns and says, "Here comes the science bit" where a male voice then patiently explains the *why* of the shiny and the glossy and the weightlessness, mostly using made up words, the implication being that women only care about shiny hair and not the stuff in the shampoo that makes it shiny? Well, now you do.)

Here's what's going to happen now: I'm going to tell you how to do all the techie bits of self-publishing: building an online platform, publishing an e-book, publishing a POD paperback. But it'll only be later, in the part about *selling* self-published books, that I'll be able to tell you what we're going to *do* with them.

For example, I have a theory about how to sell self-published books. It involves using blogging, Twitter and Facebook to build up a group of supporters, our "first readers", who will then buy our book when it comes out, pushing our book out of the shadows on Amazon and into the light where other people can see it, leading to more sales, and to reviews, which lead to more sales. And we'll keep the momentum going by regularly adding new, valuable content to the internet that will both grow our author platform and get people interested in buying our book, and we'll build a fanbase using a mailing list service so that when our *next* book comes out, we have an added booster rocket to get things going.

But I can't go into too much detail about it at this stage, because you may not have a blog. You may not have a Twitter account, or you may have one but not know how to use it right. And, crucially, you don't yet know how to self-publish your books, or how long it'll take to publish them, and if you've been reading this book straight through without stopping, you might also have forgotten your own name because I've bombarded you with so stuff that your brain is flashing "Error: not enough available disk memory to complete this task."

So I'm going to tell you all that stuff first and save the Big Theory of Everything Self-Publishing for later, when you're familiar with all the key players. Think of it like learning how to play the guitar: you start with the individual chords, so that later we can put a few of them together and play a song.

This section is about how to **create and maintain a blog**, **build a mailing list**, **use Twitter** and **create a Facebook fan page**. In other words, the basic foundations of an author's online platform. What we're going to *do* with these things in order to sell our books will come a bit later on.

The "What Are You Trying To Achieve Here?" Speech

Line up, my lovelies. It's lecture time. (Again...?)

I'm about to start telling you how I think you should blog, tweet and use Facebook. This will involve me saying things like, "Don't ask for more Twitter followers", "Don't blog about how your boyfriend just dumped you" and "Don't poke me or anyone else on Facebook", and you saying things like "Don't be such a party pooper!", "I can blog about whatever the hell I want!" and "But I LIKE poking people!"

Let's get something clear right here, right now. I am not here to tell you how to blog, tweet or use Facebook to entertain yourself, connect with friends or become a champion poker. If those are your goals, you're right: you can do whatever the hell you want. What I'm telling you is how to do it *and sell books* and yes, party pooper or no, this will involve curtailing your poking, because in a professional arena, poking is not only *un*professional but *extremely bloody annoying*. I'm not trying to put a stop to your fun, or prevent you from talking about your loser boyfriend with your Twitter friends, or implying that blogging about quilting isn't worthwhile. All I'm doing is telling you what works for me as both a writer and a reader, and trying to help you to sell your book.

So hold off on the angry "But a blog is SUPPOSED to be personal!" and "But what's the point of Twitter if you don't TALK to people?" e-mails. For the moment, anyway. At least wait until the end of the book to see if there's anything you can be *really* annoyed about.

Chances are, I will also tell you not to do things that some of you are already doing, and then you will take this personally and imagine that I've been reading your blog and that that's where I got the idea to tell everyone else not to do it from. (Rest assured that even when I seem to be talking about specific people, I have in fact drawn on details from several people and/or changed all identifying details, in order to avoid this very event. Except for that bit where I was talking about *you*.) You might argue with me in your head something along the lines of, "Well, *I* do that and I have loads of followers" or "I actually *prefer* bloggers who do that" and in doing so, you'll be missing the point.

For instance, I'm going to say that those chain-letter style blogger awards ("Most Pink Blogger" and the like) bestowed upon bloggers by other bloggers, who are then obligated to bestow it upon a specified number of other bloggers, have no place on the blog of a professional writer, or a writer who is trying to look professional. Now, I've received a number of these, and maybe you even sent me one, and if you did you'll have seen that while I appreciated the acknowledgement, I never put another link in the chain and I certainly never put the little MS Paint "award" image in my sidebar. Do I think if you do this you'll never sell a single book or make a living as a writer? No. But do *I* do it? No. And what is the whole point of this book? Telling you how *I* did what I did.

If things are going really badly, you might also get the impression that I want to drain all of the fun out of your blogging, tweeting and Facebook-ing and make it a clinical, dry and boring experience. Nothing could be further from the truth. I don't do anything that isn't fun for me — or at least, I don't do it for very long (see *dieting* for more examples of this) — and I certainly wouldn't have ploughed so much time into this if I didn't enjoy it. I truly love blogging, I have some fantastic Twitter friends (some of whom have even become friends in real life) and whenever Facebook isn't threatening to sell my home address to the highest bidder, I like Facebook too. I have a *great time* with social media. It's enriched my life. But I use it without doing things like asking for more Twitter followers, blogging about the terrible date I had last night or virtually poking you, and I find it works better that way.

What's With The Be Professional Thing?

Why do you need to act like a professional? Why can't you smear your emotional crap all over the place? Why can't you do whatever it takes to get to a nice round number of Twitter followers? Why can't you virtually poke me in the eye, especially when after reading this far, you really, *really* want to?

You Have Something To Prove

Self-publishers, in the eyes of the discerning reader, start off fairly low on the Book Ladder. In fact for some, we're not even *on* the ladder. The ladder is leaning against a house and we're across the street and five doors down from it. Before the discerning reader will give our book a chance, we have to convince him or her that we have the potential to be just as good as anything the top-selling, most lauded, international-superstar-authors have to offer, and that just because we're associated with a group known for bad quality doesn't necessarily mean that we've gone down that road as well.

How can we do that? By sending *I'm-not-crap* signals at every opportunity. On the book, this is the cover. On our Amazon listing, this is the product description. And online, this is how much our blog looks like the website of a professional author, maybe even one who has someone else to make and maintain their website for them, someone with a website manager. (The dream!) When you're a self-published author, everything you do online is a reflection of the quality of your book. *Everything.* Because even when no one is watching, Google is.

The More... The Merrier?

When you first start blogging, you feel like it's just you and the screen. Then a few people leave comments, and you feel like it's just you and them. Even though you know, intellectually, that whatever you type on those posts is entering the public domain, it doesn't feel like it at the time. Even when your site stats say a couple of thousand people are visiting your blog on a regular basis, it still feels like a little group of friends, gathered together over a coffee every morning, chatting about quilts or whatever. It's nice. It's intimate. It's *safe.*

It's only when something from the real world pierces the bubble of your blogosphere that you realise how many people can, potentially, read your every blogged thought, and who some of those people might be. Maybe you write a post about how your family don't believe in you, and then Aunty Joanne brings it up at your cousin's wedding. Maybe you tell people the resort you're going to on holidays and, while you're there, someone comes up to you by the pool and says, "Are you the Quilting Queen of the Universe? I read your blog!" Or maybe you bitch about how your boss is clearly a devoted disciple of Satan, and then the next day you get fired.

And not to get all serious and sinister, but a lot worse can happen than that.

Your social media presence requires your personality, but it shouldn't include your personal life. The easiest way to ensure that we keep one but exclude the other is to behave ourselves, and act the same way a professional writer — who knows, right from the outset, that lots of people, including reporters, agents and editors, are reading his/her every word — would do.

Dress For The Job You Want

You've heard that, right? Dress for the job you want, not the job you have? The same applies to your online presence. If you want to be a professional writer some day, start acting like one now.

At least on your blog.

A Few Words About Being Nice

Another great rule in life, treat others as you would like them to treat you, is especially important in social media. You'll only get out of it as much as you put in, and that isn't confined to blogging on a regular basis or always responding to any comments your posts may get. I'm talking about *outside* of your blog, or *outside* of your own Twitter profile. Always be nice, kind and generous. Hopefully this will lead to people being nice, kind and generous to you.

When author Talli Roland (*The Hating Game*) started building her blog following a year before her book came out, she knew how important it would be to read other blogs and comment on the posts. In fact, whenever someone left a comment on her blog she would make a point of reciprocating. In the beginning she was visiting an average of *seventy blogs a day!* Now that's dedication. If you visit Talli's fantastic blog, you'll see that every single one of her posts gets loads of comments, and she has thousands of loyal blog followers. And if you're not yet convinced, *The Hating Game* was an Amazon bestseller on the day of its release.

A Few Words About Being Genuine

As I'll be explaining — and hopefully *proving* — in more detail later, I believe that the best chance of self-published success is a promotional strategy that involves an online platform, i.e. a blog, a Twitter account that sends traffic to it and a Facebook page that taps into already assembled groups of potential readers. It's the only *free* way to do it that I know of. I also believe that the best way to maintain that success and to enjoy the fruits of it is to have a direct connection with your readers through the same tools, and that blogging, tweeting and using Facebook is *fun*.

(*Way* too much fun, sometimes.)

With so much of our time spent online these days, author platforms are becoming increasingly important, especially in the traditional publishing world where marketing budgets are being cut and competition for review space is fiercer than ever. That's why, every now and then, a traditionally published author who has previously shied away from every internet-related activity except e-mail and booking cheap flights feels forced to sign up for Twitter and steps, blinking, into your stream with something like, "*Erm, my new book, I Don't Want To Be Here and Resent The Fact That I Feel I Have To, is out on July 18. So... buy it?*"

There are also certain books and seminars out there encouraging writers to abuse online platforms, i.e. write specific types of blog posts and send specific tweets to hoodwink readers into connecting with them and their books. This is just plain dishonest and manipulative. Social media is all about making a connection, and that connection *has* to be genuine.

Please don't do this if you don't want to. Don't do it just because I said you should. Now, I'll be honest with you: I don't know how you can do this without an online platform. But I *do* know that it definitely won't work if your heart isn't in it. The rest of us will be able to tell.

Privacy Issues

I came home from Florida once for a visit to find that the family PC had about fifteen new icons on the desktop. Turns out that in my absence, my parents had hired some cowboy to come and "spring clean" the computer to speed it up and he'd managed to convince them to pay him to install a whole host of anti-virus, anti-malware and anti-spyware software. My parents, not knowing enough to realise that the best way to avoid viruses was to refrain from clicking on things called "happy.exe" and the like, readily agreed, and now our PC was so clogged with anti-virus programs (there must have been upwards of ten things just auto-running at start-up) you couldn't use the internet anyway, as you'd have to wait half an hour for every page to pass their anti-virus scan and load.

This was a few years ago now, and these days the Really Scary Thing about the internet has become privacy, or lack thereof. But while invasion of privacy is a genuine concern online, chances are you're worried about the wrong *kind* of invasion of privacy. And all you need to do to avoid it is to exercise some common sense.

If I write a Facebook status that I think will only be seen by my Facebook friends and Facebook dump it out into the internet at large, allowing Google to catalogue it so that it shows up in their search results, that is an invasion of privacy. That is something to *actually* be worried about. (Although whenever Facebook does something like this behind its users' backs, the beady-eyed among us get all angry and riled up, and they get it sorted for the rest of us. So we don't *really* need to worry about it.) But someone getting your credit card details because you've signed up for Twitter? Publishing your home address because you've got a WordPress blog? Finding out about all those knitting books you bought from Amazon through your Facebook fan page?

Um... *no*. Those are things we don't need to worry about, unless we're stupid enough to, say, post our home address in the "About Me" section of our blog.

I often hear social media phobes say things like, "I know I should have a blog, but I don't want one. I don't want people reading every little thing about me", or "I'd sign up for a Facebook page, but I don't want everyone knowing where I am all the time." The eye-rolling I then indulge in — behind their backs, because I'm a coward who hates confrontation — is nobody's business. *You* control what goes on your blog. *You* control what you tweet. *You* control what goes on your Facebook fan page and it won't be connected in any way to your personal Facebook profile if you don't want it to be.

Don't do a Hollywood actor on it and say that you're only "interested in the art." You'll *have* to be interested in something other than the art if the art doesn't pay any money, and people can't go to see movies (or buy books) if they don't know they exist, so you're just going to have to go tell them about it.

Blogging

The blog is where it all starts. This is the main hub of your online platform, the place where people can come to find out more about you, to hear more from you or, let's be honest, satisfy their curiosity about what you look like. It's one big advertisement for you as a writer, and a snapshot of your personality in HTML.

Why start a blog? Because blogging is so much FUN. You get to tell people what you think about things and they can't interrupt you. It doesn't cost anything but your time, if that; I write most of my blog posts while simultaneously watching TV. (True story: I'm writing the first draft of these very words with one eye on a late night showing of *Jackie Brown*.) The true magic of blogging is that you have no idea of the fantastic places it'll take you—new friends, free stuff, bestseller lists, speaking engagements, VIP events—but rest assured, it *will* take you somewhere.

The Best Things In Blogging Are Free

Don't pay for anyone to design, host (store) or maintain your blog, website or blogsite (a term I'll explain in a second). You don't need to, and the less money you spend, the more of your profit you get to keep.

Right now I have a WordPress blog that also acts as my website. (See? A *blogsite*.) It's adorable, I love it, everybody else loves it too and it's all free. The blog is free, the space online for the blog is free and the theme (the design, the template) is free too.

The only thing I pay for is called a customised URL upgrade, and it costs about $17 a year per blog. This upgrades the free URL that came with the site (www.catherineryanhoward.wordpress.com) and changes it to something I want (www.catherineryanhoward.com). You don't even have to do this, but I recommend that you do. I'll explain why and how later on.

Blogger.com is free too, but I think in most cases it looks it. I recommend that you use WordPress. You may find it a bit tricky to use in the beginning especially if you've been using Blogger.com, but stick with it because it is so worth it. I have never seen a Blogger.com blog that looks as good as one WP can do.

(You might hear people talking about WordPress.com versus WordPress.org. "Org" is the self-hosted version of WP; you use their software but you pay for your blog. We're going to stick with WordPress.com, the free version.)

The Benefits Of A Practice Run

The best way to figure out how to use social media effectively is to start *using it*, as you'll quickly get an intuitive sense of what works and what doesn't. We all make mistakes right out of the gate, and there's a wealth of articles online called things like "10 Things I Wish I'd Known When I Started Blogging" because the top bloggers learned everything they know on the job. Still, you might not want to make all your rookie mistakes on the blog you've just worked incredibly hard ·to get thousands of people to visit, which is why it's best to have a bit of a practice run in semi-private first.

I started Catherine, Caffeinated on February 1st, 2010, but I started The Scribbler in September 2009. You can still go have a look at it now, if you like (www.cathryanhoward.blogspot.com) but before you all run off, I've already deleted the most embarrassing bits. So there.

Now I may have an unhealthy relationship with Catherine, Caffeinated I love it so much (it's pink! there's a typewriter! the name refers to my favourite thing to do—drink coffee!), but even if I was just being generous, I'd still say The Scribbler is the Primark (Target, my American friends) knock-off version of what my blogging is today, if even that. It was *truly* craptabulous.

What was wrong with it? Well, for a blog it was fine. It did the job. But for a blog that's supposed to be the hub of an effective online platform, an advertisement for me and my writing and a snapshot of my personality in HTML... well, let me count the ways:

- It was on Blogger.com. You can argue with me all you want, but 9.9 times out of ten, WordPress blogs look infinitely more professional. Not all Blogger.com blogs can be tainted with the same brush of course, but even though both platforms are free to use, Blogger is the only one that looks it
- It was a muddy green. Yuck!
- It didn't reflect my personality *at all*
- It had a name that implied I was writing for fun and not because it's all I've ever wanted to do with my life

- It was updated on a schedule that boasted the same regularity as Oreo cookies breaking the way you want them to, i.e. with no regularity at all
- It was just a blog, i.e. it had no pages or sections, e.g. "About", "News", "Contact", etc.
- It had mismatched and wrongly-sized widgets in its sidebar (the column that goes down one side of your blog, usually the right, where you can put links and stuff), which is my pet blogging hate — and back then, I was actually doing it myself!
- It was so lacking in focus, it was practically blurry.

Luckily no one was reading it except for real-life friends I forced to on pain of death or being forced to watch my Floridian memories DVD *again*, and one teenage boy who seemed oddly obsessed with me. So even though I was doing the blogging equivalent of flailing about in the water and screeching "I can't swim!" (fun fact: I actually *can't* swim), only a couple of people were around to see it and thankfully none of them had video phones.

Crucially, it was only after I started The Scribbler that I started reading other people's blogs, something I *insist* you do before starting your own. You wouldn't attempt to write a book without reading as many books as you could first, right? The same goes for blogs. Sign up for something like **Google Reader (www.google.com/reader)**, that allows you to add as many blogs as you'd like, and then delivers their new posts to one convenient place — your GR account — each day. (This is the only way I can read blogs; visiting them all individually would be a nightmare and *so* time-consuming.)

When I knew I'd be self-publishing *Mousetrapped* and thus raising my own blogging stakes, I decided to take everything I'd learned from reading other people's blogs and having no one read my own, and move to WordPress.com where I'd start a new, free and very pink blog, Catherine, Caffeinated. Today that blogsite is the hub of all my online activities. It's where people come if they want to find out more about me, find out more about my books, sign up to my newsletter, see what news they've missed, contact me and/or read my blog posts, current or past. And it costs me next to nothing, as you'll see in a minute.

Books and blogs have another thing in common. Just as you should write the book you want to read (but don't see on the shelves), you should create the blog you want to read (but can't find on the internet). That's exactly what I did with my blog, and I think that's largely why it's been so successful. So try to imagine the kind of blog you'd like to read. What would it look like? What would the tone be? What topics would it cover? Then think about how you can create that blog.

With regards to separate websites and blogs, I don't believe in them. Many authors have static websites where not much changes on a weekly or even monthly basis, and then entirely separate blogs. I think they should all be together, in one spot. (Or at least *look* like they are.) I don't want to go to the trouble of looking up an author online, finding their blog and then having to make yet another hop onto their website. And if someone does land on our website, why wouldn't we entice them to read some of our latest musings by having them right there? Attention spans are getting shorter; we have to do what we can as *quick* as we can to keep browsers interested.

Make things easy for your visitors and yourself: have everything together, in the one place.

Get Yourself A Blog

Signing up for a free WordPress blog is easy and can be done in less than a minute. Simply go to **www.wordpress.com**, click the "Sign Up Now" button and on the page that appears, fill in:

- Your desired blog address. This should be your writing name, e.g. catherineryanhoward. As soon as you type it in, WP will run a check to see if it's available. If it's not, try putting the word "writer" after it, or stick in a middle initial. We're going to upgrade this once our blog is up and running, so we'll be changing it eventually anyway.
- Your username. Keep this the same as what you've entered in the box above. When you comment on someone else's WP blog, this is the name that will appear, so it's not a good idea to have that saying something totally unconnected to your own blog, like "angelwings1980" for example.
- A password.
- An e-mail address.

After you click "Submit" you'll be brought to a second page that tells you to go check your e-mail. It also prompts you to fill in some profile information, but we're going to leave this for now.

Instead, go to your e-mail account where there should be an activation message from WordPress waiting for you. Click on the link in it.

Then, congratulations! You now have a free WordPress blog. Log in to it. At the top of your screen you'll see a dark grey bar that begins with "My Account." Next to it is "My Blog." If you put your cursor over it a drop-down menu will appear. Select "Dashboard."

The WordPress Dashboard.

You are now on your WordPress Dashboard, the nerve centre of your blog. If this is the first time you've seen it, a yellow box will be prompting you to watch an introductory video, read tutorials, etc. But we don't want an overload of information so look for the "Hide this" link in the bottom right-hand corner.

You will now be looking at your dashboard as you'll normally see it every time you log in (as it is in the picture above). It's here we'll return to whenever we want to do something to our blog over the rest of this section.

What's In A Name?

Unless you're already a household name, you're going to need a name for your blog.

Most people find new blogs to read in lists of recommended blogs on other people's blogs ("blog rolls").

Normally these blog rolls look something like this:

Blogs I Like:

John Smith's Blog
Jane Murphy
Claire Richardson's Musings
Mary Jones
The Blog of Edward May

Now I may be looking for new blogs to read but I don't have the time to click into all those links to see what those blogs are about, or if they're the kind of thing I'd like to read. But imagine if the blog roll looked like this:

Blogs I Like:

High Heels and Book Deals
A Newbie's Guide to Publishing
How Publishing Really Works
Help! I Need a Publisher
Pimp My Novel
Organic Growing Pains

How much more inclined would you be to click on those blogs? Answer: a LOT more. They're already sinking their blogging teeth into you with their clever and pithy names, telling you that they're exactly what you need and have been looking for.

So give your blog a name, something short and sweet, and either informative ("How Publishing Really Works") or funny and cute ("High Heels and Book Deals"). You can even incorporate your own name if you like ("Catherine, Caffeinated") or award yourself a subtitle ("Coffee and Roses: Life as Eternal Optimist"). This really is a shortcut to lots of blog readers, because most people don't do it. And so on most blog rolls I find myself on, it's me in a sea of names like this:

Blogs I Like:

John Smith's Blog
Jane Murphy
Catherine, Caffeinated
Claire Richardson's Musings
Mary Jones
The Blog of Edward May

If you could only click on one blog there, which one would it be? Who sounds like they might be *ever-so-slightly* more fun than the others? (Just sounds like. Not saying it actually is. That's the next step!)

But what, you're protesting now, if someone is looking for my blog or website by name, because I've become oh so famous that people outside of my family, friends, co-workers and postman actually know who I am? Well, fear not, because your name is going to be in your URL, or blog address.

And While We're On The Subject Of Names...

I have a confession to make: my name isn't Catherine Ryan Howard.

It's actually just Catherine Howard, but I added in Ryan, my mother's maiden name, because there's another Catherine Howard, and she gets a *lot* of Google search results.

Catherine Howard was the fifth wife of Henry VIII of England, and if you Google "Catherine Howard" you get 2,780,000 results. I haven't checked, but I'm fairly certain that if I do pop up anywhere, it would be so many pages down that anyone looking for me and not her would have given up long before they got to it.

Google "Catherine Ryan Howard" and you get 1,040,000 results. Although eventually they go off into things that have "Catherine Howard" in one place and "Ryan" in another, I'm the top result. (It's a link to my blog.) Better yet, you have to get to the bottom of the fifth page of results before you get a result that's not related to me.

If you have a very common name or you share your name with someone famous, seriously consider changing it or adding something in. Even an extra initial might do the job. It might not make that much difference in the beginning, but what if you end up on, say, the radio? People will hear you talking about your book while they're driving, or cooking their breakfast, or trying to act like they're concentrating on the customer who's talking to them at work. They won't be able to write anything down; they'll just make a mental note of your name. Later, they'll enter it into Google. If they don't find you easily, they won't go looking again or they'll forget about you before they think to. And you can't exactly change your name halfway through, because then you'd have to start all over again.

This is why I despair when I see authors—traditionally published authors, I might add, whose publishing houses should know better— recycling titles, using titles already used for movies or even other books. This is a bit silly in the Google Age, but it's downright stupid when the movie or book they're borrowing from is infinitely more famous than theirs, and has been around for a long, long time, thus allowing years and years of Google friendliness (links, pathways, etc.) to build up.

Take *Some Like it Hot,* for instance. On Amazon.co.uk, the top result is a special edition of the DVD of the movie that's so well known and so popular and has been around for so long that it should never have been used as a title for anything else, but there are also other editions of the movie, a companion book to the movie, another companion book to the movie, a memoir by Tony Curtis about making the movie, (at least) two erotic novels and then there's *Some Like it Hot* by Amanda Brobyn, which was released by Poolbeg here in Ireland late last year. Now *Some Like it*

Hot happens to be a great title for the book, but I went through five pages on Google Ireland and got no mention of it. If I'd heard her interviewed on the radio or something but didn't catch her name and went looking for the book afterwards, I might well give up on page five. Or even before it.

For traditionally published authors, this isn't that big of a deal. They're also in bookstores. There'll be plenty of other chances for us to find out about their books. But for self-published authors, we're only online. If someone only has the title of our book and Google doesn't help them find us, there may never encounter a mention of us again.

Just something to think about before you name your book—and yourself.

Getting A Customised URL

WordPress offers you the opportunity to take the free URL they gave you when you first signed up (that has the word "WordPress" in it, e.g. www.catherineryanhoward.wordpress.com) and upgrade it to a customised URL that can say anything you want, provided it is available. This upgrade costs $17 per year.

I strongly recommend that you do this, and that the URL you upgrade to is www.yourfullname.com, where the name is the same as the one you're going to put on your books.

Why?

- Let's be honest: having your own domain name feels good, doesn't it? It's like having a little home of your own on the magical interweb
- It's easier for people to remember a yourname.com address
- It fits better on a business card, the back of your book, a poster, an advertisement for your "using social media to sell books" workshop and on the forearm of someone who loves your blog so much they want to get its URL tattooed on their body
- Having a .com address is more—what's that thing, again?—oh, yeah: PROFESSIONAL!

This way, if someone googles the hilarious name of your blog, they find your blog. If they google your name, they find your blog. And if you meet them in the street and tell them your blog address, they'll remember enough of it to find your blog when they get home.

Using Google Apps, there is another huge benefit to upgrading to a customised URL with WordPress: an e-mail address that ends in the same domain. This will be at no extra charge to you and will be accessed through Gmail. So if you upgrade to a domain that reads www.janemurphy.com, you can then get email addresses like info@janemurphy.com, books@janemurphy.com, etc. Needless to say, this is a far more professional-looking thing to put on your business card than, say, makemineaventi_1982@yahoo.co.uk.

Upgrade To A Customised URL

To upgrade to a customised URL, go to your WordPress dashboard and look for "Upgrades" on the left-hand side of your screen. Click on it. You will now be brought to a page displaying all nine of the paid upgrades WordPress offers its users. "Add a Domain" is the first one; click "Buy Now."

On the next page, enter your desired domain into the box under "Add a Domain", the one that has "http://" just in front of it. It doesn't matter if you put "www" in front of it or not; both will work. For example, I entered "catherineryanhoward.com" in that box when I was purchasing my domain upgrade, but if someone types "www.catherineryanhoward.com" into their browser, it still works. WordPress offers domains that end in .com, .net and .org, but I strongly recommend you stick with .com. (And anyway .org is associated with organisations.) If the address you wanted wasn't available when you signed up for your blog, it might be available now. Let's say you wanted "karenblack", as in www.karenblack.wordpress.com. But you couldn't have it, because another Karen Black already had a WP blog. (How very dare she!) But perhaps that Karen didn't upgrade, and so now you can have www.karenblack.com which, like, hello? Is *so* much better anyway.

When you've entered the domain you want, click "Add domain to blog." If the domain is available, the next page will prompt you to enter your personal details and register the blog. If it's not, this page will suggest available alternatives. Select one of them or come up with something else yourself.

By the "Register" button you'll see an option to make your personal information private for an extra $8; this will keep your details off public domain registries which are sometimes used by spammers and cold callers. I would either pay it or, ahem, *modify* your address and telephone number so that either way they don't end up on public record.

Once you've purchased your domain, wait a minute or two for it to kick in. In my experience, it'll go live almost immediately and at most, it'll take five minutes. If you'd rather manually renew this domain when it expires in a year, you can click the "Disable auto renew button." (Don't worry — WordPress will send you plenty of reminders!) Then change your primary domain to the one you've just purchased and click "Update Primary Domain."

NB: The $17 price is broken down into registration ($5) and mapping ($12). Registration is, not surprisingly, the registration of your new domain name to you. Mapping basically means redirecting. If you already own your own domain, you can just purchase the mapping service from WordPress. Prices are correct at time of writing and are of course subject to change.

Get An E-mail Address For Your Domain

This is going to read like it's a *really* long process but honestly, it *is* straightforward. Just think how fabulous your new e-mail address is going to look next to your new blog address on your business cards. And remember that you only have to do it once, and you don't have to have any idea *why* you're doing these things. (I certainly don't!) Just follow the instructions. It should only take about 15 minutes.

To begin, you're going to need to go to Google Apps (**www.google.com/apps**) and click the blue "Sign Up Now" button. On the next page you'll be asked to enter a domain you own, i.e. the domain you just upgraded to. Then click "Get Started."

Google Apps set-up wizard: verification screen.

Fill in your personal details on the next page, and then click continue. Now you should be on a page with "Set-up—create your first administrator account" at the top. The first box to fill in here is marked "username." **This combined with your domain will be your e-mail address.** So if you're Karen and you enter "contact" here, your new e-mail address will be "contact@karenblack.com." I think you only need one e-mail address, and it should be an "info" address, e.g.

"info@karenblack.com." This works for everything and avoids the confusion of too many e-mail accounts. Create a new password and accept the terms and conditions to move on to the next step.

When complete, you'll be brought to a page that says "Google Apps Setup Wizard." Click next until you come to "Let's verify that you own your domain" and then click next to begin verification.

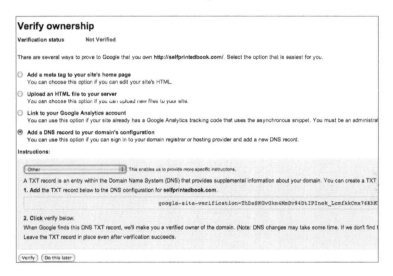

Generate your DNS TXT record.

On this page there'll be four options to choose from. Select "Add a DNS record to your domain's configuration." (Good news: we never need to figure out what this means.) In the drop-down menu below it, select "Other." A chunk of gobbledegook text will now appear with the words "google-site-verification" in it. Copy it.

Keeping this window open, open a new window and use it to go to your blog's dashboard. Scroll down until you get to "Domains" in the list on the left-hand side (it's towards the end, under "Settings") and click on it. Next to your freshly purchased domain you'll see a blue link that reads "Edit DNS." Click it.

The page you'll now see has a large empty text box. In it, type "TXT", leave a space and then paste the code Google has given you. Click "Save DNS Records." Close this window.

Go back to your Google Apps window (which you've kept open) and look for the "Verify" button at the end of the page, under the blue box. Click it. You'll now return to the main Google Apps page. Look for the "Dashboard" tab and on the dash, look for "Email." Underneath it you should see a blue link that reads "Activate email." This bit is a bit weird but just remember: you don't need to know *why* you're doing what you're doing. (I certainly don't and I've done this about five times.) You're now on a page that's headed "Set up email delivery" and, underneath that, "Changing Mail Exchange (MX) records." Scroll down until you come to a list of records that look something like "ASPMX.L.GOOGLE.COM 20." Select all of them and copy. Don't close this window.

Open a new window and go back to your Domains page on your WP dashboard and your old friend, the "Edit DNS" button. Now in the text box, beneath the line that begins "TXT" that you typed earlier, paste the text.

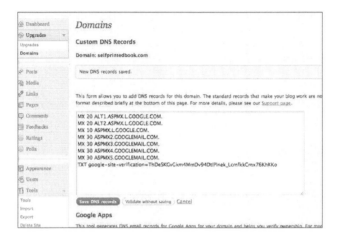

Paste your MX records into your DNS records form on WordPress.

Each line needs to begin with "MX" and then a space. When I pasted in my records, the priority number (double digits, like 10 or 20) was at the end, but it needs to be immediately after the space instead. So make sure now that each line reads MX, space, number and then code, e.g. MX 20 ΛLT2.ASPMX.L.GOOGLE.COM (as it does in the image above). Then click "Save DNS records."

Back in the Google Apps window headed "Changing Mail Exchange (MX) records", click "I have completed these steps." It will now take Google up to 48 hours to verify that you indeed own this domain and can set up an e-mail address for it.

Once they've done that, you'll be able to access your new e-mail account through Gmail, or at: **http://mail.google.com/a/example.com** (where "example" is your domain, e.g. janemurphy.com).

Tip: I've done this for each domain I've purchased, just so I can have a matching e-mail address to put on promotional material and to filter incoming mail by book/blog. BUT no one wants to be checking four different e-mail accounts every day, so in your main account (for me, my blog) go to Settings –> Add Account and add any additional e-mails you've assigned yourself to the "Incoming Mail" list. This way, all your e-mail comes to the same account but all your sent mail gets sent from the same account, i.e. your main one. I know it doesn't sound like it from reading this paragraph, but that's the simplest way to do it. Trust me!

Say No To Rainbows: Your Blog's Appearance

Now for something a bit more fun: picking a theme for your blog and then making it look pretty. Professional-looking themes are WordPress's strong point and you'll have plenty of them to choose from. But we have three requirements for our theme that are non-negotiable:

- We need a customisable header (we need to be able to insert our own picture at the top)
- We need a theme that is readable (no navy blue text on a slightly lighter navy blue background)
- We need a theme that allows us to put "Pages" (sections) across the top or down the side.

If you've ever visited my blog, you'll know that it's colour co-ordinated to within an inch of its virtual life. (And if you've ever seen my house at Christmas or received something gift-wrapped from me, then this will come as no surprise.) This isn't just me being anally retentive, but pushing what my free WordPress blog can do to the max.

Visitors might not be able to say exactly why, but they'll leave my blog thinking, *well, doesn't that look nice?* (Or perhaps, *why does that blog look like something you drink when you're nauseous?* But let's hope it's the first one.) If you had a website designed by a professional website designer, do you think he or she would give you a red background, purple text and a blue header? No. They'd give you a site whose elements match, co-ordinate or complement each other. So because we're aiming for that same professionalism, we're going to make ours match as well.

The easiest way to do this is to find a header photo that not only reflects the content of your blog, but also matches the colour scheme, e.g. the pink typewriter. (You can find these on the same stock photo websites you went to to look for cover images. Or take one of your own.) I also got real lucky, in that WordPress happened to have a free theme (Bueno) whose header was in the same font (Impact) as the cover of *Mousetrapped*. Yes, you can imagine how much *that* discovery satisfied my co-ordination-loving soul.

My pretty-in-pink blogsite.

Many WordPress themes allow you to change the colours of the theme; try to pick one that does. Then you can really take your colour co-ordination to the max.

If colour co-ordination isn't your thing, that's irrelevant. Don't fall into the *Selling Houses* mentality where you think that just because your blog looks good to you means it'll look good to everyone else. At least aim for *cohesiveness*. It's also worth remembering that blogs aren't set in stone. Play around with them. Change them up until you're happy. I didn't start off with a Bueno theme; I started with something completely different that was just all wrong. I didn't realise *how* wrong, though, until I changed my theme.

Customising Your WordPress Blog: Title, Theme And Header

First things first: if you haven't already given your blog a snazzy name and tagline, here's how. On the Dashboard, scroll down until you come to "Settings" on the left-hand side. In this menu you'll see "General." Click it.

On this page you can add the title of your blog (e.g. Catherine, Caffeinated) and a short tagline that gives the reader some idea of what it's about or who you are (e.g. "Writer, astronaut, skinny: Catherine Ryan

Howard wouldn't mind being any of those things"). You should also set the blog to your local time zone so that when you schedule a blog post for 9 a.m. on Tuesday, it posts when it's 9 a.m. on Tuesday wherever in the world you are. Once you're done, click "Save Changes."

When you signed up for your blog you were assigned the default theme by, um, default. Now you can go back to your Dashboard, scroll down until you come to "Appearance" on the left-hand side and then, in that menu, "Themes." Click it. You will now be in the WP "Manage Themes" page. Browse the themes to find the one you like best for your blog. When you do, click "Activate." For these instructions we're going to activate "Bueno", the theme I use myself, and then go back to our Dashboard.

This time we're going to select "Header" in the "Appearance" menu. Now you can upload a photo to put across the top of your screen but bear in mind that its dimensions will change depending on your theme, so you might have to upload a few photos and see how they look before you find the right one. Click "Choose File", find the photo you want on your computer and then click "Upload." On the next page, drag the pre-sized selection to the area of the photo you want to display on your blog. Then just click "Save Changes" and you're good to go.

You can now tailor the colour scheme of your blog to suit the photo, which Catherine Co-ordinated As Well As Caffeinated *highly* recommends that you do. Right under "Header" in the "Appearance" menu you should see "Theme Options." Click it. You're now on a page where the third option down is "Colour Scheme." Select the colour that predominantly features in your photo and select it. (If there isn't one, change your photo!) Then click "Save Changes." So after all that, this is what our blog looks like now:

(The post you see, "Archives" widget in the sidebar and "About" link on top are all put there by WordPress by default. We'll get to sorting them out in a minute. And the picture is Minnie's Country House in Mickey's Toon Town Fair in Magic Kingdom. You know, in case you were wondering.)

The Small Print

To protect yourself and your blog, make sure you have all the small print you and your blog require. You can insert these into your sidebar or footer by using a text widget. You'll need:

A copyright notice. It should be obvious that stuff you write belongs to you and that if someone else copies and pastes it into an e-book they're charging $9.99 for, it's stealing (although not very profitable stealing, as you and I both know that $9.99 e-books don't sell). Just because something's on the internet does not mean that it's free for anyone to use. But just to make sure, put a copyright notice at the bottom of your page. NOT at the bottom of individual blog posts, mind you, because that will make you look like a bit of a tool. One at the bottom of the site itself is sufficient.

Mine reads:

All text © Catherine Ryan Howard 2009–2012. Linking? Good. Encouraged even. Copying and pasting into the e-book you're going to make money from? Bad. And illegal.

I've never, to my knowledge, had a problem with this, but it doesn't hurt to put it up there. And guess what else it does? You got it in one: it makes you look *professional*!

A comment policy. This is like a nightclub reserving the right to refuse admission to very drunk and/or aggressive people. On your blog, it's you reserving the right not to publish (or to delete) comments left on your blog by pissy people. I can't say I've had much problem with this, but I do know some bloggers who have had terrible trouble with people who have nothing better to do with their time than verbally abuse people they don't even know, about subjects they either know nothing about or are taking WAY too seriously.

The first version of mine read:

So here's the thing: this is my site. It's not a democracy. Neither is it a place where we discuss The Big Issues of the World Today. Every post is written with a wink; that's why it takes me so long to write them. Therefore if you insist on leaving abusive or annoying comments, I will delete them, because I can. Please note I am also not free advertising for your crappy and/or spammy site, nor am I host to comments run through a translation program and/or written in Adolscnt Txt Msg Englsh. First-time commenters (or is it commentators?) are moderated. Now, how do the rest of you take your coffee?

Today, several, ahem, *incidents* later, it reads:

So here's the thing: this is my site. It's not a democracy. Neither is it a place where we discuss The Big Issues of the World Today. Every post is written with a wink; that's why it takes me so long to write them. Therefore if you insist on leaving abusive or annoying comments, I will delete them, because I can. Please note I am also not free advertising for your crappy and/or spammy site, nor am I host to comments run through a translation program and/or written in Adolscnt Txt Msg Englsh. Do NOT put links in your comments unless they are relevant. Even if your book is great and your business is reputable, please don't use my site to advertise them. I reserve the right to remove any links. First-time commenters (or is it commentators?) are moderated. Keep it short—we're already spending too long on the internet as it is. Now, how do the rest of you take your coffee?

My blog is light-hearted, and so you wouldn't expect there to be much cause to assert this right—and there isn't. But it *has* happened. I can think of three times in the last year when I've refused to publish a comment, and these were the reasons why:

- I wrote a book review about a non-fiction title that detailed a famous crime. The prime suspect committed suicide before his trial could begin, and there are as many people who think he was innocent as they are who think he was guilty. Crucially, the FBI and other investigating authorities are in the latter group. A man who had never before commented on my blog stopped by to leave a comment accusing *the author* of the book of perpetrating the crime, and then went on to list "evidence" of his guilt. He was clearly (i) unhinged and (ii) either had a personal beef with the author or was a friend of the prime suspect. Whatever his story, he had no right to accuse innocent people of murder on my blog, so I deleted his comment and then posted a comment of my own saying something like, "[Crazy Man]: your most recent comment has been deleted. This is a book review and not a discussion about who committed the crime. See my Comment Policy below for more information."
- A human spammer left a link-filled comment on my blog. Spammers are normally robots who run around the internet leaving nonsensical comments on blogs with links to sites that will

sell you cut price Viagra or whatever, and you don't have to worry about them because WordPress has an excellent anti-spam feature (Akismet) that catches all these robots in a net. You do have to contend with human spammers, however: idiots who leave comments on your blog, very thinly disguised as a genuine comment but really all they want to do is get people to come to their own site or buy their book. An example of this would be something like: "Thanks for this post about book trailers. I made my own book trailer [link to book trailer] for my book, Talking Purple Unicorns [link to book's website] which will be out on April 1 but in the meantime is available to pre-order on Amazon [link to Amazon]. Love your blog!" In all likelihood this person never came to your blog before and will never come again, and as far as I'm concerned, it's the virtual version of stroking yourself in a public place. So DELETE.

- Text message English. I don't expect my blog comments to be in the Queen's English and written in calligraphy, but I expect them to be *readable*. This comment went something like: "dis cud hapin in real life u dnt no u cnt say it wdnt." Indeed. D-LEET.

A disclaimer. If you review products on your blog that you've received for free, are paid by any outside party to blog about specific topics or you are connected with a company or brand in some way that may appear on your blog from time to time, tell people that upfront. If they find out later, trust is broken and your readers will no longer believe anything you say.

For instance, let's say you're a mummy blogger who is always recommending a certain brand of nappies (diapers). Your readers love you, believe everything you say and so rush out and buy this brand you're championing. But then it emerges that the company who makes them keeps you in stock of them for free; that puts your blog posts in a whole new light — and not a good one. Be honest from the start.

I don't have anything like this on my blog, so I don't have a disclaimer.

I do receive free books to review, and at the end of the review I usually put something like "Thanks to [publisher] for my copy", both to thank the publishers and to alert the reader to the fact that I got it for free.

Wonderful Widgets

The sidebar of a blog is, you won't be surprised to learn, the bar running down the side of your blog. In it, you can put "widgets" such as:

- A blog roll: a list of your favourite blogs
- Text widget: does exactly what it says on the tin, can be used for everything from a welcome message to your comment policy
- A Twitter widget that will automatically show your last five tweets
- Images, and images you can embed links in (e.g. I have the cover of *Mousetrapped* in mine and when you click on it, it brings you to the *Mousetrapped* page)
- Other links, such as Most Popular Posts or a "tag cloud" that will show your most used tags (keywords or phrases, such as "writing" or "coffee")
- Archived: a shortcut to previous month's posts
- Calendar: previous posts arranged by date.

(Image above right: homemade widgets on Catherine, Caffeinated.)

WordPress doesn't allow most "outside" widgets, but if you use Blogger you can have a whole host of these, such as a word count progress bar, a miniature Amazon bookstore, a local weather widget... The list goes on.

I *hate* these kinds of widgets. They make blogs look messy, they're very hard to size correctly and – yes, I'm going to say it – they *don't match*. I also think that if you fill your sidebar with them, you're invoking the impression that you're an amateur. A couple is okay, but I've been on blogs where there are so many different widgets of all shapes, colours and sizes (and some of them are flashing on and off as well), that it looks like something you'd see on the back of your eyelids after someone punches you in the head.

And there's a better way to do it. On Catherine, Caffeinated, I mostly make my own widgets. I use MS Word or Apple's Pages to make a little sign, I take a screenshot of it, upload it as an image widget and embed the link I want readers to be taken to when they click on it. You can also do this with pictures of your book covers. Simples.

(And yes, to answer your question, I was one of those children that wouldn't allow baby-sized dolls into Barbie games because they weren't the right size.)

Creating Sidebars, Footers & Widgets

Depending on the theme you've chosen, you will have a space called a sidebar running down one or both sides of your blog, and possibly a footer running along the bottom as well. To put widgets into these spaces, go to your Dashboard and click "Widgets" in the "Appearance" menu. Here you'll see your spaces (sidebar, etc.) and the widgets you can put into them. Just click and drag the widgets you want into the spaces where you want to put them, and then do the same to order them however you want.

The Widgets page on the WordPress Dashboard.

Each widget will ask you to fill in some information, or choose settings.

I'm just going to go through the main ones you should have, but what you need will of course depend on your blog.

The non-complicated ones:

Twitter widget. Will automatically show your five most recent tweets. Just enter your Twitter username and check the box that says "hide replies." Click Save.

Blog subscriptions. Add this widget so that readers, should they be so inclined, can click the "Sign me up!" button and receive new posts by you right to their inbox.

Text widget. Use one each for your comment policy, disclaimer (if applicable) and copyright notice. These should go in the footer if your theme has one. (Pictured below.) You might also use this for a welcome message at the top of your sidebar.

COMMENT POLICY	DISCLAIMER	DON'T BE STEALING STUFF
This is my blog and I can do whatever I wanna.	I gets stuff for free.	All text and hilarity copyright Catherine Ryan Howard © 2011.

The slightly complicated ones:

An image widget. Slightly complicated because you have to upload the image first and then link to it in the widget. To upload the image, select "Media" (in your Dashboard menu) and then "Add New." Follow the instructions on screen to upload a new image and copy and paste the link where the image will be stored. Then paste this link into the image widget where it says "Image URL." You can resize it to fit by altering the width and height and just below that, you'll see a place to enter the link you'd like to take your blog reader to when they click on the image. (So if it's your book cover, you might want it to take them to the Amazon listing.)

A link widget. Again, you have to save the links ("Links" in Dashboard menu) and then select which ones you want to display. This link widget is what you use for your blog roll, or list of recommended blogs.

Building A Blogsite

A blogsite, as I've said already, is a free blog that masquerades as a website, or a website that incorporates a blog.

Ours is going to be a little bit of both.

A blog is just an online journal that's updated regularly. You'd log on, find a pretty picture (a header) going across the top of the page, the blog posts themselves taking up most of the space below with the newest one on top, and a column (sidebar) of links, pictures and weird flashy things (widgets) going down the right-hand side.

This type of thing is fine if you're sharing your adventures in quilting, but if you want to sell books, you're going to need something a tad more sophisticated, or a **blogsite**.

The big difference between a blog and a blogsite is that a blogsite has sections or **pages**. On Catherine, Caffeinated, you can see my pages running across the top, just below the title and just above the header picture of the typewriter:

They are: About, Books By Me, Self-Printing, Videos, News, Newsletter and Contact.

Make sure you chose a WordPress theme that allows you to display your pages across the top (above or below the header) or at the very least, down the side. You want readers to be able to instantly access them without having to go looking.

What pages or sections should you have? This will vary depending on what you decide to blog about, but as a professional writer, aspiring or otherwise, you should always have:

- An "About" page where you write a little bit about yourself, i.e. an author bio and your author photo
- A "Books" page listing all your available books and detailed information about where to buy them
- A "News" page. You might not want to do this until you actually have some news to put on there, but keep in mind I'm not talking about news that's been announced at six o'clock on TV. Go have a look at my News page and see the kind of things I put on there (clue: all kinds). Another benefit of having this page, I've discovered, is that you can read back over it to see how far you've come whenever you're in need of a little encouragement or motivation

- A "Contact" page. WordPress allows you to insert a form really easily that will ask people to fill in their name, website, e-mail and whatever else you specify and then hit "Submit" to e-mail you. This way, they don't see your e-mail address unless you respond to them from it. Initially I had my e-mail up on this page, but that just seemed to be an invitation to the crazies. Stick with the form, but make sure people have *some* way of getting in contact with you. My contact page is how I ended up on radio and in the newspaper; the producers and reporter contacted me through my site.

Creating Pages In WordPress

To make pages or sections in your WordPress blog, go to "Pages" in your menu and click "Add New."

Whatever title you give your page is what will be displayed across the top of your homepage, so keep it short.

To the right-hand side you'll see a box with a zero in it labelled "Order." This lets you change what order your pages appear in across the top of your page. When you're done, click "Publish."

To insert a contact form, click the last icon in the row of icons after "Upload/Insert" just above your formatting bar.

You can also create a hierarchy of pages. Let's say you have a "Writing" page/section, but you want to split that further into a page/section for each of your two books. Create a new page for each of them, but before you click "Publish" select "Writing" as the "parent page" in the drop-down menu to the right of the screen.

Keep your page titles short, so that they all fit in one row across the top of your homepage. If they don't fit, make them shorter. I'm insisting on this. Because please, FOR THE LOVE OF FUDGE people—PLEASE!—do *not* do this:

I can't even look directly at it.

Would a web designer return a homepage to you that looks like that? Only if he or she didn't want to get paid. Maybe I'm a bit OCD about this, but landing on a blog or website that has an overhanging menu like that makes me come out in hives—okay, so maybe not come out in hives, exactly, but I sure don't stick around to read it.

We make our blogsites pretty and well-organised for the same reason we format our manuscript perfectly before submitting it to an agent or an editor: because *we don't want to distract from the content*. I'm sorry but even if you have the funniest, cleverest blog posts ever, interspersed with shirtless pics of Josh Groban (sidenote: does such a thing exist? I've never seen one. And I've *looked*...), all I'm going to see is the overhanging menu, flashing widgets and clashing colour scheme.

So make it look real nice, okay?

The Author Photo

There is one thing you're going to need across all social media platforms, and that's a profile picture. Here on your blog, you're going to put it on your "About Me" page. And what am I going to say about this? Yes, you've guessed it: make it a *professional* one.

If you can afford it get one taken, but that's not quite what I mean. I have never had photos taken; every one I've ever had on any of my sites has been taken with the tiny little camera above my Mac's screen. What I'm getting at is don't use that picture of you drunk and making an obscene hand gesture that was taken in Ibiza when you were 21, sunburnt and three (or thirteen) sheets to the wind—unless, of course, that's what your book and blog are about.

A good profile picture is usually a close-up of you; better yet if it's just your head and shoulders. Try and take it against a blank background, or at least one that doesn't interfere with your pretty face. For maximum Catherine Brownie Points, wear something that co-ordinates with the colour scheme of your blog.

Comment Moderation

All free blogging platforms allow you to moderate comments that are left on your blog posts, i.e. hold them for publication until you have a chance to read and okay them. There are several schools of thought on what's the best way to do this, and I can see pros and cons to them all.

You can either (a) not moderate comments; all comments are published except those identified as spam which are held for checking, (b) moderate first time commentators; the first time you leave a comment, it's moderated, but if that's approved, all future comments from you will be published immediately, or (c) moderate all comments no matter what.

On Blogger, you can also set your blog so that all commentators have to pass a "Are You Human?" test which involves retyping a word or phrase into a box before they can submit their comment.

Some bloggers don't like moderating comments because it might discourage people from commenting (as they perceive that there are too many hoops to jump through before they can, or that you don't trust them not to be crazy) and it takes time to go through them and decide if they can be published. Also, if you go on holiday or don't have access to the internet for a while, they build up, and commentators begin to wonder why their comment hasn't shown up. But then if you don't moderate comments at all, you might end up with more junk on your blog than anything else.

Personally, I only moderate first-time commentators, and I find this works for me.

To change your comment moderation settings in WordPress, go to "Settings" and then "Discussion." You can then choose the actions you want taken — or not — whenever someone leaves a comment on one of your blog posts, as well as getting e-mail notifications about comments, etc.

To *get* comments, end your blog post with a question. Most of the posts I write don't really invite commentary, as they're instructional. But if you want to get a discussion going in the comments, end your post with something like "Have you had any problems with this?" or "Is it just me?" But don't do it *just* because you want some comments. And if you get any, *respond* to them.

What Am I Supposed To Blog About?

Oh, yeah. *That*.

I can't tell you what you should blog about because that has to come from you. I can only recommend that you read lots of blogs, identify what you'd like to read about on a blog but can't find (or can't find it written about in a way that you like) and then get to it. But because we're being professional, we're going to *focus* our blogging, or at least narrow it down to a few topics or areas that we'll return to again and again.

For instance, almost everything I blog falls into one of the following categories:

- **Astronuts**: stuff about NASA and the Space Shuttle, which is a topic in my book
- **Catherine's Bookshelf**: book reviews and book news
- **Mousetrapped**

- **News**
- **Self-Printing**
- **Novely**: novel writing, tips and advice
- **Special Guest Stars**: guest posts
- **Twittertastic**: blog posts about Twitter or Twitter-related topics
- **Video**: blog posts that contain video embeds
- **General Randomness**: a catch-all category for everything else, it's further divided into A Crafty Catherine Christmas (festive crafting ideas), Catherine's Coffee Breaks (coffee reviews), Couch Potato (blog posts about TV), and LOST (when the show was on, I used to blog about it here and on a LOST fan blog).

Why stick to a certain number of topics? Because then people know what to expect. For instance, I'm known as a blogger who posts a lot about self-printing. If I suddenly stopped doing that, my following would be wondering what the fudge was going on. A blog I follow can be relied upon to be about books, writing and reading. Sometimes there's an unrelated post in there, but because I like the blogger, I read that too. But the reason I'm following the blog is for the books, writing and reading, so if one or more of them doesn't show up once in a while, chances are I'll stop following.

Maybe *your perspective* is focus enough. By that I mean that maybe you have a unique take on things and/or are hilarious (get you!), and so you can blog about anything from writing a novel to *American Idol* and we'll all just lap it up.

Don't worry too much about how to blog. Just create a blog you'd like to read. We'll talk more specifically about how we're going to blog about our book in the Selling Books section.

Anatomy Of A Blog Post

(To post a new blog post in WordPress, just click one of the many "New post" buttons you'll see on the dashboard. It doesn't quite need its own instructional section, now does it?)

A good blog post has an interesting title, well laid-out text divided into paragraphs, perhaps with headers if it's a really long post, and a relevant link to something else by the same blogger at the end. For instance, if I write a post about self-publishing, I put something at the end of the post like, "Click here to see all my self-printing posts", or "Click here to find out more about *Mousetrapped*, the book I self-printed."

A lot of bloggers don't do the relevant link and I think it's because they don't think about *where* most people will read their blog posts because, newsflash, it won't be on their blog. Many people use blog feeders (like Google Reader) and will never or rarely see your lovely blog with all your links, etc. in your lovely sidebar. If they want to read more, give them a link right there that they can click on to get it.

(If you're asking yourself now why we go to the bother of making our blogsite pretty when most people are reading our posts somewhere else, it's because (i) not everyone is and (ii) that's probably where they first saw one of our posts, and a professional-looking blog will help convince them that the post we wrote and they liked today was not just a one-off — more quality content can be expected from us in the future.)

You'll find loads of social media "guru" posts telling you the best ways to get people to read your posts, down to the font size, number of words and the exact time of day you should post them, but I think that's taking things a tad too far. Just follow this piece of advice instead: make 'em *interesting*. And perhaps don't post them in 16pt Wingdings.

Also: tag your blog posts with relevant keywords (search terms) so if someone is looking to read about this very subject, they'll find your post. It's also a good idea to sort your posts into categories, which you can create in the "Categories" section of the dashboard and then select from the "New post" window.

New WordPress users: remember to delete the "Hello World!" blog post that WordPress puts on your blog by default.

The Regularity Rules

How often do you need to blog? It's entirely up to you. I blog between 3-5 days a week, never on the weekend if I can help it (I don't do *anything* online on the weekend, if I can help it) and never more than one blog post per day. But I follow blogs that post short pieces several times a day, or just once a week, or with no discernible schedule whatsoever. It just depends on the blogger and the blog.

I think if you're just starting off, you should aim to blog three times a week, spreading them out, e.g. Monday, Wednesday and Friday. The reason I say this is because every time you release a new blog post out into the world, you create a window of opportunity in which people might find you for the first time. You create a new Google search result, someone might post a link to it on Twitter, someone else might repost that link, or you might stumble onto the kind of blog post that suddenly brings a tidal wave of new followers racing to your blog. So if you're only producing one new blog post a week then you're really limiting your opportunity to grow your audience. And just like anything else new, the beginning is when you need to spend the most time on it.

I usually write my blog posts ahead of time, and then schedule them to publish throughout the week.

The Blogging Community

One of the best things about becoming a blogger is finding your place in the blogging community, and making loads of new blogging friends. For now, they'll keep you entertained with their brilliant blogs and start interesting discussions with comments on your blog, and in the future they might write you a guest post, host your guest post on their blog or help you with giveaways, reviewing your book or recommending your blog to their readers. And if you have a blogging-related problem, they might be able to help.

Remember those blogs we added to your Google Reader that you've been reading? Well, start commenting on them. Follow the bloggers on Twitter and chat to them there.

Run along now children, and go make some blogging friends.

Statistically Speaking

It's very easy, in this blogging business, to become obsessed with numbers. WordPress offers you fantastically detailed statistics that are accessible from your dashboard whenever you like. You can see:

- how many people have visited your blog today
- how many people have visited your blog this week
- how many people have visited your blog this month
- the most visited or read posts
- the most visited or read pages
- links that people are following to your blog
- links that people are clicking in your blog
- every other stat you could possibly want, and then some.

As numbers are really the only way you can chart your progress as a blogger, at least in the beginning, it's easy to become a tad obsessed with them. And while I do recommend you keep an eye on them, they're not telling you the whole story, or even most of it. In social media, people love to play the numbers game, but it's all about quality, not quantity.

For example: by summer 2010 I was getting about 1,500 blog hits a month. Okay, but not anything special. But one of these readers was the writer Jane Wenham-Jones, who wrote the hilarious *Wannabe a Writer?* She got in contact with me about contributing to her next book *Wannabe a Writer We've Heard Of?* — a question to which I said yes before she'd even finished asking it. So now my social-media-book-selling tactics (and my blog URL and my book's name) are in a proper book. Better yet, a little bit after that, Jane recommended my blog to readers of her column in *Writers' Magazine*, one of the bestselling writing magazines in the UK and Ireland. So did it matter how many people were reading my blog at the time? No. It only mattered that someone like Jane was.

The other thing to remember here is that for most people, blogging success takes time, builds slowly and is cumulative. You'll have hardly any readers in the beginning but if you keep at it and do it at least sort of right, you'll start to build a following. Great blogs don't go unread; someone finds them, and then that someone tells all their friends, and then *they* tell all *their* friends, and so on and on. But just like your self-published book, you may need to give your blog at least a year to find its feet and its audience.

Tip: WordPress has a "hit count" widget that shows how many visitors the blog has had. Don't add this until it's a big number. You can check how many hits your blog has had at any time, but we don't need to be telling everyone *else* that number until it's a figure we'd like them to know.

Monetising Your Blog, Or Trying To

Numbers aren't the only obsession to sweep the blogging world. Another one is *monetising*. Yes, you can "monetise" your blog, or earn money from it. If you're on Blogger.com, this usually means enabling Google Ads on your blog, so if you post about, say, Florida, the reader will see a list of Florida text ads down the side of the page or in between posts. Anytime someone clicks through to one of these ads and buys something, you get paid. Another popular way to monetise is to sign up for Amazon Associates, which is a system where you can put links to Amazon products on your blog (say, your book) and if someone clicks that link and goes on to buy that product or others, you get paid. If you have a popular blog, you can also go the old fashioned way and charge people to put ads on there for a fee, but you'd have to be *really* popular to do that.

WordPress.com does not allow this type of activity on its free blogs. They're giving you an amazing service for free, and in return all they ask is that you don't use it for commerce, or to make money in an obvious way. (This is the reason why a lot of widgets that work on Blogger.com do not work on WordPress sites, and why you can't put a 'Buy' PayPal button on a WordPress.com site.) But that's fine with me because I think trying to monetise your blog is a waste of time, and your ads hurt my eyes.

Unless there are millions of people visiting your blog and thousands of them are clicking on your ads and buying things, you're not going to make any money from these schemes. You're just *not*. I follow a hugely popular book blogger who advertises all the books he reviews with

Amazon Associate links. He blogs on a daily basis, is well known in the book world and is well established online. In other words, if anybody could make money in this way from their blog, it'd be him. But he said that what he earns in a year from Amazon Associates amounts to "the price of a packet of biscuits." The percentages are so small (you're getting a commission) and the people making online purchases linked to your blog so few, that if you made $5 or $10 in a calendar year, you'd be doing well.

And what do you get in exchange for this? Ugly ads on your blog. Ugly ads that (noooooo!) don't match your otherwise co-ordinated blog. Ugly ads you have no control over. For instance, if I had ads on my blog, do you know what they'd be for? Self-publishing companies of the kind that I believe rip people off. (The ones who charge you $3,000, give you a cover that looks like something someone coughed up and then attempt to sweeten the deal with 10 FREE copies of your own book! How nice of them.) And that would bother me. But even if the ads were for, say, Starbucks (who I *lurve*), they would still bother me, because they'd clog up my blog, distract from its content and, as I think we've established, not match. And considering the money you're likely to make from them, I don't think it's a fair deal.

Now if you have a little quilting blog, maybe monetising it—or trying to—is a good idea for you. But we're not here to make a pittance out of the three people each year who buy a book or a computer cable through your site. We're here to build an online platform and then use it to help sell copies of our book, and then use *that* as a foundation on which to make us a living as a writer. So we don't need to do things like monetise our blog with a few pennies from Amazon or Google every now and then, because we'll be making real money from selling our books.

And while we do, everything on our blog will match. Phew!

NB: WordPress does put *some* ads on its blogs, but a very small number and if you're logged in as a WP user, either on your own blog or someone else's, chances are you won't be subjected to them. (I've been using WP for a year and I've never seen a single ad.) They offer a $30 upgrade that guarantees ads won't appear on your blog, but I don't really think there's any need to purchase it. I haven't.

Buy Me A No-Foam, Extra Hot Venti Latte

There is something you can do to earn money from your blog, on Blogger *and* WordPress.com, that won't mess up your aesthetics or risk advertising things you don't agree with: you can install a virtual tip jar.

Sign up for a PayPal account and get a "Donate" button to install on your blog. (WordPress allows donate buttons.) Most bloggers I've seen do this do it with a picture of a cup of coffee and a sentence like, "Hey there! Like my blog? Buy this blogger a cup of coffee!" The idea is that if people like your blog or find it useful, they "tip" you a dollar or two.

I think this is worthwhile if, for instance, your blog is truly useful to a lot of people and releasing your book is a year or more away.

But be *very* careful how you do it. Don't beg your blog readers to keep your lights on. They didn't ask you to start your blog so don't ask them to keep it going.

(And yes, no-foam extra hot venti lattes are indeed my drug of choice.)

Preparing For A Post-Social Media World

Ten years ago I was twenty, and most people I knew had a Bebo page. *A what page?* you say. A Bebo page. It was a precursor to Facebook that, for some reason no one has ever quite been able to pinpoint, took off in Ireland quicker than a new recipe involving potatoes would. Not long after that, everyone I knew had a Myspace page. When I started blogging, people were desperate for Google Wave invites and the people who *had* them were treated like demigods. Now no one remembers Bebo, no one cares about Myspace and Google Wave has been shut down. So who's to say where the likes of Twitter and Facebook will be a few years down the line?

My guess would be still around, but you never know. So what if you devote all your time to building up an impressive and engaged following on Twitter, only for it all to disappear a bit further down the road? What happens to your 50,000 followers then? How do you let them know that you'll still be writing books, and that as luck would have it there's a new one out soon?

The only thing we can really rely on to be around forever is *e-mail*. Therefore it's important to establish a mailing list, and to establish it early on.

Sign up for MailChimp (www.mailchimp.com), a free service that enables you to build a mailing list and then send newsletters and other announcements out to the people on that list whenever you like.

Here you can create a new mailing list and design a sign-up form so people can join it. MailChimp's design features are a little tricky to use, I find, but they have "auto-design" wizards that make it easier.

Your sign-up form will have a unique link; if anyone clicks on that link, they'll be brought to a page with only your sign-up form on it, like this:

Put a link in your sidebar, or use WordPress custom menu function to build a direct link between "Newsletter" in your Pages list* and the sign-up form. You'll find the custom menu option under Appearance –> Menus in your WordPress dashboard.

A word or fifty on mailing list etiquette: it's illegal to send people mass e-mails from mailing lists they haven't signed up for. You can't sign anyone else up for your MailChimp mailing list—they have to do it themselves, and then confirm their subscription by verifying a link in a subsequent e-mail. Avoid harassing or pushing people into signing up for it. They will if they want to. If they don't want to, they're not going to read them anyway.

You also cannot collect e-mail addresses and then send out messages to them about your book or anything else manually. That's still spam, *extremely* annoying and 100% guaranteed not to get you anywhere.

We'll get to *sending* newsletters later.

Obviously if it's a direct link to the sign-up form, it's not technically a page.

Before You Get Out Your Catherine-shaped Voodoo Doll...

So now that you know in some detail all the things about blogging I don't want you to do, you are no doubt swearing at me in your head again. Or perhaps even out loud. Maybe your blog is exactly as I've described in my "don't do this" sections, or your favourite blog is. Or you know of an author who has sold trillions of books, is so rich he can wipe his rear end with hundred dollar bills and has the most popular blog on the web since the dawn of HTML, and at last count he had seventy widgets in his sidebar and they were *all flashing*. To which I say: good for him.

I attended a talk a few months ago about how to get published, and at it an editor at a major Irish publishing house told the story of how he had received the manuscript of a memoir on dog-eared pages, not only formatted the wrong way but not formatted at all, and filled with grammatical errors and misspellings. He wasn't even going to read it, but he did, and only a few pages in he realised that the story of the author's life was utterly gripping. *So* gripping that he offered the writer a book deal, and put an editor to work on getting the manuscript into acceptable shape.

Knowing this, would you send the manuscript of your book to that editor in the same condition? Of course not. You'd make sure it was spell-checked, printed out fresh on bright white paper, double-spaced and in a readable font. Why? Because you'd want to put your best foot forward and give yourself the best possible chance of getting a "Yes, we'd love to publish this!" And that is what I'm saying here about blogging. No, you don't have to do as I say. No, there is no one right way to blog. Yes, all of this has been poured through a filter called *my personal taste* and yes, all of this is based on just me and my failure and success. No, it wouldn't qualify as a scientific experiment. And yes, you can have twenty multi-coloured flashing widgets running down the side of your blog that, if you look at them long enough, will hypnotise you into an LSD-like trance and still get blog followers, or even sell books.

Perhaps you've done it before.

Perhaps you're doing it right now.

But if you want to put your best blogging foot forward and give yourself the very best chance at succeeding at this using social media and selling books thing, I *recommend* that you don't.

So you've set up your hilariously named, all matching, blogsite-like blog and you've been reading and commenting on a few other blogs in an effort to start your little corner of the blogging community going. There might even be a trickle of people stopping by your blog every day.

But how can we turn that into a steady stream?

Welcome, my friends, to Twitter.

Twitter

Unless you use Twitter or have in the past, you likely have no idea what it is. That's fine. What's *not* fine is thinking that it's a place where Stephen Fry or Ashton Kutcher tells us what they put on their toast, which for some reason is the impression the non-Twitter-using folk of the world have got of it.

This is the way I always explain Twitter, and I have assurances from Twitter-using people (*tweeps*, or *tweople* if we're being *really* annoying) that it bears some resemblance to the way Twitter actually is: Twitter is like a 24/7/365 cocktail party. It's always going on, and if you've chosen your guests wisely, it'll only ever be filled with people you find funny, interesting, strangely attractive, into the same things as you are or all of the above. You can dip in and out of it as much or as little as you like, and you can stay for five seconds or the whole day. When you *do* dip in, you can:

- Lurk in the corner, saying nothing
- Join in a conversation
- Strike up a conversation with a particular guest
- Respond to a question a particular guest has asked, e.g. "Where are they hiding the good beer?"
- Whisper something in someone's ear that you don't want anyone but them to hear
- Stand in the middle of the room and say something that does not require a response
- Stand in the middle of the room and say something that does not require, but welcomes, a response
- Stand in the middle of the room and say something with an eye to getting a good old discussion going
- Stand in the middle of the room and show everyone this amazing YouTube video you've found of cats standing like humans. (This is where the analogy breaks down somewhat, but you get the idea.)

Twitter 101

Twitter, if you look it up, will be described as a "micro-blogging" site, where you have to say whatever it is you have to say in **140 characters** or less. (That sentence was 154 characters, so that'll give you some idea of the length we're talking about.) I don't think of Twitter as having anything to do with blogging though; I think of it more like a "chat" application.

What Twitter looks like to me when I sign in: on the left, the "Compose new Tweet..." box is where I can write tweets and on my right is my tweet stream, i.e. the tweets of the people I'm following.

You sign up for a free account and "**follow**" whomever's tweets you want, and so whenever they send out a 140-character thought into the Twitterverse, you'll see it in your Twitter "**stream**", an ever-updating list of tweets from the people you've followed.

Hopefully someone will think that they'd like to read what *you* have to say, and so they will follow you. Whenever you tweet, everyone following you will see that 140-character nugget appear in *their* Twitter stream.

If you see a tweet that you think your followers will be interested in—say, the answer to the question "What is the meaning of life?" or a link to a YouTube video montage of cats sitting like humans—you can "**retweet**"(RT) or repost that tweet, making it appear in your Twitter stream. Anyone who follows your tweets will see this retweet just as they would one of your own hilarious musings, but they'll also be able to see that it was penned by someone else.

Some programs do this automatically for you, but to do it manually you'd type "RT @[username of the original tweeter] and then what they said, e.g. RT @cathryanhoward: 'Give me 10ccs of caffeine. STAT.'"

You can also add a comment to the RT if there's room, e.g. "RT @cathryanhoward: 'Give me 10ccs of caffeine. STAT'—LOL! Hilarious, as usual."

@AverillB
Averill Buchanan

RT @cathryanhoward: Next week I'll be telling you about 2 Super Secret New Self-Pub Projects I'm working on wp.me/pK3Dz-1CR

21 Mar via HootSuite   ☆ Favorite   ↨ Retweet   ↻ Reply

Tweeter @AverillB has manually retweeted a tweet of mine which, incidentally, is a link to my WordPress blog that WP generated automatically for me when I hit "Publish" on the post.

@twisst35
TwisstISSalerts

@cathryanhoward ISS will cross your sky early in the morning. It comes up in the South at 06:54. Details: http://twisst.nl/9404

19 hours ago via Twisst.nl   ☆ Favorite   ↨ Retweet   ↻ Reply

An "at reply" to me. I'll be the only one to see this appear in my tweet stream UNLESS someone is following both me and @twisst35.

If you see a tweet that you'd like to respond to, you can reply to the tweeter with an **"at reply"**, so called because to do that you begin your tweet with the "@" symbol and then put their Twitter username, e.g. "@cathryanhoward I know all this already. BOR-ing." (If you *do* know all this already, feel free to skip ahead.) This is how you can have a conversation on Twitter, going back and forth with "at replies." Your followers will not see these tweets UNLESS they are also following the person you've directed it to.

Christine Locke
@wrtrdoll

🐦 Follow   👤▾

An amazing blog for indie authors...wish I'd seen it sooner! SELF-PRINTING: Posts wp.me/PK3Dz-2Fz via @cathryanhoward #writerswednesday

↩ Reply   🔁 Retweet   ★ Favorite   ≋ Buffer

Christine Locke "mentions" me in one of her tweets. Anyone who follows @wrtrdoll will see this in their tweet stream, and I'll see it in my "Mentions" list.

If you want to "**mention**" someone in your tweet , or direct their attention to a tweet about them while making sure that everyone who's following you can see it too, you do the same thing (the "@" symbol followed by their username) but NOT at the beginning of the tweet, e.g. "OMG that @cathryanhoward is so unhinged" or "Crap. All @cathryanhoward's talk of #coffee has made me want to get one myself!"

Notice the hashtag (#) in that tweet? That's called... well, a **hashtag**. Hashtags have two main purposes on Twitter: search and comedy.

Let's say you and fifty of your friends want to have a conversation on Twitter. How are you all going to keep track of the tweets? By all using the same pre-agreed hashtag like, say, #writing. (A very popular Twitter hashtag that, by the way.) Then you go to Twitter's search function, plug it in and instead of seeing your usual Twitter stream (of people you follow) you'll see a stream of tweets tagged with #writing. Or say you're watching *The X-Factor* and you want to find out if anyone else thought that last girl was singing like a bag of strangled cats. Search for #xfactor and you'll soon know the answer. (Twitter, while we're on the subject, makes watching reality TV at least *twice* as entertaining as watching alone.) Whenever I post a link to one of my self-printing blog posts on Twitter, I always tag it with something like #selfpublishing or #ebooks, so that if people are interested in those subjects they might happen upon my tweets.

Hashtags are also used for laughs, e.g. "I'm never going to drink again. #liesItellmyself" or "I seem to have forgotten to wear pants today.

#imaybearrested" or "I just watched 'Dear John'. What an amazing movie! #sarcasm." Feel free to make these up. I remember once upon a time I did this—I can't remember what the hashtag was—but a guy who must have been new to Twitter sent me a tweet, deadly serious, accusing me of making up my own hashtag. Um, yeah. Like, *duh*.

Tweeter @rebeccaberto tweets a link to one of my blog posts, including the hashtags #Ebook, #publishing and #authors.

If you follow someone on Twitter and they follow you back, that's not only a beautiful thing but you can also communicate with each other by **Direct Message (DM)**. This is like a miniature e-mail that no one else but you two will see, and you get a whole 160 characters for it. Just make sure you don't do the accidental DM/tweet shuffle; *so* many people have got in trouble for that...

You can actually send a DM to anyone who is following you, but they won't be able to reply unless *you're* following *them*, so if you're not then doing that would just be cruel.

Your Twitter Profile

As well as dropping 140-character gems of knowledge, wisdom and hilarity into the Twittersphere, you'll also have a Twitter profile. This is the little section of information about you that people can see alongside your tweets, and encompasses your username, actual name, location, profile picture, bio and website address.

First, let's talk about your **username** and **actual name**. There are space limitations (that's why my actual name doesn't have spaces, and my username is cut back to "Cath") and just like our blog address, we want something that's easy for people to remember. You also have to choose something that no one else is using.

I highly recommend that you stick with your name or some

derivative of it, and not something like, say, @oodlesofnoodles. Now is not the time to be cute.

CatherineRyanHoward

@cathryanhoward

Writer, astronaut, skinny—Catherine wouldn't mind being any of those things...

Cork, Ireland · http://catherineryanhoward.com

My Twitter profile:
profile pic, real name, username, location, short bio and website URL.

Here are the usernames of some writer-type Twitter accounts I follow—including Andrea from *Mousetrapped!*—with their actual names in brackets:

@mduffywriter (Maria Duffy)
@ckingwriter (Claire King)
@Andrea_Summers (Andrea Summers)
@joefinder (Joseph Finder)

You don't have to put in your **location** but if you do, make sure you make it general. Use the same **profile picture** (sometimes called an "avatar") as you did on your blog. Cohesiveness, people. Cohesiveness!

Along with your tweets, your **Twitter bio** is an opportunity to convince people that you are oh so very interesting and should be followed at once. Take up all the space they give you (160 characters, so only a little bit longer than a tweet) and refrain from using it just for advertising. For example, my bio line used to be something like "author of MOUSETRAPPED, BACKPACKED and SELF-PRINTED." Well, great. But why would anyone follow me? Isn't "Writer, astronaut, skinny..." a much better line and far more likely to convince someone to follow me than a boring bibliography?

(Unless of course you've written *A Brief History of Time* or *Twilight* or something.)

You might also want to ensure that this line is in keeping with your whole "professional" author appearance. Not too long ago I happened upon the profile of a published author that read, "I have publishes 12 novels."

Indeed.

There is only one thing that should be in your **website address box**:

your website address. Do not link to a Facebook page and, dear god, do not link back to the very Twitter page the person clicking on the link is already on. (I've seen people do this.) And do put something in there, so if people want to know more about you (and why wouldn't they?) they have somewhere to go.

What Now?

Now you start to follow people. Begin with me (@cathryanhoward) and then after lurking for a while, you'll find loads of other people you want to follow. You can also search for them by name in the Twitter search box. Each new person you follow might lead you to follow someone else, e.g. you might see them chatting to someone or retweeting a *right* joker all the time.

Tweeter @AshleyHenschel lists her recommendations
for #ff, or Follow Friday.

Another great way to find people to follow is **Follow Friday**, designated by the hashtag **#ff**. On Fridays, if you are so inclined, you can recommend tweeters to your followers. So let's say you want to recommend me (and you *better*). You'd tweet something like "Because she said I had to: #ff @cathryanhoward." The people you follow will be doing this too—recommending other tweeters—so keep an eye out for any that take your fancy, and then start to follow them.

There is very little point in following celebrities, unless they're particularly funny or something. (Or they're Josh Groban. We're *always* allowed to follow Josh Groban.) But it is a good idea to follow people connected with this book world of ours, such as book bloggers, writers, book publicists, publishers, agents and booksellers.

Twitter = World

Twitter is completely public. Every tweet you tweet can be read by anybody and may even show up on search engines such as Google. You don't even have to have joined Twitter to read someone's tweets, i.e. even if you're not on Twitter you can go to www.twitter.com/cathryanhoward right this second and see what wondrous musings I've failed to come up with today.

But this is what we *want*; we want as many people as possible to find out about us and our writing.

You can "protect" your tweets, which means that no one will see them unless you okay their follower request—which is the same as opening a hotel and then refusing to let anyone make reservations. I'm guessing you can infer from that sentence what I recommend you do about *that*.

Earn, Don't Ask

If you were at a party, would you stand in the middle of room, call for quiet and then say, "Wow! I have *so* many friends. Five hundred and forty-two to be exact. I'm, like, SO popular. Can I get one more?"

Hopefully the answer is *no*. And just as we shouldn't do this in real life, whether we're popular or not, you shouldn't do it on Twitter either. As a general principle (I was very careful there not to use the word *rule*) you shouldn't acknowledge your follower count at all, or only do so in very special circumstances. The reason I say this is not because of how you'll come across or how you'll be perceived or the fact that there are people on Twitter who, as a rule, unfollow anyone, friend or foe, who dares break the fourth wall and draw attention to their follower count (which, I think, is a *bit* of an overreaction). It's because of *what happens when you do*, and how what happens is utterly pointless and no help at all to you or your cause.

Some people are obsessed with getting followers. They follow as many people as Twitter will allow them to (there's a limit based on your follower-to-followed ratio as a deterrent to spamming), hoping that they will follow them back and thus raise their follower number. Others will offer "follow backs" like they're something *to* be offered. They're not. There's the follower-fishing tweet: "I only have 56 followers... feeling very unpopular here! Can I get 300 by midnight?" and its friend, the friend-follower-fishing tweet: "My friend @pain_in_the_ass has only 99 followers—can we make it 200 in time for her birthday tomorrow?"

We could, but what would be the point? The people who click

"follow" won't be doing it because they dig your disarming charm; they'll be doing it because you (or your friend) asked them to. They might never read a tweet of yours again, or unfollow you tomorrow. And what's the point of having 10,000 Twitter followers if none, or most of them, aren't even reading your tweets anyway?

A sideline to this is the Follow Me and I'll Follow You extravaganza, where people either use the offer of following to sweeten the deal—you'll occasionally see in Twitter bios something like "I always follow back!" or "Follow me and I'll follow you back!"—or take offence because you don't follow everyone who follows you. Twitter is about following people you're interested in, not pretending to be interested in the people who follow you. Just yesterday I saw someone I follow on Twitter say, "Having a clear out. I'm following WAAAAY too many people on here who don't follow me back. Time to say bye-bye." To which in my head I said, "What are you, dude, *twelve?*"

And anyway, how many Twitter followers you have doesn't matter. How you engage with the followers you *do* have, or how they engage with you, is all that does. Anyone can have thousands or hundreds of thousands of followers; it doesn't mean anything. (We live in a world where a washed-up, drug-addled TV star in the midst of a mental breakdown just broke the record for acquiring the most Twitter followers in the shortest space of time.) We're not here to collect numbers; we're after *engagers*. And you'll get them—without even trying—if you're a tweeter worth following.

You shouldn't have to ask for anything in social media; you should *earn* it.

If you really want to get your friend more followers, do it in an organic way. Twitter-chat to her or mention her in your tweets ("Oh my god @so-and-so and I were SO drunk last night. You wouldn't BELIEVE what she got me to do to that dustbin!"); your followers will see you talking to this new mysterious tweeter and because they think *you're* interesting, they'll assume they're going to find her interesting too. Recommend her for Follow Friday. Post an interesting link to something on her blog.

And if *you* want more followers? Tweet interesting stuff. Simples.

The flip-side of this is the "What Did I Do?" tweet which draws attention to the losing of followers, e.g. "OMG I just lost a follower! Maybe it was all those tweets about how many followers I have..." Twitter is constantly in flux: people sign up, people delete their accounts, people get booted off for being spammers, people protect their tweets, people realise that protecting their tweets is stupid and either unprotect them or delete their accounts instead, etc. etc. Your follower number is going to constantly change, especially once you get over a couple of hundred, because the chances that there's a spammer in there who'll be booted off in the coming days is extremely high. So if your follower count drops by one or two, that's what's happened, and you asking why it happened shows not only that you have a tendency to overreact, but that you have one eye on that follower count at all times.

Just don't worry about it.

The Discerning Retweeter

I once had a bit of an obsessive Twitter follower who *literally* retweeted everything I tweeted, including "at replies" I sent to individuals. His Twitter stream ended up looking just like mine but on a delay, and interspersed with the odd tweet of his own which would go something like, "I know I'm RT-ing like, everything @cathryanhoward says, but I agree with everything she says!" Really? You do? *Really?* You mean you agreed with what I said to my friend Andrea, i.e. "@Andrea_Summers I know! I just emailed you those details, BTW."

(I blocked this person, needless to say.)

Be discerning with your retweeting. I retweet things that I think are funny or interesting and that I suspect my followers will find funny or interesting too. But keep in mind there's nothing stopping your followers from following the person whose every thought you're copying into your stream and if they *are* following that person, they'll see all those tweets twice.

What if you want to be retweeted? Well, just as with our followers, don't ask for retweetage. (Unless it's for a good cause or part of a competition or something.) For instance, there is an otherwise lovely tweeter in my stream who, when he posts a blog link, puts "PLEASE RT PLEASE RT PLEASE RT THANKS" at the end of it. I don't retweet them, and not because I find it annoying, although I do. I don't retweet his links because his blog posts just aren't interesting to me.

If you want to get retweeted, tweet something that's *worth retweeting*.

How Do I Tweet Links To My Blog?

You can:

- set up WordPress so that whenever you publish a new post, a tweet from your account is automatically tweeted with a link
- click the "Tweet" button at the end of the post (automatically inserted into your posts by WP)

- do it manually, i.e. copy and paste the link from the address bar into a new tweet.

Facebook offers an option to repost all your tweets automatically as Facebook statuses but <u>DON'T</u> do this. Twitter is used more often than Facebook, and so what seems like a handful of tweets may be a ridiculous overload on a Facebook wall. Depending on the content of the tweet, they might also make little sense to someone on Facebook, especially if you're using hashtags and/or if the person reading it doesn't use Twitter at all.

Connect Your WordPress Blog To Twitter

Let's hop back to WordPress for a second and set up our blog so that it connects to Twitter in every way possible.

Go to your Dashboard and find "Sharing" in the "Settings" menu. On that page you can:

- Set WP to tweet links to new posts as soon as you click the "Publish" button. At the top of the page you'll see a Twitter icon and below it, a link that says "Connect to Twitter." Click it and follow the instructions. Once it's set up, you'll see a check box marked "Twitter" just above the "Publish" button when you're in the New Post page.
- Add share buttons to your posts. This is very important: it lets other people share your posts on their Twitter pages with just one click. Drag the share buttons you want into the "Enabled Services" box. Do them all.

Then hit "Save Changes" at the end of the page.

What Am I Supposed To Tweet About?

To begin with, whatever you want. I always recommend that you "lurk" for a while before you say something, to get an idea of the kinds of things other people are saying on there and how they use the platform.

I will say this: if you have nothing to say then don't say *anything*. Don't force yourself to get on Twitter just because people like me have said it's a good way to build a platform and sell books, because you won't be any good at it unless you're primarily doing it for fun. And the I'm Tweeting Against My Will Brigade stand out on Twitter like sore twumbs. (See what I did there?)

With regards to tweeting about your *book*, we'll get to that later.

Before You Get Out Your Catherine-Shaped Voodoo Doll Again...

When I was 14 my school friends and I merged our "gang" (there was like, three of us) with a group of boys who lived in our neighbourhood, who we thought were *oh so cool*. They all smoked. One day, one of them gave me a cigarette and because I thought that I too could become oh so cool by smoking it, I put it to my lips and took the shallowest of breaths. As a plume of grey smoke left my mouth, one of the Oh So Cool Boys laughed and said, "You didn't even *inhale!*" and in that moment I certainly didn't feel cool, but stupid. I felt like everyone else knew how to do something except me. I wasn't "in" on it. It wasn't a nice feeling, and not just because my mouth was filled with smoke.

Sometimes when people are told to not ask for Twitter followers, retweet too much or protect their tweets, they feel as if there is a Twitterati Club, a sort of Premium Class lounge for clued-up tweeters where they can look out at those who don't know how to tweet the "right way" and laugh. And because these people *do* do things like ask for more followers, they feel like they're in the group being laughed at. They feel like they're fourteen again, not inhaling, and a group of "cool" boys are sneering at them.

It is not my intention to make you feel like Twitter is something that only an elite group of people "get" or know how to use, or make you question whether or not you're using it "right." There is no secret manual to using Twitter and no right way to use it. As I said about blogging, if you want to make your blog one gigantic flashing widget, please do, and if you want to tweet nothing but how many followers you have, please do that too.

What this book is about is how *I* used Twitter, as an author, to effectively build an online platform and then later, sell books. I also spend a lot of time on Twitter as a reader and therefore I see, from the other side, what works for tweeting authors and what doesn't. I've bought a huge number of books because I've encountered the authors on Twitter, but I haven't bought books from all the authors I follow on Twitter and it's not just because I'd be broke if I did. Some of them are just better at convincing me that their books are worth checking out through their tweets. Maybe some of those authors don't care whether or not anyone buys their books after reading their tweets. Maybe for them, Twitter is just a place to chat about *American Idol* or whatever, and not to advertise their work. And that's *okay*. But if you just want to use Twitter as a place to chat about *American Idol* and don't want to use it to sell books, why are you reading this book? (So don't hate me, is what I'm basically saying.)

Facebook

If your head is swimming with terms like *at replies, retweets* and *follow Friday*, fear not: this section is going to be very short and super sweet.

Let's get one thing straight first: when I talk about Facebook, I don't mean a personal profile where people can add you as their "friend" or send messages or subject you to 500 photos of their third holiday this year in an attempt to make you jealous. I mean a **public page**, one where Facebook users click a "Like" button to say *I'm a fan of this.*

Mousetrapped's *Facebook "fan" page.*

I thought you had to be someone famous or own a certified business to set up one of these pages. I presumed that even if you passed the celebrity/business test, you'd have to provide some sort of proof that you were worthy of asking people to like you. Turns out, anyone can set up one of these pages for anything at all, as long as it's not offensive or something weird.

And guess what? *You're* anyone!

So let's set up a Facebook fan page.

Separate Yourself

But before we do, let's separate your existing Facebook profile (your personal page) from the new fan page you're going to create.

The thing is, you need to have a Facebook profile to set up one of these pages, but the profile used will be linked to the page as the page's administrator. So set up a new Facebook profile, under your writing name if it's different to your real name, and use that to set up the fan page.

Why not just use your existing profile? Because trust me when I say that you'll want to keep them separate. It may not seem like a big deal now; it may not seem like a big deal for a long time from now, or possibly ever.

But it's better to play it safe, because:

- If you are already connected to your real-life friends with an existing Facebook profile, they do not deserve to be subjected to your book promotion especially since, if they are really your friends, they'll already know all about the book and have bought a copy for every single person they know.
- People who don't know you in real life will "like" your page, see you listed as the administrator and then request you as a friend. Not everyone will do this (thankfully), but lots will—not least of all because there are Facebookers obsessed with friend numbers just like there are tweeters obsessed with follower numbers. You can ignore them, of course, but that might make you seem mean, and what if the requester is someone you've met in real life, say, at a writing event?

Things can start to get complicated. It is far easier to take your existing profile and set it to private (so that if people search for your name, they won't find you) and then create a new one under your writing name from which you will create the fan page, i.e. the new profile will be the appointed administrator of your fan page.

That way, if someone does find you through the fan page and requests to add you as a friend, you can accept without reservation.

NB: I don't *use* the profile I created to make my fan page. It's an empty shell. Everything I do in Facebook as an author I do on the fan page itself.

Creating A Fan Page

Once you've made your new "author" Facebook profile, you can go to the main login page and click "Create a page" which is just below the green sign-up button (pictured below.)

Now you have to make a decision: do you want to create a page where people become a fan of you as an author, or a fan of your upcoming book?

Initially I set up a page for my first book, *Mousetrapped*, but when it came time to release another book, I thought maybe an author page would be better instead. But the author page is growing cobwebs and the *Mousetrapped* page is a hive of activity, so I'd say whatever you start out with, stick with. The question is which one to start out with. It's easier to build a fan base around your book, if only because you'll be less embarrassed asking your real friends and family who are on Facebook to "like" a page about your book than a page all about you. But then you can put more content on a page about you, because people who "like" your book page will be expecting content about the book. And all the already famous writers have pages about *them*, not their books...

Oh, it's a toughie. What to do? I think if you're only planning to release one book for now and that book is non-fiction, then set up a *book* page. Anything else — a series of books, other types of writing or novels — then set up an *author* page.

Unlike a Facebook profile, anyone can see a Facebook fan page. That's kind of the idea. So needless to say, no home address, no telephone numbers and no photos of you on holiday.

Why Do I Need One Of These?

There are two and a half good reasons for setting up a Facebook fan page:

Reason no. 1: *Find One, Find Them All.* If your book is about a specific subject, you *have* to infiltrate Facebook somehow because somewhere on there are people who are interested in that same subject and have already organised themselves into groups. These are ready-made readerships that you need to connect with, and Facebook is the easiest way. Even if you have, say, a thriller novel, you can target fans of such books, or similar authors. (And when I say "target" I don't mean in a spammy way. I *never* mean in a spammy way.) One day a Facebooker found my *Mousetrapped* page, posted a link to it on his own page and like magic, I suddenly had 50 new fans and sold about that many paperbacks in one afternoon. Turns out he was a Disney podcaster and all his Facebook friends were huge Disney fans. I'd managed to tap into a group of ready-made readers simply by making a Facebook page.

Reason no. 2: *Everyone's on Facebook.* At a self-publishing conference I spoke at a while back, I asked the 50 or so attendees how many of them had blogs, had Twitter accounts and had Facebook pages. About a third had a Twitter account, about half had blogs but nearly everyone had a Facebook page. Not surprising considering it's the most commonly used social media platform in the world with over 600 million active users. (Twitter, by comparison, has an estimated 190 million.) If you're trying to alert the world at large to the existence of your book through social media, don't you think it'd be a good idea to do some of it on the largest social media platform there is? Um, YEAH.

Reason no. 2.5: *Roping in Friends and Family.* When you start your fan page, you can rope all your friends and family who are already on there into clicking the "Like" button on your page, enabling you to create a customised address.

Customised Address

Once you have 25 or more fans, you can customise the URL or address of your Facebook fan page.

For example, when you first sign up, the page will probably have a URL like www.facebook.com/qetv9984user_wei91 or something equally catchy. But once you get your 25 fans, you can change it to actual words, e.g. mine is www.facebook.com/mousetrappedbook.

Getting More Fans

We've already talked about not being fixated on numbers, but here on Facebook I wouldn't even worry about trying to get fans; it'll happen organically. Put links to your Facebook page on your blog and maybe in your Twitter profile, and between that and your friends and family breaking news of it by "liking" it (an action that will appear on their Facebook walls), you'll soon see your fan numbers go up.

* * *

So that's how we get ourselves a blog, a Twitter account and a Facebook page. In a little bit I'll be telling you what you need to *do* with them but for now, while you and your editor are putting the finishing touches to your manuscript, all you need do is get used to using them.

And try not to get *too* addicted to Twitter.

Next up, the main event: self-publishing our books.

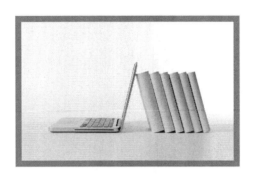

PART 3:
Publishing An E-book

All About E-books

Aren't you excited that we're finally getting to actually *publishing* your book?

Where's your manuscript? By now it should have been edited and proofread. Chances are it's in a word-processing document, double-spaced and on a virtual A4 or letter-sized page. Make two copies of it, marking one "e-book" and one "paperback." It's important you do this now, before you start formatting either of them with a specific edition in mind, and not later, when turning an e-book scroll-type document into a paperback interior will give you a week-long headache.

We're going to start with e-books, the bandwagon *du jour* of the publishing industry.

The bandwagon we're about to hop onto. Oh yes we are.

I still laugh at the fact that I "accidentally" published e-books after seeing someone tweet about Smashwords, and now two years later they account for more than 95% of my sales. And the market is *growing all the time*. So while I think it's okay for you to publish an e-book but not a paperback, I think there is little point in publishing a paperback but not an e-book. You could be doing yourself out of the majority of your potential sales. And e-books are so much easier to sell than their print equivalents.

The good news is that producing an e-book is far less complicated than producing a paperback. It's also completely free. You won't need to order anything or pay for any kind of expanded distribution plan.

The bad news is that the steps you *do* have to complete are a bit trickier and involve that horribly painful thing you may have already heard about, formatting your e-book. *Ugh.*

Formatting Versus Conversion

One little thing while we're on the subject: I may say "formatting our e-book" but I don't *mean* formatting our e-book. Not technically. I mean formatting our manuscript document so that when we upload it to, say, Smashwords, and they run it through their conversion software, it comes out the other end looking like it should. Like we wanted it to. I mean *optimising our document for e-book conversion*, but that takes ages to type and I'm lazy. So I'm just going to say formatting, okay?

You can convert your document into all sorts of fancy file types before you upload to an e-book publishing site, including things like ePub, plain text, RTF, zipped HTML...

Blah, blah, BLAH. I'm bored already. (And a little stressed.)

Amazon KDP accepts Microsoft Word documents. Smashwords

accepts Microsoft Word documents. You and I both know how to use Microsoft Word, and the document we're going to be working with—our manuscript—is already in that format. So we're just going to stick with Microsoft Word.

Why Do E-Books Need Formatting?

Why do e-books need special formatting? Why can't you just upload your manuscript as it is now, or use the Word file you just used for the interior of your paperback? Because in e-books, there is *no such thing as the page.*

If you buy the paperback edition of my book and turn to page 36, you'll see exactly what I intended for you to see, which is whatever I put on page 36 when I was making the book. But if you buy the e-book edition of my book, there is no page 36 and even if there was, I could only guess as to what would be on it.

E-reading devices—Kindles, iPads, Barnes and Noble's Nook, to name a few—allow readers to customise their reading experience. When they download your book, they don't have to read it as you've uploaded it, e.g. Times New Roman in 12pt. They can change the font, the font size, the paragraph alignment and the line spacing. They can read it in portrait or landscape view. And before we even start changing things, how many words fit by default on a Nook screen is not the same as how many fit by default on a Kindle screen.

In this environment the only way that the book will retain its readability and not descend into total gobbledegook is to make the e-book like a *scroll*. Remove the idea of the page altogether. Make them irrelevant. Let the text *flow*.

The other thing is that there are several different e-book formats: Kindle uses .mobi, Sony Reader uses a format called LRF and ePub is the most widely used or industry standard. So when you upload your manuscript to a site like Smashwords, it has to put it through its conversion program (Smashwords's conversion program is called, suitably, "Meatgrinder") and crank out not one but several different versions of your e-book.

So between the I-can-read-my-e-book-however-I-want scroll thing and the my-e-book-has-to-be-converted-into-several-different-formats thing, your e-book MS Word document has to go through a lot. And if you've filled it with page breaks, blank lines, seven different font types, twenty-seven different font sizes, tables, shapes, clip art, headings, sub-headings, sub-sub-headings, a partridge and a pear tree, it's going to end up looking a *right* mess. (Or, as Smashwords puts it, do it wrong and Meatgrinder will turn your book "into hamburger.")

That's why we need to format it in a *very* specific way.

I Feel Your Pain

Formatting your e-book is going to be tough, and not just because it can get really annoying, depending on the complication level of your book and the amount of patience you started off doing it with, but because it feels utterly unnatural to be removing formatting from your book.

As I type these words in the first draft of this book, I'm not formatting it at all. I'm just typing it. When I have to go onto a new section, I just hit the return button and start typing. I'm doing this to make it easier for me later on, when I'll take one copy of this document and go off and make a paperback, and use another to make an e-book.

But doing it this way is *killing me*. I am *itching* to copy and paste everything I've done so far and move it into the Word template I've downloaded from CreateSpace, the one that matches the size of my book, and start laying it out properly.

ITCHING, I tell you.

But I *must* resist.

If you've never formatted a document with imminent e-book conversion in mind, you'll feel the same way when you start to do it. You'll want to make it look all nice and *pretty*. You'll want to give your chapter headings their own page and centre them, vertically and horizontally, and maybe sprinkle a cute little line underneath it, or insert a piece of clip art. You'll want to put in bullet points and blank lines and pear trees, but you can't. You *must resist*. Do it for yourself—it'll cut down on the migraines later—and for your readers, who'll delete your book in disgust when they find that trying to read it is like staring at the sun.

Change Your View

It's easier to resist making everything Real Book Pretty if you do one simple thing: *change your view*. Most people use Microsoft Word in "Print Layout" view or as it will appear on the page when you print it out. Well, when we're trying to ignore the very fact that there is a page, this isn't a good idea. It'll mess with our heads. So instead, go to **View -> Draft** to look at your entire document on one, scrolling screen (see image on opposite page).

NB: I work on MS Word for Mac, so your menus, etc. may look slightly different and there may be a slightly shorter or longer series of steps to complete the tasks. The principles are all the same however.

I should also advise you here to make another copy of your manuscript and name it "ebook2."

Just in case everything goes *horribly* wrong...

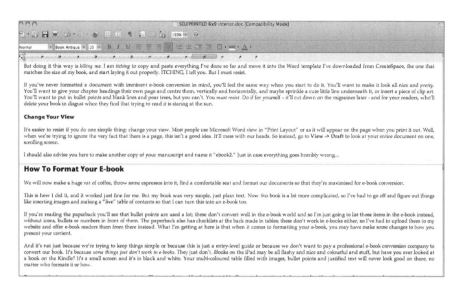

Looking at this page in "Draft" view on MS Word.

How To Format Your E-book

We will now make a huge vat of coffee, throw some espressos into it, find a comfortable seat and format our documents so that they're maximised for e-book conversion.

Unless you have a straightforward novel, chances are you will have to make some changes to your book in order for it to work as an e-book. If you're reading the paperback edition of *Self-Printed* you'll see that bullet points are used a lot; these don't convert in the e-book world and so I'm just going to list those items in the e-book instead, without icons, bullets or numbers in front of them. The paperback also has checklists at the back made in tables; these don't work in e-books either, so I've had to upload them to my website and offer them to e-book readers from there instead. When it comes to formatting your e-book, you may have to make some changes as to how you present your content.

And it's not just because we're trying to keep things simple or because this is just an entry-level guide or because we don't want to pay a professional e-book conversion company to convert our book. It's because *some things just don't work in e-books*. They just don't. iBooks on the iPad may be all flashy and nice and colourful and stuff, but have you ever looked at a book on the Kindle? It's a small screen and it's in black and white. Your multi-coloured table filled with images, bullet points and justified text will never look good on there, no matter who formats it or how.

To go one further, *some books just don't work as e-books*. Photography, cookbooks, other richly illustrated or intricately formatted guides: the way things are at the moment, there is no way for an individual to convert these properly without professional help, and on e-reading devices like the Kindle (which is black and white) they can't be fully appreciated.

So if you've written a novel, thank your lucky stars right now. Because for you, this bit's going to be *easy*.

Stop Tracking Changes

If you've been working with an editor on your manuscript, you might have Word's "track changes" feature enabled. Make sure now that it's switched off by going to Tools –> Track Changes.

If you're still seeing sections underlined in red where changes have been made, go to Tools –> Track Changes –> Accept or Reject Changes –> Accept All.

Lose the Dead Wood

Let's get down to business. The first thing we have to do is to prepare our manuscript for e-book conversion. This means losing anything that won't work in an e-book, and everything that has no relevance in an e-book. You either let them go completely, or leave the pure text in there to do a little work-around on later, e.g. take the text out of any text boxes you've use, delete the text box and put the text back in as an italicised paragraph instead.

If you've been working with the manuscript as it was when it came home from the Editor Hospital, you won't have much to do here. Maybe you'll just have to lose the title page. But if you're working with something that was once destined to be the interior of a print book, you need to lose nearly all the front and back matter.

The following items have to go bye-bye:

- Reviews (you can keep one or two review extracts, at most)
- Copyright notice (we have to change it)
- Title pages
- Table of contents (numbers only; keep the chapter headings, etc.)
- Index
- Any "extras" like advertisements or other information at the back of your book (just keep About the Author, Acknowledgements, Further Reading and Author's Note, if you have one).

The following are e-book no-nos:

- Text boxes
- Headers and footers, including page numbers
- Columns
- Tables
- Bulleted or numbered lists
- Any other fancy word processing stuff.

Then click Edit –> Select All –> Copy.

Go Nuclear

MS Word is the devil's word processor, sticking in all sorts of extra, unseen stuff we didn't want added. So now to ensure that what we see is all that's there, we need to do what Smashwords calls "going nuclear": we need to strip our document of all formatting and take it back down to bare bones.

Yes, this includes italics. If you're like me and use them a lot, you may now emit a groan of frustration. You have my permission to emit another one of them later when you're painstakingly adding all the italics back in. But just think of it as one last proofread. Who knows? You might spot something on screen you didn't spot before.

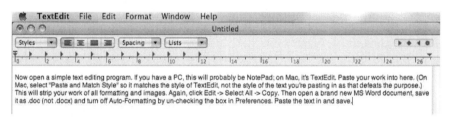

Our newly non-formatted text pasted into Mac's TextEdit.

Now open a simple text editing program. If you have a PC, this will probably be NotePad; on Mac, it's TextEdit. Paste your work into here. (On Mac, select "Paste and Match Style" so it matches the style of TextEdit, not the style of the text you're pasting in as that defeats the purpose.) This will strip your work of all formatting *and images*. We don't want the images to copy and paste, because copied and pasted images won't convert with our e-book; we have to go back and insert them from file.

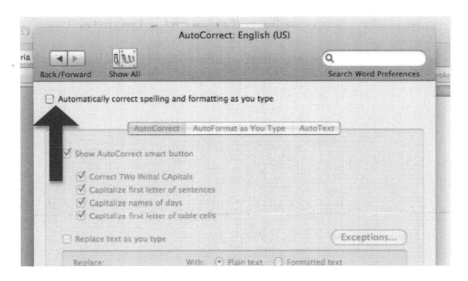

Turning off AutoCorrect and AutoFormat in MS Word's Preferences.

Once you've done that, click Edit -> Select All -> Copy. Then open a brand new MS Word document, save it as .doc (not .docx; look for the option from the drop-down file type menu in the Save As box) and turn off AutoFormatting and AutoCorrect by un-checking the boxes in Preferences.

Paste the stripped text in and save.

Close It Up

Close up your text so that everything is together, i.e. there are only two blank lines between the end of one chapter and the beginning of a new one, and within your chapters, only one blank line between the end of one section and the start of another one.

It's unwise to use block paragraph style, i.e. where each paragraph is separated by a blank line. Unwanted blank lines come with e-books like ketchup packets come with fries—whether you want it or not, there's always at least one—so adding additional blank lines is a bad idea. Indenting is the most effective way to mark the beginning of your paragraphs, so that's what we're going to do. So remove all blank lines between your paragraphs now.

This should leave you with absolutely no blank pages and at most, two blank lines together at a time.

Activate Show/Hide And Go Tab Hunting

Word's Show/Hide feature is designated by the "¶" mark in the toolbar. Click it. You will now see all "non-printing characters" in blue—things like paragraph returns, tabs and section starts. We'll use this feature to help us format our book from here on in.

Formatting e-books makes me feel: ¶
¶
→ (a) Stressed ¶
→ (b) Angry ¶
→ (c) Homicidal. ¶

But first, we need to eliminate every *single* tab in our document. They're nasty little things; even *one* of them can stop our e-book converting correctly. Remove them using the Find and Replace function, putting ^t in the Find box and nothing in the Replace one.

Then, just to make absolutely sure, go through your document to make sure there isn't a *single* blue right arrow, as in the image above.

Style It Up

Working now in this new, stripped-of-formatting, tab-free, no-more-than-two-blank-lines-anywhere MS Word document, and again with all text selected (Edit -> Select All), go to Format -> Style.

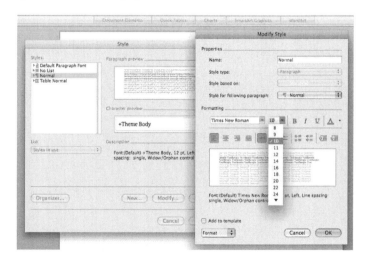

Your style will be set to Normal, but chances are that normal won't be what you want. (It's that damn horned demon again.) So click Modify and make Normal **Times New Roman, 10 point, left-aligned and single spaced**.

No exceptions.

Click Okay to modify that style and then Apply.

Troubleshooting tip: If you're working on a Mac, for some reason I can't fathom it seems to work better if rather than use "Normal" style, you change everything to "Plain Text" instead.

Keeping all the text selected, then go to Format –> Paragraph and make the settings single line spacing with no extra space before or after, left-aligned with first line indent to 0.3". So that it looks like this:

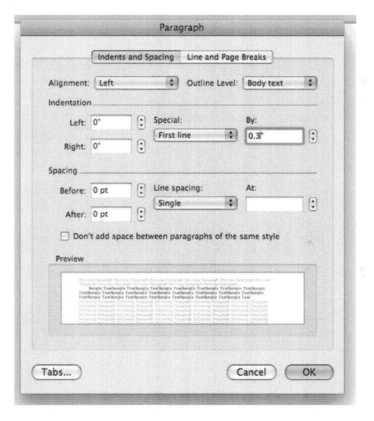

NB: If there are lines you don't want indented, set the indent to "0.01." We have to do this because the Kindle automatically inserts indents whether you want them or not. We can work around this by setting the indent to a size that will ultimately be imperceptible on screen.

Your book should now be looking like this to you:

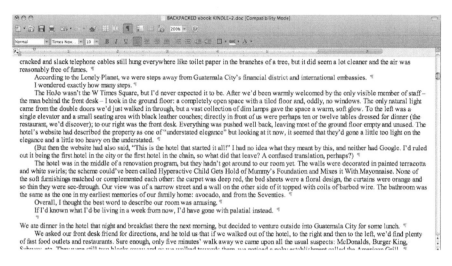

If it is, save your document, pop back up to the top of it and then go make some more coffee. This is where the work really begins.

Add Your Sparkly New Front Matter

What goes at the front of your e-book is not the same as what goes at the front of your print edition. You should have (and *only* have):

- The book's title
- Your name
- Whether it's a Kindle or Smashwords edition
- Copyright symbol and date
- Copyright notice (modified to reflect that it's an e-book)
- Licence notes.

And guess what? You're allowed to *centre* this text. I know, I know, I'm spoiling you. But—and this is a big but—do not just centre the text by selecting it and hitting the centre button. Doing that will make me shake my head and make tut-tutting noise, and it might also undo all the work you've just done. Because MS Word is the devil, and it's only kidding that that text is centred. We need to make sure that it's been centred at its core. So instead, create a new style that will (a) not indent your paragraphs and (b) centre your text. Call it "Front Matter" or something like that. Then select the text you want centred at the beginning of your book and set it to that style, just like we did a few steps ago when we changed all our text to Normal.

This is what it should look like:

Note: no blank lines. The whole thing is bunched up together. We do this for two reasons. First, I've already mentioned how during the conversion process, blank lines just lurve to appear out of nowhere. Therefore adding unnecessary blank lines is just asking for trouble. Second, e-books allow you to download a free try-before-you-buy sample. If a reader gets hooked on our free sample, they'll pay to read the rest of the book. The more they read, they greater the chance of getting hooked, and so the less space we take up in our sample with stuff that isn't our book, the better.

You'll need to save one "Kindle edition" version and one "Smashwords edition" version, but you can do that at the end.

Reviews

In our print edition we might put some reviews at the start, but do we *really* need to put them in our e-book?

I don't think so, no. A print copy might be picked up by someone who has never seen our Amazon listing whereas an e-book purchaser *has* to see our listing (where we'll put reviews once it goes live and, crucially, we get some) before clicking that "Buy" button.

It also delays them getting to the start of the book.

If you really want to put in some reviews, keep them short (1–2 sentences and who they're from) and keep them limited (1–3).

Whip Your Book Into Shape

Now we're going to go through our book, working as we go. We're going to:

I don't think so, no. A print copy might be picked up by someone who has never seen our Amazon listing whereas an e-book purchaser *has* to see our listing (where we'll put reviews once it goes live and, crucially, we get some) before clicking that "Buy" button. It also delays them getting to the start of the book. ¶

- **Insert page breaks**. To insert a page break, click Insert –> Break –> Page Break. It will appear as a thick blue line across the screen that says "page break" as in the image above. If you are also seeing some thin blue lines that don't say anything, don't worry about them. That's just MS Word showing you where your text would split onto another page if you were printing it out, which we'll never be. There are two rules for page breaks: (i) ONLY insert them in between chapters or parts/sections and in the place where your front matter meets the start of your book—absolutely *nowhere* else and (ii) every page break has to have one paragraph return above it and one paragraph return below it, as in the image above.

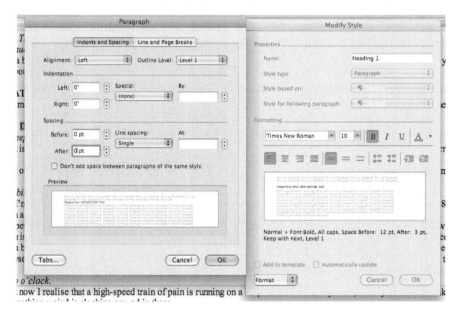

Modifying the "Heading 1" style so there's no extra space above or below the text and it's left-aligned.

- **Make chapter headings**. Keep your chapter headings simple as you possibly can. I usually left-align mine right above the beginning of the chapter, set the font to all caps and make it bold. But remember: we can't just do that from the formatting bar. We need to do it through styles. So go into Styles, find "Heading 1" and modify it until it's what you want, i.e. Times New Roman, size, bold, all caps, left-aligned. Check the "font" tab to make sure there's no kerning added, and the paragraph tab to ensure that no extra space has been added above or beneath your heading's text. The beauty of this is that by setting our chapter headings to "Heading 1" style, we're telling the conversion program that this is where our chapters begin. This means that when our readers download a copy of our book, their e-reader will help them navigate from one chapter to the next based on where we've put our heading styles. Tip: if you have parts and chapter headings, make the parts "Heading 1" style and the chapters "Heading 2" to show that they're one level down the hierarchy.

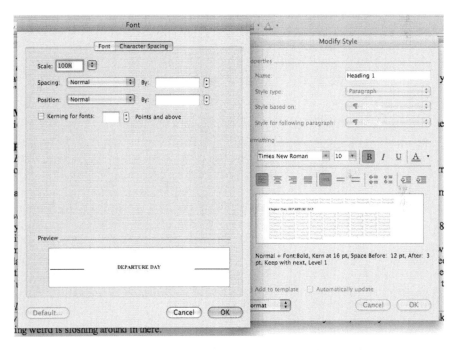

Modifying the "Heading 1" style; note the "Kerning for fonts" box is unchecked.

- **Remove the paragraph indent from your first lines**. When we did our whole Select All–>Normal a while back, it gave every paragraph in our book an indented first line. But we don't want that, because the first line in a chapter or section shouldn't be indented. I used to remove the indent by selecting the line and dragging the ruler back across to the left-hand margin, but this doesn't always work—you might end up with some weird paragraph alignments in the finished e-book. So instead, create a new style, based on your existing paragraph style but with no indent. Call it "first paragraph" or something. Then as you go through your book, set the first paragraph of each chapter or section to this new style.

•

mails, caught up on missed sleep, snacked on things made of high fructose corn syrup and watched BBC World News, the only English-language channel in our room. ¶

I also spent an hour rooting through my backpack for items I could lose, and said goodbye to two impractical T-shirts and the travel hairdryer. ¶ (*Noooooooooooooo!*) ¶

By the time the morning of our third day rolled around, we were restless with cabin fever. Luckily the exhaust fumes we inhaled during the forty-five minute taxi ride out of the city and up into the hills calmed us *right* back down, and so we arrived in Antigua relaxed and ready to *really* start our backpacking adventure. ¶
¶

| ¶
¶

Chapter Three: THE CORRECTIONS ¶
The colonial town of Antigua is nestled in the Guatemalan highlands with only the peaks of volcanoes breaking the blue sky above its brick-red roofs. With its adobe houses, cobbled streets and beautiful Parque Central, it's everything Guatemala City is not: quiet, pretty and relatively safe. ¶

I'd found a hotel online called Casa Cristina, and had booked us three nights there before leaving Florida. We planned on staying in Antigua longer than that, but figured that by the time those three nights were up, we'd have sussed out somewhere cheaper. Of course, Casa Cristina was cheap compared to say, anywhere else of its kind in the Western World, but by backpacker standards it was an indulgence. ¶

It was nice though. A typical Antiguan home from the outside, the doorway led into a tiled hallway filled with natural light. The colours on our room's walls were not, perhaps, what you'd like to see first thing on a hungover morning, but the beds were comfortable, the bathroom was en-suite and there was even a TV. On top of the Casa Cristina was a roof terrace with panoramic views of the town and the countryside beyond, and Parque Central was only steps away. ¶

Memories of Guatemala City's stinky, screeching, smoking metropolis were already fading away. ¶

The beginning of a chapter in my e-book, Backpacked. *Note: one page break with at least one paragraph return on either side (but no more than two), left-aligned bold/caps chapter heading (set to Heading 1 style) and no indent on the first line of my first paragraph, but all first lines indented after that.*

• **Put back in any italics or bold text**. We can just do this from the Format toolbar, i.e. just select the text and then either hit the "Bold" or "Italics" button. Thank fudge for that, eh?

• **Make all hyperlinks live**. The beauty of e-books is that if you're reading one of my books on your iPad, for example, you can click a link to my blog and be taken there immediately by Safari (Apple's internet browser). But in order for that to happen, we need to make the links live. To do this, select the text you want to make a live link, e.g. my website or www.mywebsite.com, and click Insert –> Hyperlink. Type the URL into the box provided and click "Okay."

• **Re-insert images, if necessary**. Ah, images. I really do wish people would leave them out. Do me one favour, will you? If you're planning on inserting images, mock up a little MS Word document with one of your favourite images in it, send it to a Kindle in PDF and view it on the Kindle screen. And not a fancy new Kindle Fire, but a normal Kindle, one where the screen is in black and white. Now, how does it look? Good? No. It looks crap. It's small, and it's in black and white. Plus, adding images to your book makes your file bigger, and Smashwords has a rather small 50MB limit on e-book files. But sometimes you *have* to insert images (as I did in this book), so the way to do it is to insert them from file, i.e. Insert-> Picture. You CANNOT copy and paste them. You must also make sure that all your images are set to "in line with text" in the Format box. (Right-click your image and select "Format Picture" from the menu that appears.) If you can drag them around the screen, they're not. Keep in mind that all e-reading devices have different size screens and since the user can choose the font size, your book will look totally different on each one. So will the images in them. Make them a reasonable size — I usually stick with 3-4 inches across, max — to give them the best chance of displaying correctly.

- **Remove excess blank lines**. Listen to me VERY carefully: under no circumstances should you have more than 3-4 empty lines anywhere in your e-book. Trust me, this will be difficult to implement. You'll really, really, *really* want to leave some after your copyright notice, or after the last line of each chapter, but you need to be strong! Don't do it. When you press Return to make a blank line, you'll get a little "¶" mark just as you do at the end of each paragraph. Make sure you have no more than four of these together anywhere in your book.

Some things to remember:

- When inserting hyperlinks, make sure that only the text you intended to be a live link becomes one. Conversely, if you've copied and pasted text into your e-book from an online source like your blog, go through to remove any wayward live links.
- Don't mention any retailer other than Amazon in your Kindle edition, and try not to mention *any* retailers in your Smashwords edition other than putting "Smashwords Edition" in your front matter. Do you really think Barnes and Noble wants links to your Amazon listings *inside* your book?
- Do not change your font size, or use more than one. There's just no need. I know it goes against all your formatting instincts, but trust

me on this. The simpler our e-books are the better, and this is one area where we can save on complication.

Add Your Sparkly New End Matter

Do you have the words "THE END" at the end of your book? If not, type them now. Oh, go on then: you can centre them too. (Using the "Front Matter" style, needless to say.)

If you have an Author's Note, Acknowledgements and About the Author, put them here and put them together, i.e. only have one line between them. Insert links to all your online homes, and make them work, i.e. Insert –> Hyperlink. Then type three hashtags (###) to show that now your book has really ended, and there is no more.

It should look like this:

And they all lived happily ever after.

THE END

Author's Note
Something very important I have to tell you about my book and not just something I made up because I really wanted an author's note.

Acknowledgements
I don't understand why I have to thank anyone for helping me write this book, as no one did. But maybe I'll sell a few more copies if I put loads of names here, so let's do it. Thanks to Mum, Dad, the guy who sells me my venti lattes in the Starbucks on Market Street, the Mars Foods company for making Snickers bars and the person who invented Sky Plus, without which I'd get nothing done at all...

About the Author
Up until recently, E-Book Author was drinking copious amounts of coffee and working on her second novel. However, after spending a weekend attempting to format this e-book correctly, she had to be transferred to a secure mental health facility for the safety of the people around her. She's currently considering embellishing her experiences there á la James Frey's *A Million Little Pieces*. Her agent thinks she's on to something... Oh, wait. That should have been *on* something.

Find out more on www.amillionlittleformattingerrors.com

www.myblogsiteURL.com
www.mybooksiteURL.com
###

Creating A "Live" Table Of Contents

In an e-book there's no point having a table of contents unless it *works*, i.e. when you click on or select "Part 5: Bubbles", it takes you to Part 5. (Remember there are no page numbers.) So how do we do that? We insert hyperlinks into our table of contents text, but instead of typing a URL, we select one of the headings we've already made.

Before we start this, ask yourself do you need a table of contents? Unless your book is non-fiction or instructional, I'd say no. If your answer is yes, ask yourself if you need as lengthy a table of contents as you have in your print book. For example, in the paperback version of this book, the table of contents lists every part, section and sub-section. It runs for a few pages but because it's a print book, the reader can just flip ahead and see where the actual book begins. In the e-book, I've scrapped the sub-sections, because if I don't the table of contents will run on and on, and because the e-book reader can't "see" ahead, they might not bother clicking their way through it all. We want the actual book to start as soon as possible on an e-reader and having a 100+ item table of contents is going to ensure that that doesn't happen.

Go back to the start of your book and type your table of contents. Insert it just before the point where your main book begins. You can either use numbers like:

TABLE OF CONTENTS

Chapter 1
Chapter 2
Chapter 3

or names like:

How to Self-Publish an E-book: Contents

Prepare Your Manuscript
Remove Tabs
Normalise Text

Now you're going to link these to the headings you've created. Highlight the word(s) you want to link the heading to, e.g. "Prepare Your Manuscript" and click Insert->Hyperlink. What happens next will depend on what version of Word you're using and if you're using a PC or Mac, but look for "Document", i.e. the option that will enable you to link to anchors or points that already exist in the document you're working on. From the list that appears, look for "Headings." Then select the heading you want the text to correspond to.

It's *way* simpler than it sounds, believe me.

This is what it looks to me on MS Word for Mac:

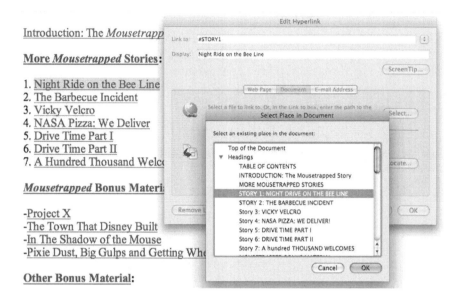

If you want to be *really* organised about it, you can also make your Table of Contents a heading and then link it to a "Back to top" or "Return to Table of Contents" phrase at the end of every section.

If you do that, consider yourself the teacher's pet in this classroom.

And that's it! Our e-book is formatted. If you've done it correctly, you'll never have to come back to this again. If you're in the majority of people who do this, you'll be looking at your document again real soon, trying to sort out some problem with the conversion, the cause of which you just can't figure out. But for now, let's think positive and say we're done with e-book formatting.

Now we just need to sort out a cover.

Your E-book Cover

Your e-book cover (also called your "Product Image") is just the front cover of your print book. If you're getting your paperback cover professionally designed and sent to you as a PDF, all you need to do is select the front cover area and Save As in JPEG format.

Your e-book cover file should be 1000 pixels wide on the longest side and ideally a height/width ratio of 1.6 and for best quality. Amazon recommends 2500 pixels on the longest side for best quality.

I don't know what this means; I just pass this information on to my cover designer.

If you don't know what this means and you're planning on trying this cover designing thing yourself (*nooooooooooo...!*), then try Catherine's Patented E-Book Cover Resizing Method:

1. Try to upload your cover image
2. Make it slightly smaller or bigger and try to upload again
3. Repeat until cover image is accepted and uploads.

Optimising Your E-book Cover

If your planned print cover has a lot of detail or very small text, you might want to consider producing a separate front cover that's optimised for e-book sales. You know how big a book cover looks on an Amazon listing? That's how big anyone who is considering buying your e-book will ever see it and most people will see it looking even smaller than that—and in black and white—on their e-reading devices.

I haven't made a separate e-book cover for *Mousetrapped* but if I was going to, I'd lose the tagline text at the top of my cover and make the title, subtitle and my name all much bigger, because they're too small to be readable in a thumbnail image.

Keep in mind though that you'll be linking your paperback to your e-book on Amazon and so you don't want the covers to look so different that they seem like different books.

Making A DIY E-book Cover Using MS Word

Perhaps you're only going to publish an e-book and so you don't already have a print cover. While I *strongly* recommend that you get that professionally designed too, there is a way you can produce a cover by yourself. It won't win any design or beauty awards, but it will do the job. And if you start to sell books, you can use the profits to get a proper cover designed later.

(NB: This cover will have a low resolution and will not hold up well if you print it out or zoom in. But it'll look fine on a thumbnail preview such as the one your readers will see on the book's Amazon listing. Depending on how low a resolution it is, you also run the risk of it NOT being accepted by some e-book retailers.)

1. Open a blank MS Word document with the same dimensions as a book cover (use a CreateSpace template for a 6 x 9 book; that works well).
2. Visit stock images websites (listed at the back) to find pictures or images. You'll have to pay to use them. Alternatively, use ones you already own or photographs you've taken yourself.
3. Insert your chosen image into your MS Word document. This works best if the image can also serve as the background. Stretch it out so that it covers the entire page and extends beyond it. (You need a high-resolution picture to do this; it can't be blurry.)
4. Using "no-fill" text boxes, insert your title, subtitle, author, etc. Remember this is for an e-book, so no tiny text.
5. Save the MS Word document as a PDF. (You might have to go into the Print menu and then Save As –> PDF to do this).
6. Open the PDF and save *that* as a JPEG file.

These are three covers I made using this method. (The images still say the name of the stock photo website I got them from because I didn't pay for them; once you do, that disappears.)

Fun fact: I use this same method for mocking up cover ideas for my cover designer.

NB: If your e-book cover is white, put a grey border around it as it will look a tad ridiculous against the white background of its Amazon listing.

Upload To Amazon Kindle Direct Publishing (KDP)

We're going to do the easy and most important bit first: upload to Amazon Kindle Direct Publishing, or KDP from here on in because, as we've established, I'm lazy.

I say easy because for some reason, formatting goes a hell of a lot more smoothly on KDP. This is probably because it's merely converting your MS Word document into one thing (the Kindle .mobi format) whereas Smashwords has to multi-task. I say important because this is where almost all your sales are going to come from, in my experience.

The very good news is that this is one of the best user interfaces in existence, which is a fancy way of saying it's *super* easy to use.

Create A KDP Account

Go to the KDP website (**kdp.amazon.com**) and register for a free account. If you already have an Amazon.com account, you can create your KDP account with that.

Once you've signed in, you'll have to click "Agree" on a couple of terms and conditions notices and then you'll be brought to the KDP dashboard, where up in the right-hand corner a yellow box will remind you that you haven't set up your account information yet. Click on "Update Now."

Here, you'll have to fill in your name and address—make sure it's correct; it's where your cheques will be sent—and your US tax information. If you don't have a US Social Security Number or tax number, leave this blank. (We're going to address this tax issue later on when we talk about getting paid.)

It will also ask you to specify whether you'd like to be paid by cheque or bank transfer (subject to location).

Add New Title

After you sign in, you'll arrive at the Dashboard (pictured at the top of the opposite page). Across the top you'll see four items: Bookshelf, Reports, Community and KDP Select. "Bookshelf" will be in bold because that's where you are.

Once you upload a book, it'll appear here.

Click "Add New Title." You will now be looking at a screen that looks like this:

Now, we get filling in.

(Don't) Enrol In KDP Select

KDP Select is a programme whereby you can make your book available for lending from the Kindle Owners' Lending Library (KOLL). In return for this, you get compensated for borrows out of a pre-determined fund—the giant $600,000 visible in the screenshot of the KDP dashboard—and you get to promote your book as free for up to five days out of every 90-day period.

We're not going to worry about this until we come to selling our book, so leave the "Enrol this book in KDP Select" box **unchecked** for now.

Book Name

Fairly straightforward: enter the title of your book. And yet, some people will not follow this instruction. I know they won't, because I've seen the evidence.

All books have titles. Some books have titles and subtitles, although that is almost exclusively reserved for non-fiction. That—a title, or a title and a subtitle—is what belongs in this box. NOTHING ELSE.

But Catherine, you're wondering, what else would anyone put in this box? What is not a title or a subtitle that could be confused with one?

Oh, *plenty*.

Taglines, most commonly. What is a tagline? Besides being NOTHING THAT BELONGS IN THE TITLE BOX, it's a little snazzy phrase that is supposed to entice you to read the book. A sort of slogan. You see them on a lot of thrillers and crime novels. They come from Hollywoodland, where no self-respecting movie is released without one. (*Jurassic Park*: An adventure 65 million years in the making. *Jaws*: Don't go in the water. *Finding Nemo*: There are 3.7 trillion fish in the ocean. They're looking for one.) I saw a self-published book on the Kindle store whose title was "VOLCANO—you need to Run." Presumably "you need to Run" is the book's incorrectly capitalised tagline, and it has no place being anywhere *near* the book's incorrectly capitalised title.

Once upon a time authors were adding things like "for fans of Patricia Cornwell" to their titles, which was a cute (and highly effective) marketing ploy until Amazon noticed and promptly put a stop to it. So don't do that either.

I would avoid telling people what your book is in the title box, e.g. "Presumed Dead: A Thriller" or "Talking Purple Unicorns: A Supernatural Steampunk Mystery." If they can't tell the genre of your book from your book cover, your book cover isn't cutting the mustard and needs to be re-designed. The only exception I would make here is if you have a novel that might be mistaken for non-fiction. Let's say you've written the book version of *How To Lose a Guy in 10 Days* (ignoring for a second the lawsuits you'd be slammed with as soon as you released it unless you changed the title). Well, we don't want anyone to purchase our book because they want *instructions* on how to lose a guy in 10 days. So in this instance, it would be acceptable to make the title of your book "How to Lose a Guy in 10 Days: A Novel."

If you were thinking of putting something like "Buy me, please!" in the title box, please:

1. Read ahead to the end of this numbered list
2. Close the book
3. Hit yourself with it repeatedly.

So, enter your title in the box marked "Book name." Do NOT enter it in capital letters; enter it as it would be written, e.g. Mousetrapped, A Wrinkle in Time, Fifty Shades of Mind-Boggling Levels of Repetition. (What...?)

If you have a subtitle, enter it after a colon, e.g. Mousetrapped: A Year and A Bit in Orlando, Florida. Don't make up a subtitle just because you think it'd be cool to have one.

If on your print edition you used a long subtitle, there's no room for it here. It'll just look weird on your product listing, because Amazon will dump the middle of it, i.e. *How To Lose a Guy in 10 Days: A Dating Plan for ... and Leg-Shaving.* We'll just stick it in our product description instead.

Series/Series Title/Volume Number

If your book is part of a series, check the box marked "This book is part of a series" then put the name of the series in the box beneath it. Add the book's volume number, if applicable, in the box provided.

For example, if your book was *Catching Fire*, the name of the series would be "The Hunger Games Trilogy" and the volume number would be "2" or "II".

Edition Number

Chances are you'll upload newer editions of this book in the future (when you find mistakes, change your website address, produce more books and want to link to them, etc. etc.) so it's an idea to put a '1' in here, and change it accordingly as you update the book.

Description

You have 4,000 characters (about 700-ish words) to describe to us what your book is about. This is where you put your **back cover blurb** and nothing else, even if your blurb is only 154 words. Just because you have space to spare doesn't mean you should start filling it with stuff; only put a short, relevant description of your book. Keep in mind that this is what will appear, *exactly* as you enter it, on your Amazon listing.

Your blurb is a *very* important selling tool for your book. I was at a talk recently where an editor at a major publishing house said that she believed the blurb was more important than the cover design. I think it's *as* important, but maybe she knows what she's talking about more than me, because she knows how difficult it is to sell all sorts of books all over the world.

She even went so far as to say that self-publishers should *hire copywriters* to write their blurbs for them before they think about hiring cover designers, but I can't say I agree with this, especially because blurbs is an area where I see traditional publishing fall down a lot. (Just an example that comes to mind: the blurb for *The Drop*, the last Michael Connelly novel I went to the store on the day of publication to buy, had a blurb that gave away a twist at the end. Yeah.)

I think you should write it yourself, because no one knows your book as well as you do. This isn't something you do as you upload your book to Amazon — you should spend a week or so drafting and redrafting, going away and coming back, seeing what works and what doesn't. Don't rush the blurb. Think about what will happen: you've managed to convince someone to go visit your Amazon listing to check out your book (an achievement in itself), then look at the price, think *okay*, they look at the cover, think *okay*, they come to read the blurb. If it's interesting enough, they'll buy it. If it sucks, look at all the time and effort you've wasted getting them to your Amazon listing, only for your blurb to trip you up at the last hurdle.

Your blurb should:

- Be very short, about 100–300 words
- Be written in the same style/voice as your book
- Entice people. After they read it, people should think, "I *really* want to read that book!"

Your blurb should NOT:

- Give away the ending
- Be your author bio — that's a separate thing
- Include physical details unless the book is exceptionally short. If you're charging 99c for an e-book of 20,000 words, that's 80,000 words less than most e-books that are sold for 99c. So as not to disappoint your readers, add something like "Please note: this e-book is 20,000 words long" at the very end of your blurb. DO NOT take this the other way though, i.e. trying to convince readers that

99c is a bargain because your novel is a bargain because it's 160,000 words. You *could* do it with a reference book because in that case, the length of the book *is* relative to the value of it, because people are buying it for information. So maybe add a line like "Over 200,000 words of great advice" or something. Just try to avoid sounding like a jerk while doing it, because remember: this is a self-published book. Everyone who reads the blurb will know that *you* wrote it about *your* own book.

This is the original blurb for *Mousetrapped*:

When Catherine Ryan Howard decides to swap the grey clouds of Ireland for the clear skies of the Sunshine State, she thinks all of her dreams—working in Walt Disney World, living in the United States, seeing a Space Shuttle launch—are about to come true. Ahead of her she sees weekends at the beach, mornings by the pool and an inexplicably skinnier version of herself skipping around Magic Kingdom.

But not long into her first day on Disney soil—and not long after a breakfast of Mickey-shaped pancakes—Catherine's Disney bubble bursts and soon it seems that among Orlando's baked highways, monotonous mall clusters and world famous theme parks, pixie dust is hard to find and hair is downright impossible to straighten.

The only memoir about working in Walt Disney World, Space Shuttle launches, the town that Disney built, religious theme parks, Bruce Willis, humidity-challenged hair and the Ebola virus, *Mousetrapped* is the hilarious story of what happened when one Irish girl went searching for happiness in the happiest place on earth.

That's 175 words. This is the blurb for my next book, *Backpacked*, which is 241 words:

Catherine Ryan Howard isn't the backpacking type. Working for one of the world's largest hotel chains, she and her employee discount have become accustomed to complimentary bath robes, 24-hour room service and Egyptian cotton sheets. As for vacations, Catherine likes places that encourage lying—lying on the beach, lying by the pool, lying in bed...

She's been on what feels like one long holiday in Florida when her fearless best friend, Sheelagh, announces plans to backpack across Central America. With Catherine's US visa about to expire, no desire to return home to Ireland and her common sense, evidently, on a day off, she agrees to go along. After all, how bad can this backpacking thing be?

Um... very bad, actually. Catherine soon finds herself showering with the threat of electrocution, living with mutant cockroaches, sleeping on wooden planks, suffering from all but one of the side-effects listed on her anti-malarial tablets (liver failure, in case you were wondering) and riding a horse up the side of a smoking, lava-filled volcano.

And that's just the first week.

Picking up where her bestselling memoir, *Mousetrapped: A Year and A Bit in Orlando, Florida*, left off, *Backpacked* is the wry tale of what happened when one very reluctant backpacker hit the backpacker trail and discovered that beyond the mosquitoes, bad coffee and flea-infested hostels lie even bigger mosquitoes, even worse coffee and flea-infested hostels with no doors on any of their bathrooms.

(Fiction blurbs, by the way, are usually *much* shorter.)

There is plenty of advice online and in "How To Write a Book" books about how to write a blurb or short synopsis for your book. You can also seek out books similar in genre to yours and study their blurbs to get an idea of what's the norm, structure, length, etc. It is vital to your success that you have a good one and if you have any concern about your ability to write it, you can hire a copywriter to do it for you. But personally, I think the best person for the job is the person who wrote the book, because who else knows the story better than you do?

Remember: you have blog readers and Twitter followers. Chances are, most of them read a lot of books. Why not post your blurb or multiple versions of it and ask them what they think? This is not only helpful to you, but makes them feel involved in your project as well.

Do NOT add anything moronic like ***BUY ME PLEASE*** or THIS BOOK IS AMAZING!!!!

The Best of Catherine, Caffeinated: Caffeine-Infused Self-Publishing Advice [Kindle Edition]

Catherine Ryan Howard (Author)

★★★★★ (7 customer reviews) | Like

Kindle Price: **$2.45** includes VAT* & free international wireless delivery via *Amazon Whispernet*

- Length: 314 pages (estimated)
- Don't have a Kindle? Get your Kindle here.

Contributors

What's weird here is that they don't automatically make you, the registered owner of the KDP account, the default contributor. (I suppose it's because it would only work for self-publishers...?) So you need to add yourself as a contributor. Click "Add contributor", enter you first and last names in the box provided and then select "Author" from the drop-down menu. Then Save.

Then close the box in which you add contributors. *Immediately*. Quick, do it now!

Because for some unfathomable reason, self-publishers *love* abusing this Contributors thing. They treat it like a kind of cast list or, worse yet, their acknowledgments. But it's not a cast list and it damn sure isn't the name-drops in your acknowledgements. It's what will be shown at the very top of your Amazon listing, for all to see, as in the image on the previous page.

Abusing Contributors makes you look like an amateur, because crediting everyone who worked on your book is not what this is for and if you *weren't* an amateur, you'd already know that.

So just add yourself as the "author" and fill in your name. Don't use all caps and make sure you enter the right part (first name or surname) in the right box. Just stick with your first and last names unless you're Bret Easton Ellis or Michael Jackson III.

If you are using a pen name, enter the pen name. And for the love of fudge, don't put "Mr" or "Mrs" anything!

There are only four exceptions to this rule of listing yourself as the author and nothing else:

1. If someone famous who might help sell your book has written a foreword or an introduction for you, e.g. you've written *How To Get Rich Writing Children's Books* and J.K. Rowling has liked it so much that she's agreed to write an introduction to it. In that case you could add J.K. Rowling and select "Introduction" or "Foreword" from the drop-down list.
2. If you are publishing a collection of short stories and someone other than you has collected and assembled them. In that case you could add that person's name and then select "Editor". ***This is what is meant by the role called "editor" in the drop-down list***. (Yes, bold, italics *and* underlined. I'd put it in flashing lights if I could.) It does NOT mean the freelance help you got editing your book.
3. If your book contains original illustrations or photographs all made or taken by the same person. In that case you could add that person's name and "Illustrator" or "photographer" but ONLY if the illustrations/photographs play a major part in the book, as they might do in a children's title or a cookery book, for example.

4. If your book was written in a language other than English and someone translated it into English for you. Yes, you've guessed correctly: "translator."

Language

Select the language the book is written in from the drop-down menu.

Publication Date

You can select a past date you'd like the book to have officially been published on here if you wish, but you cannot select a date in the future. I'd recommend leaving it blank, making its publication date today.

Publisher

The instructions for filling in this box say, "The publisher name can be the name of the author or the name of the publisher" and "If you are the book's author, you can enter your own name or the name of your publishing company."

Remember how we talked about pretending we weren't self-publishing, and making up fake publishing company names just because we could? Well, do you *have* a publishing company? Have you *registered* that company's name? Does this company *exist*? Yeah, I didn't think so.

This box is optional. So just leave it blank!

ISBN

You don't need an International Standard Book Number (ISBN) to publish on KDP so leave this blank.

If you happen to have an ISBN, I wouldn't waste it on your Kindle book because, again, you don't *need* one to publish to KDP.

(You don't *need* one, okay? Jeez Louise.)

Verify Your Publishing Rights

Check the box next to "This is not a public domain work and I hold the necessary rights."

Target Your Book To Customers

This is every bit as important as the name suggests. It's how we're going to help your potential readers to find your book.

The first thing you have to do is assign up to two Book Industry Standards & Communications (BISAC) Categories. These are genres and other categories standardised throughout the world to help identify books by type and group like with like. Choose from the list available the two best categories that describe your book. It might be something as simple as Fiction –> Thriller or it might be more like Reference –> Practical Guide –> Arts and Crafts –> Wool Crafts –> Knitting Ugly Jumpers.

Later on, when we become bestsellers (!), it's in these categories it'll happen first. For instance, I am frequently #1 on the Kindle store in Travel –> North America –> United States –> Regions –> South –> South Atlantic. (I know, right? The first time it happened, that was the day I knew I'd made it... Not.) Now if I'd written an erotic novel about cupcakes, it's category would be Fiction –> Erotica. But if I was being a smart arse, I could also put it in the Cooking –> Courses and Dishes –> Cakes category where, because fiction sells in much higher numbers than cookery books, I'd have a greater chance of getting to #1.

DON'T DO THIS. It's not smart, it's not clever and it's probably going to leave some cupcake makers *very* upset and/or all hot and bothered. Putting your book in the wrong category is just the same crime as false advertising, and it's not going to help readers find your book.

Once you've picked two (correct!) categories, you can enter up to seven keywords or search terms that will bring readers to your book. Try to imagine finding something about your book on Google. What search words would you enter in the search box? Think of seven, and add them here.

Upload Your Product Image

This is your e-book cover that your cover designer has already sent you, or you've already made. Browse your computer for your image and hit upload.

If KDP doesn't like your cover, it'll tell you now. Otherwise it'll say "Upload successful."

We Need To Talk About Digital Rights Management (DRM)

You'll see that the next item you have to decide on is whether to enable Digital Rights Management (DRM) or not. DRM is a device that "intends to prohibit the unauthorised distribution" of your book or, to put it simply, it aims to prevent piracy. And we are NOT going to put it on our book.

I know that sounds crazy but trust me, we don't want DRM. It will make your e-books more expensive, cut into your royalties and make me roll my eyes in exactly the same way as I do when I see copyright notices at the end of blog posts about choosing a brand of butter, or hear of idiots submitting manuscripts to agents and publishers with copyright symbols on the title page.

Unless you're an internationally bestselling author, the chances of your book being pirated are between so-slim-you-can't-even-see-it and none. You should be so lucky that people think your book is so amazing that they'd go to the trouble of hunting down an illegally obtained copy of it instead of just paying $2.99 to buy the thing.

Puh. *Leeease.*

I also think inserting DRM is a bit of an insult. You're basically saying to your readers: "Thanks for buying my book, but I don't trust you and suspect that you might steal from me, so I've taken counter-measures." What's next—putting a notice in your print editions prohibiting lending to friends? And that's not all: DRM prohibits readers who *have* paid for your book from reading it when and where they want. Let's say I've bought your book to read on my computer and then I get a present of a dedicated e-reading device like a Kindle or Nook. Shouldn't I be able to transfer that book, seeing as I've paid for it? Indeed I should, but DRM won't let me.

DRM also can affect "text-to-speech" features—where a reader can set their e-reading device to read your book aloud to them—which discriminates against readers with vision problems who may rely on these features to enjoy your book.

And here's the kicker: *DRM doesn't work.* It doesn't prevent piracy; there are ways around it. So basically there isn't one single reason why you should apply DRM to your book.

If you think you need DRM, you're (a) wrong and (b) suffering from our old friend Peter Paranoia. I wouldn't dream of putting DRM on an e-book and I don't even worry about piracy. In fact, writing this section is the first time I've given it any thought. It is the scourge of the bestselling author, yes, but it's nothing to do with us. Especially since we're charging such reasonable prices for our e-books.

If it helps you sleep at night, set up a Google Alert for your book's name and your name. That way if it shows up on a file-sharing site or something, you'll find out about it and can take action.

(But it won't.)

Upload Your Book

Select your book's document from your computer and hit upload. NB: Make sure you are uploading the file that says "Kindle Edition."

Wait; it usually only takes a couple of minutes. Then you'll see (hopefully!) "Upload Successful" and a button inviting you to preview your book.

You can preview your book using either Amazon KDP's Simple Previewer or their Enhanced Previewer. The Enhanced Previewer is really for people smarter than us who have done all sorts of fancy e-book stuff, so we're just going to stick with the Simple one.

Click "Preview book".

Now a virtual Kindle will appear on screen and you'll be able to click through your whole book. What fun! *So* much fun that you might forget you're supposed to be checking that the thing has converted correctly...

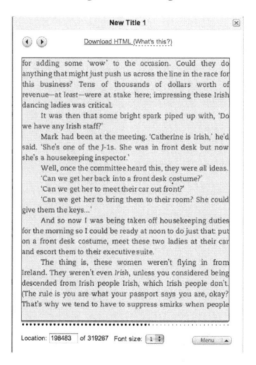

The "virtual" Kindle preview.

Chances are it won't be 100% perfect. There might be a couple of extra empty lines here and there, or your About the Author is now centred instead of left-aligned. I wouldn't worry about these things; I would just worry about the main body text being readable and well-presented.

If you see any of the following you're going to have to go back and re-format, I'm afraid:

- More than one font within a section or within a paragraph
- Extra space between lines within a paragraph
- Variable line spacing
- Every second paragraph in italics
- Paragraphs switching from left-alignment to centre or right-alignment or justified
- Only one paragraph on every page
- Any unreadable text
- Any other crazy stuff.

If you're happy with what you see, click "Save and Continue" to move on to Page 2 of the upload process, Rights and Pricing.

On To Page 2

Verify Your Publishing Territories

This is asking you within what geographical regions you have the rights to publish this work. Since you wrote it and no rights to it have ever been sold, select "Worldwide Rights — All Territories."

If you are a traditionally published author self-publishing a book that remains in print somewhere in the world, check with your agent or publisher which territories you can legally publish the e-book in. If it's not all of them, manually select the relevant territories from the list.

Choose Your Royalty

Here you select whether you want to make 35% off the sale of your e-books, or 70%. It's a toughie, isn't it?

No, it isn't. We want 70%, and as I've already argued I think $2.99 is the right place for each standard length self-published book to start off from. (Note: when I say standard length I'm talking about not selling pamphlets for $3. I'm *not* talking about charging $5 because your book is longer than most.)

The catch: in order to qualify for the 70% rate, your book has to be at least $2.99 and no more than $9.99, and you'll only get the 70% for books purchased in the US, the United Kingdom and the handful of other countries that have their own Kindle stores. (For purchases from all other countries you'll get 35%.) The good news is that in all likelihood, the majority of your sales will come from there.

If your book is 99c or $1.99, you have no choice but to go with 35%.

This is also where you enter the list price. If it's more than $4.99 I'll find out, you know.

You can also manually set your British pounds and Euro prices, or have KDP calculate it automatically based on your US price. In the interests of fairness, I say calculate it automatically.

NB: You must select a royalty and then a list price, and it will only let you enter a price that agrees with your selected royalty. So if you find yourself unable to enter 99c without getting an error message, make sure you've checked the "35% royalty" box.

Kindle Book Lending

Kindle owners can lend a Kindle book they have purchased to a friend and you have to let this happen if you want your 70%.

This is another thing that tends to lead to knicker-twisting, but it shouldn't. It's not that different from me buying a book, reading it and then lending it to a friend. Kindle owners can also only lend each book once. Just leave the box checked and let's move on.

Publish

Once you've completed everything on the page and are happy to do so, click "Publish."

Tip: you don't have to do this whole thing all at once, if you don't want to. You can save your changes without publishing by clicking "Save as draft" at the button of the "Book Details" and "Rights and Pricing" pages.

What Happens Now?

First of all a little dialogue box will appear telling you that you've successfully published your book and that it should make an appearance on the Kindle store in 12 hours or so.

If you return to your Bookshelf, you'll see your title has appeared there. It will say "In Review" for a while, and then that will change to "Publishing", and then that will change to "Live." You'll also see that it has been assigned an Amazon Standard Identification Number (ASIN) which is Amazon's own version of an ISBN, and the reason you didn't need one to publish on Amazon KDP.

So now we wait for our book to appear on Amazon. And while we wait, we get busy:

Uploading To Smashwords

Now we move onto Smashwords where a successful upload will put our e-books, potentially, onto the Smashwords website, Barnes and Noble's e-book store, Sony's e-book store, Kobo, Diesel and Apple's iBooks, among others, and where if your book isn't correctly formatted, you're about to know *all* about it.

(I recommend taking a good long coffee break between KDP upload and Smashwords upload or, preferably, doing them on different days. Best practice for patience levels.)

Create A Smashwords Account

Go to **www.smashwords.com** and register for a free account. Click the "Join" button near the top of the homepage.

Fill in all the details on the first page, and then go to your e-mail account to collect the message containing the link you need to finish the process.

Update Your Bio

After verifying your e-mail address, you'll come back to Smashwords where the site will ask you to update your bio and upload a profile picture.

NB: This is *your Smashwords author profile* which will be visible to the public and, more importantly, potential purchasers of your book.

Enter all your online addresses in the boxes provided (website, Twitter, Facebook, etc.) and copy and paste the Author Bio from your book into the "Bio" box here. Smashwords allows you to upload videos; if you have a book trailer or a recent video blog you can upload it here. Use the same profile pic you've used elsewhere; I haven't said this word in a while but remember, we're being *professional*, and that means giving all our online homes a form of cohesiveness.

On your profile page you'll also see a link that reads "update payee information." Click it and fill in as much information as you can. Again, if you don't yet have US tax information, leave that section blank for now.

The beauty of Smashwords is that they pay directly into your PayPal account. If you don't have one, sign up. Smashwords provides a handy link here for you. Money that goes into your PayPal account can be spent anywhere PayPal is accepted, or you can transfer it into your bank account.

Publish New Title

Once you've saved all this information, return to the homepage and click "Publish." You will now see a screen like the one pictured at the bottom of this page.

Title

Again, here we have no specific box for a subtitle so, if you have one, put both it and the title here.

(And don't even *think* about adding anything else...)

Short Description

Not all e-book retailers allow 4,000 characters for a book's description, so you need to provide a shorter, summarised version here. You have only 400 characters, so perhaps sum up your book in a sentence or two.

Think about your book's "elevator pitch", i.e. how you would explain to someone what your book is about if you were in an elevator with them and only had the time it takes to move between floors in which to do it. Again, this is very important to future sales of your book, so don't just scribble down the first thing that comes into your head. Work on it.

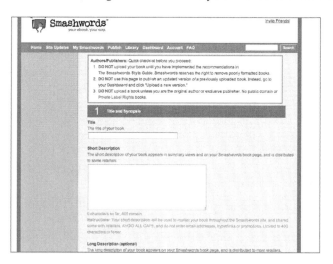

Longer Description

This is just like your CreateSpace and KDP product description: you have 4,000 characters and you should copy and paste the back cover blurb.

Language

Set the language the book is written in and then ...

Contains Adult Content

... select whether or not your book contains adult content. (Remember we're talking soft porn here, not kissing!)

Set Your Price

Ignore the "make my book free" (not recommended) and "let readers set the price" (???!!!) options and check the "Set price" option. Enter your list price in the box provided.

NB: You <u>MUST</u> set your e-book to the same list price on <u>BOTH</u> Amazon KDP and Smashwords. If one site finds out you are offering the same book at a lower price elsewhere, they can remove your book or worse, price-match it. We'll be talking about the endless migraine-inducing problems *that* can cause later.

We Need To Talk About Sampling

When KDP puts our book live on Amazon, anyone will be able to download a try-before-you-buy sample to their e-reader device or computer for free. This is the e-book equivalent of taking a book down from a bookstore shelf and having a flick through to see if you like it and since Amazon didn't even mention it to you, you had no option but to let them do it.

For some reason, Smashwords not only gives you the option of setting what percentage of your book you'll allow sampled, it also gives you the option of opting out of it altogether. And just like DRM, I am about to unleash hell on anyone who thinks that disabling or limiting sampling is a good idea.

Well, maybe not *hell*, exactly. But I *am* going to tell you not to do it.

I'll try and say this nice, okay? *If you limit or disable sampling you are telling me that you know absolutely nothing about e-book publication, haven't listened to a word I've said (or read a word I've typed) and are almost definitely doomed to failure.* A little harsh, perhaps. Or maybe not harsh enough. I say this because of the *reason* writers limit or disable sampling: it's because they don't want anyone to get any of their words for "free." It's a bad attitude, and shows plain ignorance about how this whole e-book thing works.

I once saw an author complain online that Amazon were "giving away too much" of his book for free by way of the free sample. "It's the whole first chapter!" he said. "There's way too much valuable information in there!" So, what you're saying is, if this was available in paperback, it'd be shrink-wrapped in all the stores? Because that *is* what you're saying, you utter moron.

Sampling should be 25% *minimum*, and 30% is better. After spending the time it takes to read a quarter of the way through your book, there is a far greater chance of the reader shelling out money to finish it. And remember our friend the Premium Catalogue? Well you can't get into it if you disable sampling.

And if you're worried about sampling because after reading that much people won't want to pay for the rest because they'll have realised your book isn't worth their time or money and you'd rather pocket their cash before they find out you aren't that talented a writer, that's called *being dishonest*.

Tags & Categories

You get one category selection, and I entered 17 search words and there was still no sign of anyone stopping me from entering more.

You know what to do.

Select E-book Formats

Next up you'll see a list of e-book formats like this:

ePub
Sony Reader (LRF)
Kindle (.mobi)
PalmDoc (PDB)
PDF
RTF
Plain Text

and all of them will be checked, showing that you want your book converted into all these formats. Which you do, so leave them all checked.

But haven't we already published in Kindle format, back at Amazon KDP? Yes, but we're still going to publish in .mobi here. That way if someone goes to Smashwords to buy your book, it's available in every format they could possibly want.

Upload Your Cover Image

Um... upload your cover image.

Upload Your Book

Upload your book document, ensuring that you're uploading the one that says, "Smashwords Edition."

Publish

Once the file has been uploaded, check everything is filled in and click "Publish."

What Happens Now?

Unless you're uploading at crazy o'clock in the morning and you live on the Irish side of the Atlantic Ocean, you won't be the only one who has just uploaded your e-book file, and you'll have to wait in a queue while your e-book converts. Depending on how busy the site is, this could take minutes, hours or no time at all. So leave the site and either check back later, wait for the e-mail with the subject header "Conversion Results" and just keep your eyes on the screen and wait for the conversion to begin.

Once the book has converted, it'll appear in your Smashwords dashboard as a published book. Under the column heading "Premium Status" you'll see something like "In review, submitted [date]." Your book won't pass that review unless you assign an ISBN to it, so go to Smashwords's ISBN Manager link in the sidebar or click "Assign an ISBN", follow the instructions and when the time comes to pick one of the options available, *go with the free ISBN.*

Don't make me start *that* lecture again. Please.

Then, with any luck, in a couple of weeks your book's Premium Status will change to "Approved" and a few weeks after that, your book will start popping up on iBooks, Barnes and Noble and a whole host of other online e-book stores.

Checking Your E-books

You've already checked your Kindle upload in the little Kindle preview mid-way through your KDP upload, and as far as I'm aware it would be highly unusual for your book to turn out looking significantly different than that. To be absolutely *sure* though, we're going to download a copy to check for ourselves. However, we can't do this until the book appears on Amazon, so for now we're just going to worry about Smashwords.

With Smashwords, one of two things will happen now. Either Smashwords will e-mail you to say that all is a-okay, your e-book converted with no problems and all is right with the world, or they'll tell you what's wrong with the document you uploaded, e.g. tabs were found or the font size used was too big.

Sometimes you've followed all the guidelines to the absolute letter and you *still* get formatting issues. I know: it blows.

But if Smashwords tell you that something specific is wrong with your book, thank your lucky stars because the only thing that blows more is when they tell you everything is all right and then you download your book to see if it is for yourself and you discover that it bloody well *isn't*. Chapter one is upside down, every other paragraph is in underlined italics and your table of contents links to someone else's book. (I should say these are things that actually cannot happen; I was exaggerating for comedic effect.) And you have *no idea* what's gone wrong.

The first e-book edition of *Mousetrapped* had 1,300 pages because there was a page break at the end of every paragraph. Smashwords told me it was fine. And not only did Smashwords tell me everything was fine with that book, but it bestowed upon it the illusive entry to its Premium Catalogue. (In their defence, this was more than two years ago, and with their constant improvements and upgrades I highly doubt it would happen now.) That's how it ended up for sale in Barnes and Noble's e-book store, where a customer ultimately posted a review saying, "This book has 1,300 pages!" (meaning he had to click "Next Page" 1,300 times because, as you and I both know, e-books don't have pages!), which was the first I had heard of this problem.

Anyway the reason it was the first I'd heard of it was because *I didn't bother checking all my formats*. Once Smashwords had converted my book and said it was okay, I almost didn't do anything at all, but then in a spurt of enthusiasm (a short, mild one) I went to my Smashwords dashboard and checked the "Online Reading" version of my book. It looked okay to me, so I considered my e-book work done.

Here's what I *should* have done and what I recommend you do now.

Download Adobe Digital Editions

The most widely used format of your book will be ePub. To check this, we're going to download a free copy of **Adobe Digital Editions,** download a copy of your own book in ePub format from Smashwords (where you can download your own book for free) and use the first one to check the second.

You can get it here: **www.adobe.com/products/digitaleditions.**

Adobe Digital Editions is the best place to check if setting our chapter headings to "Headings 1", etc. has actually worked. If it has, you should see a list of your chapter/section headings displayed down the left-hand side of your ADE screen.

Amazon's Kindle Application

Amazon has a free Kindle application you can download to Mac and PC. Download it, and then download the .mobi edition of your book from Smashwords. After that, connect to the Kindle store (once your book goes live) and download the sample or buy the whole book if you want.

(You can't download your own Kindle book for free from Amazon.)

You can get the Kindle application here:

(For PC) **www.amazon.com/gp/kindle/pc**
(For Mac) **www.amazon.com/gp/kindle/mac.**

NB: You can download .ePub and .mobi editions of your own books for free from Smashwords once you're logged in, but you can't download a free Kindle version of your own book. You have to buy it.

Ask Your Friends

I think checking the ePub and Kindle versions is enough, but never miss an opportunity to see what your book looks like on a specific e-reading device. Does your friend have a Kindle? Ask to borrow it for a sec so you can look up your book. On my last visit to the States, I popped into a Barnes and Noble, went straight to the Nook stand and used a demonstration model to check out what *Mousetrapped* looked like on there.

Troubleshooting

So what if chapter one *is* upside down? What do you do?

As I said already, if Smashwords have told you something specific is wrong then: hooray! You know exactly what you need to change. Go back and change it, and then upload the file again.

If you don't know, check to see if you've committed any of these cardinal sins, otherwise known as the Top 5 Most Common E-book Formatting Errors:

Improper Indents

There shouldn't be so much as a *hint* of a tab in your entire document. Paragraphs have to be marked by a first line indent and a reasonable one at that; don't indent your paragraphs so much that the first word is pushed more than halfway across the page.

Repeating Paragraph Returns

You should have no more than one or two blank lines together and you *can't* have more than four. Do you have too many blank lines together? Could you just not resist putting a big fat chunk of blank lines between your copyright notice and the start of your book? Did you keep pressing return because you didn't want "The End" and "Acknowledgements" to appear on screen together?

Improper Paragraph Separation

I told you not to use block paragraph style but to indent the first lines of your paragraphs instead. Whatever you do, it has to be one or the other. You can't do both. If you *must* use block paragraph style, make sure you don't have an indentation going on somewhere else, and you haven't used tabs to make a space between them. (You need to set the space between them automatically, in Paragraph settings. Or just do what I told you, which is *don't use block paragraphs!*)

Font And Style Mistakes

Have you used the same font throughout with absolutely zero exceptions, stuck to a very small range of font sizes (no more than 2 or 3 in the entire document) and refrained from using text bigger than 16 point—14 point if you can help it?

Copyright And Licence Notes

Have you forgotten to put your copyright notice in? Forgot the licence notes? Referred to the wrong e-book publisher in either of them?
One more time, the following will NOT work in an e-book:

- tables
- text boxes
- columns
- headers
- footers
- automatic footnotes.

I didn't get my e-book right first time, and it was because:

- I had about a thousand page breaks
- I used too large a font for my chapter headings
- my paragraph style wasn't set to "Normal" throughout
- my paragraph style was set to "add extra space between paragraphs."

Fix whatever you can find and re-upload your book until you get it right.

If at some point you experience an overwhelming urge to take your computer and throw it into the path of a moving car, then either:

- take a break of at least 48 hours from trying to fix your e-book and then go back to it
- find someone else to do it and reward them handsomely.

E-book Conversion

What I've been talking about in this section up until now is publishing an e-book by formatting your MS Word document in a very specific way, uploading it as a .doc to Amazon KDP and Smashwords, and letting them convert it automatically with one of their magical e-book-making programmes. You are the publisher and you can access your sales figures, royalty info, etc. at any time. All you need do to update your book is log on to your KDP or Smashwords account and upload a new file in place of the old one.

But here's the problem: Smashwords. It's practically easy these days to format a book for Kindle conversion on KDP. Follow my instructions and you'll have no problem. But Smashwords is another kettle of HTML entirely, because Smashwords has a much bigger job to do: not only does it have to take your MS Word document and convert it into multiple formats, but one of those formats, ePub, has to be readable on numerous e-reading devices, all of which display the text in a slightly different way.

Sometimes no matter what you do, you can't get your book to look right on all of Smashwords's platforms, and that makes *you* look unprofessional.

So is there a way from MS Word to ePub that doesn't go through Smashwords? Yes. And although it costs money, it *is* better. I've invited Diana of Ebook Partnership to explain more. (*I should say I chose Ebook Partnership for this because I've heard great things about them, both from bestselling e-book authors and publishing professionals, and because their services are comprehensive and in my opinion, very reasonably priced. I haven't received any financial incentive for recommending them here and there are other conversion/distribution services available.*) Over to Diana:

"If you would like to manage your own e-book conversion, there is a wealth of advice and resources available to writers. As previously outlined, if you follow guidelines and take advantage of the generosity of pioneer authors like Catherine, Word to .mobi is straightforward. Amazon is continually refining the KDP system, and it is a great tool for authors.

ePub is a slightly different prospect, and can induce a level of frustration that may impact on your writing productivity, but if you recognise this at the outset and invest in the marvellous Liz Castro book *ePub Straight to the Point* you may be able to add e-book formatting to your author toolbox quite quickly. Liz explains the complete process for creating an ePub file from Word and InDesign files. You can also find Liz on Twitter (@lizcastro), and if you follow the #eprdctn stream, you can pick up tips from ePub specialists also.

However, there are several reasons why you may want to enlist the help of a professional e-book conversion service for some, or all elements of the project:

- You may have successfully mastered the Kindle file conversion and upload, but would like an ePub file that does not contain any coding errors (which can lead to a title being rejected by a retailer) and allows you to sell on Apple, Barnes & Noble, Waterstones, Kobo, and other e-book sales outlets around the world
- Your book has complex formatting, many images, or needs to be converted to a fixed layout rather than a standard flowing e-book
- Perhaps the terms *html*, *CSS*, or even *zip file* induce instant anxiety and an urge to move away from the PC or Mac
- You would like to simply send the manuscript to someone and get conversion done quickly and efficiently to meet a specific launch date
- The ePub file you created has been rejected by a retailer and you cannot identify a fix
- The only copy of your book is a print version and you need a scanned version with extracted text that is recognisably English

(or whichever language it was originally written in), rather than a collection of unfamiliar characters and symbols

- Your self-publishing company created an e-book version of your book on your behalf, uploaded it to Amazon, and promptly went out of business, or refuses to return your calls or send you the e-book files. Sadly, we have received calls from a number of authors with this predicament in the last two years.

These are some common scenarios, but whatever the reason for investigating other options, look for relevant experience in all file formats, including fixed layout. Check for credible client testimonials and do not be afraid to ask as many questions as you need to. E-book conversion is a relatively new field of expertise and there are varying levels of competence!

eBookPartnership.com is a service provider, we advise and support authors, and they pay us for the services they require, rather than enter into a long-term revenue share arrangement. If we also manage distribution for authors looking for wider distribution, we charge a set-up fee and low annual fee, and pay 100% of royalties received from the retailers directly to the writer or publisher. This applies to writers or publishers who do not individually meet new account set-up criteria for Waterstones, or Apple, or Barnes and Noble, for example.

Other companies will offer different levels of involvement and royalty share, and it is vitally important that you understand any agreement before you sign a contract.

Questions to ask your e-book conversion professional:

1. Can you provide a contract, and details of terms and conditions?

Obvious, but a good place to start. Make absolutely sure that you retain all rights to your work, that your files are being securely stored, and that any distribution agreement for the e-book is crystal clear. Once converted, you should receive copies of the e-book files, and if you wish to, you can then upload these files to retailers yourself. If you have paid for cover design, the cover then becomes yours, check that any images used are correctly licensed and that the use of the image is not in any way restricted.

2. Will I get a review copy of my e-book?

It is essential that you see the e-book files before publication. Ideally you would then view them on a Kindle or iPad, or Kobo reader for example, but you can use a PC-based reader if you do not have access to an e-book reader.

It is worth emphasising at this point that the file you submit prior to conversion should be the final file, as if it were going to print. If you receive your review copy and decide that you need to make editorial changes, you will be charged for the time it takes to recode the e-book.

Of course, if there are errors in formatting, the conversion specialist should correct these without charge.

3. Are there any extra costs I should be aware of?

Standard pricing may apply to books of a certain length (up to 300 pages for example), or may only take into account a maximum number of images, included in the price. You may have to submit your file in order for an accurate quote to be provided. Images take time to get right—they need to be optimised and placed correctly within the text—so you may find that you incur extra charges for including more than a specified maximum number.

4. Do you help me to promote sales of the e-book?

Do not assume that your conversion company will be able to offer you marketing services as part of the package, unless it is specifically stated. This is a specialist area and one which needs the same focus and research as the conversion. We keep a close eye on industry news and often circulate articles and resources that we find, and our authors and publishers feed back information too.

5. I want to upload my e-book myself to retailers. Can I do this?

Once your e-book files are created, they are yours and you can decide which retailers you would like to upload to. Managing your own account on Amazon is easy, many authors like to take control of this and have access to sales information, and to have the ability to make changes or manage their KDP Select campaigns. This is not the case for all retailers however, and it may be that you need to use a company like eBookPartnership.com to upload your books via their accounts, and have the royalties paid to you by them.

Feel free to call us on +44 845 123 2699 for a chat (or Skype DMHorner). We are delighted to work with authors at any stage of their e-book adventure. Our website has lots more information: **www.ebookpartnership.com**."

Thank you, Diana. If you're interested in conversion, you can find a full list of eBookPartnership.com's prices on their website.

* * *

So there we have it: we've published our e-books. I would love to tell you that the hard part is done, but the hard part is only beginning. (Sorry!) The good news is that next, when we get to work bringing our POD paperback baby into the world, we've already done a lot of the tricky bits, like writing a blurb...

Okay, so we've done *one* of the tricky bits.

Now might be the time to make some coffee.

PART 4:
Publishing Your Paperback

Welcome To CreateSpace

Oh, the humble paperback! The realisation of our book in the flesh! (Or at least, on paper.) We didn't grow up dreaming of seeing our name on a Kindle screen, but most of us probably did dream of seeing it on the spine of a book. Well, now you get to make that book, and if at any point it starts to feel like hard work, just imagine opening the cardboard package marked "CreateSpace" a couple of weeks from now, seeing your shiny cover for the first time and then calling in sick to work and cancelling all social engagements so you can gaze at it adoringly until the novelty wears off.

(Which it won't. *Ever*.)

For our Print-On-Demand paperback, we're going to use CreateSpace, the POD service owned by Amazon. As I've already said, I'm not going to tell you how to use other services or recommend that you do because this book is about what *I* did, and I used CreateSpace. Two years on, I'm still extremely pleased with the service, especially the quality of my book, their prompt payments and their speedy and helpful responses to any issues I may have had cause to e-mail them about.

And I should say here, in case you were getting suspicious, that I have absolutely no ties to CreateSpace other than the ones you'll learn about in a minute, i.e. I published my book with them, and I receive nothing in return for telling readers of this book that you should go with them, except the warm, fuzzy feeling I get from helping you. But I'm not opposed to bribes and should the situation change, I'll be sure to let you know. Promise.

The order of what follows may seem a bit odd to you, like formatting our interior before we've even seen a mock-up of a cover, but stick with it and you'll see why this is the easiest way.

Head on over to **www.createspace.com**, sign up for a free account, fill in your payee information (so they can send you some cheques) and let's do this thing.

Title Set-Up

The first thing we're going to do is set up our title.

You can either begin by clicking "Create a Book" in the "Publish" section of the site, or select "Add New Title" from your Member Dashboard (the screen you see when you log in that shows your titles, monthly sales, etc.).

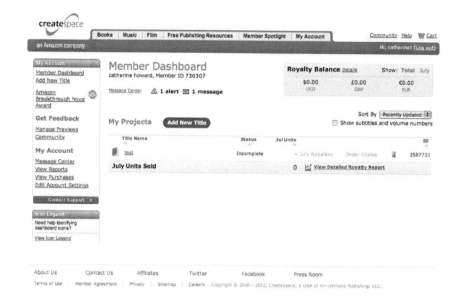

CreateSpace's Member Dashboard.

Under the heading "Start Your New Project" you'll then be asked to enter:

- Your book's title (you can change it later)
- What type of project you want—select paperback
- Which set-up process you want to use. Because you have me and this book, you're going to select **Expert**. Don't be scared: all this means is that you're going to work with one page as opposed to being guided through it section by section in a process so over-simplified that it'll drive you crazy. You also won't be able to use this book to get through it. So from now on, consider yourself an expert!

You will then be brought to a screen that looks like the one pictured on the next page.

We are now going to work our way through this process, but not all at once; when you need to leave the page, find the "Save Progress" button (scroll down) so that everything you've entered will be there when you return.

If you want to access the Member Dashboard at any time, click "Return to Member Dashboard" (top left-hand corner).

You can also view all the information you've entered about your project (and get an idea of what will appear on its listings) by clicking "Return to Project Home" (just above the Dashboard button), although remember to save any changes before you do.

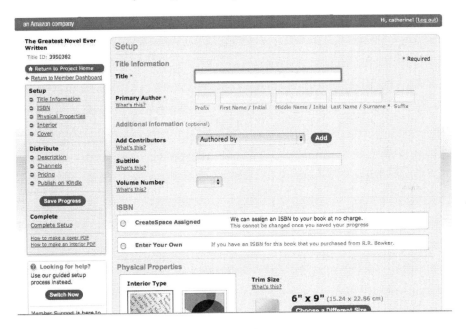

CreateSpace Title Setup

Title Information

As we begin to fill things in, I want you to keep something in mind: however you do it here is how it'll eventually end up looking on Amazon and any other retailer that sells your paperback online. So all this information is not only telling CreateSpace what you want to produce, it's going to form your book's online retailer *listings*.

So don't do anything stoopid, okay?

Title

Fairly straightforward: enter the title of your book. You know what to do. (Or rather, what *not* to do.)

Primary Author

That's you, by the way.

Again, don't use all capital letters and make sure you enter the right thing in the right box, and just stick with first name and last name unless you're Bret Easton Ellis or Michael Jackson III.

Leave that "prefix" box alone unless you're Dr. Oz and you've written a book about some new, even more disgusting part of the digestive system.

Add Contributors

CreateSpace just don't make it easy for people writing "how to self-publish books" books, do they? You could do some damage on KDP, sure, but here you can enter all *sorts* of things: created by, from an idea by, memoir by, preliminary work by, revised by, compiled by, as told by, prepared for publication by, assisted by...

And that's only a *selection* of the fanciful contributor titles they have on offer.

This is because CreateSpace also produces POD audio CDs and DVDs. It is not for you. So just ignore this completely, unless you can prove in a court of law (Catherine's law) that you have a reason that is identical to one of the exceptions to the rule listed on page 165.

NB: You've already listed yourself as the author in the "Primary Author" bit.

Subtitle

Your POD paperback gets its very own space for a subtitle. Treat it with the respect it deserves, i.e. only enter a subtitle here if your book actually has one.

If you need to put "A Novel" after your main title, you can put that here.

Volume Number

Leave this blank unless your book is part of a series.

If your book *is* part of a series, I would still leave it blank unless this is a volume other than the first. There's little point in having a book for sale listed as "Volume 1" of something when there isn't yet any other volumes to confuse it with. You can always come back later, when you *do* have a second volume, and update this with a "1" then.

ISBN

Check the box next to "CreateSpace assigned — We can assign an ISBN to your book at no charge."

Physical Properties

Now we come to the real important stuff: what kind of book do you want? What size do you want it to be? What colour pages do you want? You can't change these later, so now is the time to decide.

Interior Type

Select "Black and White" because that's what you want: a black and white interior. This will make all text black and any images black and white.

The only exception to this is a fully-illustrated title, like a cookbook, which is not the kind of the book *this* book is designed to guide you through creating. Full colour interiors are a lot more expensive, so Print-On-Demand isn't the ideal way to bring a book like that to life.

Sometimes you see books, particularly non-fiction, that have a number of glossy photo pages in the middle while the rest of the book is black text on plain paper. This is not an option here. In the second edition of *Mousetrapped*, I put photographs in the middle but did it on the standard paper, and it looked fine. Not *great* or as good as it would've on photo paper, but it did the job.

Paper Colour

You can choose either bright white or cream coloured paper. Before we go any further, go to your bookshelves and see what colour the pages are in most if not all of the paperbacks there. I'll save you the bother: they're *cream*. And because we want our books to look as close to "properly" published books as possible, we're going to choose cream too.

There is only one exception, as you may have guessed from the page you're currently reading this on (if you're reading the paperback): if your book cover is predominantly white (especially at the edges where it meets the pages), then I'd choose white paper, because the cream colour might look dirty or just off-white against a bright white cover.

While we're on the subject of paper, you may be wondering what the paper is like, i.e. does it feel thick or flimsy? According to the CS website, the interior paper they use is 60#. This may mean nothing to you or me, so let me tell you this:

- It's the paper you have in your hands right now (unless you're reading this on a Kindle!)
- It's of a similar quality to mass produced, traditionally published books
- It'll do the job just fine.

Self-publishers love doing silly things like upgrading to premium paper (which, coincidentally, you can't do on CreateSpace). The books your readers are used to reading are not produced on thick, high-quality paper; some books on my shelf have pages so thin you can see through them, and they work just fine. Furthermore, the higher the quality of your interior paper, the heavier it will be and shipping charges are decided by weight. So pick a colour and don't worry about the rest.

Trim Size

CS offers a whole range of trim sizes, but you can't use them all. In order for your book to be eligible for Amazon.com and other online retailers, it needs to conform to industry standards and to do that it needs to be one of the following (all in inches and width x height):

- 5 x 8
- 5.06 x 7.81
- 5.25 x 8
- 5.5 x 8.5
- 6 x 9
- 6.14 x 9.21
- 6.69 x 9.61
- 7 x 10
- 7.44 x 9.69
- 7.5 x 9.25.

It'll also have to have a minimum of 24 pages and a maximum of either 828 (for white paper) or 740 (for cream). All of the above trim sizes are also listed in centimetres on the CreateSpace website.

This is confusing, right? Anything with lots of options is. So instead of focusing on all the different sizes you can potentially make your book, think about just one thing: what size do you *want it to be?* If you're about to self-publish a novel, go measure some. See what their trim size is, and then see if it or something similar is available on CS. The same goes for other types of books.

(If you can find a book the exact size or almost the exact size as the trim you've chosen, be it traditionally or self-published, hang on to it. We're going to need it in a minute to check something.)

When it came to picking a size for *Mousetrapped*, I ordered a let's-just-see-what-this-is-like proof copy in 6 x 9 because that seemed to be the most popular. But when it arrived, it was thin, floppy and screaming "I'm a crappy self-published book!", because with more space on each page, my page count was under 200. It's hard to judge at this point how thick your book will be, but the smaller the trim size, the thicker it will be. And thickness is just as important to its overall appearance as anything else. I ended up making *Mousetrapped* 5.5. x 8.5, which in turn made it about 230 pages.

This book, however, could not be 5.5 x 8.5, because the number of pages I'd need to use to print at that size would make the book too expensive, both for me to sell and for you to buy. (It's 6 x 9.)

Nothing here is "locked" until you order a proof copy, so we can change the trim size later if we discover that our book is going to be too thin with our current choice. However, this will generate extra work for you – you'll have to format your interior twice – so do your best to make an educated guess at this point.

Get Your ISBN And Your Interior Template

Now that you've filled in your title set-up information, opted for a free ISBN and told CS what trim size and paper type you want, scroll down to the very end of the page and click "Save Progress." Then scroll back up to where you were.

You will now see your ISBNs displayed in thick, bold type. There'll be two of them, a 10-digit one and a 13-digit one. Make a note of them both.

Underneath these will be the "Physical Properties" section and to the right of it, a navy blue button that says "Choose a different size." Underneath *that* will be the words "Download a Word template" and two options: to download a blank template or a formatted one.

What's happening here is that CreateSpace is giving us a MS Word document sized exactly to be the interior pages of our book in whatever trim size we've opted for. Not only is it perfectly sized, but its margins are optimised for the layout of a book, i.e. they allow for the differences of odd (right-hand side) and even (left-hand side) pages.

We're going to download the **blank** template. Open it in MS Word, rename it to something including your book's title and the word "interior", and then check in "Page Setup" that your page properties match those of the template, i.e. if you have a 6 x 9 book and you've just downloaded a 6 x 9 interior template, is Word showing a 6 x 9 page under "Page Size" in the "Page Setup" box? If it's not, change it, making sure that you preserve the margins. You might have to add a new paper size ("Custom Size") to achieve this.

Log out of CreateSpace for now.

NB: We're about to make the interior of our book in a MS Word document. We will then convert it to PDF format and upload it to CreateSpace. It will appear in the printed book *exactly* as you have laid it out, so be careful. If you make a mistake, there's no one but you to catch it and correct it.

Fontabulous

Pick a font for your book that is readable, looks good and resembles or matches fonts you have seen used in actual, proper books designed by professional book designers. This is not the time to profess your love for Mistral, Brush Script or a font you designed yourself based on scans of your own handwriting. Industry standards are industry standards because they *work*. I recommend that you pick one of the following: Times New Roman, Book Antiqua, Georgia or Garamond.

Your main font size should be either 10, 11 or 12 point (pt). Which size you decide upon will depend on what font you pick. For instance, this book is Book Antiqua 10pt, but if it were in Garamond, 10pt would be a bit small. (*Mousetrapped* is in Book Antiqua 11pt.)

Remember how we found a real book the same size as our chosen trim size? Go get it now. Copy and paste a few paragraphs into the template you just downloaded and print out a page. Then cut the page so it matches the finished trim size and slip it into the book to see what it will look like. Is it readable? Does it look good? Will my eyes be hanging out of my head if I look at it for longer than five minutes? Is it a similar size to what's actually been used in the book?

The simpler you keep things like fonts and font sizes, the easier you make it for yourself. In *Mousetrapped* I made the chapter headings all capital letters and bold but kept them in the same font and just went one size up, and I think this worked fine. In this book, where there are a far greater number of headings and sub-headings, I used a different, contrasting font. However, in both cases I tried to keep things as simple as possible, which is better for my brain and your eyes.

NB: The most common font problem in self-published books are fonts that are too large. I'm guessing this is because it's hard to judge on screen how the font will look on the page, and this leads to needlessly large fonts.

That's why it's important to print out a test page, because if the font is the wrong size on your proof copy then you'll just have to go and order another one. (And pay for it).

Format Your Interior Text

Now open your manuscript document (which has been edited, proofread and set to first line indent instead of starting paragraphs with tabs), select all text, copy it and paste it into the MS Word template you downloaded.

NB: Do *not* copy headers and footers from your manuscript into your interior template.

Then:

- Delete anything that may have belonged in your manuscript but does not belong in your book, like contact details
- Justify all text
- Set all line spacing to single
- Set it to the font and font size you've decided on.

The Front Matter

Pick up any traditionally published book and open its cover. What's on the first page? What's on the second page? And what's on the page after *that*?

Books don't just begin with Chapter One on page one. Before that there are a few other things we have to worry about.

The First Page

I recommend one of two options for your first page. If this is your first book and it has yet to be reviewed, then put an "About the Author" on it. This should be short, relevant and written in the same tone as your book.

By relevant, I don't just mean leave out the fact that you were Under 8 Munster Disco-Dancing Champion in 1991. (Even though I was, thanks for asking. My winning routine was to that musical classic, *Do the Bartman*.) I mean *tailor it to the content of your book*.

For example in *Mousetrapped*, my About the Author reads:

Catherine Ryan Howard is a frequently over-caffeinated twenty-something from Cork, Ireland. As well as working in Walt Disney World, Catherine has administrated things in the Netherlands, cleaned tents on a French campsite, established a handmade card company and answered telephones in several different offices. She wants to be a NASA astronaut when she grows up.

But in *this* book, my About the Author is going to look more like this:

Catherine Ryan Howard is the coffee-guzzling twenty-something behind the popular blog, Catherine, Caffeinated. In March 2010 she self-published her travel memoir, *Mousetrapped: A Year and A Bit in Orlando, Florida*, using the Print-On-Demand service CreateSpace, Amazon's Kindle Direct Publishing and Smashwords. Using free promotional tools like blogging, Twitter and Facebook, she managed to make *Mousetrapped* an Amazon bestseller and sell 4,000 copies within a year. Her success story has been featured in *The Sunday Times* and *The Sunday Independent* newspapers, and Catherine has been interviewed on BBC Radio Ulster, Newstalk and RTÉ Radio's Marian Finucane Show. Known for her pragmatic approach to all things self-publishing—and her dislike of the word "gatekeepers"—Catherine was chosen to deliver the first ever self-publishing course at Faber & Faber's "Faber Academy" in Bloomsbury, London, in February 2012. She lives in Cork, Ireland, where she currently divides her time between her desk and the sofa.

Why is the second example so much longer? Because for a book like this, I have to convince you that I'm *qualified* to write it, that I have sufficient experience to advise you on how to self-publish your book. So I start by listing my accomplishments. But because this book is a bit irreverent, I put a bit of humour in there at the end. (And besides, I've wanted to put that "between her desk and the sofa" thing in my bio for *so long*, I can't even tell you.)

If you have previously released a book or have reviews you can quote for this one, then you can put them on the first page instead. Make sure you attribute them and *a name is not enough*. I'll be lecturing more about endorsements in due course.

For now, as examples, here are three reviews from the first page of the second edition of *Mousetrapped*:

"I really loved *Mousetrapped*. It was sweet, funny, charming and inspiring. Particularly the chapter in which Ryan goes to Kennedy Space Centre—it made me cry and it made me feel like anything is possible."—Keris Stainton, author of *Jessie Hearts NYC*

"*Mousetrapped* is a unique book by a brilliantly witty, instantly loveable author. I couldn't put it down. Catherine Ryan Howard is highly talented and has the ability to make the most dire of situations sound funny. [This] is an absolutely wonderful read."—*Trashionista.com, Top 10 Reads of 2010*

"[Catherine] writes with wit and humour about her time in Orlando, and you get a true sense of what living in a town dominated by a massive theme park really feels like. Thoroughly enjoyable and a great read!"—Talli Roland, author of *The Hating Game*

Notice that in each example the source is named and who they are is explained. These reviews all appeared on blogs or sites belonging to the reviewers, and I asked each of them for permission to include them in the book, and checked that they were happy with how it appeared.

Put "Praise for [your previous book's title]" or "Praise for [your name]" at the top of the page.

If you decide to put reviews on this page, we'll relegate the About the Author to the back.

(As for *getting* reviews, we'll talk about that later.)

The Copyright Page

Your copyright notice should be the next thing to appear, and it should be on an even-numbered or left-hand page. It should begin with both your ISBNs, then your copyright symbol and name, and then the copyright notice itself. Like this:

ISBN-13 978-14515222921
ISBN-10 1451522924

Copyright © Catherine Ryan Howard 2010

All rights reserved. No part of this publication may be reproduced, stored in a retrieval system or transmitted, in any form or by any means, without the prior written permission of the author, nor be otherwise circulated in any form of binding or cover other than that in which it is published and without a similar condition being imposed on the purchaser.

If your book is non-fiction, you might need additional lines such as "Although this is a work of non-fiction, some names have been changed by the author." Find a book similar to yours, be it a novel, an instructional guide or a memoir, and see what its copyright notice says. But change it around a bit—don't just copy someone else's copyright notice because the infinity loop of irony would cause the planet to implode.

You can also put things like your blog URL, Twitter username and Facebook page address on this page, and maybe even give a shout out to your cover designer.

NB: Before you can order a proof copy, you'll have to submit your book for "processing", which means that CreateSpace's computers will go through your files checking that your cover file is the right size for the number of pages, etc. They will also check that the ISBNs they assigned you appear on your copyright page, so it's imperative you put them in there.

The Title Page

Opposite the copyright page, and so on the right-hand side, i.e. an odd-numbered page, should be your title page. This is simple: your name, the title of your book and subtitle, starting about a quarter of the way down the page and centred. This should be in a larger font than your main text.

CATHERINE RYAN HOWARD

MOUSETRAPPED
A Year and A Bit in Orlando, Florida

Also By

If this isn't your first book, you should take the opportunity to list your other titles. These should be on an even page, or on the left-hand side.

Also by Catherine Ryan Howard

Backpacked: A Reluctant Trip Across Central America

Self-Printed: The Sane Person's Guide to Self-Publishing

If you need to insert one of these pages, put a second title page opposite it, but this time just put the title, i.e. leave out the author name and subtitle.

Table Of Contents

If you want to put a table of contents in your book, do so on an odd page between two titles. Put the chapter name to the left of the page and the corresponding page number to the right, using tabs (yes, you're allowed use tabs!) so they both line up evenly, like:

1: The Call of the Mouse.................................... 9
2: Arrival..15
3: Mousetrapped..21

If your chapters or sections are not named, just numbered, you do not need a table of contents. I actually took my table of contents out of the second edition of *Mousetrapped* because I came to believe it was utterly pointless. But in a book like this one, it's essential.

Start Your Book

Make sure that the main text of your book starts on an odd, or right-hand side, page. So to recap, the beginning of your book will either be:

Page 1: Reviews or About the Author
Page 2: Copyright Notice
Page 3: Title Page
Page 4: Blank
Page 5: Book starts

or

Page 1: Reviews or About the Author
Page 2: Copyright Notice
Page 3: First Title Page (Author, Title, Subtitle)
Page 4: Also By
Page 5: Second Title Page (Title Only)
Page 6: Blank
Page 7: Book starts

or

Page 1: Reviews or About the Author
Page 2: Copyright Notice
Page 3: First Title Page (Author, Title, Subtitle)
Page 4: Also By
Page 5: Table of Contents
Page 6: Blank
Page 7: Second Title Page (Title Only)
Page 8: Blank
Page 9: Book starts.

You can play around with it a bit—this very book doesn't exactly conform to any of those three lists—but only a little. Remember that we want our book to conform to book standards, and the standards are that because they *work*.

Creating Chapters

Now we're going to go through the main text of the book checking that all text is justified, new paragraphs are indented and all text is correctly sized. Use something simple but effective to delineate the start of a new chapter. Here's what I did with *Mousetrapped*:

- Start each new chapter on an odd page (the page that's on your right as you hold the book)
- Press return until you're approximately 1/4 down the page (check the ruler to see the exact position so you can put it in the same place each time. In a novel, chapters should never start at the very top of a page)
- Type the chapter number in words (i.e. 'One') in 12 pt italics. Press return
- Type the name of the chapter in 14 pt bold, all caps. Press return twice
- Start your chapter.

Try to avoid being overly ambitious with your interior text. In a traditionally published book, you might see some artwork or an illustration accompanying chapter headings, or chapters beginning with a "drop cap", where the first letter of a chapter is much larger than the text around it. But traditional books are laid out by professional book designers; we're just going to concentrate on making ours look good. As we're self-publishers and doing it all ourselves, that means keeping it simple.

As you go through your book, try to avoid having pages where only half of one line appears. This does *not* look good. I went so far as to edit lines out of chapters so this wouldn't happen. You can also use MS Word's "Widow/Orphan control" function to help you avoid this. Select all text, then Format->Paragraph, and then select "Line and Page Breaks" tab. Check the box next to "Widow/Orphan" control.

Always start new chapters or sections on the odd page, i.e. the right-hand side. You will end up with some blank pages; this is perfectly normal.

Please don't try to close everything up or use a smaller font just because you want to save yourself a few cents on the extra pages. Not having a well laid-out interior will cost you more in the long run than the few cents you'll save now by doing that.

The End Matter

The back of your book needs some thought too—typing "THE END" and then having nothing but a cover to close is a wasted opportunity. Imagine you are the reader and you get to the end of (what we hope!) is an enjoyable book that piques your interest in both the author and the subject matter. Don't you want to give them something more?

In the first edition of *Mousetrapped*, the words "THE END" appeared on page 227, but that wasn't the end of the book. Still to come after that was:

Author Note

You may want to tell the reader something about the book outside of the book itself. Use these sparingly and only if you have to, i.e. don't try to think of something to put in an author's note just because you want one.

In *Mousetrapped*, I used it to explain that yes, I was aware that Walt Disney World was not "the happiest place on earth" (Disneyland California is; WDW's Magic Kingdom is in fact "the most magical place on earth") but that since "What could go wrong in the resort that has a theme park in it that's called the most magical place on earth?" wasn't anywhere near as catchy a headline, I took some licence with it instead. I also told readers that a number of places mentioned in the book (a movie theatre, a bookstore, etc.) have since closed down.

Acknowledgements

This is where you thank all the people who helped you with the book who, if you don't thank them, will never speak to you again.

Tip: don't scrimp on the Acknowledgements. If your name is in a book, you'll buy it. But keep them within reason; if you start listing the phonebook, we'll know something's up.

Further Reading

Mousetrapped touched on a lot of subjects, including the history of Walt Disney World (very lightly touched because I actually trashed that chapter before it went to print), NASA's Apollo program, and that little obsession of mine that is Celebration, Florida, otherwise known as the town that Disney built. Should the reader, having got to the end of my book, want to read more about those subjects or read the books I referred to during research, then here was a handy list of those titles.

Bring Your Readers Online

As we're doing all our promotional work online, it's highly unlikely that anyone will pick up your paperback book before they encounter your blog or Twitter account—but it *could* happen. It's also likely that most of your e-book readers will find your book by accident or through a keyword search, and so will know nothing about your online presence. To make sure we snare every reader in our social media trap (or, you know, something less unpleasant and mean-sounding), we need to *link our book to our online platform*.

In the simplest terms this means *give them an incentive to look you up online*.

In the first edition of *Mousetrapped*, I had a page at the back describing *The Sane Person's Guide to Walt Disney World*, a light-hearted and not at all comprehensive guide to touring the world's most famous theme parks. (And, as you may have guessed, the inspiration for the title of this book.) It was only a short little thing, maybe 30 pages, that I'd uploaded to the *Mousetrapped* website in a PDF. It was free and anyone could download it. This is what the page said:

THE SANE PERSON'S GUIDE TO WALT DISNEY WORLD

Walt Disney World is a place of happiness, magic and wonder, but a family visit there can also induce a nervous breakdown and sow the seeds of divorce. Drawing on her experience as a WDW Front Desk Agent and her own visits to the theme parks, Catherine dispenses Disney World advice in easy-to-swallow, Mickey-shaped chewable tablets, the theme being 'Relax—and that's an order!' Sprinkled with sarcasm, and fun but useless facts (did you know, for example, that Magic Kingdom's trash is emptied every fifteen minutes?), Catherine's Disney guide provides just the right amount of information for a magical Mouse visit, the kind of family vacation your children will not be recalling for a mental health professional some day in the far off future.

The Sane Person's Guide includes everything you need to know about Walt Disney World, but not as much as a particle of pixie dust more.

Mouse Manuals: Do you need one and if so, which one?
Disney World 101: Everything you need to know before you go
Into the Parks: A quick rundown of each of Disney World's four theme parks
Frequently Asked Questions: What time IS the 3 o'clock parade?

Visit mousetrappedbook.com to view Catherine's photo albums and videos and to download your FREE e-book edition of The Sane Person's Guide to Walt Disney World.

Hopefully this would lure people to my *Mousetrapped* website, which would then bring them to my blog, which would then bring them to my Twitter account and so on. You might be wondering why I'd bother, when they'd already done what I wanted them to, i.e. read my book. But here's the thing: our followers are not disposable. We want them to hang around. We want them to engage with us online so that when we release another book, they find out about it and, hopefully, buy that one too.

I took that guide out of the second edition and tried something different. By this stage a year had passed since I'd released *Mousetrapped*, and it was looking like least another six months before another book of mine was ready to join it. So I decided to put some new, *Mousetrapped*-related content out there but only make it available to a specific group: people who joined my "More *Mousetrapped*" mailing list.

I used MailChimp for this, setting up a new list, creating a sign-up box and putting a link to it on a "More *Mousetrapped*" page on my site. Then I put this in the back of the second edition:

Want More *Mousetrapped*?

Visit mousetrappedbook.com for lots more *Mousetrapped*, including:

Photos and videos of all *Mousetrapped*'s sights including
inside the Walt Disney World parks,
the town of Celebration and **Kennedy Space Centre**

Mousetrapped's video book trailers:
The Story of *Mousetrapped* and ***Mousetrapped* in 60 Seconds**

Catherine's tongue-in-cheek (free!) e-book,
The Sane Person's Guide to Walt Disney World

Look inside **Catherine's Walt Disney World scrapbook**
and listen to her **Florida playlist**

and from April 2011,
get a new 'More *Mousetrapped*' story every month!

Visit Catherine's website and blog at www.catherineryanhoward.com

Follow her on Twitter at
www.twitter.com/cathryanhoward

Find Mousetrapped on Facebook at
www.facebook.com/mousetrappedbook

The beauty of this idea is that we're both getting what we want. The readers are getting more of the book they liked, for free and delivered straight to their inbox, and I'm getting a mailing list. Of course I never used it for anything but sending out the stories (it would be unfair to, and you'd probably lose all your subscribers), but each story e-mail came with footers and sidebars where I shared news, including the date my next book comes out.

Sidenote: last month I released a little e-book containing all these More *Mousetrapped* stories, along with some new material, some previously unpublished material and an exclusive preview of my next book, *Travelled*, that's coming in November. I'm only charging 99c for it so it's not exactly a money maker but it's more virtual Amazon shelf space taken up by me—which means I'm a slightly larger needle in that particular haystack—and it's a permanent home for those stories. It also means anyone who didn't want to read them off their computer screen in an e-mail can now buy them in book form for their Kindle. Clever, eh?

About the Author

If you've put reviews at the front, put your About the Author back here.

News Of Your Other Books

If you have other, related books available you might want to mention them here, or even include a teaser chapter.

Now if I'm reading a paperback and I see a teaser chapter at the end introduced with something like, "Read the opening scene of Big Author's next novel, coming May 2014" then I don't bother reading it, because I don't see the point when I have to wait *ages* to read the rest of the book. But what if the book was out already? I think as long as you're not eating into your profits with too many extra pages, sticking a preview of another book in here isn't a bad idea.

Inserting Images

As I've already said this book isn't aimed at self-publishers looking to produce richly illustrated books (because I don't know anything about doing that, but I know enough about the cost of POD to think you'd be better off not producing your full colour book this way) but if you want to put a handful of images into your book, you can.

In the second edition of *Mousetrapped*, I inserted about nine photos across 5 or 6 pages in the middle of the book. All I did was insert the images as I normally would in any MS Word document, set their layouts to "tight" and after I'd converted to PDF, checked they were all still in the same places. (They were.) Even though they were colour photographs, they of course appeared in black and white in the book because I'd chosen a black and white interior.

I did the same thing with the images in the paperback version of this book.

Technically-speaking, CreateSpace say: "Images may be CMYK or RGB color. All images should be sized at 100%, flattened to one layer and placed in your document at a minimum resolution of 300 DPI." But I have literally no idea what any of that means, so I just Insert –> Picture and hope for the best!

NB: Be careful how many images you insert. CreateSpace will not accept your interior file if it's bigger than 400 MB.

Page Numbers And Running Headers

So up until now formatting our interior document has been pretty easy, right? Well now, as we put the finishing touches to it, we have one *ickle* complicated bit that might drive us a tad insane.

But it'll make our book better and we only have to do it once, so try and stick with it. It'll be worth it in the end.

Our book—obviously—*has* to have page numbers and it *can* have running headers, if you want.

A **running header** in fiction is when the title and the author's name appear in the header of each page, with the title on the even, left-hand pages and the author's name on the odd, right-hand pages. Like this (quite simplistic example):

Backpacked

glean from this trip? Would I get anything out of it at all, other than mosquito bites, an increased immunity to malaria and a bronzed tan?

And how much longer, realistically, could I maintain this pretence of enjoying myself, acting as if I wanted to talk to potentially psychotic strangers, murmuring my consent every time someone suggested white water rafting whilst bound, blindfolded and tied to bricks, and do it all only feet away from the one person who could read me like a book, my very best friend, the person whose trip I'd tagged along on? And do it

Catherine Ryan Howard

my legs. The room is dark, although a faint blue glow in one corner is enough bright to reveal a backpack lying on its side by my feet with a wad of folded paper, a bottle of anti-malaria pills and a Florida licence plate half-in, half-out of it. They must have made a bid for freedom while I slept.

I prop myself up onto my elbows and see the phone. Having switched off the alarm, I bring it close to my face to read the time. 4:00 a.m.

In non-fiction, the running header reminds the reader what section or part they're reading, so it might be the book's title on the even page and the current section's name on the odd one.

Page numbers can go in a number of places but for simplicity's sake, I'm going to recommend that you put them in the footer, and that you put them in the middle of it, i.e. centre them at the bottom of each page.

You're thinking, *that sounds simple enough. What's all the fuss about it?* Well, that *does* sound simple enough—but that's only the half of it. The thing is, we don't want a page number on every page. And we don't want our running header on every page. And on some pages, we'll want page numbers but no running headers. Yet, if you insert a footer or a header into your document, it happily appears on every page. So what do we do?

We're going to use **the sections feature of MS Word**. This is technically something that's quite easy to do, but in practice it takes a few extra brain cells to master. And trust me when I say that writing all this down makes it seem a *lot* more complicated than it actually is.

Let's make a list of what we need to achieve. We need:

- A header with the title of our book on the even-numbered or left-hand pages
- A header with the author name on the odd-numbered or right-hand pages
- Our page numbers centred in the footer.

But we also need to make sure that:

- Page numbers don't start until our book does, i.e. there shouldn't be any page numbers until you get to the first page of chapter one
- If there isn't a page number, there shouldn't be a running header either
- Blank pages, like the ones we left blank so each chapter would start on a right-hand, odd-numbered page, should be *completely* blank, i.e. no page number or running header
- Title pages in the midst of your book, e.g. the "Part x: xxxx" pages in *this* book, shouldn't have page numbers or running headers
- The first pages of chapters should have page numbers but *not* running headers
- Pages numbers should end when our book does, i.e. there shouldn't be any page numbers amongst the end matter.

So in practice that means that we're going to divide our book up into the following sections:

- The beginning <=> the first page of chapter one
- The first page of each chapter <=> the last page of each chapter
- The page that says "The End" <=> the end of the book
- Each blank page will be its own section.

To create a section, go to the last line on the page before you want the section to start and click Insert->Break->Section Break (next page).

But if you put a page number in the footer of a page in your first section, it will still appear on the pages in your second section. This is because unless you tell it otherwise, MS Word assumes you want every page to be the same.

So, how do we do *that*? When you create a header (or footer) in a particular section, you have the following options:

- **Different first page**. This means that the first page of your section will be different to the rest of it, and it's ideal for the first page of chapters that need a page number but *not* a running header.
- **Different odd and even pages**. We need this so that the title of our book appears in the headers on our even-numbered, left-hand pages, while our name appears in the headers on our odd-numbered, right-hand pages.
- **Link to previous**. When you create a new section, MS Word assumes you want it to follow the same heading/footer style as the one before it. If you don't want it to—for instance, if the previous sections had running headers and page numbers and you don't want this to have them—uncheck the "link to previous" option.

These options will be in "Edit Header/Footer" (right-click in the header/footer) or if you're working on a Mac, in the Toolbox.

A word of warning: "link to previous" is what makes this complicated. If you forget to uncheck it and start deleting the page numbers off blank pages, Word will assume you want to delete the page numbers in the previous section too. This is why you need to have all your wits about you for this. If you've never worked with sections before, I suggest you make a copy of your interior document and practice on it for a while until you get the "knack" of working with them. After a few sections, you really do get into a rhythm.

If you want to keep things as simple as possible, forget about the running headers altogether and just stick with the page numbers instead.

If you need to remove a section break, switch to Draft View. You'll easily spot it as it'll now be visible as a double blue line marked "section break". Simply highlight and delete.

Collect Your Cover Template

Now that you know how many pages your book is going to be, you can collect your cover template and get your cover designer started on your paperback's jacket design.

Go back to the CreateSpace website and either click Publish -> Books on Demand -> Cover (tab) -> Submission Requirements -> Download Cover Templates, or go straight to:

www.createspace.com/Help/Book/Artwork.do

Here you'll find a cover template generator. Enter your interior type, trim size, choice of paper colour and number of pages, and CreateSpace will generate a perfectly sized cover template for your book which you can then download immediately.

In the ZIP file that you download will be a Photoshop template, a PNG template and instructions in a PDF file. Don't worry about what any of these are; just send them off to your cover designer who'll know what to do with them.

There are some stipulations about what goes on your cover. The name and author name must appear *exactly* as they have been entered in the title set-up process, and you need to ensure that there is nothing important in the lower right-hand corner of the back cover, because that's where CreateSpace will insert the barcode for you. (This area will be marked on the template so your designer will know not to put anything there.) If your book is less than 120 pages, CreateSpace recommends nothing goes on the spine. The finished file, i.e. the PDF of your cover that's ready for you to upload, must be **40MB or less**.

Even though I strongly recommend that you *don't* use the Cover Creator, ahem, "wizard", I realise that some of you may have no choice but to, so I will include instructions for that too. But we'll do it later, when we upload our files.

Finalise Your Interior File

As I've already explained, before you can publish your book on CreateSpace you need to order, pay for and approve a proof copy of it. There are two elements to this: cost and time. The cost isn't much (I paid around €12 or $10 for mine and I live in Ireland; if you live in the States it might cost as little as $5 or $6 to get your proof copy shipped to you—and that's including the cost of the book itself), but it takes time to print and ship it.

Let's say you order your proof copy on a Monday. CreateSpace are busy, and it might be Wednesday before they print it and Thursday before they ship it. If you pay for economy shipping it might take another week or more to get to you, depending on how far away from South Carolina you live, and even if you pay for express shipping it'll still take a couple of days. Now what if, when the proof copy arrives, there's something wrong with it? You'll have to go through the whole proof copy process *again*. And again and again, until you get a proof copy that's perfect. This can cause serious delays and maybe even interfere with your planned release date.

So do whatever you can to ensure that when that first proof copy arrives, it's already perfect. And one of the things we can do is to *print out our interior*.

Page Versus Screen

It's a fact that mistakes are easier to see on the page than they are on the screen. Just ask any writer. On paper, we'll also have the added benefit of seeing what our book's interior will look like *before* we've shelled out money for the proof copy. I can't stress enough that waiting for the arrival of your proof copy to see your book in the flesh, so to speak, is a very bad idea and will in all likelihood cost you time *and* money — more money than the ink cartridge and ream of paper we're going to use to print it out now.

Don't be tempted to scrunch up all your text or change the font size when you do print it out in order to save ink and/or paper. We're not just looking for mistakes; we're checking to see how the interior of the book looks, feels and reads. Go through it slowly, marking mistakes with a bright highlighter so you'll see them. Correct the interior file and make any changes you feel are necessary, such as increasing or decreasing a font, or changing a heading.

When you are *absolutely positive* that you can correct no more, convert your file to PDF. In Word, click "File -> Print" and then "PDF -> Save as PDF." If the PDF is A4 or letter-sized paper, you haven't changed your page size to your book's trim size in Page Setup.

If you want to be super thorough, you can do another print-out here, or maybe ask your editor to have a look over the final file. (This would have had to be agreed in advance, of course, and included in the price.) Alternatively, get a trusted friend (who reads and can spell!) to have a look over it, as chances are you're getting a bit sick of looking at it by now.

At the very least, flip through the entire interior in its PDF form to check that it has converted correctly and looks exactly as you intended it to.

If it doesn't, fix the problem and convert again.

What file size is your PDF? If you have inserted photos or other images you need to check now, because **the largest interior file CreateSpace will accept is 400MB**.

Peter Paranoia Pops Up Again

I once got an e-mail from a self-publisher chastising me for recommending CreateSpace when, according to him, they were the world's worst self-publishing service. He claimed that on three different occasions he'd sent them a perfect interior file, only to find mistakes in the proof copy that subsequently arrived. Their motivation was to make more money out of him, he said.

A PDF file cannot be changed and at CreateSpace, everything is done automatically. Only a computer sees your interior file before it goes to the printing press, and even that computer can't do anything to change your PDF file. That, if you weren't aware, is the *whole point of PDF files*. So if there's a mistake in your proof copy after you uploaded a "perfect" PDF, it's because the PDF wasn't as perfect as you thought it was.

Finalise Your Cover File

Once you're happy with a cover design, your cover designer should send you the cover in a PDF file no bigger than 40 MB and that has been built using the template you (and CreateSpace) provided. It'll be slightly wider and taller than it will eventually appear on your physical book (because it has a "bleed" area around the edge that will get cut off) and it'll be missing its barcode, which CreateSpace will insert. This is what mine looked like:

If it's small enough to fit on a single page, it's a good idea to print this out too. Of course quality-wise it won't look anything like it will on your book, but at least you'll get to see how the size of the text works, etc.

It's also a good idea to save a copy of your cover as a JPEG or other image file, and then crop the front cover out of it. Then you'll have it to upload to your blog, your Twitter account, your Facebook page, the postcards you're going to make, the back of your business cards, etc. etc. It can also serve as your e-book cover.

So now you have an interior file and a cover file, both in PDF and both perfect, or just a perfect interior file because despite everything I've said, you're going to go ahead and use the Cover Creator.

Now we go back to CreateSpace and upload them.

Upload Your Files

Pop back to your Member Dashboard and click on your book's title. You'll then be brought to a page called "Project Homepage." On it, find "Title Information" and click on it. Now we're back on the Title Set-Up page that we left after getting our ISBNs.

Scroll down until you find the next incomplete section: Interior and Cover. Upload your interior file, and select "ends before the edge of the page" under "Bleed." This means your page will appear exactly as it appears in the PDF file, or as we want it to.

CreateSpace has something called an Interior File Reviewer, which shows you what the inside of your book will look like by showing you an approximation of each page on screen. I don't really get the point of this, because *that's what a PDF does*, and you've just uploaded in PDF after checking it again and again. But it's fun to play around with if you've time to spare.

Next, upload your cover file. Or if you don't have a cover file, click "Launch Cover Creator." Oh boy.

Using Cover Creator

Don't do it! But if you absolutely *must*, here's how. (I will try to keep my feelings about this out of the rest of this section. *Try*, mind you. I can't guarantee it.)

When you launch Cover Creator, the first thing you'll have to do is choose from one of approximately 30 "designs" or (craptabulous) templates. (Sorry!)

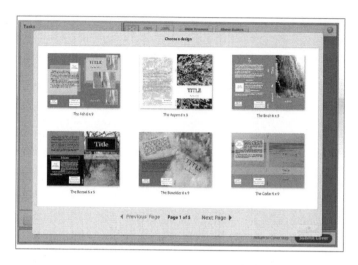

Selecting a design for your cover in Cover Creator.

After you select one, you'll be brought to the main screen, where you can make (some very limited) changes to the design. After you complete a section click "Next" to move on to the, um, next one. You can move back and forth until you finalise your design, so have a play around.

(Not that it'll help.)

(Sorry again!)

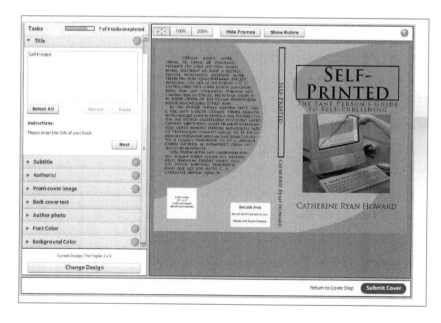

(Previous page) This image is a screenshot from Cover Creator using their design "Poplar."

Here are the modifications you *can* make:

- Themes. Each design has within it several themes, each with their own font type, style (whatever that means—used ironically, perhaps?) and stock image
- Title. CreateSpace will have automatically imported the full title you entered in the Title Set-Up process. If you want to edit it (perhaps shorten it, etc.) you can do so now
- Cover image. Upload your own or use one of CreateSpace's stock images (for free)
- Back cover text. You get to enter some—hooray!
- Background colour
- Font colour.

Here are the modifications you *can't* make:

- Font type (outside of picking a style)
- Font size
- Paragraph alignment
- Move the template's elements (you can only hide or show them)
- Anything else.

Do you understand what I'm telling you here? When you use Cover Creator *you can't even centre the text on your back cover blurb*. Or do *anything* at all to it, for that matter. And this is in addition to the fact that because all the templates are craptabulous, your book's cover is going to be that way too.

So please, for the love of Josh Groban, DON'T USE COVER CREATOR. Hire yourself a cover designer. Hire *my* cover designer. Hire an art student. Hire anyone you can find who can use Photoshop and potentially will accept chocolate as payment. If you can't find them, advertise online. Do whatever you can to avoid using Cover Creator because if you do use it, you're setting you and your book up for failure. And what is all this for if you're going to go and do that?

But if you *have* used it, click the "Submit Cover" button in the bottom right-hand corner when you're done.

[Sad sigh.]

ARCs, Or Why Cover Creator Isn't Completely Useless

It's *almost* completely useless, mind you, but it can have one very good use to you in your self-publishing adventure: you can use it to make ARCs.

An ARC is an Advanced Reader's Copy, sometimes called an Advanced Review Copy. A few months before a book comes out, a publishing house will print up a stack of these to send out to reviewers.

Because the book itself is not finished yet — it may still be getting typeset or even edited, and the final cover might not be done — these ARCs are like sub-par versions of the finished book. For these reasons they'll always say something like, "Uncorrected proof copy. Not for re-sale."

Why not wait until the book is ready? Two reasons. First, reviewers can't just drop everything and read the book you sent them on Tuesday so they can write their review to coincide with its release on Friday. Reviewers need time, so rather than wait, the publishers print up the ARCs and send them out instead. The reviewer knows it isn't the finished product, but they'll still be able to review the book. The second reason is that if there's time, the publisher might be able to stick one of these reviews on the finished book or in other promotional material. For instance, I was lucky enough to get an ARC of *Cuckoo* by Julia Crouch, a fantastic psychological thriller, and I blogged my review a couple of months before the book came out. When it did come out, my (glowing!) review was quoted on its press release, under the heading "Early Praise."

As I'm typing these words, I'm planning to send out an ARC of this book to several "beta readers" or trusted types who know a bit about books and/or self-publishing. I'm going to ask each of them for a short review, if they want to give it, and then potentially use a quote from that review either in the finished book or to promote it, e.g. on my blog or in my Amazon listing. These ARCs will have a (craptabulous) cover that Cover Creator made because I won't have finalised the *actual* cover yet.

Complete Title Set-Up

So you've uploaded interior and cover files, and are now ready to complete your Title Set-Up, starting at the section headed "Distribute."

Here what's left to fill in, most of which we'll be familiar with from our Amazon KDP and Smashwords adventures:

Description

You have 4,000 characters (about 700-ish words) to describe what your book is about. This is where you put your **back cover blurb** and nothing else, even if your blurb is only 154 words. Just because you have space to spare doesn't mean you should start filling it with stuff; only put a short, relevant description of your book. Keep in mind that this is what will appear, *exactly* as you enter it, on your Amazon listing.

Book Industry Standards & Communications (BISAC) Category

Choose from the list available the best category that describes your book. You can only choose one here, so choose carefully.

Author Biography

Copy and paste your author bio as it appears in your book into the box provided. You have up to 2,500 characters, which is about 450 words. Or, more than enough. This, too, will appear on your Amazon author listing under "About the Author."

Book Language

Enter the language the book is written in.

Country Of Publication

Enter the country in which you want the book to be listed as published, i.e. your own or wherever you happen to be living.

Date Of Publication

Leave this blank; it'll automatically become the day you click "Approve Proof." You can't set it to a date in the future.

Search Keywords

Very important. These words or phrases will be how your customers find your book on Amazon and in internet search engines, so choose wisely. You can enter up to five, separated by commas. (Once your book goes live on Amazon, you'll be able to add more, so just pick the five most important ones for now.)

Contains Adult Content

Check the box if your book contains adult content. This doesn't mean sex or swearing or things you don't think you'd like your 15-year-old niece to read. It means "could be mistaken for soft porn." So unless you're writing erotica, your book doesn't contain adult content.

(Although after *50 Shades*, I fear *everyone* reading this book will be writing erotica...)

Large Print

Check this box if your book has a font size large enough to qualify as "Large Print."

When it says "Large Print" it means that section of the library where there are special editions of books that cater for those with poor eyesight. It does not mean "Well, I used 16pt *most* of the time."

Sales Channels

The last thing we have to do before we submit our book for processing is select our sales channels, i.e. how many places we want our book to be available to buy online.

Select them all, and fork out the extra cash for Expanded Distribution if you'd like.

Set your list price, keeping in mind everything I said in the section on pricing our book.

Kindly Refrain From Doing These, Please

Oooh, we're about to submit our book! Are you excited? I hope so, because it *is* exciting. But before you click that all important button, I just want to put one last stop sign in front of you. (Some of you might need to be whacked over the head with said sign. We'll see.) Before you set your book in stone — for the moment, anyway — I want you to have one last look over everything: the interior, the cover, the description, your chosen BISAC category. *Everything*. And make sure that you're kindly refraining from doing any of the following things:

Using Cover Creator

Hopefully, now that you've seen what it can (or can't) do, you'll have decided to refrain from doing this all by yourself.

Inserting An Order Form

I've never understood order forms in books. If I want more copies, I'll go online and buy them, thanks very much. Filling out a form and posting it to some place with a cheque is practically prehistoric, and I'm not sure that they even did it back then.

Overzealous Interior Formatting

I once read a self-published book that could easily have been called *Watch As I Fit Every Formatting, Styling and Paragraph Alignment Feature of Microsoft Word into This One Book!* Simple is always best when it comes to the pages of your book.

Sticking It To The Man

Don't you just hate how book pages are numbered sequentially? How chapter twelve always seems to come after chapter eleven? How the text is justified, big enough to read and has the first line of each paragraph indented to exactly the same length? Don't you think it's so damn boring and, like, pitifully conformist?

If you want to stick two fingers up to the industry standard of *books people can actually read*, feel free to. But don't expect anyone who buys books to read them to buy yours. Likewise don't expect them to pay more for your book because you couldn't chop it down to less than 900 pages, or to keep reading even if chapter one bores them because "the best bits come later." Stick to the established principles. They work.

Quoting, Lifting And Unauthorised Copy/Pasting

You know when you pick up a novel and it has song lyrics or a poem printed in the front or elsewhere in the text, and then you look at the copyright page and you see something like "The lyrics to Really Relevant Song by Relevant Singer Dude appear with permission of Relevant Records"? That's because the author and/or the publisher got permission to reprint them. And newsflash: permission doesn't always mean "permission." Sometimes it means "they permitted me to use it in exchange for the wad of cash I gave them."

You might get away with a line of a song or your character saying the first line of a poem but if you can, avoid it. I wouldn't even take the chance. If you have *anything* in your book that came from another source either get permission to reprint it (which may well involve a hefty price tag) or get rid of it altogether.

Libel And Slander

It's also a good idea to avoid libel and/or slander while we're at it. If you have a non-fiction book that talks about real people and places either be nice or change all identifying characteristics. If it's fiction and you've based your characters on real people, change all identifying characters a *lot*.

Obviously quoting without permission or committing libel is something that should be avoided in both your paperback *and* e-book.

A DIY Index

Don't attempt to put a DIY index in your book. Compiling an index may seem like a straightforward thing you can attempt to do yourself, but it is not. It is far more than an alphabetical list of words or topics, and it is best done by a professional who hasn't written the book they're creating an index for. So either don't do it, or hire a professional indexer to do it for you.

You can find British and Irish indexers at www.indexers.org.uk. Consult the all-knowing Google for indexers in your area.

Printing Contact Information

Keep all personal contact information out of your book, including your e-mail address. If people want to contact you they can do so through your website, and they don't need your e-mail address to do that because you'll have inserted a nifty WordPress contact form.

Hyperbole

I could devote an entire book to this subject, but I'm going to do my best to keep it short here. When you self-publish, everyone knows that whatever is on the book's cover or inside its pages was put there by *you*. Therefore you should refrain from making grandiose claims, including quotes that say your book is the best thing since people started using the phrase "the best thing since sliced bread", and comparisons to other authors, living or dead, or indeed to other books. Don't sell yourself short, but don't be a jerk either.

And jerk is a very nice version of the word, or combination of words, that I'm using for this type of person in my head.

And whatever you do, don't make up a review or get a friend to say something glowing, because guess what? We can tell that's what you did. If I read a review that says Hemingway would have never written a word if he'd read any of your work because he would've known, instantly, that he could never do better, and then I open your book and the first paragraph reads like something an automated translation program coughed up while it was malfunctioning, I'm going to know something's up. Furthermore, I'm going to think you're dishonest, a liar and have your head so far up your own arse that when you open your eyes you see the back of your teeth.

This is a review I recently read on the press release of a self-published novel I had the misfortune to receive a copy of. I've changed it enough so the author can't identify it (hopefully!) but I haven't changed its level of cringe-inducing, I-got-paid-to-write-this, my-best-friend-is-the-author or I'm-not-real-the-author-made-me-up super stinky BS *one little bit.*

(I should also point out that this "review" is attributed to someone I've never heard of, with no explanation of who they are. I don't think anyone else knows who they are either, because when I googled them I couldn't find anything. So.)

"When an advanced reader copy of *The Best Novel Ever Written* arrived at my door, I was filled with the warmth of a thousand sunny springtime mornings, so grateful was I for this opportunity to feast my eyes on and direct my synapses towards this wondrous tome, one I am certain will take its rightful place on the bookshelves of every forward-thinking man, woman, child and household pet across all lands, societies, races, continents and dimensions. I was on page 13 when it struck me: this is not a debut novel. It just *couldn't* be! Based on the facts with which I am presented and the calibre of the writing before me, I could only surmise that the author had devised a clever way to turn back time, write several novels before this and then return to the present to begin work on *The Best Novel Ever Written*; that is the only explanation for the skill, wisdom and experience he shows in putting one word after the other. *The Best Novel Ever Written* is not only an entertaining novel that fans of Dan Brown will find a significant and pleasing improvement on the work of their favourite author, but also an allegory for the state of the world yesterday, today and tomorrow. It not only illuminates the path we must now all take as we move into the future; it shines new light on the past as well. It's *multitasking*. It should be required reading for every human, and broadcast into space by NASA in binary code so every other being can read it as well. And yet within its shining diamonds of pages lies unexpected humour, a brand only seen in comedy classics like *Fawlty Towers* and *30 Rock*. But there is real emotion too; I am reluctant to admit I had to send the butler out for Kleenex on page 341 and again on page 1,394, but will do so to comprehensively explain to you the stirrings I felt in every last molecule of my self as I read this book, although "book" seems like too small a word to describe the experience I just had with *The Best Novel Ever Written*. Truly a masterful, important, entertaining, amazing, hilarious, touching, dramatic and intelligent work. I recommend it with the conviction of a thousand convinced men. Superb."

Indeed. (And for the record, I read a bit of this book. Maybe 25 pages. And the only thing I was convinced of was that this "reviewer" clearly read some *other* book.)

Submit Your Book

Once you've completed everything on the Title Set-Up page and double-checked you haven't done anything silly like put an order form at the back, click that "Submit Your Book" button. What will happen now is that magical CreateSpace computers will check that everything is okay and if it is, they'll invite you to order a proof copy.

What kind of things are they checking are okay? It's kind of hard to say, because there's no list or anything that I know about. There are the obvious things like does the page count fit with the size of the cover, and is your ISBN on your copyright page and correct. Then there are some other grey, blurry things they might be looking for and if they find them, they'll let you know.

In my experience there can be a 24–48 hour delay between submitting your book for processing and CreateSpace coming back, saying everything is okay and inviting you to order a proof copy.

Order A Proof Copy

Um, order a proof copy.

You can't change *anything* after you order a proof copy without having to order another proof copy, so make sure you're good to go before you do.

Your proof copy will look exactly like the finished product EXCEPT that it will say "Proof" on the last page. I was once on a forum for self-published writers when I saw a complaint about this that went along the lines of, "Ugh! My proof copy says 'proof'. Why? Why would they print something in my book I didn't tell them to?" Well, this may come as a shock to you but it's because *it's a proof copy.*

Also, you can only order up to five copies of any one proof.

If you make a change in between submitting your book for processing and CreateSpace saying, okay, you can order a proof copy, you'll need to submit it again after you make the changes.

You may notice that CreateSpace offers a "skip a printed proof" or "proof a digital copy" option. You may also ignore it. If you want people to pay money for a physical copy of your book, the least you can do is check a physical copy of it before you sell it to them.

Publish Your Paperback

In all likelihood it'll take around a week for your proof copy to arrive on your doorstep. Once it does, you'll have to set aside time to check it thoroughly and then gaze at it adoringly for hours on end while saying "That's my book! *My* book! Look at how pretty it is..."

When your proof copy arrives, go through it with a fine-tooth comb and a highlighter. Then go through it again. And *again*. Then once more.

When you're 100% happy with it inside and out, go back to CreateSpace and your book's "Project Homepage", take a deep breath and click "Approve Proof."

* * *

There. You've just *published your book*. Congratulations! So now we've built the foundations of an online platform, published an e-book and published a POD paperback. Phew! I need a lie down. The good news is that you probably could squeeze in a nap. The bad news is that... well, I'm afraid we *still* haven't got to the hardest part.

That's selling books.

And that's next.

PART 5:
Selling Self-Published Books

How To Sell Self-Published Books

So, how do you sell self-published books? Well, isn't *that* the million dollar question.

There are a number of guides on the market right now with enticing titles like *How I Became a Trillionaire in Only 7 Minutes a Day: A Guide to E-books, Message Boards and Jedi Mind Tricks* that all promise to contain some hitherto unknown, sure-fire way to sell thousands upon thousands of self-published books. Their advice ranges from common sense to things you could get arrested for in some parts of the world, but they all have one thing in common: the only secret they reveal is how *their author* sold his or her books. In terms of usefulness to other self-published authors, yes, reading them is great motivation and tales of astronomical success always provide great fodder for our wildest daydreams—but that's about it. Because the methods they describe are so grandiose, hyper-specific and time-consuming, the average self-published author neither has the time nor inclination to even half-heartedly adopt them. Even if they *did*, the original results are never replicable; anyone who has sold hundreds of thousands of e-books has *luck* to thank, whether in whole or in part.

I think this kind of thing is overthinking it. It's like me and dieting. I know, intellectually, that in order to lose weight you have to spend more energy than you consume. In other words, eat less and move more. I *know* this. I know that it's a scientific fact. And yet instead of doing that, I read countless diet books and blogs, watch TV shows, pay for weight management programmes, buy all manner of shakes, bars and Chemical Stuff Masquerading as Food and tell myself that I'm going to start using the treadmill in the garage every single day, come Monday. No, really. I *swear*. Why do I do this? Because I want to believe that there's some magic secret to weight loss that's just waiting for me to discover it, and I want to believe it because I don't want to do the hard work. So instead of *starting* the hard work, I keep searching for the secret while, in the meantime, the circumference of my thighs continues to be in direct proportion to my love of Toblerone cheesecake.

This is exactly what happens to self-published authors, minus the cheesecake. Instead of considering the time, hard work and common sense that has led to hundreds of self-published authors making money but not necessarily headlines, they dream of emulating the handful who did little other than upload to KDP before they found themselves sleeping on mattresses stuffed with cash.

We're not going to do that. We're going to get our arses on the treadmill right *now*.

The Science Of Book Selling

If the science of slimming is eat fewer calories and exercise more, what is the science of book selling? What events have to take place in order for someone to purchase a book? What had to happen in order for you to buy the last book you bought?

1. You had to find out that the book existed.
2. Something about the book made you care, i.e. made you stop and think, *Hmm. That sounds interesting* (instead of ignoring/not caring about it like all the other books you found out existed)
3. You were convinced enough by the information you had about the book to believe that you'd like it.
4. You found a place where it was on sale.
5. A combination of the blurb, book cover, price, etc. cemented your decision and you purchased it.

Every single book sold has been through this process, unless it was purchased by mistake. It wouldn't be too bad if everyone who was at #1 made it all the way to #5, but of course, that's not the case. The number of readers at #5 are only a *tiny fraction* of the number who were with us back at #1; potential readers drop away at every step.

Let's say that on a particular day 100 people found out that our book existed. Of them, maybe only 50 cared enough to stop and pay attention. Of that 50, only 25 became convinced the book was something they might like. Of that 25, only 10 made an effort to find a place where it was on sale and of those 10, only one ended up purchasing our book. That's a conversion rate of 1%, which I'd guess is at *least* ten times what the actual conversion rate of hearing about a book/buying that book is in the real world. So how can we improve our chances? The good news is that we can improve our chances easily, and we can do so at every step. Consider, for example, how the conversion rate would be affected if:

*   The people at #1 was a huge number
*   The people at #1 were established fans of books quite similar to ours
*   *All* the people at #1 were given good reason to think, *Hmm, that sounds interesting*
*   The information at #3 was presented in such a way that sent nearly everyone who read it onto #4
*   Your Amazon listing (product description, cover, price, etc.) got almost everyone at #4 onto #5.

We can also set mechanisms in place that will mean we don't have to be constantly working to inform new people that our book exists—eventually someone *else* will start doing it for us, and doing it for us while we sleep, work on our next book or watch *I Didn't Know I Was Pregnant*. And that someone will make sure *only* to tell people who they know for a fact are interested in books like ours, and they'll promote our book for free.

Actually, buying a book by accident isn't the only way a book sale can bypass this process. I love the likes of Michael Connelly, Karin Slaughter and Belinda Bauer, and buy every single one of their books when they come out without steps #1-#5. I just buy it. That's because at some stage in the past I went through the process above and liked the book enough to say to myself, *I want to read all the books this author has written*. When the next book came out, there was only one step for me:

1. Find out about the new book.

That was sure to happen because I had "liked" the author's Facebook fan page, or because I was joined their newsletter mailing list, or because I was regular visitor to their blog or website. For now we're only selling one book but we have to think of the long term too, so whenever a reader makes it to #5 and reads and likes our book, we need to make it easy for them to find out about future releases. Then when we come to release that book, we not only have all the ways we can get to #1 we used with our first title, but also a ready-made audience of #5s just waiting to hear that the book is out.

Wasn't Publishing It Enough?

Once upon a time, a newly self-published author sent me a tweet that said, "How will people find my book on Amazon?" Setting aside for a moment the fact that it's *unbelievably* annoying when people ask you questions via tweet (or e-mail), the answers to which are all over your blog, thus confirming that they haven't bothered to even go look and instead think you've nothing better to do with your time than to repeat yourself, this tweet is quite frightening. It's frightening because the author seemed to think that the answer could be provided in 140 characters or less, just like the questions *What's the URL for Amazon KDP?* and *If I charge $2.99, how much do I get to keep?*

Make your peace now with the fact that this is the hard part. It's going to take time, energy, imagination, dedication and patience to get your book selling. It's entirely *your responsibility*; no one else, Amazon included, is charged with promoting your book.

And as self-published authors—as any kind of first-time authors— we've our work cut out for us because, by default, no one gives a tiny rat's arse about our book.

No One Cares About Your Book

No one cares about your book. They really, *really* don't. They couldn't give a monkeys. Even people who should care, like friends and relatives, don't. Not one bit. In fact, if they cared any less, they'd probably pass out. This is something a lot of self-publishers fail to grasp, not least of all because it's a horrible thought that no one wants to believe. But it's the truth. If you understand one thing in this entire guide, understand this: *just because you wrote a book does not mean people are going to want to read it.*

Sounds suspiciously like common sense, but as I've said before, common sense isn't as common as you might think.

Think of all the books you hear about on a daily basis. Think of all the books you see when you walk into a bookstore, or through the book isles of supermarkets. Think of all the books that pop into your line of vision while you're on Amazon. Do you buy them all? Are you even *interested* in them all? Or are you like me—and, I'd suspect, most book-buyers—buying and ultimately reading just the very cream of the crop, the top 0.5% or less of the books we know about, just the ones that get us interested in them and wanting to read them, i.e. just the ones we care about?

At least once a day I receive an e-mail from an author I don't know saying "I've written a book. Will you review it?" If this author knew that every week Oprah's Book Club sends me an e-mail recommending several books—books that, this being Oprah's Book Club, are hugely publicized, high advance, this-is-gonna-be-big traditionally published books—and that, on average, I make a note of maybe two of them and ultimately buy maybe *one* of them for every five or six e-mails I get, do you think they'd do anything differently? Do you think they'd put more effort in than, "I've written a book. Will you review it?"

I'll say it again: just because you wrote a book does not mean people are going to want to read it. There is no inherent entitlement here; you aren't entitled to readers just because you managed to type 100,000 words. Telling people, "I wrote a book" isn't a strategy. It has to come with something else, and that something else has to be a reason for us to care.

Before you take a *single* step in this book promotion business, you have to acknowledge that. Why? Because this is the kind of thing that happens if you don't:

I am a member of Goodreads (Facebook for readers, if you've forgotten) and one of the features of Goodreads which self-published authors delight in abusing is the "Events" feature, whereby an author (or reader) can create an event and then invite other Goodreads users to attend. I'm fairly certain this is supposed to be for things like book-signings, live web chats with your favourite author, etc. but these days it's a wasteland of free book promotions, blog tours and the like, to wildly varying degrees of success. Recently one self-published author, who shall remain nameless, sent me this via Goodreads Events:

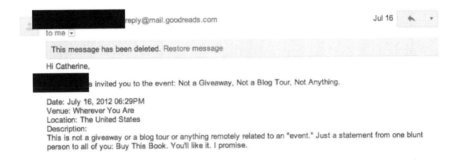

The text reads, "This is not a giveaway or a blog tour or anything remotely related to an 'event'. Just a statement from one blunt person to all of you: Buy This Book. You'll like it. I promise." The book is, of course, the author's own. Underneath that [not pictured] are two endorsements so glowing that I momentarily lost the vision in my right eye — they include words like "masterpiece", phrases like "great American novelist" and the sentence "a saga that blasts away the outer layers so we can gaze into the soul where humanity is one" — but they *aren't attributed to anyone* (!), and underneath them is a fairly unremarkable synopsis.

Now I don't mean to pick on this author; on the grand scale of self-published authors' crimes, they'd get away with merely a warning. They just had the misfortune to send me a perfect example of the point I'm trying to demonstrate here while I was writing this book. Because not only is this message spammy, but the author openly admits to their abuse of the Goodreads Events feature ("this is not a giveaway or a blog tour...") and, most importantly, doesn't give me a *single* reason to go read the book.

This is because the author doesn't know that no one cares about it. They've assumed that because they've written a book, they're already several steps up the ladder of book selling. The lines "Buy this book. You'll like it. I promise" are irrefutable proof of that. But that's *not* how it works. You have to *make* people care, and care enough to stop and think, *Hmm, that sounds interesting*, to give your book some time instead of just breezing on by it without a second thought like we do with the overwhelming majority of books that enter our line of vision.

Just sending them a synopsis and a "buy me!" plea isn't enough.

It is *very* hard to get people to care enough about your book that they go and buy it. It's the hardest part of this whole thing. And before you can even do that, you have to get them interested in it, and before that you have to let them know that it exists. But by embracing the fact that, by default, no one gives a rat's arse about your book, you'll have a much clearer idea of what you're working with, and that'll help you recognise the lengths you have to go to in order to make a sale happen.

Why Promoting Your Book Online Is (A Bit) Like *Fight Club*

The first rule of Fight Club is that you do not talk about Fight Club. The first rule of effectively promoting your book online is that you do not promote your book online.

By which I mean, you do not *blatantly* promote your book online.

Some self-published authors take offence at being told that they shouldn't regularly send out tweets like "My book, YOUR EYES ARE GLAZING OVER, is on Amazon now, just $2.99. PLEASE RT! OKAY? THANKS!", or that they should avoid working the title of at least one of their books into every comment they leave on someone else's blog, or that they shouldn't send e-mails to people they don't know or don't know really well trying to flog their book because, even if it's done manually, it's still spam. They stubbornly want to do things their way, and that's fine. Maybe a trillion-selling 99c e-book author did the same thing and now they're convinced that's the secret to success. Maybe they're just not that bright.

Whatever their reasons, leave them to it. But I don't want *you* to do it that way because *that way doesn't work.*

Did you hear me? IT DOESN'T WORK. So yes, of course, you're free to do whatever you want. But personally, I'd rather just do stuff that is at least *likely* to work. Otherwise, it seems like it would be a massive waste of time to me.

The reason it doesn't work is because people aren't using social media because they love being sold stuff. They're using it, I think, for one or more of the following three reasons:

- Because they want to be **entertained**
- Because they're looking for specific **information**
- Because they want to **connect** with other people (connect as in *virtually meet*, but also as in *relate to*).

From what I've seen over the past two years, both in trying to sell my own books and watching what other self-published and traditionally published authors have done to try to sell theirs, is that your promotional efforts have to have a value of their own, and that value has to satisfy one or more of the demands in the list above. Online promotion works best when the book actually comes *second* to the content's main objective.

Say *what* now?

To put it another—hopefully clearer—way, your goal should be to improve the internet, above all else. Make it a better place than it was five minutes ago by writing a great blog post, posting a funny tweet, using a tweet to direct your followers to a great blog post you just found, uploading a video that helps people perform a task, uploading a video that makes people laugh while they're procrastinating to keep from doing that task they're supposed to do... You get the idea. Adding a mention of your book to this content might also sell a few copies of it for you, yes, but that's secondary. That's not the most important bit. We need to create stuff to put on the internet that would still be something useful and worthwhile even if we took the selling books bit out of it.

Book trailers—good ones, anyway—and other book-related videos are a really effective way to demonstrate what I mean.

The book trailer *Love in the Time of Amazon* is one of my favourites. It's a short film about a woman who secretly starts buying copies of her husband's book to raise his Amazon sales ranking and also, what with him obsessively watching his Amazon sales rankings, his mood. It's also a book trailer that advertises the authors' books.

The point is that if you took the advertising books bit away—if you just imagined for a second that this was just for fun, and that those are actors and those books don't really exist—it would *still* be a video you'd have a little giggle at. It would still be a video you'd post on your blog, share with your Facebook friends and/or tweet a link to. Especially if your friends are published authors, because we can so relate. (And so—added bonus—connect.) It's been viewed over 8,000 times, I saw countless links to it on Twitter, I've posted about it myself several times and it got picked up by high-traffic sites like Media Bistro.

My own video, *How Much Editing Backpacked Needed*, is nothing more than a sped-up scroll through of *Backpacked*'s manuscript after it came back from the copy editor. It's been viewed over 1,000 times and passed around numerous editing and writing blogs. At the very end of it, there's some info about the book. But if I didn't name the book that was being edited and took that info at the end out, the video wouldn't lose any of its value. It would still have the same number of views and have been passed around and shared just as much. Because this isn't a video about me wanting you to buy my book. This is a video that, first and foremost, contains useful information and/or is interesting.

My self-printing-themed posts contain information that some people might need. Fun, chatty tweets that bemoan the pain of having to put words on paper are something any writer can relate to, and over time we might make a connection with the person writing them. Anything that makes us laugh, mutter, "Hmm. Interesting...", holds our attention for longer than a few seconds or could be considered "just for fun" falls into the entertainment category.

And after they've entertained, informed or made a connection, they've also informed a new person that our book exists, which is the first step in getting someone to buy it. (Making them interested in the book is the step in between.) Obviously the number of people who know our books exist is far greater than those who actually buy it, but as the first number increases, so does the second.

Am I silly enough to think that everyone who reads my blog is going to run straight over to Amazon and buy up all my books? No. I don't think that anyone is going to run over there and buy one of them. I'm not trying to open and close the deal in the same shot. My main priority is to make my blog a good blog. Above all else, I want new people to keep discovering my blog, and I want the people already reading it to keep doing so, and I want everyone to find it useful with a side of occasional giggles, even if they don't like pink.

Below that on my list of priorities is selling my books. Over time, a very small percentage of blog readers become book readers, but because I have a lot of blog readers, that's enough for me to feel a little thrill every time I check my KDP units-sold-to-date report (which I do at *least* four times a day).

How do blog readers become book readers? These are some of my theories:

- They like the way I write; they want to read more
- They want to get my book to see how it's turned out (after reading about its production)
- After hanging around there for ages, they read the About page or My Books, and one of my books catches their eye
- They buy a book of mine as a thank you for me helping them with their book (through my posts)
- One of the above, combined with me telling them I have a free promotion on, and perhaps reading one for free leads them to buy another one
- Then they might write a review, recommend me to a friend, etc. etc. leading to other, "outside" sales

- After reading the blog from the beginning and following me through the release of four books, they just can't resist my Jedi mind tricks anymore…

Let's say that instead of writing blog posts, I just stuck up a picture of a book of mine with an Amazon link and a price tag. And I did that every day, without fail and without deviation. Where do you think I'd be then? I'm pretty sure I'd have zero blog readers. But yet people treat Twitter *exactly* in this way, and expect not only people to stick around and put up with it, but also to go buy their books. Put down the crazy juice and have a cup of coffee instead.

Think about it: what does you tweeting "Another 5* review for MY BOOK on Amazon! Here's the link so you can go read it and marvel at the praise I have received…" achieve out of those three? And no, it doesn't fall under information, because the information has to be useful. If you're going on a blog tour and you have five guest posts lined up to send to your kind hosts, ask yourself: are these posts good by themselves? Are they likely to entertain, provide information, have readers relating to them, or is the only point they make something like buy my book and buy it now?

Let's return to the word rule. You—I—can't really say "never do this" or "as a rule, don't do that." Sometimes you have to tell the internet something, even if that something doesn't achieve one of our three aims. There's little point, for instance, in your book being free for Kindle for a few days if you can't tell people about it. (Although, in my opinion, the opportunity to get a free book falls into the information category. I'm slow to admit this thought because I JUST KNOW that someone will take it a step in the wrong direction and assume tweets on the hour, every hour about how his book is "just $1.99" falls into the same category. IT DOESN'T.) And what if you get a review from, like, someone amazing? What if your writing hero says she likes your book and says it on the internet? You couldn't keep news like that in, even if it doesn't do anything but make the rest of us sick with jealousy. So sometimes, it's okay to break the rules or not follow the principles. But only in extreme moderation. Because remember, the hard sell doesn't work. No one is listening to it because that's not why they're there.

Over time, what's considered valuable information will also change. For instance, if I pick 1,000 people at random and tell them that I've released a new book and go buy it now, please, thanks, I'd probably get into trouble for spamming, or at the very least, I'd have wasted my time. But what if those 1,000 people had already read a book of mine and signed up to a newsletter so they could find out about my future releases, and they were happy to hear from me because they were fans of my work?

Then "my book is out now!" becomes valuable information to them, because finding that out was exactly why they signed up to the mailing list. BUT—before you bring it up—this isn't the same as me following you on Twitter. I didn't follow you on Twitter to be constantly told about your new book. I'd like to know if you have a new book, sure, but I want it to come on the side with the real reason I'm on Twitter in the first place: to be *entertained, informed* or *connected.*

We're Not African Princes

We've all received an e-mail (or three hundred) from some poor unfortunate royal family member on the continent of Africa who'd make us both millionaires if only we'd agree to some shady stuff involving a wire transfer. *Why do they bother?* you wonder. *No one in their right mind would fall for this!* Unfortunately people *do* fall for them—there was a woman on Oprah once who received a fax version at the office and thought it was genuinely from a friend of her boss, who was away on holidays at the time, so she sent the money, thinking she was doing the right thing. And that's the whole point of these spam e-mails: if they send out 500,000 of them and only *one* person falls for it, they've achieved their objective. They've made a profit.

If you're thinking something along the lines of *well, I'd like to sell 1,000 books. If I tell 1,000,000 people about my book, chances are I'll get those 1,000 sales. So why don't I just send a tweet with my Amazon link to the first 1,000,000 people I can find on Twitter? Or collect e-mail addresses from around the web and mail out 1,000,000 press releases at random? Or [insert some other hare-brained idea]?*, then please, stop. We're not going to do any of those things because:

- It's all **spam**, which is at best effortlessly ignorable and at worst, utterly illegal
- It's a gigantic **waste of everyone's time**: yours, and the people you target
- The **only sustainable growth is organic**. Going back to our dieting analogy, I could probably drop 20 pounds in ten days if I followed Emily's diet from *The Devil Wears Prada* ("I don't eat anything and then right before I think I'm going to faint, I eat a cube of cheese."), but I'd gain back 40 in five once I started eating normally again. Similarly, I could probably get a few thousand people to buy my book using a variety of shortcuts—like spamming, super low prices, etc.—but not all of them would bother reading it, and even fewer would remember my name in a week's time. This isn't just about getting as many people to buy our first book as we possibly

can. This is about slowly but steadily building a readership over time.

A note: a couple of months back there was a scandal involving an author who had sent out thousands of e-mails in a bid to sell his book. There was a question mark over whether or not he had done it manually or used a mailing list/e-mail collector programme of some sort, and one person (a friend of his, I think it'd be safe to assume) was quite vocal in arguing that if it *was* manual, it *wasn't* spam. This is like saying that because you secured an upright knife to the floor and stuck out your leg to trip your victim causing him to fall onto it, it wasn't murder. The person is still dead, and the "buy my book" e-mail is still something that thousands of people received against their will. Don't waste your time clinging to a technicality. We'll all be *very annoyed with you* and guaranteed *not to buy your book* regardless.

But I Just Want To *Write*!

As I write this section, my fellow "platforming" self-publishers and I have been stung by an article in a major UK newspaper that basically says the e-publishing bubble will burst just like the Dot Com one did, that author platforms are useless and don't work, and that building them eats into writing time and ultimately detracts from the work. It was extremely snarky in tone and used the phrase "self-styled" to describe virtually every self-publisher mentioned in the piece. And it was *completely* wrong.

People who think Twitter et al doesn't sell books don't understand *how* they sell books. The usual anti-using-social-media-to-sell-books argument goes something like this: *"Well, Johnny X has 10,000 Twitter followers but he's only sold 500 books. Conclusion: Twitter doesn't sell books."* But that is an observation about advertising, not building an online author platform.

The clue is in the term *social network*. This, more than anything, is about networking. It's about connecting with other writers, other readers and people who can help us to promote our book without actually buying a copy themselves. It's about meeting the people that matter without even leaving the house.

As for how time-consuming it is, that's up to you. Obviously you'll be spending a lot more time on it in the beginning than you will in the long term, and later I'll be sharing some ideas for managing your social media time.

When writers moan about wanting to write all the time, my eyes begin searching for some sort of heavy object I could hit them with while my hands clasp themselves behind my back so I won't if I find one. The *only* way to write all the time is to sell books, and the only way to sell books is to promote them. If you don't sell books, you have to have a job. And if you have a job, you can't write all the time.

This guide isn't about dropping everything to turn ourselves into lean, mean marketing machines. It's about dividing our time between trying to promote the books we've written and writing more of them.

But you can't "just write." You never could. Because if you don't make money from your writing, you will have to do something else — probably for eight hours a day, five days a week.

Pick A Release Date

Before we start any marketing, we need to know when the book has to be finished by. You need **a release date** for it.

In self-publishing, this is a date you get to pick and, as it's practically impossible to know in advance the *exact* date your book will pop up on Amazon, and it's *actually* impossible to make this coincide with the date your e-book pops up, it's pretty much arbitrary. But you should have one. Remember that we're trying to make our self-published efforts look as professional as possible, and traditionally published books have release dates. So we're going to have one too.

We'll decide on an actual date a bit later on, but for now we'll just work out what month we're aiming to release our book in. It depends, of course on where you are with your book, but assuming that nearly all of the work is ahead of you, your schedule will look something like this:

- Sourcing an editor and cover designer: 1–4 weeks
- Editing your book: anywhere from 1 to 6 months
- Cover design: 2–4 weeks
- Formatting and uploading paperback's interior: 1 week
- Formatting and uploading e-book's interior: 1 week
- Waiting for e-book to appear on Amazon, etc: 1 day–1 week
- Waiting for proof copy to arrive: 1–2 weeks
- Checking proof copy: 1 week
- If there are problems with the proof copy allow another: 2–3 weeks
- Waiting for book to appear on Amazon sites after you approve proof: 1–2 weeks
- Waiting for book to appear on other retailers: 2–8 weeks.

These times can vary greatly and you might be able to do some of these things concurrently, saving time. (For instance, I formatted and uploaded my e-book while waiting for my paperback proof copy to arrive.) You'll also have a much better idea of when you and your book will be ready by the time you get to the end of *this* book.

Or at least, that's the idea, anyway...

Be warned: some people take things like release dates *way* too seriously. Someone once took the time to e-mail me because they'd spotted a book of mine for sale on Amazon even though "it's not supposed to be out until next week?!!?" If you are a regular book buyer—and considering that *you're* considering self-publishing a book you wrote, I sincerely hope you are—you'll know that sometimes, books appear in stores sooner than the author said they were supposed to. It's not a big deal. Your release date is less about availability than it is a focus for your promotional efforts.

And before the thought even forms in your head, self-published books cannot be set up for "pre-order" on Amazon. I'm not even going to bother to explain why because this book costs me by the page and I don't want to devote any space to such stupidity. All you need know is that every time a self-publisher wonders aloud about how they can get their book set up for pre-order on Amazon, at least one fairy dies. FACT.

I mentioned already that the contents of this book aren't in the *exact* order you need them. Therefore, about half of what I'm about to describe takes place in the months leading up to the release of your book, and half of it afterwards. You'll be doing some of it while simultaneously editing and preparing your book, and for some of it, you'll need finished copies. The bulk of your promotional efforts will take place in the three months before and after your launch date. From then on, it'll just be a matter of maintaining them.

We'll talk more about a specific timescale or schedule towards the end of this book.

So we've talked a lot about what we're *not* going to do. But what *are* we going to do? How are we going to sell our self-published books?

Find Your First Readers

So you have a (colour co-ordinated, hilariously named WordPress) blog, Twitter account and Facebook fan page either dedicated to your imminent book release or to you as a writer. You've been finding your blogging feet, making blogging friends and are getting at least *some* non-accidental hits. You've started following people on Twitter, chatted to them, retweeted the links they post to adorable YouTube videos featuring animals acting like humans, and made sure they all know where to find your blog if they want to read longer versions of your priceless witticisms. You've coerced all your friends and family already on Facebook into "liking" your page and then insisted that all *their* friends and family on Facebook do the same. All the accounts have the same profile pic, link to each other and look—

here it comes again—*professional*, i.e. the social media presence of a (soon-to-be) world famous author-type.

Fast forward now to approximately three months before your book launches. You're having the time of your life with your blog readers, Twitter followers and Facebook fans, and you're having it (bonus!) in the comfort of your own home, in your pyjamas and without a scrap of make-up on. (And thinking, *This is the life...*) But now we need to tell these people that we have a book coming out, that we are self-publishing it and that, if they come along for the ride, there's at least a *moderate* chance they'll be occasionally entertained.

It's All About You

I've already talked about how much easier it is to get people to buy your book because they're interested in or by *you*, as opposed to the content of the book itself.

When we walk into a bookstore or browse Amazon listings, it's things like the cover art, the blurb, the genre, etc. that help us decide whether or not we'd like to buy a particular book. And no wonder, considering that this is our first contact with the author of the book. But on social media platforms like blogs and Twitter, the first thing we meet is the author in their blog posts and tweets. If their personality shines through and it's a personality we *like*, we might then go and look at their book.

I've bought books I would never have otherwise read in a million years because I've been following the authors on Twitter and either am interested in how their book has turned out (including traditionally published authors) or because I like them and so want to support their writing. I've bought books outside of genres I like just because the author's blog is hilarious. I've bought books because someone I follow on Twitter liked an author's blog and/or book and recommended it to their followers. In all of these examples, the author is my first point of contact; the details of their book (what it's about, who has published it, what genre it's in) comes second.

There are huge benefits to winning readers because of you and your writing rather than because of a specific book. For instance, I love all things NASA so I picked up *Packing for Mars* by Mary Roach which I found out about after seeing Roach interviewed on *The Daily Show*. She seemed funny and her book was about NASA, so I bought it. I loved Roach's writing. Turns out she's a famous science writer in the States and really funny to boot—an odd combination, I'm sure you'll agree. So I ran out and got all of Roach's other books which, even though they're not about things I'm particularly interested in, I now want to read because I so enjoy the author's writing, and she makes technical details so easy to understand

and the science so entertaining that I'm willing to bet that I'll like them too. So with the subject of one of her books, she sold me one book, but with her writing, she sold me the whole set. And if I wasn't interested in NASA or if she hadn't written about it, I might never have picked up any of her books.

Now chances are, you and I are not going to get invited on to *The Daily Show* to chat with Jon Stewart, so we need to look for other places we can sell ourselves. That's where your blog, Twitter account and Facebook fan page come in.

Look at my own experience. The weekend *Mousetrapped*—a weird little book if ever there was one—came out, I sold about 50 copies of it. In *paperback*. Nearly all of them were to blog readers, Twitter friends, etc. who had been following my progress and/or chatting to me (about coffee, probably), and now wanted either to see how the book had turned out or to support me by buying it.

So how do we advertise ourselves? Well, really it's our *personality*, our *perspective* and our *writing* (or "voice") that we're pushing out into the world. When you write a blog post or type a tweet, you can't help but display all these things. It just occurs naturally.

I was once asked if anyone could sell their books through social media, or if it only suited certain personality types. It was just after giving a talk during which, because it was late afternoon and I was attempting to combat the effects of an exhausting holiday and lingering jet-lag with more coffee than a human being should reasonably drink, I came across as "bubbly." Thus the implication for some was that non-bubbly types wouldn't produce very bubbly blogs. And indeed they wouldn't, but there are more than bubbly folk out there in the world (thank fudge) and you certainly don't have to be that way to sell books. Just be *you*.

Be you, be honest and offer something new and/or different, and don't worry about the rest.

... But Not an Annoying Version of You

There is a big difference between introducing the world to us (and by *us* I mean our *personality, perspective* and *voice*) and forcing news of us down the throats of everyone we can find.

In other words, no one likes a shameless self-promoter.

But Catherine, you'll argue now, *isn't blogging in itself a type of shameless self-promotion?* No. Millions of bloggers are out there doing it because they like blogging, and anyway they have nothing to sell. (This is like the argument that by blogging, you're assuming people want to listen to what you have to say and in this way, are a certifiable egotist. It isn't about the listening; it's about the *saying*.) Most people who follow your blog will probably not buy your book, or even consider doing so. They're just there for your blog posts, which is fine because it's a *blog*. Likewise, while I may find out about a lot of books on Twitter, I'm not there to find books. I'm there, first and foremost, to be entertained, encounter interesting people and get links to YouTube videos where animals are acting like humans.

(Cracks me up every time. That and babies laughing like adults. FUNNY.)

So as we move forward we're going to incorporate promoting our book into our online activities but always politely, in moderation and while still catering to the folks who have been reading our blog or following us on Twitter because of the content we've produced to date, and not because they want to buy our book, now or ever.

Your Unique Selling Point

Any highly-trained monkey can start a blog, join Twitter or set up a Facebook page, and writer-types are especially good at it. As a result there are thousands if not millions of other people out there doing the social media equivalent of tugging on your sleeve and trying to get your attention, and it's in this environment that you have to find a way to be heard.

Tip: it's not by shouting the loudest or shouting the most often. It's by saying the most interesting, most original, or the funniest things, or if you can't manage that, saying something completely unoriginal in a funny or interesting way. Find a gap and then figure out how to fill it. Work out what will be your *unique selling point*. This doesn't need to be related to your book, but your book needs to fit into it.

My favourite piece of writing advice is "Write the book you want to read." I think this can be applied here too, and in fact it might be the easiest way to find that illusive gap. What's the blog you'd love or need to read? Who's the Twitterer you think you'd enjoy following? What would be on the kind of Facebook page you'd be interested in "like"-ing?

Back when I had no clue how to go about this self-publishing thing, I did some research online. I quickly discovered that most of the posts, articles and sites about the subject, while helpful, all came served with a large side of evangelism. That is, their authors all championed self-publishing above all else, used the word "gatekeepers" in every other sentence and spoke about "the Big Six" (the large US publishing houses) as if they were minions of the devil himself. If they weren't shouting, "Down with Big Publishing!" they were deluding themselves into thinking that by uploading their book to CreateSpace or Lulu, they were going to be topping the *New York Times* bestseller list by the end of next week.

Yes, I was self-publishing after traditional publishing had said no, but only as a sideline while I pursued my Real Dreams of getting an agent, a book deal and a well-paying job I can do in my pyjamas, and I was brutally realistic about what the results of it were likely to be. So where were the blogs and websites for *me*? Where was there helpful information, good marketing ideas and clear instructions, but relayed with a level head, zero bitterness or resentment and a prevailing mood of sanity?

So I decided that's what I would blog about. That's *how* I would blog. My first post explained why I was calling what I was doing self-*printing* instead of self-publishing, and that set the tone. And it worked. It wasn't related to the subject matter of my book, but it gave me the opportunity to tell people about it. It also gave me plenty of material to blog *about*.

Don't try to tell me that because you've written a novel, you'll have to take a different approach. I've had people tell me this in person about their self-published books and all I can think when they do is, *You're just lacking in imagination*. And since you've written a novel, you must have *some* imagination, so the only excuse that leaves is laziness. There must be *something* about you or your book that's interesting. If you can't think of one single thing, then maybe you have bigger problems than I can help you with.

Let's have a little brainstorm.

How did you write the book?

Every writer can blog about how they wrote their book. All you need to do here is find a new way to do it. For example, I read a blog by a UK writer who has started a weekly video blog entitled "A Year in the Life of a Book", where she'll take us, her blog readers, right along with her as her next novel goes from idea to finished book. I read lots of writing blogs, but hers is the one I make sure to visit every week, because no one else is doing that.

What were you doing before you wrote the book?

Were you an astrophysicist in a previous life? Once voted America's Sexiest Man? A NASA astronaut? (If you were all those things, CALL ME.) The story of how you came to write your book might be the interesting thing about you, enabling you to make *you* the real story and the focus of your social media efforts. Let's say you were enslaved in a corporate cubicle and you wrote a novel about being enslaved in a corporate cubicle. Well, you need to start blogging about being in and then finding a way out of a corporate cubicle. Put a satirical slant on it, or write the next *The Four Hour Work Week*. If you do it well, people will be attracted to your book, and now that they know your background, they'll know it's going to be authentic too.

What is the book about?

Are you a feisty pathologist who has written something like Patricia Cornwell's *Point of Origin*? A bereaved widow who has written something like Anita Shrieve's *The Pilot's Wife*? A recovered drug addict who has written something like James Frey's *A Million Little Pieces*, except you haven't made it all up? If you can connect your life to your book, then you're golden. Or maybe the fact that you *can't* connect your life to your book is going to be your story. Stephanie Meyer was a Mormon housewife when she started the Twilight series, for example, and I'm pretty sure that the lovely (and hilarious—if you don't believe me, sign up for her newsletters!) Karin Slaughter doesn't commit or investigate murders. Maybe there's something there.

Ask yourself *what makes me different to everyone else?* Maybe your personality is enough of a focus. Or maybe you already have a blog about quilting and you plan to slip mentions of your upcoming book in there, ninja-like, between the photos of your stitching. And it goes without saying that self-publishing your book is something to blog about all by itself.

Whatever it is that you decide on, make sure it's unique. Or at least considerably different to most everybody else.

Meet My Book

When it comes to introducing your online readership to your upcoming book, it's not so much about *how*, it's about *what*. We want content that's about our book but that also offers a value of its own so that a reader who has no intention of *ever* reading a book of ours isn't left behind.

What, Why, When, How

The fact that you've decided to write and self-publish a book—or self-publish the book you've been trying to get traditionally published up until now—generates content for your blog posts, tweets and Facebook page in itself.

Make an announcement. Tell the story of why you wrote the book. Explain how you came to this decision. Blog about your self-publishing adventures. Start a countdown to publication day.

Release The Blurb

Share the blurb of your upcoming book. If you're having trouble writing it, ask your blog readers for help. Even if you're not, a focus group would be beneficial and fun. Post a few versions of it; ask for feedback. Involve your readers, followers, etc. in the self-publishing process. Chances are they're readers too, and their opinions will be highly valuable.

Share Your Book's Cover

Mousetrapped's cover had four incarnations. Before I decided which Print-On-Demand company to go with, I ordered one proof copy from Lulu and one proof copy from CreateSpace. Each of these had a cover on them generated by the relevant site's cover creation software. I wasn't happy with either of them, so I mocked-up a cover myself using MS Word. Finally that went to the cover designer I hired who turned it into the cover you see on the book today.

The incarnations of Mousetrapped*'s cover. The first two were made by cover creation programs (Lulu's and CreateSpace's, respectively), while the third is a MS Word mock-up. The fourth is the actual design used.*

Not only did I show my blog readers each version of the cover, but I asked them which one they preferred. When my proof copy arrived, I told them how exciting it was (the initial reaction) and then all the things that was wrong with it (terrible paper, weird size, etc.). When I'd decided on one, I "revealed" it on the blog too, and then tweeted links to the post and invited people to *ooh* and *ahh* over it.

Blog about how you came to decide on a cover. Share where you or your cover designer got the idea for it in the first place. Tell them what you especially love about it, or how long you've spent gazing at it since you got the final proof. (*Hours,* if you're anything like me.)

Release Your First Chapter

When your manuscript has been finalised, convert the first chapter to a PDF and upload it to your blog. (WordPress lets you upload PDFs just as you would an image.) Then point everyone in the known universe in the direction of it.

This is a *major* advertisement for your book. A number of readers told me that they bought my book after reading the first chapter online and, crucially, liking it.

Warning: if you're thinking something along the lines of *I'd rather release my third chapter, because the first one isn't really the best advertisement for my book,* put down *this* book immediately and go back to working on your own, because it's not ready yet.

Book Trailers

A book trailer is essentially a short video (1–3 minutes) that advertises your book in the same way a movie trailer does for an upcoming feature film release.

Book trailers are a relatively new addition to the book world and as there's no one way to make a book trailer or any particular thing you're supposed to put into it, the only limit here is your imagination. They vary in quality from DIY to slick and professional, and you can upload them to video sharing sites like YouTube and Vimeo. After your book comes out, you can also add them to places like your Amazon Author Page and your Goodreads Author Profile.

I don't believe that book trailer views convert directly to sales, but I do think a good book trailer can encourage someone to go look up your book, check your blog or start following you on Twitter and, since you'll have such a stunning-looking book, colour co-ordinated blog and hilarious tweet stream, *that* might lead to a sale. Book trailers also have a huge "share" value, i.e. there is a much better chance that someone will post your book trailer on their Facebook wall or tweet a link to it than something plain and unexciting like the text of your preview chapter. Some book trailers even go "viral" and end up with hundreds of thousands, if not millions, of views.

I love making little movie mementoes of holidays, trips and other experiences with programs like Windows Movie Maker (PC) and iMovie (Mac), so it wasn't that much of a stretch for me to make a book trailer, especially since my book was non-fiction. You can watch it on the *Self-Printed* website.

If you can't use those programs and don't want to learn, there are alternatives. Ask a friend, or maybe find an editor who's looking to build a portfolio. If you want to be really professional about it, write a script, hire a camera and audition actors (who will work for free when they're starting out in exchange for something good they can add to their CVs and show-reels). This is exactly what author Gemma Burgess did for her novel *The Dating Detox*, and the result is a fantastic book trailer that is an excellent reflection of her book. And it's got thousands of views and helped her second book, *A Girl Like You*, become a bestseller.

If none of those options appeal to you, there's always Xtranormal. This is a website that lets you make animated movies simply by typing instructions. No technical knowledge is required whatsoever and if you use it well, it can make an excellent book trailer.

I don't recommend spending a lot of money on a book trailer, or any at all if you can help it. Buying your camera operator or actors lunch is one thing, but don't go paying a crew of people to produce a three-minute Hollywood-style movie of your book. As I said, I don't think views convert directly into sales and sinking money into something that isn't proven to sell books just isn't a good idea.

A word of warning: I recently saw somebody advertising their book-trailer-making talents online and charging a not insubstantial amount of money in exchange for them. What was laughable was that the trailer they'd made to show how great they were was *terrible*, and something I — or any other person who has figured Windows Movie Maker or iMovie out—could have knocked together in less than five minutes. What was even *more* laughable was that this person's own video book trailer, which they'd made for their novel, was even worse, and in my opinion could only serve to *dissuade* people from buying the book. My father turned 60 recently and for the occasion I made a little movie to play at the party, which basically consisted of a slideshow of photographs I'd scanned into my computer, playing to music. The people watching it thought it was a wondrous thing, but I knew it was just a simple slideshow, something anyone with a bit of patience could do. When you watch video book trailers, don't get distracted by their apparent shininess or sleekness. Ask yourself, what am I looking at? How was this done? I'll tell you right now, both my book trailers are only *slightly* more complicated affairs than a simple slideshow.

So please, don't get conned by people who only know a *tiny* little bit more about a thing than you do. Instead of paying them money they don't deserve, see if you can do it yourself first. You probably can, and you can probably do it better.

Video Blogs

If making a book trailer sounds too much like hard work or is beyond your technical capabilities, consider a video blog. You should be able to point your laptop's built-in camera in your direction (or plug a webcam into your PC), hit record and *go*.

Video blogs (or *vlogs*, if we're being painfully up to date) are just video versions of your blog posts: say what you would've otherwise typed out. The beauty of video blogs is that they can be much more exciting for your blog readers (as there's the novelty of hearing you speak and seeing you in the flesh) and you can show them things, like the room where you write, or the proof copy that just arrived, or your book launch shoes.

You can also work your video blogs into a series. Ali McNamara (*From Notting Hill With Love... Actually*) started a video diary when she signed the contract for her debut novel and then took her blog readers right the way through the experience until her book launch party. It was fantastic because it showed her meeting with her publicist, seeing her book getting printed and putting her proof copies in the space she'd reserved on her bookcase ever since she'd first dreamed of seeing a book of hers in print. Bestselling chick-lit author Miranda Dickinson (*Fairytale of New York*) is currently doing a video blog series called "A Year in the Life of a Book" where she takes her blog readers from writing the first draft through edits to seeing the cover, proof copies, etc. right up to the book being in stores.

I bought Ali's novel purely because after watching her video diaries, I wanted to see what the book was like, and I'll buy Miranda's new novel when it comes out towards the end of the year for the very same reason.

Twitter Events

As *Mousetrapped*'s release date got nearer and nearer, I was spending more and more time doing *Mousetrapped*-related things. This, in turn, gave me more and more *Mousetrapped* things to tweet about. Not all of these were promotional in motivation, but I was still afraid that I was bombarding my followers with yawn-inducing self-promotional tweets, or that they'd think I was. So I decided to put a cap on them, limit them to between 3–5 tweets one afternoon a week and label them for full disclosure, which I did with the hashtag **#mousetrappedmonday**.

I was amazed when what started off as a warning about me yapping on about my book (again) became a thing that people actually enjoyed, and got in on. They retweeted my #mousetrappedmonday tweets to their followers, and if I forgot to do it or did it late, they'd ask where it was.

To top everything off, I released the book on a Monday, making the final #mousetrappedmonday its publication day.

(I know. I'm like, *so* clever. Can I have a gold star?)

Twitter is the ideal venue for a virtual party, live discussion or giveaway. Set your imagination to work on how you might use it.

Meanwhile, On Facebook

The main purpose of your Facebook page is really to get as many interested people to "like" it as possible, and to keep those people updated about what's happening with your book.

Post links to your blog on the days you share the cover, first chapter, etc., upload photos of you proudly holding your proof copy and encourage interaction on the page by asking questions that encourage answers, e.g. *I'm trying to decide on a price for the paperback. What do you guys think? What do you normally pay for a paperback book?* If you have a Real World event like a book launch or signing, you can also list it as an "event" on Facebook. This enables you to invite specific people or leave it open to all, and attendees can RSVP.

Keep in mind that depending on the user's settings, if someone RSVPs to an event of yours, it'll be visible to all *their* friends on the profile page and maybe even in the News Feed. The same goes for answering questions, posting comments or "liking" photos and statuses. Therefore the more activity you encourage on your Facebook page, the more likely it is that even more people will find it.

When Does Me Promoting My Book Get Annoying?

Quickly, if you do it wrong. It's been my experience that you are far better off focusing on providing the internet with a quality blog and an entertaining or interesting tweet stream, rather than concentrating on getting people to buy your book. If you do the former well, the latter will take care of itself, to a point.

This is, again, where the idea of getting people to like *you* rather than your book comes into play.

I think there's a line, and you should be able to judge for yourself where that line is. Saying "don't promote your book in your tweet stream" is a needlessly broad statement, as Twitter is a great place to find out about new books I want to read and I wouldn't find out about them if everyone thought there was a rule about not mentioning them. There are also a number of writers I follow on Twitter purely because I want to know about their upcoming releases, signings, TV appearances, etc., because I'm a fan of theirs. But on the other side of the coin, there are writers I'm following because they're funny or they can always be counted upon for animals-as-humans YouTube videos, and if their stream suddenly becomes choked with tweets like "My book is out March 3. Just $9.99. Pre-order it here! PLEASE RT PLEASE RT PLEASE RT THANKS!" then I'll get annoyed.

If you're unsure where your line is, ask yourself:

- Why are all these people reading my blog and following me on Twitter and while I promote my book, *am I still giving them that?* (The most important question)
- What's the ratio of my promotional tweets to my non-promotional tweets? Does it seem high?
- Have I lost a significant number of followers or blog subscribers since I started promoting my book?
- Am I doing anything that when I see someone *else* doing it, it annoys me?
- Am I even starting to annoy *myself?* (Time to rethink your strategy!)

Remember too that all anybody is really interested in is themselves. A cynic's view of the world maybe, but a rule of thumb when it comes to advertising. Think about what your followers will ask themselves: Will *I* like this book? Will *my* money be well spent on it? What's in purchasing this book for *me?* So you have to make engaging in your self-promotion worth their while. This is where the content you're offering becomes an important factor.

I used to work in an office, and every so often someone from a stationery company would come around and try to sell me stuff, or get me to buy stuff in the future from them rather than someone else. Usually it was a guy in a suit with a sheet of A4 paper listing their special offers, or comparing their prices with a competitor. To which I would say, "Yeah, thanks" and then never think of them again. But sometimes a guy would come in with a sheet of A4 paper listing their offers, a glossy catalogue (I LOVE me a good stationery catalogue) and free stuff: notepads, pens and Post-Its all embossed with their logo and phone number. Since I was getting something out of the deal—free stationery, woo-hoo!—I would think of them whenever I next needed to place an order.

Online, you're selling *entertainment.* Tweeting a link to your Amazon listing is boring with a capital 'b' and doing it repeatedly, all day every day, is grounds for unfollowing. But tweeting a link to your book trailer which will give me something to do for three minutes and maybe even make me laugh, or showing me pictures of you holding your book in your hands for the first time (something we all dream of, and understand the excitement of) will entertain and maybe even inspire me, and I probably won't even notice that in doing so, you're trying to sell me a copy of your book.

What's My Goal Here?

Your book isn't for sale yet, so at this stage we're not trying to get people to run off and buy it. Our goal here is to build a group of supporters, friends and fans who will help us launch our book by helping us spread the word about it online, maybe even buying it, or both. (The people who do *that* get gold stars and our undying gratitude.) These are the people who will help pull our book out in front of the millions like it and shine a great big torch in its direction. We'll love them forever, and owe them *lots* of chocolate.

We want to:

- Let people know that your book exists and will be out soon, especially targeting people who might be interested in it because they're fans of that genre or interested in its subject matter
- Get these people to spread the word about our book, tell their friends, etc.
- Bring people along on our self-publishing ride so that when the book is released, they want to see how it turned out
- Build anticipation so when these same people realise the book is now on sale say, "Oh, I must get that! I've been looking forward to reading that book"
- Do all this without annoying, or worse, losing the people who love our blog and tweets but have no interest in buying our book.

Do not rush this step. One of the most common mistakes I see self-published authors make is telling us on Monday that they've a book coming out and then telling us on Tuesday where we can go buy it. This part needs time. It takes time to get used to Facebook, time to build real relationships on Twitter and with other bloggers, time to have any sort of readership at all stopping by your blog on a regular basis. You wouldn't get the painters in while your builders were digging the foundations, so don't release your book while you're still building anticipation about it. Wait.

One final word of author platform warning: this isn't about telling people stuff. It's about *connecting* with them. Try to remember that *before* you click "Send" on a "MY BOOK IS OUT SOON PLEASE PLEASE RT PLEASE RT THANKS OKAY LOVE YOU!" tweet.

Launching Your Book

This is crunch time. Sure, you've built a successful (and colour co-ordinated) blog, Twitter following and snazzy Facebook page, and you've produced a fabulous paperback and e-book that you're confident are as good as they can be, and you are clued up on every aspect of the book-selling experience. (And, most importantly, you haven't used the word "gatekeepers" once during the whole operation. Hooray!) You've even made some new friends who are kind enough to retweet links to your book-themed blog posts, offer support when you moan about the scourge that is e-book formatting and appreciate hilarious cat-themed YouTube videos as much you do. Maybe one or two of them have told you that they're looking forward to reading your book.

But all this will have been for nothing if you don't give your book the launch it deserves and needs. Think of your book's launch as its breakfast: if it ain't a good one packed with fibre, caffeine and that wholewheat stuff that releases energy slowly, then it's not going to set your book up for a very good day.

Rockets Versus Matchsticks

When it comes to your book's launch I have two golden rules for you that I discovered the hard way: (i) don't pick a specific date too far in advance and (ii) don't diffuse your own momentum.

We need to ensure that by the time we're telling people "My book is out March 14th" it'll actually be available to buy on March 14th, and that when we come to launch our book, we're lighting the engines of a Saturn V moonrocket and not desperately blowing on a damp matchstick.

The Problem With Being Specific

If I had my time over again, I wouldn't say anything more specific than "my book will be out in March." If pressed, I'd say, "my book will be out towards the end of March." Then I'd quietly upload my e-book and paperback files, wait for them to appear on Amazon, etc., make sure everything is absolutely perfect and ready to go, and then I'd set a launch date a week ahead, e.g. "My book is launching next Monday, March 29th." This takes the pressure off you, and will save you having many a sleepless night if something goes wrong and there's a not insignificant delay.

The alternative is disaster. Say my paperback listing *didn't* go live in time for my launch. I would have either had to tell everyone that the launch was postponed, or launch anyway but explain that only the e-book was ready to buy. Doing either of those things would have diffused the momentum I'd worked so hard to build up and turned what should have been an exciting launch into a damp squib. It would have looked amateur instead of professional, and I would've been *mortified*.

On our release date, we want the people we've got excited about our book saying to themselves, "Finally! That book I've really been looking forward to reading is out. I must go and get a copy." If we get enough people saying this, the excitement begins to spread and thus the excitement surrounding our book's release begins to gather momentum. If all we can do is get people to say, "I was looking forward to that book coming out... but now it's been delayed" or "I was going to buy that book today... but it's not available yet in the format I want", then you're just sticking a big fat needle in your own balloon.

Don't Diffuse Your Own Momentum

I've seen self-publishers do amazingly well at building up anticipation and excitement around their book and then ruin it all by telling me beforehand where I can go buy their book right now. I know that when your listings go live you want to scream it from the rooftops, but *don't*. Resist the urge and don't tell anyone. If they find it, then so be it, but chances are they won't go looking until you tell them that it's time to. Every day of the week I see a self-publisher on Twitter say something like, "The e-book of [TITLE] is available now — the paperback should be out by my launch day!" and every time they do, they let a little air out of their balloon.

A good balloon needs to be filled with air, and a good launch needs to be filled with *concentrated anticipation*. Save everything for your big day, i.e. the day of its release. Think of it this way: you're opening a new clothing store and you've set your opening date for May 1st. On opening day you plan to have special offers, free champagne and finger food for customers, and the first twenty-five people in the door will get vouchers to use in store. You're doing all this because you want opening day to be an exciting event that everyone's talking about, one the local newspapers and radio stations are covering. This will help spread the word about your shop, and ensure a steady flow of customers in your opening weeks. Are you going to open your shop beforehand and put things on special offer? Are you going to hand out those vouchers in dribs and drabs? Are you going to offer champagne and finger food every day? No, because if you did, it wouldn't be anything special. It would just be what you do every day. And what you do every day isn't exciting, and it certainly isn't news.

But That's Not What the Professionals Do!

A traditionally published author will in all likelihood spend their publication date at home, signing for the flowers their publisher sent, drinking a celebratory glass of champagne and then writing 2,000 words of their next book. They'll have told their Twitter followers about their

Amazon listing months ago, or as soon as it could be pre-ordered, and they'll have already blogged about their new e-book. They can do this because they'll have a launch party, interviews, TV appearances, signings and other events coming up that will help spread the news that their book exists, and you can now go buy it. Even if they're *not* doing any of these things, their books are still in bookstores, where I might happen upon it during my weekly browse.

You and your book, on the other hand, only have the opportunities you can create for yourself, which will probably be confined — for now anyway — to social media. People cannot chance upon your book; they can either hear about it from you or from someone who heard about it from you (for the most part). You need to grasp hold of anything you can which will give you something to blog about, tweet about or post as a status on your Facebook wall, and this means making an event out of your release date.

The good news is that you can be at home drinking champagne *and* blogging at the same time.

Reviews

Reviews are both the best thing and the worst thing about sending something you wrote out into the world. I've had reviews so wonderful they've made me cry, and reviews so scathing that I've felt as if someone reached into my chest, pulled out my heart and tore it to shreds right in front of me. (And if you're about to tell me not to take it personally, you clearly haven't yet experienced the acidic, burning pain of a bad review.) Thing is, reviews are *very* important to self-published books; much more so than they are to their traditionally published counterparts. With no editor or agent to vet the quality of the work, the potential customer has to look elsewhere for promises of quality. Your cover is one, your blog or website is another — even how your Amazon listing is laid out can sway a person's mind. But none are as convincing (or as condemning) as your book's reviews. A 2012 survey of self-publishers also found that the most successful self-publishers had, on average, won three times as many reviews for their books as their less successful counterparts.

There are three types of reviews we're going to talk about here:

- **Blurbs and endorsements**, where someone important is happy to lend their stamp of approval to your book, usually pre-release
- **Reviewer reviews**, which for self-publishers usually means getting impartial book bloggers to read and review your book
- **Amazon customer reviews**.

NB: *Never* pay for a review. There are services out there run by everyone from off-shoots of well-known literary reviews to callous cowboys, offering to impartially review your book for a fee. Not only is this a gigantic waste of money, but the resulting "reviews" are likely to be far less impressive than those you'll get from your actual readers.

Blurbs And Endorsements

Blurbs and endorsements are short quotes from People Who Matter that you can use to convince the book-buying public that your book is indeed the bee's knees.

These are normally sought pre-publication so that the blurb can go on the cover of the book or inside it. (That's where those Advanced Reader Copies, or ARCs, come in.)

A Person Who Matters, or a PWM, if you will, for the purposes of blurbs and endorsements, is:

- a famous or well-known author, highly-respected and/or selling loads of books
- a highly-regarded expert in a field related to your book
- a well-known, respected newspaper, magazine or literary review.

Even though the following people may be important to *you*, they are so *un*important when it comes to endorsing your book that they are basically irrelevant:

- your mother
- your best friend who reads, like, *all* the time
- anyone who the majority of the book-buying public has never heard of (with *one* exception, which we'll come to).

Let's look at some examples of this blurbing business that I found on my own bookshelves:

- On the cover of *You're Next* by Gregg Hurwitz, *New York Times* bestselling thriller writer Harlan Coben says "Pure stay-up-all-night suspense"
- On the cover of *If I Never See You Again* by Niamh O'Connor, internationally bestselling crime writer Tess Gerritsen says, "Gripping, terrifying. If you like Martina Cole, you'll love this" (which is a double-whammy, because Martina Cole is also a bestselling crime writer!)

- On the cover of *Mennonite in a Black Dress* by Rhoda Janzen, phenomenon starter, recipient of much Oprah love and author of *Eat, Pray, Love*, Elizabeth Gilbert says, "Not just beautiful and intelligent but also painfully — even wincingly — funny"
- On the cover of *Postcards from the Heart* by Ella Griffin, mega-mega-selling author and reigning queen of chick-lit, Marian Keyes, says, "A fresh, funny voice. Ella Griffin can make you laugh and then cry in the turn of a page"
- On the cover of *The Immortal Life of Henrietta Lacks* by Rebecca Skloot, author of the Booker Prize winning *Wolf Hall* Hilary Mantel says, "No dead woman has done more for the living... A fascinating, harrowing, necessary book"
- On the cover of *The Redbreast* by Jo Nesbo, the *Independent* newspaper says, "The next Stieg Larsson" [Editorial note: he's not — he's better!]
- On the cover of *The Demon in the Freezer* by Richard Preston, the *New York Times* says, "[Preston] turns a story about science and medicine into a theme-park ride of a thriller"

and finally, in what is by far, far, *far* my favourite example:

- On the cover of *Moondust: In Search of the Men Who Fell to Earth* by Andrew Smith, the late Arthur C. Clarke, author of *2001: A Space Odyssey*, simply says, "Splendid!"(Sometimes just one word is enough if the right person is saying it!)

Thing is, as a self-published author, you can't just run off and *ask* for these blurbs, in that you can't just fire off an e-mail to, say, Stephen Fry, and ask him if he'd read and endorse your book. (Well you *could*, of course, but I'm guessing you wouldn't get a reply.) Chances are you will only get one of these if you know a PWM. Here in Ireland, this might actually be the case, what with everyone being about half a degree of separation away from everyone else, but it might also be the case if you've been making blogging and Twitter friends. Are any of them PWMs? Do you think they'd consider it? Could you ask without not being able to sleep for a week beforehand because you're so sick over the thought of asking? Then maybe you'll get a PWM to write an endorsement for your book. *Maybe.*

I said there was one exception to your PWM being a name recognised by a the majority of the book-buying public, and that's if they're an expert or highly-respected leader in a field related to your book. Then whether or not they're a household name doesn't really matter, as long as you can relate their PWM status alongside the blurb.

Let's pretend you've written a novel in which the central character has mental health problems, and you deal with that issue in a realistic and sensitive way. In that case, you could get someone prominent in the field of psychology to write a blurb. As long as you could quantify who they were, you could put that blurb on your cover.

For example:

"A heartbreakingly sensitive portrayal of manic depression that, while fiction, will surely help the ever-growing number of very real sufferers of this condition out there today."

-- Prof. Stephen Jones
Dean of Psychology at Johns Hopkins University

With cover blurbs and endorsements, **it's not so much** *what* **the quote says (because they're all positive; otherwise they wouldn't be used) as** *who* **is saying it**. That's what lends weight to the endorsement, and what convinces the potential reader to go ahead and buy.

In my experience, this crucial difference is the bit that self-published authors struggle to grasp, or ignore altogether. You can put the best sentence that anyone has ever said about any book in the history of the world on your front cover, but it won't matter a damn unless we know the person who said it. (And I don't mean know because you tell us. I mean know because they're a PWM.)

Take the professor's blurb above. Using *the exact same review,* here are three ways that this review would sink into irrelevancy on the cover of your book.

"A heartbreakingly sensitive portrayal of manic depression that, while fiction, will surely help the ever-growing number of very real sufferers of this condition out there today."

-- Stephen Jones

"A heartbreakingly sensitive portrayal of manic depression that, while fiction, will surely help the ever-growing number of very real sufferers of this condition out there today."

-- Stephen Jones,
Undergraduate at Lancaster University's Psychology Department*

"A heartbreakingly sensitive portrayal of manic depression that, while fiction, will surely help the ever-growing number of very real sufferers of this condition out there today."

-- Stephen Jones. He reads like, a LOT, so he'd know.

*This isn't a dig at Lancaster University, by the way, where I was once an undergraduate myself for three whole weeks.

Or take these *actual* "endorsements" I've seen on self-published books (I'm not kidding; these are real):

"Funny and original. I read it all in one go."—*Jack, aged 16*

"I am your number one fan."—Emily, Manchester

"A magical journey into a wonderful land. Brilliant!"—Person with Same Last Name as the Author

They don't have *quite* the same gravitas, now do they?

Some people know some people who are famous, and they think that getting them to say something about their book is a good idea. If this Someone Famous is in no way connected to books, or is only connected to them because once upon a time they hired a ghost writer to scribble their autobiography, then no, it's not. And it's not clever either. This is the fictionalised equivalent of a review I saw on a self-published book recently:

"This book has pages in it. Hooray!"

— *Justin Timberlake*

(To be clear: this is *fictionalised*, but inspired by real events. I did see a self-published book that had a pointless review on it from a musician. No real Justin Timberlakes were used in the making of this example.)

If you think after reading all that that the chances of you getting a blurb or endorsement for your book that passes the PWM test are between slim and none, then you'd be right. It is almost a certainty that you won't, unless you've had the foresight to make friends with Stephen King in the last twelve months. So why am I telling you all this if there's little to no hope of it applying to you?

Because self-publishers *love* putting blurbs and reviews on their covers by non-PWMs. And putting a non-PWM endorsement on your cover might do worse than just not matter—it might actually *harm* your book's chances of getting read, because the subconscious message you send out by doing it is that you don't know *what* you're doing, and that doesn't bode well for the rest of your work, i.e. the book itself. So unless your blurb is from a certifiable PWM, don't put it on the cover of your book.

Some blurbs and endorsements can be neither irrelevant nor from PWMs. These could be reviews from traditionally published authors who aren't household names, self-published authors who have sold a gazillion books but who nobody's ever heard of, or from bloggers and blogs.

Getting these is *great* and we're going to use them to do fantastic stuff, but they don't belong on your cover.

And now, on Catherine's Cynics' Corner...

Yes, I know: a lot of the super famous authors who write blurbs for books are paid to do so, and many of them don't even bother reading the books before they put their names to endorsements of them.

They don't have the time, and the publishers don't care what they say anyway—they just want their name on the cover. And if that isn't the case, then the new author is likely to be one of the mega-selling author's friends or have photographs of them that could potentially be very damaging if they ever got out. And, yes, sometimes when you buy a book because your favourite author told you on the cover that it is the greatest book he'd ever read, it turns out to be about as entertaining as a big pile of poo, and even less memorable.

YES, I AM WELL AWARE OF THIS, thank you.

But what has any of this got to do with *you*? You are a self-publishing author, in case you've forgotten, because the making of your paperback and e-book was, like, two whole sections ago, and you need to do everything you can to convince people that your book is better than the majority of self-published books, i.e. not crap, and, on top of that, that it's something they want to read and will hand over their hard-earned cash in order to buy.

Getting Your Book Reviewed

The best way for a self-published author to help launch their book and secure its subsequent success is to offer review copies of their book to:

- book bloggers
- other bloggers
- genre-specific book review sites, e.g. crime or chick-lit websites
- published authors they know with blogs
- owners of websites related to their book
- Amazon Top Reviewers

and put the resulting reviews (if they're good!) on places like a "Reviews" page on their dedicated book site, the "News" section of their blogsite and in the "Editorial Reviews" section of their Amazon listing. They can also quote from these reviews on promotional material, such as press releases, or even on a "Praise for..." page in their next book.

In the first edition of this book, I advised against offering e-book review copies. A year ago most book bloggers, reviewers, etc. refused to accept e-books to review, and I felt that offering them one sent a message to the reviewer that their time wasn't "worth" the cost of one of my paperbacks to me. But things change fast in the book world, so now my advice would be:

- **To offer at least a small number of paperback ARCs** that you've had made by CreateSpace (with Cover Creator, if you want) if possible. You could send these to the reviewers who matter to you the most, i.e. a reviewer who you think is likely to actually review your book and whose review would be widely read by people interested in books like yours. If you are only releasing your book in e-book, this review-only ARC idea also works for you.
- **To offer e-books, not PDFs.** PDFs are not e-books. They're PDFs. They're difficult to read on most e-reading devices—if the devices read them at all—and the only alternative is to read them on your computer, which is not ideal. Instead, upload your book to Smashwords and, after conversion, download an ePub and .mobi (Kindle) version to your hard drive. (You can download your own books for free from Smashwords whenever you're logged in.) If this is weeks or months before your intended release date, just click "unpublish" once you've done so, preventing anyone else from buying them; when you're ready to release, you can just come back and click "publish" again. Now you can send these Smashwords edition to reviewers via e-mail as attachments, just like you would any other file.
- **To not send anything else.** At least once a week I get an e-mail from a newly self-published author offering me a coupon that will allow me to download their book from Smashwords for free. (Smashwords allows authors to generate coupons offering percentage discounts to readers, including 100% discounts that translate into free books.) Would you send an agent a link to a website where he or she could go read your manuscript? No. You'd just send it to them, because when it comes to them reading and liking your work the odds are already stacked against you, so you don't want to add any additional hurdles that might make things even worse. So don't send coupons. Send the book.

NB: It is perfectly acceptable to send out copies of your book for review before the text has been finalised, i.e. before your proofreader is finished, as long as (i) you make it clear to the reader and (ii) the copy editor has already completed his or her work. Just put something like "uncorrected review copy—not intended for sale" at the front of your paperback or at the top of your e-book document. In the publishing world reviews are collected months before the release date; reviewers are used to receiving ARCs with simplistic covers and a few typos here and there.

Bad Review Attitude Syndrome

I just took a very deep breath because writing this section is going to be very, very hard for me to do without GETTING VERY MAD and directing that madness at you, dear innocent reader. I do apologise. It's just that I have seen some horrors in my time in this self-published-authors-trying-to-get-reviewed arena, let me tell you, and I have seen for myself the reaction of self-publishing authors' faces when I tell them how they have to go about this business of getting their book reviewed.

A great number of self-publishers I have encountered in my time (and I concede that maybe I just need to change the places where I hang out) have held one or more of the following beliefs about getting their book reviewed:

- by giving away a free copy of my book I am depleting my profit, so I don't want to do it
- if someone wants to read and review my book, they can go and buy a copy
- to save money, I'll only offer PDFs of my book to review—that'll do
- by giving someone a free copy of my book, I am doing *them* a favour
- I only want to give copies to bloggers who have a minimum number of monthly hits; otherwise I'm just wasting my time
- since they didn't even *pay* for my book, the least they can do is give it a positive review.

Now that, my friends, is just horse faeces. FACT. And here's another fact: **when you give someone your book and they review it for you, *they* are doing *you* a favour**. It's *never* the other way around.

Think for a second about what the reviewer does. First, they choose to read your book over the piles and piles of other books they've received to review. If you don't believe in the piles and piles, consider this: I'm *extremely* small fry in the book-blogging world, and I currently have six books piled up that need to be read and reviewed. And when you get a book to review, you don't *have* to review it, so the reviewer has decided to spend their limited reading time on your book above others. Then the reviewer spends anything from four to eight hours of their life reading your book, and then another hour or two thinking about what they thought of it, and then another hour on top of that putting those thoughts into words in the form of a written review. If the reviewer is a book blogger, they then have to turn this review into a blog post and put it up on their site. If they aren't strictly a book blogger but just review books as part of their personal blog (like I am and do), then they are giving your book a post that they would otherwise use for their own cause. And even if they *are* strictly a book blogger, they're still doing all this for *free*, and just because they love books and reading them.

And if that doesn't convince you, then let's look at it this way: what do the professionals do? We are trying to come across as professional authors, so let's see what professional authors—or their publishing houses—do to get their books reviewed.

A few months ago I received an e-mail from a book publicist who had come across a review of *The Snowman* by Jo Nesbo that I'd posted on my blog. She said that she too had read *The Snowman*, and thought that if I enjoyed that, then perhaps I'd be interested in reading a crime novel by a debut author that was coming out in a month or two, and a crime novel by an author already established in another genre. She included brief blurbs of both these books, and invited me to e-mail her back if I'd like to receive copies of them to review. She also said that she realised that I was probably "inundated" with review copies and would understand if I didn't get around to them; there was no obligation to ultimately review. I did e-mail her, and she did send them. Each came with a single A4 page that told me a little bit more about the book, a little bit more about the author and logistical details like when it was going to be published, in what format, etc. I never had to contact her again but I did, just as a courtesy, when I posted the review of the first book on my blog. I still haven't got around to reading the other one, but it's not out yet, so I still have some time to get to it. But if I never get to it, it's not a problem.

Now I will acknowledge that there is one major difference between a traditional publishing house and you, a self-published author: *money*. Obviously you do not have the resources to send out hundreds of copies of your book to people who may never review them; you and your budget (and profit) just can't afford to take a hit like that.

But here is what you *can* afford to do, and what I highly recommend: **send between 10–50 copies of your book to people who you think are** *likely* **to ultimately post a review on a website, blog or on Amazon.**

Remember, this isn't "lost" money. Far from it. We're going to get great mileage out of any reviews we get, and that's not even considering how many new readers we may get just by people hearing about our book through these reviewers posting about it on their blogs or websites.

And if you claim you can't afford to send ten copies of your book out to potential reviewers in a move that will practically guarantee that many sales and potentially many times more than that, then I have *no idea* why you got into this self-publishing thing in the first place.

The Reviewing Principles

Here are the principles I strongly recommend you abide by as you seek reviews of your book:

- *There is never any obligation to review.* Never send out a copy of your book in exchange for a review. If they find the time to review it, great, but if not, we'll all still be friends.

- *There is never any obligation to write a positive review.* Do you want a review, or do you want your ego stroked? The whole point of reviews is to find out what books are like. Lies are not only pointless (because they'll soon be found out and then cast a very bad light on both the lying reviewer and the egotistical author) but dishonest. Book bloggers are very professional people; if they don't like your book, they'll explain why and they'll be more than reasonable about it. Them not liking your book is just a chance you'll have to take.

- *There is never any obligation to be timely, or work to a schedule.* Yes, it would be nice if they could read and review your book before it comes out or before you send out that e-mail in which you want to put all the quotes, but you can't ask them to. They'll get around to it whenever they can.

- *You find reviewers, reviewers don't find you.* If you send out a tweet saying something like, "Anyone interested in reviewing my book hit me up for a PDF!" then you can be sure that you'll get lots of people reading and perhaps even reviewing your book, but who will these people be? Publishing houses sometimes tweet looking for book bloggers, but as I've already said, you do not have their resources. You need to be a bit more discerning, so you need to go looking for reviewers. Also, don't expect them to do the legwork of finding you.

- *If you use the review, link back to it.* If you put the review somewhere, be it a quote or the whole thing, make sure you link back to wherever the review was originally posted, i.e. the book blogger's blog. Similarly, if you put the review anywhere offline, credit the reviewer and include their blog address, like: "Thoroughly enjoyable. I'll be looking out for this author in the future." -- *Romance Central, www.romance-central.co.uk.*

- *Say thank you.* ALWAYS thank reviewers for reviewing your book; being courteous goes a very long way. Either leave a comment on the review if it was posted on a blog or website, send them a thank-you tweet or do your thanking in an e-mail.

Finding Reviewers

The easiest way to find potential reviewers for your book is to google "review" and the name of a recently published book that's very similar to yours. You should be able to see in the search results book review websites and book bloggers who reviewed the book, and then you can e-mail them to see if they'd be interested in reviewing yours.

This is also where your blogging and Twitter friends can be a HUGE help. Offer them review copies. Since you've been subjecting them to blog posts about the book for the last six months, they'll definitely read it just to see how it turned out. (And — bonus — shut you up about it too!)

If your book has a very specific subject matter, search online for websites, podcasts, forums or online magazines devoted to that subject, and then contact them to see if they'd like a copy.

To give you some idea of who I targeted to review *Mousetrapped*, here is a selection of them (not all of them wrote reviews):

- An author who was looking for prizes to give away on her blog; I sent her a copy for herself as well, and she wrote a post about it
- A journalist with a blog that reviewed memoirs
- Two 'chick-lit' review blogs that also review non-fiction
- The book blogger of a site specialising in women travelling
- The editor of a newsletter that lists work-travel opportunities
- The editor of a directory about working abroad to which I had contributed
- A website that reviews all genres of books, TV and movies
- A Disney news blog
- A Disney podcaster.

Amazon's Top Reviewers

You can find Amazon's Top Reviewers — the Amazon customers who review the most and whose reviews get the most helpful votes—on (surprise, surprise) Amazon. There are two top reviewers lists: the best contributors at this moment in time, and "Hall of Famers" based on all time contributions. If you go to Amazon.com, you can find both lists here: **http://www.amazon.com/review/top-reviewers**

Each Top Reviewer has a profile, and it's links to these profiles that appear in the list. In order to find suitable reviewers for your book, you'll have to investigate the reviewer's previous reviews (to see if they read books like yours) and you'll have to find reviewers who include their e-mail address in their public profiles (so you can contact them). This process, therefore, is extremely time-consuming, but if even *one* Top Reviewer reviews your book, it'll be worth the effort, because not only will you have a review of your book, but that review will be by someone who Amazon customers know they can trust.

Skip the *New York Times*

Here is as good a place as any to explain to you why the *New York Times* isn't going to review your book. Well actually, the *NYT* isn't going to review your book for lots of reasons, so let's just concentrate on a local or national paper where you live instead. Why are books reviewed in the press? It's not for the good of the newspaper's health, let me assure you. No—it's for the readers of the newspaper, just like the rest of the stuff in there. And the space allocated to book reviews is small as it is and shrinking all the time, so why would they review a book that their readers cannot find in bookstores? Why would they review a book that has zero hope of making an impact on the bestseller lists because it's not in bookstores? And why would you, as an author who is almost totally focused on activities online, even pursue this "Real World" review?

Don't send copies of your books to newspapers and magazines unless it's in a significant number of brick-and-mortar bookstores; that *is* a waste of money.

How To Ask

Once you've found your book reviewers, you now need to contact them to see if they'd like a copy of your book. E-mail works best for this; I wouldn't approach reviewers on Twitter or Facebook.

If you can't find an e-mail address, see if they have a "Contact" page or form on their site.

Here is the kind of e-mail you should write:

Dear [first name]

I recently published *Mousetrapped: A Year and A Bit in Orlando, Florida*, a travel memoir of the eighteen months I spent living in Orlando and working in Walt Disney World.

As book blogger for RelevantSite.com, I wondered if you might be interested in reading it?

If so, I'd be happy to send you a complimentary copy. There is, of course, no obligation to review but if you like it, you might consider mentioning it in one of your posts. But as I said, there is <u>no obligation</u>.

You can read the synopsis below and, if you wish, find out more about the book at mousetrappedbook.com.

If you are interested in receiving a copy, please forward a postal address and I will mail one to you immediately.

Kind regards,
Me

or

Dear [first name]

I saw your review of [similar book] on RelevantSite.com and wondered if you'd be interested in a copy of my travel memoir, *Mousetrapped: A Year and A Bit in Orlando, Florida*.

If so, I'd be happy to send one to you. There is, of course, no obligation to review but if you like it, you might consider mentioning it in one of your posts. But as I said, there is <u>no obligation</u>.

You can read the synopsis below and, if you wish, find out more about the book at mousetrappedbook.com. If you are interested in receiving a copy, please forward a postal address and I will mail one to you immediately.

Kind regards,
Me

If you have any proof that you're a good writer or that this book is more likely to be good than bad, put it in here.
Like:

Dear [first name]

I saw your review of [similar book] on RelevantSite.com and wondered if you'd be interested in a copy of my novel, *Title Goes Here*.

If so, I'd be happy to send one to you. There is, of course, no obligation to review but if you like it, you might consider mentioning it in one of your posts. But as I said, there is no obligation.

You can read the synopsis below and, if you wish, find out more about the book at titlegoeshere.com.

A little bit about me: I've been writing short stories for several years, and have had them published in the likes of *Short Story Magazine*, *Stories People Have Written* and *Snooty Literary Stuff Monthly*. While a student of Very Famous University's English Literature department, I was shortlisted for the Famous Short Story Award and last year, placed second in Equally Famous Write a Novel competition. Famous Author of Books Like Mine, who was on the judging panel, said of *Title Goes Here* that it was "an accomplished début whose ending left me bereft."

If you are interested in receiving a copy, please forward a postal address and I will mail one to you immediately.

Kind regards,
Me

Here is the kind of e-mail you should NOT write:

Dear Blogger,

I really need to get my book mentioned on RelevantSite.com and am wondering if you're the person to make that happen. If you are, I'd be happy to send you a FREE copy of my book, *Mousetrapped: A Year and A Bit in Orlando, Florida*.

Before I do though, I'm going to need a guarantee that you will post a review of it. Perhaps you could send me your passport? I'll send it back after my (positive!) review goes live. I also need you to do it ASAP. Like, yesterday. I got bills, y'know?

I'm also gonna need a signed declaration—notarised, obviously—that you'll accompany my review with links to my blog, website, Twitter feed, Facebook profile, Flickr albums and Goodreads page, and that you won't use any photos of me in which my left side predominantly features.

That's what's up.

LATERS,
Me

And just because I'm still reeling in shock, this is an e-mail I received last week asking for a review — and this is the e-mail in its *entirety*:

Catherine,

My book, *Yes, This is Happening*, needs to be read.

Seriously. That was it. No sign-off, no further information about the book, not even a *link*. I mean... REALLY?!

When To Do It

If you're being *super* organised about this and have printed up ARCs especially, I would say three months before your planned release date.

(Was *I* this organised? Excuse me for a moment while I roll around on the floor laughing, would you?)

In reality, any time from then until about a month after your book is published is fine.

Should I Say I'm Self-Published?

This is a tricky one. Some might not want your book based on this fact alone (and we can't say it's unfair because it is a fact, plain and simple, that the majority of self-published books are stinky poop), and in fact some book-blogging sites specify that they do not review self-published books. But the self-published world is losing its stigma more and more every day, so you never know, it might not be a problem for most reviewers in the future.

I would say check if the site says anything about it, and if they say they don't review self-published books, then don't approach them with yours. Otherwise you don't have to point it out, but don't lie about it either. Notice in my e-mail example I said "I recently published..." which doesn't contain the phrase "self-published" but is the truth: I'm the one who published the book.

Chances are the reviewer will click on the link to your book site or blog and use what they find there to decide. And because we've all worked so very hard to look *professional,* chances are it will convince them to say *yes.*

Do NOT consider lying. What would be the point?

Sending The Review Copy

If someone says, "Why yes! I'd love to read your book!" then send out a copy of your book no later than the very next day.

(It goes without saying that should you not be in a position to send a copy of your book out the very next day, then you shouldn't be sending reviewers e-mails yet! But I've said it anyway.)

If you're sending a paperback, make sure the book is in perfect condition, and new. CreateSpace covers are glossy and collect fingerprints; give it a wipe with a cloth before you put it in the envelope. I even went so far as to buy polybags (the clear plastic envelopes that seal at the top that handmade greeting cards tend to come in) that I then put my paperbacks in before I sent them out, but then maybe you're not as crazy about books being perfect as me. (And polybags add more expense, so just get a cloth!) And while we're on the subject of envelopes, use a big enough one. Don't stuff your book in there because when it's opened at the other end, the corners will be destroyed and the book itself might be bent.

Put what we'll call an *information sheet* in with the book. This is one single sheet of paper that has your author bio, a synopsis and contact details on it. Jazz it up with photos and colour too if you can, but only colours that co-ordinate (of course!) with the colours of your book. If you're sending an e-book, attach this to the e-mail in PDF.

Never send review copies by registered post or courier service. Not because it's more expensive (although it is) but because packages like that have to be signed for, and if our potential reviewer is out at their 9-5, they'll have to traipse to the post office to pick up your book.

Your Book Getting Reviewed

With any luck, people other than the ones you've sent free copies to will also be reading your book, i.e. the ones who went out and bought it, and chances are a few of them will log on to Amazon afterwards, click that "Create Your Own Review" button and start typing. Some of these people will have liked your book; some of them won't have. Some of these people will write balanced, fair reviews; some of them won't. And some of them will go on there to give *your book* a one-star review because *Amazon* delivered it a day late, or because even though they haven't read the book, they don't like the sound of it and wished you would write fiction instead.

You'll have a honeymoon period where logging on to Amazon will be a nice experience, one that fills you with warmth. (Or perhaps the sun of a thousand springtime mornings.) Then one day you'll hit the enter button and something will look different to you. At first, you won't know what it is that's changed. And then you'll see it: your average star review, the one that's on top of the listing next to your title and is the average of all your reviews, will have lost a star. And then you'll scroll down, your stomach churning, your body covered in a cold sweat, your heart thumping in your ears, and you'll see it, right there...

A one-star review.

Someone doesn't like your book. Reading the text of the review, it becomes clear that they didn't just not like your book, they *hated* it. They detested it. They wished that the trees that died so it could live could be reborn and your book could take their place. They feel about you as a writer as they would you as a person if you drowned their puppy and made them watch, and made other puppies watch too. And while you did it you were laughing. *Hard.*

There is nothing that compares to this feeling, and having 4,124 five-star reviews beside it doesn't do anything to lessen the blow. That's the bad news. The good news is that everyone gets reviews like these— *everyone* does—and there are ways in which we can train ourselves not to take too much notice.

Before we move on I should specify that I'm not talking here about negative reviews, or three-star-out-of-five reviews. Your book is not going to be universally liked. It can't be; we don't all like the same things. What I'm talking about here are *baaaaad* reviews, vehement reviews, nasty reviews—reviews that are written in a tone that, you imagine, conveys that the author of the review would rather you die than produce another book.

(Yes, people really do leave reviews on Amazon that read like that. I've even had the pleasure of getting one of them myself. To which I can only say, *it's just a book* and, *have you considered anger management?*)

How To Avoid Baaaaad Reviews

Write a book that everyone will love and/or avoid reading your reviews.

Although I have yet to encounter a writer who has managed to do either; if you know of one, do let me know.

How To Handle Baaaaad Reviews

Here's what I recommend you do to combat the my-world-is-caving-in feeling of reading bad reviews:

- Print out or photocopy a review of your book that you really like from a source you explicitly trust and/or one whom you recall has raved about books you've loved and been blasé about the same books you've given up on. Stick it somewhere prominent, or in multiple somewheres prominent. Maybe even put an emergency copy in your wallet. Force yourself to read it immediately after the encounter of a bad review.

- Look up a book you adored on Amazon and read its reviews. This is always a good one, if only because the reasons people come up with to dislike books never cease to amaze me, not to mention the imaginative insults they heap on it afterwards. Remind yourself that you loved this book and yet BigReader874124 thought it was "not good enough to wipe my arse with in a no-toilet paper emergency—I'd rather use my hand." You can't please everyone. (And why would you want to?)
- Look up the reviewer's other reviews. On Amazon especially, this can be a very soothing exercise. Maybe they gave *Freedom* one star because it didn't have any pictures, or maybe they slated *Little Women* for false advertising once they discovered it wasn't actually about vertically-challenged females. Or maybe they thought *Never Let Me Go*, one of your favourite books of all time ever, was not good enough to wipe their arse with in a no-toilet paper emergency.
- Write a response. Bad reviews tend to linger with us because we are passionately arguing with them in our heads. *I didn't mean it literally! You took that out of context! I really did do that! You obviously don't understand what I was getting at! Did you even read the blurb? Did you even read the book?!* So put a stop to this by sitting down and typing out a response. Then delete it.
- If all else fails, pour yourself a stiff drink and ask anyone who'll listen, 'Did *she* write a book? No. I didn't *think* so."

How Not To Handle Baaaaad Reviews

Sending severed horses' heads round to these reviewers' homes á la *The Godfather* is frowned upon, I believe. Also it can get kind of messy.

The only thing to do about these kinds of reviews is nothing at all. *Don't* respond to them. Don't get (too) upset about them. And whatever you do, don't start your writing day by re-reading them.

But What If They're REALLY Baaaaad?

If a review violates Amazon's Review Guidelines then you can report the review, either through Amazon Author Central or by clicking the "Report Abuse" button underneath the review.

Common violations include:

- The reviewer admitting that they either didn't read the book at all or didn't finish it, e.g. "I couldn't even bring myself to read past page 5 this book was so terrible"
- The reviewer using the review to make a point about something unrelated, e.g. "I'm never ordering anything from this seller ever again. They delivered it a week late AND they charged me twice for it"
- Revealing crucial plot points or other spoilers. "I was enjoying it up until, three pages from the end, the main character died."

Amazon also says that making spiteful remarks about the author is a violation of its guidelines, but from what I've seen in my own and other authors' reviews, this is not something they enforce or make any effort to counteract. Or perhaps their definition of spiteful is just different to mine.

Aside from reviews that are really about the company who fulfilled them and spoilers that might well ruin the reading experience for a future reader, I wouldn't take any action against Amazon customer reviews of your book. It's a slippery slope, and you don't want to become the kind of author who does everything they can to keep all but four- and five-star reviews off their books' listings — or worse, become *known* as the kind of author who does. And the people who leave poisonous reviews are not the kind who are likely to take the removal of their poisonous reviews lying down; taking action might make the situation worse, and more widespread as they take their poison pen to their blog, their Facebook page and Twitter.

You also don't *need* to do anything about them, because most customers do not pay attention to extreme opinions, be they good or bad, and Amazon has a pretty good process for sorting the useful reviews, i.e. the balanced and honest ones, from the too-good-to-be-trues and the too-bad-to-be-reals.

When you view an Amazon listing, the review you see at the top is the "most helpful" review by default. This means that other customers have deemed it helpful by clicking "yes" next to the "Was this review helpful?" question just below it, or that a greater of number of people have clicked "yes" than have clicked "no." Comments left on reviews can also be voted upon, although the question is "Do you think this adds to the discussion?" In this way, the most helpful — or fair — review rises to the top in a kind of natural selection, albeit an elected kind.

As an Amazon customer, I know I don't take much or any notice of reviews on a product unless there's fifty of them and they are *all* bad. If I do read the reviews, I tend to side with the middle-of-the-road verdicts, the three-star reviews that say what they liked and didn't like about the book, and say it in a reasonable tone that doesn't make me think the author drowned their puppies and made them watch. And I don't think I've ever gone onto Amazon to purchase a book and then stopped because the product had negative reviews, even if, on a couple of occasions, I lived to regret it.

I was watching *The Daily Show* host Jon Stewart being interviewed by Oprah recently (one Big O Disciple, right here) and he said something really interesting that I think you should try to apply to your reviews. Oprah asked him what he thought of his almost rock-star status among certain groups (college students, for instance) and he said he thought there were people who liked him too much and people who hated him too much, and that the truth was probably somewhere in the middle. This is how I try to take my reviews. I've had some so gushing they make me blush and worry that other people will think I've bribed their authors, and some so bad I feel like entering the Witness Protection Program might be the only way to recover from them. But I think the truth of how good or bad my book actually is lies somewhere in the middle. And I'm happy with that.

Finally, getting bad reviews feels terrible, but the only way to avoid them is to not write any book at all, and I don't care what anyone says about me, my writing or the things I choose to write about: I know that that scenario would feel far, *far* worse.

E-mailed Praise

One of the nicest things about having a book out there in the world is opening your e-mail account and discovering messages from readers in far off lands, telling you how much they loved your book. Now I have no idea how many of these messages I've got, but I can tell you this for a fact: it's a hell of a lot more than I've got Amazon reviews.

Now I *love* those e-mails—I print them out and file them in a Break Open in Case of Loss of Confidence in Writing Emergency—but I sometimes wonder, if these people love my book so much and they took the time to e-mail me about it, why don't they take five minutes to give it an Amazon review and tell everyone else? As I've already said, Amazon reviews are *so* important to self-published authors, I can't stress it enough. They can make or break a sale. And so sometimes, especially after I've just got a bad or low-starred review, I come *really* close to responding to one of these messages and asking, politely, if they'd consider putting their praise in public. But I don't, because I'm afraid that I'll offend them. (And the one time I *did* do it, the praiser never posted a review. So I assumed she was offended, and never did it again.)

But I *should* and if you have the courage to, you should as well. If someone sends you a praise-filled e-mail, respond, and then at the end of your message put something like:

I really appreciate your praise and I'm so glad you enjoyed the book. If you have five minutes, perhaps you'd consider leaving a customer review on my Amazon listing? As a self-published author, reviews are extremely important to my book as they can make or break a sale. You can visit the listing here [insert link] and click "Create Your Own Review" to start.

Alternatively, you could ask your praisers if they'd mind if you copied and pasted some of their kind words onto the "Reviews" page of your book site, or onto other promotional material. This is better because the reader doesn't have to do anything except give their permission.

NB: If someone praises your book in an e-mail, that's private. You cannot reprint it without their permission. If they tweet it, paste it onto your Facebook wall or leave a comment on your blog, that's public.

Review Karma

Having said that, I know *exactly* why the people who e-mail me praising my book don't leave reviews on Amazon, and why I've had the pleasure of a review so scathing my ego wasn't merely hurt, but sandblasted. It's because of my review karma.

I am always e-mailing authors or tweeting authors or telling authors in person how much I enjoyed their book, but I can't remember the last time I wrote an Amazon review. And let's just say that when a certain author got a major book deal a few years back, at a time when my own writing career was as far away from reality as it's ever been, and she was the same age as me and had started writing last week and only after trying her hand at a succession of other jobs, and I had wanted to be a writer for as long as I could remember and was still getting nowhere, and now she was rich and famous and in *Marie Claire* and I was just broke and despondent, and when her book came out and I could only make it halfway through because it was so bloody terrible, I vented my painful jealousy into a scathing Amazon review that could have stripped old paint off walls its tone was so acidic.

What I'm saying is **be wary of your review karma**. Write Amazon reviews. Be reasonable and professional; you don't have to heap praise on every book you read, but there's never any need to get personal, mean or spiteful. If you thought something (e.g. "this book is boring"), explain *why* you thought it (e.g. "most of the chapters didn't move the pace forward, and the multiple narrators only seemed to slow it down even further.")

Always review a book *on its own terms*, i.e. don't give the latest Dan Brown one star out of five because you just read something by George Orwell that was a lot better, and don't chastise it for doing what's expected of its genre. For instance, I recently read a review of a romance novel that called the ending (after being kept apart for the whole book, girl and boy get together) as predictable. *Predictable? A happy ending in a romance novel?* Surely not!

And if you read a book that you really, *really* don't enjoy, then just keep quiet about it. Have some diplomacy. You're an author now, and everything you do online — including trash other peoples' books — can not only be traced back to you, but lasts forever — if someone gets a screenshot of it before you delete it, anyway.

And the universe *always* knows... Well, it might. Either way, I wouldn't take the chance.

(If you've got a bee in your bonnet now because I've suggested you curtail your poison pen reviews, ask yourself what you want to do here: write, publish and sell your own book, or spend the rest of your life talking about how much you didn't like everyone else's?)

What To Do With Your Reviews

Or what to do with your *good* reviews, I should say. Once they come in (and you've remembered to thank your kindly reviewer) I would copy and paste some or all of them onto the dedicated book page that you (should) have installed for your book on your blogsite. With any luck, this will be one of the top search results generated by Google if someone goes looking for reviews of your book. Remember to credit each one and link back to the original, if applicable.

Next, go to your "News" page on your blogsite, and enter a new item. You could say something like, "[Book name] was reviewed by Science Fiction Central" and then link to the review.

If it's a *really* good review and it came from a *really* respectable source, you might consider taking a line or two from it and posting it on your Amazon listing as one of your five editorial reviews, through Amazon Author Central (which we'll get to in a minute).

You can also print them out, stick them on your noticeboard and gaze at them adoringly. That's always fun.

A word of caution here: **not all reviews were created equal**. This is something that, along with what matters in blurbs and endorsements (the *who* and not the *what*, if you need a reminder), many self-publishers fail to grasp. For instance, there is an epidemic of self-published writers on Twitter who tweet every time their book receives a five-star review, e.g. "My book, *Annoying, Much?*, just got ANOTHER 5* review on Amazon!

Thanks ReadingBunny79!" If they were doing this because they were genuinely excited about getting a five-star review, I'd let them off. But they're not. They're doing it because they think the rest of us will think, "Oh, wow! That book must be *amazing*. I'm going to drop everything I'm doing and run over to Amazon to buy a copy now." (And maybe because they're excited as well. But only a little bit.) And we are never in a million years going to react that way to a "ANOTHER 5* review!" type tweet. How would you react to a tweet that said, "This girl just told me that I'm way better looking than Brad Pitt", or "My boss said if I left the company, he doesn't know how he'd cope" or "My mother just told me that I'm her favourite daughter. Suck it, sis!"? I know I'd be thinking something involving *unfollowing* and *jerk*. But I'm sorry to say that this is *exactly* what you're doing when you tweet—yet again—that you've got "another" glowing Amazon review: annoying us, and sounding like a bit of a tool. Because what's a five-star review on Amazon? Nothing. Nothing at all. It's just one, and we don't know who wrote it. It could be someone who reads a book a year and so has no frame of reference. It could be someone who only reads books we'd hate. It could be your best friend. But what it definitely is is *not important*.

But—and this is a big but—sometimes Amazon Customer Reviews *do* matter. They matter when there's a lot of them, or when they've been written by a Top Reviewer (and so, come from a more credible source). In those cases, you can use them to sell your book. For example, if I told you that my book has over 500 five-star reviews on Amazon, wouldn't you assume it must have something going for it? Wouldn't it be safe to assume that? The #1 Top Reviewer on Amazon.co.uk (who is also the #1 Hall of Famer) gave *Mousetrapped* four out of five stars, and said nice things about it. I took a quote from the review and put it in my Product Description, because the #1 Top Reviewer is as good an endorsement as a respected fellow author, or a popular review site.

This goes back to the same point I made in Blurbs and Endorsements: the *what* isn't as important as the *who* who's saying it. In the case of Amazon Customer Reviews, *how many* are saying it also becomes a factor. But individually, no matter how glowing, they just don't matter in terms of trying to convince me or anyone else that your book is good. I'm sorry, but they just don't.

As for tweeting about reviews, I'd avoid tweeting about Amazon reviews altogether. If a book review site posts a review of your book, certainly, link to it in a tweet. I'd be interested in reading what they have to say about it. If your writing hero says she loves your book, that's a big moment. If you get a write-up in the local paper or in a magazine, that's something to celebrate. But please avoid the "ANOTHER 5* Amazon review!" tweet. They achieve nothing, and we've more than enough of them already.

Release Day

The big day is finally here: your release day. This is the date, picked by you, on which you "release" your book, even if in reality it's already been on sale for a few days or even a couple of weeks. What you do on this date will capitalise on all the hard work you've put into building your online platform up until now and set you and your book on the road to success, so make sure you do *something*.

Am I Ready?

By the day of your release:

- Your dedicated book site should be completed
- Your paperback's availability on Amazon, if applicable should be "In stock"
- Your Amazon Kindle listing should be live
- Your book should be available to download in any format from Smashwords.com.

If you are self-publishing a paperback with CreateSpace and uploading e-books to Smashwords and Amazon KDP, it can be difficult to ascertain exactly *when* they will all be listed and available to buy. I understand; I've been in the same position myself—and I made a bit of a mess of it. I worked out a schedule and figured that March 29th, the eighth "*Mousetrapped* Monday", would be the best day to launch the book online. My e-book listing went live a lot quicker than I thought, so that was up and running by March 9th. My paperback took *longer* than I thought it would, because I didn't check my file as thoroughly as I should have and in the first proof there were mistakes. There was then a delay of a week while I waited for another one to arrive, and then an incredibly anxious few days during which I was searching Amazon every five minutes to see if my listing had appeared. It eventually went to "In stock" on March 26th, or just *three days* before my planned March 29th release date.

(This situation led to me making an even *bigger* mistake—selling books through my website—which I'll be telling you not to do in the next section.)

Yeah, But What Do You Actually *Do*?

What do you actually *do* on your launch day? That's up to you, but I recommend being online for most of it and doing everything you can to spread the word.

On my launch day I:

- Gave away copies of my book
- Blogged about the book finally being out
- Held a virtual launch by setting up a Facebook event, inviting everyone to it and setting the location as "online." I then posted a photo of a mojito cocktail. Even a virtual cocktail is better than none!
- Tweeted about the book (talked about it, thanked people who'd bought it, retweeted tweets anyone else posted about the book, linked to video trailers, linked to the first chapter, linked to Amazon listings, linked to other people's blog posts about it, etc. Did this get annoying? Not that I'm aware of. It was actually really exciting for me, and I think my followers saw that, and only wanted to make it more exciting for me as opposed to rolling their eyes and hitting unfollow. This was because I wasn't just throwing things at them; these were people I "knew", i.e. my blogging and Twitter friends. And they knew I would help do the same for them and their books. Plus I also *stopped* doing it again the day after.)

I would estimate that I was online that day, with the exception of bathroom and coffee breaks, from about 8.30 a.m. until 7 p.m. when I collapsed (without spilling any of my self-congratulatory Corona, mind you), exhausted but happy, and safe in the knowledge that my book's life was off to a great start.

Contests And Giveaways

The best way to drum up some excitement about your release day is to have it coincide with a contest or giveaway. In fact, this is a great way to build excitement about anything connected to your online presence, be it your blog or your book.

Blog Giveaways

Giving stuff away to your blog readers is so much fun, and really easy to do. Maybe it's a copy of your book, someone else's book or just something fun, but whatever it is, it's worth it. Not only do you reward your loyal readers for sticking with you, but you draw new readers in as well.

Ask people to enter by leaving a comment at the end of the post that announces the contest. Either specify what they should say, e.g. "Leave a comment that says 'Pick me please!' at the end of this post", or tell them that they can say anything at all. It's best if you leave the entry period open for a few days; not everyone reads blogs every day. Then at the end of the specified time, either put everyone's names in a hat or use a random number generator (**www.random.org**) to choose, say, the 16th person to leave a comment, and announce the winner on the blog. Ask them to e-mail you with a postal address and send out their prize.

Sometimes a blogging or Twitter friend will offer you copies of their book to giveaway on your blog. In this case the process is the same, but you send the address of the winner to your friend who then sends the book out.

My Coffee Contest

When I moved from Blogger.com to WordPress.com, I wanted to do something that would guarantee my new blog a decent readership right from the start. So instead of posting every day and hoping that new readers would happen upon it, I decided to spread the word about it instead, i.e. advertise my sparkly new blog.

I asked myself: what is small (and so easy to mail anywhere and at a low cost), cheap (so I could afford it) and connected in some way to either me or my blog that would make a good prize for a giveaway? Cork Coffee Roasters are a company based here in Cork, where I live, who have a lovely little café and roast the beans that make their signature blends. With my blog being called Catherine, Caffeinated and me having espresso for blood, nothing could've been more perfect. Now, a bag of this coffee costs about €6, so I was more than prepared to buy the three bags I'd need, but on the off chance they'd give them to me I e-mailed the café to ask first. And they said yes!

On the day the blog "launched" (which was also a Monday, come to think of it!), I put up the first post: Catherine's Coffee Contest. To enter you could either leave a comment, tweet a link to the blog using the hashtag #corkcoffee (which helped me find the entries *and* advertised the brand of the nice people who'd given me the coffee) or retweet a tweet of mine about it. The result was amazing. There were hundreds of entries, and one of the bags ended up in Texas!

Best of all, in the very first month of my little blog it got a very respectable 1,500 hits, a number it would have taken me far longer than a month to achieve otherwise.

Twitter Giveaways

Twitter is a great place to hold a giveaway because as entering only takes a click, you'll be guaranteed plenty of entries.

Entry in a Twitter-based giveaway usually involves doing one of three things:

- retweeting a link about the contest
- using a hashtag, i.e. "Tell us your #faveTVshow"
- following the account that's doing the giving away, or getting it more followers.

If you're asking people to retweet a link, make sure that the link is short and that it includes all the relevant information, e.g. "Giving away 3 copies of #Mousetrapped today! RT to enter." Remember: people will see your username, e.g. @cathryanhoward, in the tweet too, and so will find your Twitter profile and blog if they go looking. When you pick a winner, follow them if you're not already (so they can send you a Direct Message, or DM). Then tell them they've won by mentioning them in a tweet, e.g. "Congrats to @caroline471 who has won a copy of #Mousetrapped! DM me your address."

I like the hashtag idea, because it engages people more and might make a few other people laugh. It will also make Twitter a more interesting place, which is what you should *always* be trying to do. You can either enter everyone who does it and draw someone at random, or award the best.

My next book is about backpacking, so I could have a contest where to enter you have to tell me the worst travel experience you've ever had, using a hashtag like #MyWorstTravelStory. I could be more specific, and ask for backpacker tales, which would enable me to use the name of my book, *Backpacked*, as a hashtag.

A while back, the brilliant blog Slush Pile Hell held a Twitter contest like this where to enter you had to come up with the best worst self-help title ever. It was a fantastic idea that tied in perfectly with the theme and tone of the blog, fitted well inside Twitter's 140-character limit and some of the entries were hilarious. The winner was *A Hypochondriac's Guide to the REAL Diseases You Need to Worry About and Their Symptoms*, but my favourite was *Do It You're Self: A Guide to Self-Publishing*.

So that's retweeted and hashtag based contests and giveaways, which are both *much* better ideas than follower-related ones, which I think are pretty pointless and a bit annoying for the followers of the people who enter them. Although these are generally orchestrated by companies and businesses, I've seen self-publishers attempt to get in on the act too.

Follower-related Twitter competitions usually look like one of these:

- "If we can get 1,000 followers by 5 p.m. we'll give away a free subscription to one of them!"
- "Follow us and RT this link to be in with a chance of winning [SOMETHING CRAP]!"
- "I'm going to give my 500th follower a free copy of [TITLE]. Who will it be?"

Let's start with the first two, which are basically variations of the same thing: the Help Us Get More Followers and/or Spread Us Around Twitter Like a Virus and Then We'll Reward a Random Person Giveaway. You might get more followers and you might even spread yourself around Twitter like a virus, but in doing so you'll annoy far more people than you'll interest in your product or brand, and tomorrow morning they're all going to *un*follow you. And even if some stick around, they're just a number. They didn't follow you because they want to hear what you have to say; they followed you because you promised them the chance of winning free stuff. Remember how we talked about engagers not numbers? Those people are not engagers. And so what was the point of that? There wasn't one.

The bottom one, the I'll Reward The Person Who Makes My Follower Count a Nice Round Number, is even *more* pointless because why would *anyone* be motivated to follow you unless they saw that *they* were going to be follower number 500? Do people even *think* about these things before they tweet them? Seriously, it boggles the mind. Not only that, but due to the nature of Twitter the chances of number 500 being a spammer or someone trying to sell you something are high, and then there's the embarrassment of falling below that number shortly after you hand out your reward, which is pretty much guaranteed. Its pointlessness cannot be adequately conveyed with the word *pointless*. At least with the Help Us Get Followers stupidity you have a chance of being a trending topic or something.

Free Stuff

There is one worthwhile thing that can be taken from those examples though, and that's the idea of *rewarding* followers, readers or Facebook fans, and doing it with free stuff. This doesn't directly spread the word about you or your book, but it says thank you to the people who are already helping you do that.

Remember those Smashwords coupons? Every now and then I make one that gives the recipient a free download, and I use them to reward the people who make all this possible: blog readers, Twitter followers and Facebook fans, many of whom are also people who have read my book.

The day *Mousetrapped* sold its 1,000th copy, I put a free download coupon on my blog to thank everyone for all their help. (It had a time limit; I'm not stupid!) When my Facebook fan page was at 99 fans, I said "The next person who likes this page, fan #100, will get a free download of *Mousetrapped*!" (Note that I didn't do it when I had 79 Facebook fans.) As I write this, next week is *Mousetrapped*'s first birthday, and as well as giving away copies of its new, second edition to three readers who leave a comment on the post, I'll be offering a day of free downloads from Smashwords to "close" the week and thank everyone for all they've done for me. Yes, many people will already have read the book, but they might want to tell a friend about it, and the majority of people won't have. A free voucher might encourage them and, if they like it, they might buy my next book.

Goodreads Giveaways

Goodreads.com, which is like Facebook but for books and readers, allows authors to give away books in the easiest way possible. Pre-release or within six months of it, simply sign up to be a Goodreads Author (you can do this as soon as your book is live on Amazon), click on Giveaways and then simply tell them:

- how many copies of your book you'd like to give away. A lot of people will enter, so it's best to give away 3–5
- which countries/regions you're willing to mail them to. As a Goodreads Reader, it annoys me no end when authors have giveaways but only spring for US postage. It doesn't cost that much more to send a book across the Pond, you know. In either direction. So don't be mean and make your contest all inclusive, geographically speaking
- how long you want the contest to run for. If you scroll through the existing Goodreads giveaways, you'll see that they vary widely in length. Some run for weeks, some for months. I chose to run mine for just five days, the reason being that I wanted to tweet about it, to encourage people to enter, and five days of it is about the limit before people get annoyed

Then you can just sit back and relax. Giveaways seem to get a great response from Goodreads users: my contest had 584 entries, and some on at the same time had over a thousand. The best bit is, you don't have to pick the winners. Goodreads will do it for you and then send you their names and addresses. You pop the books in the post, confirm with Goodreads that you've sent them and that's it. Meanwhile, 584 more people know about your book than did last week, and your winners might even review your book for you too.

Giving Giveaways

I've already explained why you need to provide complimentary copies of your books to review, and the same arguments go for providing copies of your book as prizes. It helps spread the word about your book and the person who wins it might well leave you a five-star Amazon review or, at the very least, mention the book to a friend or two. You never know, so take the chance!

You'll find that your blogging and Twitter friends, from time to time, will tweet or post about looking for items to give away on their blog. (You can do this too.) Offer them a copy of your book. If someone asks you to write a guest post for their blog, offer to give away a copy of your book too. This will ensure that that post gets read and so introduces your book to a new group of people.

Blog Tours

To help publicise their book and give their readers an opportunity to meet them in the flesh, traditionally published authors embark on book tours. This involves travelling to a number of cities, sitting at a table in the middle of a bookstore for an hour or so and hoping that someone comes up to you and asks you to sign the copy of your book they've bought and not for directions to the in-store café.

Unless you're a Rock Star Author, of course, who has a queue of nervous, giggly fans (Harlan Coben, Paris, 2006: one of them was me) and the local police force on standby for potential crowd control.

Of this we can but dream.

(Of being the Rock Star Author, not of Harlan Coben. Although that's okay too.)

Book tours cost lots of money, what with travel and accommodation, and unless your book is actually in stock in the stores you're going to, there's really no point. This counts us self-publishers out, but there is a free alternative that helps publicise our books and doesn't necessitate the leaving of our own homes: a blog tour.

The idea of a blog tour is fairly simple: instead of touring cities, you tour blogs. Every day for a specified period, e.g. the fortnight after your book comes out, you appear on a different blog, courtesy of the blog owner.

What Do I Do On These Blogs?

Generally speaking, you would do one or more of these things on each blog you're hosted on:

- give away a copy of your book
- answer interview questions
- write a guest post (an original one for each blog, mind you!).

For best results, mix it up a bit. So on Monday you could be giving a copy of your book away on one blog, Tuesday you're being interviewed on another, Wednesday you've written a guest post for a different blog *and* you're giving away a copy, etc. etc.

The beauty of blog tours is that different groups read different blogs, so you are guaranteed to reach new readers. You are also having a bit of fun with your blogging friends, and now their blog readers too. And like everything we do online, all these posts are generating more Google search results for your name and your book.

How To Organise A Blog Tour

A blog tour isn't really a tour unless you have at least a week's worth of blogs to hop through, and the more you can tour, the better. The ultimate blog tour, I imagine, would be one where every weekday for a month you pop your mug up on someone's site. (Although I also imagine this would be an organisational nightmare, and require a week's bed rest to recover from.) Ideally, aim for 5–15 blogs (1–3 weeks; we never blog at weekends, remember?), and try to make it a mixture of blogs by your friends and blogs by friendly strangers. I say this because if you and I follow the same group of bloggers, I'm going to be reading about your book every day for a fortnight, and great and all as your book may be, that's a bit much. You'll also be preaching to the choir, because I'll have already heard about your book.

You can either ask bloggers if they'll host you, or announce your intention to do a blog tour and then invite people to say, "Why yes! I'd LOVE to have you on my blog. I thought you'd never ask!" Don't pick and choose based on popularity or colour co-ordination; if someone invites you onto their blog, go. Make a list of your hosts, their blog URLs and their e-mail addresses.

Next, decide *when* you're going to do the blog tour, and then pencil in a different blog for each date. E-mail each host, thank them for offering to host you, check that the date you've reserved for them is suitable and then ask if they'd prefer a giveaway, an interview, a guest post or a combination of two or more. Most will say that whatever works for you is fine, so figure out what that is. (Hint: writing 20 different blog posts about the same subject is *not* what works for you. Trust me on this.) If it's an interview, ask the hosts to send you the questions before a certain date (politely!) so that it's not all one big rush at the end.

Closer to the date—maybe a week before you're due to make your appearance—e-mail each host with the text of your post (if applicable), a high-resolution JPEG of your book's cover, a picture of your beautiful face and any other information they need, like your blog address, Twitter username, etc.

You should also give them the URL of the blog where you'll be appearing the day after you appear on theirs, and ask them to link to it at the end of the post, e.g. "Find out more about Catherine and her book tomorrow on Eva's Book Blog: www.evasbooks.ie." In this way every blog post is linked. You should also list all your blog tour stops on *your* blog, embedding links to the posts or blogs in the list.

Being A Good Special Guest Star

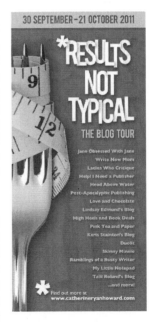

I've seen a few blog tours in my time, and I am always surprised—and, as a blog reader, disappointed—when a blog touring author doesn't *quite* get what the point of a blog tour is all about. Similarly I've hosted a few blog touring authors, and not all of them left me happy to have them back. To make sure that your blog tour achieves all of its aims and that you make a pleasant impression on your gracious host, follow Catherine's Five Steps to Being a Good Special Guest Star:

1. **Write a good post**. The number one aim of it is to *get someone new interested in you and your books*. It seems like that old common sense thing again, but in order for that to happen, you have to be *interesting*. If your book is funny, make your post funny. If your book is about writing advice, give good writing advice. For the love of fudge, do SOMETHING that makes people say to themselves, "I want to read more of *her!*" You might also want to keep it short and snappy; I once came across a blog tour post that was 5,000 words. 5,000 words! The average blog post is less than 800. Think of your

audience. You owe them some entertainment while they procrastinate instead of writing their own novels. Your host blog isn't just a soapbox.

2. **Be organised**. Your blog hosts are doing you a favour so please, make doing this favour as easy as you possibly can for them. Send your guest post in a Word document with the links already embedded and a minimal amount of fancy formatting—make it a simple procedure for your host to copy and paste the text into a new post on their blog. Make a list of all the blog tour dates and make sure all the hosts have the right one. Send them a friendly reminder a day or two out.

3. **Promote your visit**. It's not the host's job to promote your guest appearance—it's yours. You should be sending traffic to the blog you're appearing on, not hoping it'll bring traffic to your site. For the blog tour of my (since unpublished) e-book *Results Not Typical*, I even had my cover designer knock up some fancy graphics: a blog tour list to display on my blog, and a "badge" for all my hosts.

4. **Add value.** Or as a Mob guy might say in a Hollywood movie, *make it worth their while*. If you're not giving the host a copy of your book to give away on his or her blog—or even if you are—offer the host a copy of their own.

5. **Say thank you.** Most importantly of all, after you appear, send a message to your hosts to thank them for helping you to publicise your book, and say that if they ever want to appear on your blog, they're more than welcome.

(On previous page: my Results Not Typical *blog tour list. Above: the* Results Not Typical *blog tour badge for my blog hosts to display if they wished.)*

Launching In The Real World

Up until now I've only talked about launching your book online. But what about the real world? Should you try to get your face in the paper? Attempt to bribe a bookseller into stocking a few copies of your book? Perhaps even have yourself a little party?

Whether or not you launch in the real world is entirely up to you. It's been my experience that having a real world launch is good for publicity and networking, i.e. meeting people who will bring you more opportunities in the future, and it's a *lot* of fun, but it comes at a cost. It also doesn't necessarily translate into sales, which makes the cost even higher, because you can't recoup the money you spent, at least not directly.

As self-publishers of POD paperbacks and e-books, our base is online. That's where we spend all of our time, how we find our readers and where people have to go if they want to buy our books. Bricks-and-mortar bookstores are for traditionally published authors or self-published authors who have used digital printers to produce a few thousand copies of their book and then convinced a distributor to sell them to bookstores. And even if we don't have our launch in a bookstore, we still have to order in the stock that we're going to force all our friends and family to buy after we've plied them with canapés and alcohol. But having boxes of our books underneath the stairs or piled up in the hall is *exactly* the situation we hoped to avoid by going the POD route and, because we went the POD route, those books are going to be expensive to us now, even at cost price. Not to mention the fact that before we can sell them, we have to have them shipped to us.

Let's talk about how to go about this first and then I'll share with you my own experience. Then you can decide which route is the best for your book.

A Party Versus An Appearance

What sort of book launch do you want to have? Unless you have a few pots of gold you need to get rid of, it doesn't matter what sort of launch you *want*. All that matters is the kind you *need*.

An in-store launch

This is where you spend an hour or so in a bookstore, posing with your book and signing copies for all the friends and family members you've persuaded to show up and pretend to be interested strangers. Its sole purpose is to get your book in the newspapers, and this can be helped enormously by the appearance of a local celebrity. You can even make a speech, or get your local celebrity to, and you can invite as many people as you want, including actual strangers. You'll have to convince the store to stock your book, order in that stock and organise the event, but it'll be worth it if you can get a picture of you holding your book in a newspaper, or your launch mentioned on local radio. Press coverage can lead to more opportunities for you and your book. This is what I call an *economy book launch*. Personally, I think it's by far the best option for a self-publisher.

An in-store launch after hours

As above, but it happens after hours, when the store is closed. This changes two things. The first change is that there will be no one else there except people you invite, i.e. the store will be closed so there'll be no customers, and with locked or closed doors there can be no curious passers-by dropping in to make up the numbers. So if you invite a hundred people and only ten show up, there will only be you plus ten people in the store, which will be a bit cringe-worthy. *However,* people might be more interested in attending this because it's at night, has more of an "event" feel than its equivalent during the day and there'll be wine and cheese. That's the second thing. If you have your event during the day, you'll be unable to serve alcohol or nibbles because the store will be open (so there'll be no room and it'll be messy). But now you can, and people will be expecting you to. That's great and all, but *you'll have to pay for* whatever food and drink you serve, which adds to the cost.

This is a bigger deal than our first launch, but it's more expensive and dare I say, a tad self-indulgent for a POD self-publisher.

A launch party

As above, but in a private venue like a bar or hotel, and *definitely* with food and drink on offer. Of all the options, this is the one most likely to be attended by the people you invite but it is *by far* the most expensive.

A private party

Just like any other party you might have in your home with your family and friends, but this is to celebrate the fact that you wrote a book. An utterly pointless activity for a self-publisher because it does nothing to help publicise your book, but you might decide you deserve one.

If you understand that the purpose of this is fun and celebration, go ahead. But it's nothing to do with the business of selling your book.

I'm going to focus on the first type of launch, the one I strongly recommend you have if you're going to have one.

Approaching A Bookstore

The first thing you need to do is find a bookstore where you'd like to have your launch. It has to be local—so you can be A Local Author—and independent stores are best, for two reasons: first, they're more likely to agree to buy stock from you directly (crucial for your launch), and second, they have owners who can decide whether or not to host your launch without having to consult a chain of middle managers. It also helps your cause if you're a regular customer of the store, or in a somewhat suspicious but fortuitous coincidence, have suddenly become one in the last month...

Armed with a copy of your book and your best friendly smile, ask to speak to the manager. Show them the book first; if you've listened to me (and NOT used Cover Creator), this will be enough to persuade them that you're a professional operation. Explain what you want to do. If you've approached them because you're a regular customer or you have a mutual friend, or because you attended another author event at the store and were impressed, mention it. Play all your cards. And then cross your fingers that they'll say yes.

Chances are they *will* say yes, because you are going to bring customers into their store, get their store's name in the paper and (hopefully!) sell a large number of books through their tills. It's a total win-win for them. Unless:

- **Your book looks like a pile of poo**. (And if you've used Cover Creator, it does.) This is a bookstore. The people who work there are booksellers, potentially highly experienced ones. They know what real books look like, and what crappy little POD-ed pamphlets do *not* look like, and that's real books. They are not going to want to sully their store with a book that isn't really a book, can't compete with the real books already on their shelves and probably won't sell many copies, if any. If your book doesn't sell, hosting your launch holds no benefit for the store. They are running a business, not operating a charitable hosting service for unprofessional self-publishers.

- **Your wholesale price is too high**. All the books you sell the day of the launch will be sold through the store, i.e. you sell it to them and then they sell it to the people who attend your event. Ask them how much of a profit margin they need on your book, and then *agree to sell it to them for that*. Don't argue; you don't know enough about selling books to make demands, and hey, aren't you trying to get this store to host your event for you? When I went to ask my local bookstore owner about having an event there, one of the first things she asked me was how much my book retails for. I told her the truth, which was €10.99 in local currency. She then explained that their profit margin was 30%, so I'd have to sell my stock to them for €10.99−30%, making my profit (€10.99−30%)− My Cost Price. If you have to up your list price by a euro (or a dollar or a pound) to make this deal less painful, do. But don't jack up the price so much that you overcharge people for your book, especially since most people who are going to be buying it will be family members or friends.

- **You don't instil confidence that you are capable of pulling this off**. Here comes the P-word again: do you seem like a *professional* author? Do you give the bookseller the impression that you are a highly organised and motivated individual who is going to actually get people to attend this event? That you'll get out there and publicise it? Or do you come across as someone who's just doing this for kicks or, worse, expects the bookstore to do all the work? I did what I thought was the minimum an author should do for their launch (get the stock in, give the store posters to advertise it, get people to come, get the launch covered by the local newspaper), and therefore I was a tad surprised when the bookseller told me I was by far the most organised self-published author she'd ever dealt with. I'm not telling you this to gloat or show off—although if you want to give me a gold star, you can stick it on my forehead—but to prove that just by being professional, you can stand head and shoulders above the rest.

- **They don't buy stock from individuals**. Many bookstores only buy stock through distributors, so they just have to pay one person and don't end up with invoices from a variety of individuals (authors). If this is their policy, they will have to say no to hosting your event. Don't take it personally.

NB: The store will advise you on the best time for your launch. Listen to them.

Selling The Stock Through The Store

Yes, you have to.

No, you can't have a launch at a bookstore and not put your books through their tills.

The only way to avoid this is to have your launch somewhere other than a bookstore, so you can pocket all the proceeds yourself. (After you pay the credit card bill for all the stock, of course.)

How Much Stock Should I Order?

All the stock you order from CreateSpace has to be paid for outright and cannot be sent back. All the stock you give to the bookstore will be for sale or return; if they sell them, they'll pay you for them, but if they don't sell them, they'll hand them back. They might keep a couple in stock and maybe one day in the future they'll call you up and ask for more of them, but they might not, and then you'll be stuck with all of them. But what's the only thing worse than being stuck with excess stock of your own book? Having people ready and willing to buy them, and having run out.

Go through your invite list and figure out how many copies you expect to sell. Then add another 20–50 copies, depending on how many Stranger Purchasers you expect. (Not hope for. *Expect.*) Add another 10 copies for safety, and then order that amount of stock.

And order it in plenty of time. Remember the volcanic ash cloud that stopped air travel over all of Europe for a week or so? That was the week before my launch, and the week in which my books were supposed to be travelling from South Carolina to Ireland. I was just about to skip town when, *two days* before the launch, which by then had been mentioned in the newspaper and on invites sent to every single person I had ever met, a delivery van arrived with the books. It was probably the most relieved I have ever been in my life.

Fun With Printed Stuff

Stock isn't the only cost involved in this launch, and I'm not just talking about your outfit. You'll have to get invitations printed, get posters for the store and get something to give out on the day to people who come over to see what's going on but don't buy a book there and then.

I recommend a website like Vistaprint (**www.vistaprint.com**) which is really cheap, seems to ship all over the world and makes it easy for you to order different types of paper products that all match.

Printed materials can be very useful when promoting your self-published book, so long as they look professional, contain all the relevant information and get into the hands of the right people. There's no point leaving a stack of postcards on the counter of your local butchers, for instance, if your book is about vegan recipes.

To help promote *Mousetrapped*, I made myself book launch invites that doubled nicely as bookmarks, postcards and posters. I also produced an 'info page' to include with complimentary copies of my book so potential reviewers, stockists, etc. would know what it's about without having to read through the whole thing.

I like things that match (have I mentioned that?) and as all three things were going to make an appearance at my book launch, it was important they all looked related to each other, i.e. part of a brand. Online printing services are usually DIY with lots of templates, clip art, etc. but it's not always possible to get the same scheme on a postcard as it is on a business card, so the best thing to do is to make one yourself.

Here's how:

- Pick through your MS Word or iWork Pages document templates for something that looks snazzy. I chose a page of a newsletter template from Word.
- Add pictures and text of your own and remove any elements of the document you don't need. Change the colours and fonts to match or at least compliment your book cover.
- Save as a PDF document. You now have yourself a snazzy scheme.

Using this method, you can make matching JPEGs for use in your smaller items, like postcards and invites. Simply save the PDF as a JPEG and upload it to your online printing site as your own image.

I recommend you get the following items:

- **Book launch invites**. I left these in a stack on the bookshop's counter, dispersed them amongst family and friends, pinned them to notice-boards and tucked them in books.
- **Postcards**. With my book's cover on the front, a small blurb about it on the back and space to write an address, these postcards were both adorable *and* functional, if I do say so myself. I tucked them in books, handed them out on the day of the launch and sent a packet of them to friends of mine in the US, Austria and New Zealand. Global domination and all that.
- **Posters**. I used the exact same design as the invites to make A3-sized posters. These were hung around the shop on the day of the launch.

Getting Publicity

You have two opportunities to get publicity for your launch: before and after.

To get publicity beforehand, e-mail every local newspaper, free newspaper and community newsletter you can find. It helps in the months leading up to your book's release if you keep an eye out for news stories about other launches, and take note of where they appear and who writes the pieces or did the reporting. Keep a list of people and places to target.

A book launch is not a story; you need to give them something more than that. This is the actual text of the e-mail I sent out to newspapers:

Hi [name],

My name is Catherine Ryan Howard and I'm an author from Douglas. I'd like to invite you to my book launch at Douglas Books, Douglas Village Shopping Centre, on Saturday 8th May at 12.30pm.

If there is any opportunity to publicise the book/the launch beforehand, I'd greatly appreciate it.

I've included some additional information below and if you need any more/clarification, please don't hesitate to contact me. My mobile number is [number] or you can contact me at this address.

Kind regards and thanks,

Catherine

Book Launch:

MOUSETRAPPED will be launched on Saturday May 8th 2010 at 12.30 p.m. in Douglas Books, Douglas Shopping Centre. All welcome.

Book Synopsis:

Three big dreams, two Mouse Ears and one J-1 visa. What could possibly go wrong in the happiest place on earth?

When Catherine Ryan Howard decides to swap the grey clouds of Ireland for the clear skies of the Sunshine State, she thinks all of her dreams—working in Walt Disney World, living in the United States, seeing a Space Shuttle launch—are about to come true. Ahead of her she sees weekends at the beach, mornings by the pool and an inexplicably skinnier version of herself skipping around Magic Kingdom. But not long into her first day on Disney soil—and not long after a breakfast of Mickey-shaped pancakes—Catherine's Disney bubble bursts and soon it seems that among Orlando's baked highways, monotonous mall clusters and world famous theme parks, pixie dust is hard to find and hair is downright impossible to straighten.

The only memoir about working in Walt Disney World, Space Shuttle launches, the town that Disney built, religious theme parks, Bruce Willis, humidity-challenged hair and the Ebola virus, MOUSETRAPPED: A Year and A Bit in Orlando, Florida is the hilarious story of what happened when one Irish girl went searching for happiness in the happiest place on earth.

The MOUSETRAPPED Story:

Catherine wrote MOUSETRAPPED after returning to Ireland in the summer of 2008. She sent it to one agent and four or five publishing houses, and got the same response from each: they enjoyed reading it but felt there was not enough of a market for it to justify publication. Meanwhile, Catherine gave up her job at a letting office in Cork City so she could do something she'd dreamed of for years: write a novel. To help keep her in paper, ink cartridges and coffee while she did, she self-published MOUSETRAPPED.

On March 29th 2010, MOUSETRAPPED launched online, for sale on Amazon.com, Amazon.co.uk and other international Amazons, as well as through Catherine's own website. Catherine blogged about her entire self-publishing experience—the highs, the lows, the headaches—and also maintained an active Twitter account.

About the Author:

CATHERINE RYAN HOWARD is an occasionally delusional twenty-something from Douglas, Cork. As well as working in Walt Disney World, Catherine has been a student journalist, administrated things in the Netherlands, cleaned tents on a French campsite, established a handmade card company and answered telephones in several different offices. Yes, several. She is currently working on her first novel, daydreaming of a US Green Card and drinking way too much coffee. She wants to be a NASA astronaut when she grows up.

Contact Details:

[Telephone]
[E-mail]
www.catherineryanhoward.com
www.mousetrappedbook.com
www.twitter.com/cathryanhoward
www.facebook.com/mousetrappedbook

Photos Attached:

MOUSETRAPPED cover
Author photo
Launch invite
(Higher resolutions available on request.)

Some of the people I sent this to just ignored it, but I *did* get a story about my book launch in Cork's *Evening Echo*, the daily tabloid here in Cork and by far the biggest newspaper, circulation-wise, that I'd sent it to. Word of warning: they didn't contact me before they wrote the piece. They only used the information in my e-mail, and the photo I sent. So be careful what you put in your e-mail!

You can get great coverage after the launch if you can convince a social diarist to attend. This is the person who works for your local paper who has to go to events like launches, take loads of photos and chat to the attendees and then, if you're lucky, give you a two-page spread a few days later. Again, keep an eye out for coverage of other launches and events, and look for how to contact the reporter.

This is the actual text of the e-mail I sent to the social diarist of my local paper, Cork's *Evening Echo*:

Hi Martina,

My name is Catherine Ryan Howard and I'm from Douglas.

I've just self-published a travel memoir called MOUSETRAPPED: A YEAR AND A BIT IN ORLANDO, FLORIDA, and I would love to invite to you to the launch.

It will take place in Douglas Books, Douglas Village Shopping Centre, at 12.30 p.m. on Saturday 8th May. I have printed invitations and can send you one if you'd like.

I've included some information below about the book.

Thanks for your time and I really hope to see you there.

Catherine

———————————————

[Here I put the same information as in the previous e-mail—synopsis, about me, etc.]

This was really successful, because not only did Martina come to my launch, but she gave its coverage a two-page spread. I got chatting to her during the launch and offered her a free book. (Remember my free book principle?) She then offered to have me on her radio show, where I got to talk about my book and pick songs to play for an entire hour. Added bonus: there were so many pictures of the launch that another reporter for the paper took a "spare" one for her community news section, and wrote an additional story about my book.

Not bad for a few e-mails, right?

The Day Of The Launch

Check with the store to see if they want you to give them a hand setting up; if they say there's no need then show up no later than fifteen minutes before your event is due to start. Explain to your friends and family that this is not a Stop By Whenever You Can type of event, but an Everyone Has To Arrive At The Beginning one. Basically you want them to be an instant crowd, helping to fill up the store, make your event look well-attended and make passers-by curious enough to come in.

Chances are you're looking at this in black and white, but let me assure you: my cardigan, my books, my postcards, the tablecloth and even the pens are all BLUE!

If you can, wear an outfit that co-ordinates with the cover of your book. It'll look good in the photos. (Needless to say, I did! And imagine how much it satisfied my co-ordination needs when I saw that the store had put a blue tablecloth on the table I was to sit at, which matched my top, which matched my book, which matched the postcards, invites and posters. I was in colour co-ordination heaven!)

Speaking of photos, designate an official photo-taker. You won't have time, and your attendees will be too busy chatting to each other and *oohing* and *aahing* over your book. You can then post the photos on your website afterwards and attach them to future I-want-publicity e-mails.

How long it goes on for depends on the event itself but an hour is a good length, generally speaking. If someone is going to make a speech or an Important Person is there to take photos, it's best to do this first and then take a seat and sign books. (If only to get it out of the way, and your Important Person might have to dash.) Check with the bookstore before leaving—and don't forget to thank them!

After The Launch

Send the bookstore a thank-you e-mail. If they were *really* helpful, maybe even stop by with a box of chocolates and a thank-you card.

Next, find out how many books you sold. Collect the remainder from the store and then invoice them for the stock that they've sold. Warning: bookstores take *ages* to pay.

Wait with bated breath for coverage of your launch to appear in the paper. Keep a copy for your scrapbook, and don't worry too much about your eyes being closed in the photo, or your cousin's name being spelled wrong. As long as your book's name is correct, that's all that matters! Again, send a thank-you e-mail to the writer of any pieces about you that appear in the press. It only takes a second, but it's a nice gesture, and it might make getting publicity for your second book a little easier.

To Launch Or Not To Launch

Initially I wasn't going to have a launch at all. I'd wanted to be a writer ever since I found out that real, live people were behind the books I loved and so that first book launch, be it a signing or a party, was a Very Big Deal. I wanted to "save" it and not "waste" it on my self-published book which, don't forget, was nothing much of anything at the time. I wanted my first book launch to be a glittery affair, one that had an agent and an editor on the guest list, complimentary wine and the wearing of an expensive designer dress. (And to be skinny for it, but that's another story...!) I wanted it to be for a novel that a publisher had published, not a travel memoir about working in Walt Disney World, NASA and the Ebola virus that I had produced myself.

I took a baby step and informed my mother we would be having a Florida-themed party in our house to celebrate the book's release. There would be American flag bunting, tropical-themed cupcakes and shortbread cut with a Space Shuttle-shaped cookie cutter. (And it would have been *so* cool.) But we wouldn't be able to invite anyone but friends and family, and that would nix any publicity opportunities; you can't invite your local newspaper's social diarist to a party you're having in your own house. So I decided instead to have it in a bookstore.

I was terrified at the thought of approaching my local independent bookstore, Douglas Bookshop, and asking if first, they'd stock a few copies of *Mousetrapped* and second, let me have my launch there, but they couldn't have been nicer or more accommodating. And so around lunchtime one Saturday in May 2010, *Mousetrapped* had its launch-style signing in a bricks-and-mortar bookshop. It was great fun, but self-publishing is a business, and with that in mind, was the launch worth having? Did it make financial sense? Did it result in sales, or a loss of profit?

The Arguments For

- It felt good. I really enjoyed the day and it made me feel like a proper author.
- It gave my self-publishing operation a sense of professionalism. My books were in a bookstore, I had a well-attended launch and I managed to get some publicity for it.
- The event got good newspaper coverage locally, and led to a radio interview.

The Arguments Against

- It didn't result in any extra sales, and practically all copies sold on the day were sold to family and friends, i.e. people who would have bought copies anyway.
- I made less money from the sales I did make, because instead of selling them to my family and friends directly, I sold them to the bookshop who then sold them to the attendees.
- It cost money in other ways. I had to print posters, invites and postcards and order in the stock so I could sell it on (incurring shipping charges).

What Should YOU Do?

I don't think you should automatically have a launch or signing for your self-published book, but then I don't think there's anything in self-publishing that you should do automatically, without any thought. Every single book is different and needs to be treated as such. I think you need to ask yourself, *What will I get out of doing this?* and when you find the answer ask, *Is that what I want?*

If all you want is to feel like a proper author for a couple of hours, then go ahead and have whatever sort of launch/party/signing your heart desires. Buy a new outfit, hire a photographer and arrange nibbles. Invite all your friends. It'll be great fun, but be prepared for it to cost you money.

If what you want is publicity, stick with a signing or "appearance" where maybe you give a little book-related talk and then scribble your name in a few copies. Get in no more stock than you think you can sell and avoid any glossy and expensive extras, such as posters or even invites. Send an e-mail to every editor, radio show producer, social diarist, etc. that you can find and get your face in the paper, preferably with a hand holding your book up just below it. Take plenty of pictures to put on your website or blog afterwards, and maybe even rope a special guest, such as another writer or a local celebrity connected with your book or your book's subject matter, into attending and saying a few words.

If it's sales you're after, you're going to need to do a *lot* of work. Start with everything above. Then calculate all your costs and work out how many books you're going to need to sell to recoup that money. Then, get out and sell them. This means hand-selling them at the launch, forbidding anyone you know from buying a copy beforehand (so they buy it on the night instead) and getting as many people you don't know to attend as people you do.

It won't be easy but it'll all be worth it if it works.

(A sentence that doesn't just apply to this but self-publishing as a whole, when you think about it.)

The Amazing Amazon

Between your stunning pre-release reviews, exciting release day, free book giveaways and fortnight-long blog tour, you and your newly published book are doing great. People are talking about it, sales are ticking over steadily and you've even got some (nice!) Amazon customer reviews. If you've had a Real World launch, perhaps this success has even been carried over into the offline world. And well done you, because doing all that was no small feat and a *lot* of hard work.

Now we're going to take some time to make sure that our little corner of Amazon is doing everything it can to help convince people to buy our book because, if enough people start to buy it on a regular basis, Amazon will effectively start promoting our book for us.

All Roads Lead To Amazon

It is imperative, especially in the early days of your book's life, that you try to drive all potential readers to Amazon. Obviously if they own a Nook they'll be shopping from Barnes and Noble—that's not what I mean. What I mean is don't send your potential book purchasers elsewhere just because you want to earn a few extra bucks. What I mean is *don't tell people about your CreateSpace eStore.*

As soon as you approved your paperback for sale on CreateSpace, it became available to buy from your CreateSpace eStore, a page dedicated solely to your book. Your eStore has an unique URL which includes your "Project ID", the number CS assigns your book within their system. If someone buys a book from here, you make more money than you would if they bought it from anywhere else, because all the middle men have been cut out of the equation. But we don't *want* people buying our book from here. We'd rather our readers purchase from Amazon, where a sale— through improved sales ranks, etc.—can lead to another sale. Here, nobody notices.

Your Amazon Listing

One area where a lot of authors fail to take full advantage of the promotional opportunities available to them is on Amazon. They'll haunt the site day and night, clicking "Refresh" every 60 seconds on their search results and holding their breath as they reload, but once the initial excitement of seeing their book up there wears off, they'll never return to Amazon again except for the occasional has-anyone-left-me-a-scathing-review check.

The better your Amazon listing is, the more chance you have of someone clicking the "Buy" button after viewing it. So let's make it as good as we possibly can.

Amazon Speak

I'm sure you've purchased a book from Amazon before (maybe even this one!) but have you ever really studied an Amazon listing? There's a *lot* of information on there—not just about your book but about similar books and the habits of the customers who buy them. Before we talk about optimising our little corner of the biggest online book retailer in the world, let's have a crash course in Amazon Speak.

Project Image. Your front cover. For your Kindle edition, this is the cover image you uploaded. If a customer clicks on it, they get a larger version. For your paperback, CreateSpace will crop it for you. If a customer clicks on that, they'll get to "Look Inside"(which we'll come to in a second).

Pricing Information. This will usually show the list price (the price you set) and if Amazon are discounting it, the percentage discount and the amount that makes the price now. On the Kindle listing, they might compare the digital price to the print price (which is ridiculous, but anyway) as well as showing a discount, if applicable. NB: If you have a

Kindle book on Amazon.co.uk and you are signed in as, say, an Irish or American customer, you won't be able to see your pricing information. It will say something like "pricing information is not available" because only customers in the UK can see or purchase it. Sign out and go back and it should become visible to you. Remember as well that depending on the region, VAT and international delivery charges may have been added to your book; that's why the price isn't exactly the same as the one you set. But you are still getting paid the same royalties, so don't worry.

Customers Who Bought This Item Also Bought. A list of titles also bought by the customers who bought your book. This is a gold mine of information and we're going to put it to good use in a minute.

Editorial Reviews. Under the heading "Editorial Reviews" will be your product description (your back cover blurb), your About the Author paragraph and any editorial reviews you add through Amazon Author Central.

Product Details. The nitty gritty: the ISBN or ASIN (a unique identifier added by Amazon to Kindle books), how many pages in the paperback edition (shown on Kindle listing too), the publisher, whether or not lending is enabled (Kindle only) and your book's sales ranks, if any. They're a whole other story, so they're getting their own section soon.

Customer Reviews. Reviews uploaded by Amazon customers. These can either be your best friend or the reason you're crying yourself to sleep at night. The most helpful review will be shown at the top (as voted for by other Amazon customers; look for the "Was this review helpful to you?" button) and on the right-hand side the reviews will be arranged, on a much smaller scale, chronologically, with the newest review first.

More About the Author. Once you get your Author Central page up and running, this will act as a link to it.

What Other Items Do Customers Buy After Viewing This Item? Again, a gold mine of information. This tells you what people buy after they look at your Amazon listing. This is slightly different to "Customers Also Bought" because this list contains people who looked at your listing but didn't necessarily buy your book.

Tags Customers Associate With This Product. This is where customers can help tag your book so that it's easier to find on the site. And guess what? *You're* an Amazon customer, so you can tag your own book. Tip: if you have a Kindle edition and it's $2.99 or less, tag it "cheap kindle books." If it's more than that don't, because regardless of what *you* may think, it ain't a cheap Kindle book.

What Other Items Do Customers Buy After Viewing This Item?

Happier Than A Billionaire: Quitting My Job, Moving to Costa Rica, and Living the Zero Hour Work Week by Nadine Hays Pisani Kindle Edition
★★★★☆ (175)
$2.99

How to Travel Full Time by Colin Wright Kindle Edition
★★★★☆ (17)
$0.99

No Sense of Direction by Eric Raff Kindle Edition
★★★★☆ (20)
$0.99

Mousetrapped: A Year and A Bit in Orlando, Florida by Catherine Ryan Howard Kindle Edition
★★★☆☆ (45)
$2.99

> **Explore similar items**

Click to Look Inside Feature. This allows customers to look inside your book. They can choose from Front Cover, Copyright, First Pages, Back Cover or Surprise Me! (And yes, they spell it with an exclamation mark.) Customers can also search for keywords inside the book using this feature. I find this whole Look Inside thing useful but odd, and possibly damaging. While sampling an e-book gives you, say, the first 50 pages as a preview, Look Inside covers the whole book. Now because of the way it's set up you couldn't feasibly read the whole thing using it, but what if you were only interested in one chapter? If I search for "Celebration" in Look Inside, every single page of the chapter in *Mousetrapped* about Celebration comes back as a result. So if you were interested in Celebration and were only going to buy the book because of that one chapter, well, now you don't have to. On the other hand, I buy books from Amazon all the time and I don't think I've ever once used Look Inside for any of them. In fact, I've only used it to peek inside books I was never going to buy anyway, so maybe this is all besides the point...

Frequently Bought Together. If your book is frequently purchased with one or more other books, Amazon will sometimes offer all of them together in a discounted bundle. If this happens, great! Make sure you have a look around at books in your "Customers Who Bought..." list as well to see if *your* book is being offered in a FBT bundle with any other titles. [*paperback only*]

Sponsored Links. Amazon may put sponsored links on your page; mine are always for holidays in Orlando.

Popular Highlights. [*Kindle listing only*] This is one of my favourite Amazon listing features, if only because it's like looking over the shoulder of your readers as they go through your book. The Kindle allows users to highlight sections of text in any Kindle book, enabling them to mark sentences they liked, books mentioned they want to check out or words they don't know the meaning of and want to look up. That's great and all, but what's even better is that Kindle then compiles these highlights and puts the most popular ones on your listing. Hilariously, *Mousetrapped's* popular highlights includes the phrase, "if the world was inhabited by third cousins of Chucky from *Child's Play*, all of whom wear traditional dress and follow your every move with their soulless black eyes of toy darkness." Out of context, that sounds a bit weird, doesn't it? Well, fear not: I'm talking about the little animatronic dolls in the Magic Kingdom's It's A Small World attraction. Makes sense now, eh?

Where's My Listing?

Your Amazon Kindle listing will go live on Amazon.com as soon as your book says it's "live" in your Amazon KDP dashboard. It will also be visible to any Kindle user who accesses the store through their Kindle device.

Your Amazon paperback listing will take a little longer, although you should be able to find the first signs of it after about a week by using the site's "Advanced Search" feature and searching for your book by its ISBN.

Amazon listings are made up of many components and they won't all appear at once. For example when your listing first goes live, it will likely only show the product image, title and product details (like how many pages). It will also say something like, "Temporarily Out of Stock." Then a few days later the product description will appear and the stock update will change to something like "Usually ships in 1–3 weeks."

One of the last features to appear on it will be Look Inside.

Don't direct people to your listing until it is *ready*. This doesn't mean complete, but it does mean functional.

Your listing is ready when:

- Your book is listed as "In Stock"
- Your product description has appeared (your back cover blurb)

- You can find the listing by typing the book's name into Amazon's search box.

My Book Is POD: Isn't It Always In Stock?

POD books are not always "in stock." Amazon has a range of stock statuses, and from my experience they go something like this:

- In Stock
- Only x left in stock... order soon (more on the way)
- Allow an extra 1–3 days
- Usually ships in 1–2 weeks
- Usually ships in 3–4 weeks
- Usually ships in 1–2 months
- Temporarily out of stock
- Available from these sellers.

I'm guessing this is because Amazon keeps a specified virtual number of your books in its computer system and then depletes this virtual number accordingly. This is a *good thing*, because if your stock starts to deplete (virtually or otherwise) it looks like your book is hot property. And if a customer sees "Only 1 left in stock" they might buy it now rather than later.

I wouldn't concern myself with stock levels UNLESS it goes to "Available from these sellers" which basically means Amazon can't get your book. This is unlikely to happen unless you put a hold on your book with CreateSpace, which you need to do if you want to make changes to your book after publishing. Amazon is a huge operation and minute and temporary fluctuations in stock levels are just the norm. There's no point in stressing.

Back in the early days when I was watching my Amazon listing 24/7, there were times when it went to "Usually ships in 3–4 weeks" and I had a minor heart attack, only to see it pop back to "In Stock" an hour later. Likewise, my Amazon.co.uk listing could be relied upon to go from "Only 5 left in stock..." into a countdown (only four left, only three left, etc.) all the way down to one, when it would go to "Usually ships in 1–2 weeks" before popping back up to "Only 5 left in stock" so we could do the whole thing again.

So don't stress about your stock levels. What really matters is that people can order your book, not how long they're going to have to wait for it after they do.

Amazon Author Central

Once at least one of your listings is live, you can sign up for Amazon Author Central. There is an Amazon.com Author Central and an (inferior) Amazon.co.uk Author Central, but we're just going to concentrate here on the .com one, and because the tendons in my fingers are hurting and I've practically typed my fingerprints away, I'm going to call it AC from here on in.

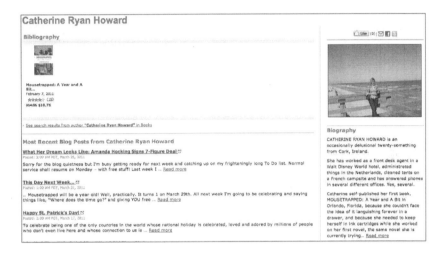

My Amazon.com Author Page.

You can sign up for an AC account and page at **authorcentral.amazon.com** using an existing Amazon account (or the one you used for KDP) if you wish. You will have to fill in your information and identify what books of yours are on the site, and then Amazon will say thanks very much, we'll be in touch. They'll go away and verify that those are your books and, a couple of days later, come back and say hooray! You're an Amazon Author now.

The Perceived Benefits Of An AC Author Page

If you have an AC page, customers can click on your name on your book's listing or the "More About the Author" section and go to a page that's just all about you and your books. This is what they'll see, depending on how many features you've activated:

- **Bibliography**. All your books in one place.

- **Biography**. An author bio and photograph.
- **Blog posts**. Your blog posts can be automatically fed to this page.
- **Events**. You can list upcoming signings, appearances, etc.
- **Videos.** Upload video blogs or book trailers.
- **Customers Also Bought Items By**. Authors that people who like you like too.

Behind the scenes, you'll also be able to see all your **Customer Reviews** listed (sort "Rating: Highest to Lowest"—it's best for the soul) and **Sales Data**, such as where in the US were those people who bought those six copies last week, and what your sales rank looks like over time on a graph. I have yet to find a use for this information, and looking at it too often can become an obsession. (And seeing my sales rank on my listing is bad enough, obsession-wise.)

Now as a customer, the only time I have ever looked at an AC page is to see how many books a particular author has published. And even then, I looked at nothing else but the bibliography. And since you can put your blog URL in your product description, you already have an About An Author, you don't want to see your customer reviews, thanks very much, and you have enough obsessive-compulsive behaviours without adding Nielsen BookScan data to the mix as well, what is the point of signing up for it?

Well my friends, I shall tell you.

The Actual Benefits Of An AC Author Page

There are two reasons you should sign up for Amazon AC—because *you can edit and thereby enhance your listing* and *you can contact Amazon.com*.

Now of course, anyone can contact Amazon.com. There are "Contact Us" and "Leave Feedback" buttons all over the site. But this particular contact button is on AC, making you an author and not just one more cranky customer amongst millions. If you have a problem with anything, don't e-mail Amazon through the site, contact them through AC. I've had nothing but positive experiences communicating with Amazon—even when they haven't been able to solve a problem for me, at least they've told me so really quickly. I've also corresponded with them as a customer and for whatever reason, it's always taken a lot longer. So assert your author-ness and use what clout you have whenever you can!

And as soon as your AC account goes live, you *need* to e-mail them to tell them to link your paperback edition with your Kindle edition like, yesterday. Always be very clear when you're contacting them about products. Include the ISBNs or ASINs and links to the listings in question, if applicable.

But back to editing your listing. This is a superb feature because it not only enables you to update information, but to put extra stuff in there too. (Very exciting, I know.)

Edit Product Description

This is a great feature that allows you to format your blurb, i.e. add bold and italics. It's also what you can use to update your product description if you get a better idea for it a few weeks after launch, or if you need to update it with new information. For me, this is the best feature of Amazon Author Central.

Your product description is vital to the success of your book. What is the point of going to the effort of informing me that your book exists, getting me to stop and think about it, motivating me to find out more and eventually leading me to your Amazon page, the final hurdle, only to have me leave again without buying anything? There is no point, only time-wasting.

Book Description
Publication Date: **August 28, 2011**

The laugh-out-loud new travel memoir from the bestselling author of *Mousetrapped: A Year and A Bit in Orlando, Florida*

Catherine Ryan Howard prefers bath robes to bed bugs, lattes to lizards and mini-bars to malaria. So why is she going *backpacking*?

She doesn't know either...

Catherine isn't the backpacking type. Working for one of the world's biggest hotel chains, she and her employee discount have become accustomed to complimentary bath robes, 24-hour room service and Egyptian cotton sheets. As for holidays, Catherine likes places that encourage lying - lying on the beach, by the pool, in bed...

She's been on what feels like one long holiday in Florida when her fearless best friend, Sheelagh, announces plans to backpack across Central America. With Catherine's US visa about to expire, her having no desire to return home to Ireland just yet and her common sense, evidently, on a day off, she agrees to go along.

After all, how bad can this backpacking thing be?

Um... very bad, actually. Catherine soon finds herself showering with the threat of electrocution, living with mutant cockroaches, sleeping on wooden planks, suffering from all but one of the side-effects listed on her bottle of anti-malarial tablets (liver failure, in case you were wondering) and riding a horse up the side of a smoking, lava-filled volcano.

And that's just the first week.

Backpacked is the wry tale of what happened when one *very* reluctant backpacker hit the backpacker trail and discovered that beyond the mosquitoes, bad coffee and flea-infested hostels lie even *bigger* mosquitoes, even *worse* coffee and flea-infested hostels whose bathrooms have no doors...

Praise for *Mousetrapped* by Catherine Ryan Howard:

"[Catherine] writes with wit and humor about her time in Orlando. Thoroughly enjoyable and a great read!" --Talli Roland, bestselling author of *The Hating Game*

⌃ Show Less

I personally believe your product description should have the following key elements, preferably in this order:

- **The answer to the question *what is this book?* in one sentence**, ideally with an incentive to buy or at least to read on thrown in too. The average Amazon browser is flicking through tens of books a minute, only glancing at the descriptions, and so we need something that they can read in a second that will (hopefully) stop them in their tracks. In the description of *Backpacked* above, this is the line "The laugh-out-loud new travel memoir from the bestselling author of *Mousetrapped: A Year and A Bit in Orlando, Florida.*" This promises: (i) a funny book, (ii) a book from an author who has already sold books and so, presumably, can write as opposed to merely type and (iii) something fans of *Mousetrapped* will like too.

- **A tagline**. Yes! We can actually put our tagline here! I know; I must be going soft in my old age. This answers the question *what is this book about?* in a sentence or three, without giving away any key plot points. If the potential purchaser of our book didn't stop reading at the sentence that describes what kind of book we have here, this line that tells them what it's about shouldn't stop them reading either—it should encourage them to read on. For *Backpacked*, this is "Catherine Ryan Howard prefers bath robes to bed bugs, lattes to lizards and mini-bars to malaria. So why is she going *backpacking*? She doesn't know either..."

- **Your blurb**. Again, don't just throw up the first thing that comes into your head; work on it. And once it's up there, play with it a bit. Try out different ones. Is one more successful than the other? Could it be improved at all? Bestselling self-published e-book author Mark Edwards attributes changing his product descriptions with his #1 bestseller success on Amazon.co.uk.

- **An endorsement**. Because "Editorial Reviews" is much further down the page—further than most potential purchasers will read, in my opinion—it won't hurt to put one or two endorsements into our actual product description.

- **Any other relevant information**. If your book was shortlisted for an award or has been #1 in a major Amazon category or has sold over 100,000 copies, I'd put a mention of it here.

NB: There is a little glitch in the system at the moment that doesn't always allow authors to edit the Product Descriptions of their Kindle books. You can e-mail Amazon through Author Central to get them to do it, but there's another glitch that means once an Amazon employee has edited the description for you, you can't do it yourself. I know: I feel a headache coming on too. Let's hope this gets sorted out soon because I've yet to see a product description that couldn't benefit from some formatting.

Editorial Reviews

These are not so much reviews as quotes or blurbs excerpted from reviews. These should be from named, reputable sources (i.e. not your mother), limited to 1–2 sentences and up to 250 characters or about 50 words in length.

You can add up to five of them, and they should look something like this: "[Catherine] writes with wit and humour about her time in Orlando. Thoroughly enjoyable and a great read!"—Talli Roland, author of THE HATING GAME.

(As for *getting* these reviews, we'll discuss that in the next section.)

From the Author

This is supposed to be a "message" from you to your readers (or potential readers) and what it says is pretty much up to you, crazy behaviour aside.

I'm considering writing one of these for *Mousetrapped* explaining that working in a hotel in Disney World *is* the same as working in Disney World, which is what my blurb says, but is different to working for The Walt Disney Company, which is what my blurb does *not* say, or that it's called *Mousetrapped* because that is the name of chapter three in which I talk about being geographically trapped in Walt Disney World because I don't have a car and Orlando's public transport system sucks, and not because some people, inexplicably, think the official definition of "mousetrapped" is working for The Walt Disney Company. (If we're being technical, "mousetrapping" is a technique practised by porn sites that keeps customers from leaving, such as endless pop-ups or windows that can't be closed. So there.) But I'm going to wait until my anger subsides and I can write it in a non-snarky tone...

Amazon suggest that you use it to write about your experience of writing the book, or how you came to write it or where you got the idea from. That sounds nice, and a better use of this feature than Bad Reviewer Retribution. Better for your karma too.

You could also look at this as an extended product description. I think when this book goes live on Amazon I'll use it to explain why I wrote this book—because all the self-publishing guides I could find came served with a massive side of "Death to Big Publishing!"—which will pull double-duty as a further explanation of what the book is like.

They give you loads of space for this: 8,000 characters, or about 1,600 words. Although, again, only use them if you have something to say—don't ramble on about how one night your main character appeared before you at the end of your bed and simply *demanded* that you write a book about them, so you hopped up, went straight to your desk and typed until the sun came up ten days later. (I cannot *stand* these kinds of stories, by the way. What actually happened to you is called *getting an idea*. Big whoop.) Don't put phone numbers, e-mail addresses or URLs, advertisements or other promotional material (like discount codes and whatnot) and for the love of vanilla-flavoured fudge, don't put anything like, "HEY, YOU GUYS ROCK! I'D LOVE SOME 5-STAR REVIEWS! LOVE AND BUBBLES 4EVER! XOXOXO!"

From the Inside Flap

Here is a whole other 8,000 characters' worth of space in which you can transcribe the text that appears on the inside flap of your book's dust jacket. Do you know what *transcribe* means? Well, it doesn't mean *make something up just because I have the space*. And your book doesn't have an inside flap, so you can't use this.

From the Back Cover

And yet another 8,000 characters' worth of space! But you *can* use this one, if you're clever about it. Our product description is only 4,000 characters, at most. Could you expand on it? Because as long as it's similar, you could put an expanded product description here.

About the Author

You can also edit your author biography from this page, and you have 2,000 characters in which to do it, which is about 400 words. This is a good feature that you should think about whenever something major happens to you, like you win something or you're on the radio or in a national newspaper. (Writing-related, I should add!)

All you need to do to add or edit any of these items is to sign in to Amazon AC, click on the book's image in your bibliography and start typing. You'll also be able to edit these items in the future.

A Gentle Reminder

I know being able to put all this information about ourselves on Amazon is heady stuff, but don't lose sight of what you're actually trying to achieve here: you want to convince people to buy your book. So avoid:

- Coming across like a jerk ("I just *had* to write this book—to save the world!")
- Irrelevant information ("I love bunnies!")
- Too much information ("I started writing page 3 at 10 p.m. on Tuesday 2nd March...)
- Hyperbole ("This is the greatest book ever written"—Person Nobody Has Ever Heard Of).

Amazon Sales Ranks

Your Amazon Sales Rank is that little (or big) number you see on your listing next to "Amazon Bestseller Rank" even though, ahem, you might be the furthest thing from a bestseller. When someone buys a copy of your book, the number goes down. It'll then rise steadily (as the sales of other books and their improving ranks push it down—or up!) until someone buys another copy. Thus, the lower the number, the better. #1,042,181? Very bad. But #201? Pretty amazing.

But of course it's not that simple, and it wasn't all that simple anyway what with a number that goes up as it gets pushed down. (My brain hurts.) These numbers are determined by all sorts of mysterious, secret algorithms, change all the time and are *not* straightforward bestseller ranks.

If my book is currently ranking at #1,505, it doesn't mean that based on the numbers of copies of all the books on Amazon that have been sold in the last few hours, I sold the 1,505th most. It's more like taking into account all of the books sold on Amazon in the last few hours, the books that are like mine that sold and how my book was selling before this number was updated, I'm the 1,505th most popular book on Amazon at this moment in time.

(Or something.)

Let me put it another way: multiple factors affect your sales rank, and they are not directly related to how many copies of your book you've sold. If your sales rank is #1000 on Friday and the purchase of one copy makes it go to #800, doing the same thing when your sales rank is #1000 on Saturday won't have the same effect. It might make it #100, #1500 or it might not change it at all, because Amazon also takes into account sales of books that are related to yours *and* the sales of all other books. And so maybe the site was quiet on Friday, giving you an advantage (or a better sales rank) with the sale of one book, but on Saturday it was busy, with plenty of other authors selling copies too, giving you no advantage and keeping your sales rank practically unchanged.

(Is this section over yet?)

Sales ranks can take 2–3 hours to update after the sale of a book has taken place.

Does Your Sales Rank Matter?

Only if it's *really* good or *really* bad. If it's really good, congrats! Your book must be doing really, really well, especially if it breaks into the top 1,000. (Or, dare we dream, the top 500. Or, dare we delude ourselves, the top 100.) Make sure you take a screenshot for posterity. The benefits of having a low (or good) sales rank is that your book becomes more visible on the site—higher up on bestseller lists, higher up on search results, more frequently recommended, etc.—and therefore has a better chance of selling even more copies; this is why sales lead to more sales on Amazon.com.

If you don't have a sales rank, no one has ever bought a copy of your book. At least not from Amazon. And if your sales rank is 1,000,000 or more, it means no one has bought a copy of your book in ages, and neither of those scenarios make you or your book look very good.

The Power Of One Sale

You'd be surprised, however, how as little as one sale can vastly improve your sales rank. Sometimes my paperback is hovering up around 500,000 (after maybe 4 or 5 days of no sales at all), and then one person buys one copy and it drops to under 100,000. If more than one or two people buy a copy within the space of a few hours, you can see your rank drop to less than 10,000, which would be brilliant for a self-published POD book.

Kindle is even better because a) you sell more copies and b) there's less competition, a situation that makes for very good sales ranks indeed. I've seen my Kindle edition of *Mousetrapped* drop below 250 on Amazon.co.uk, which was quite the coronary-inducing moment, let me tell you.

Don't Even THINK About It

Since sales ranks are so easy to affect, some people get the idea to artificially raise (or lower!) them by organising mass purchasing of their book in a very short space of time, pushing it into the bestseller ranks, making it more visible around the site and securing its future as an Amazon bestselling book, even if it's in name only and the very next day the book drops out of sight.

The most popular way to do this is to enlist friends, family, people who signed up to your mailing list, yourself and anyone else you can find with an Amazon account to all go online at, say, noon on the day your book launches and buy one copy. There is even a book (for sale on Amazon, of course) that describes in detail how to do this.

This and stuff like it is completely dishonest, pointless, desperate, moronic and pathetic, times ten. Is that really what you have to do to get your book selling? Make all your friends buy it? Buy copies of it yourself? Boy, I bet *that's* a good book.

The Non-Moronic Way To Improve Your Sales Rank

When author Talli Roland (*The Hating Game*—you've met her already) released her e-book, she "took on Amazon" with a blog splash. She got as many people as possible to blog or tweet about her book on the day it launched. Let's be clear: she didn't *ask* anyone to buy it. Not once. She just said "my book is now available on Amazon" across the platforms of her online presence and those of her blogging and Twitter friends and fans. At the end of the day, her Amazon.com sales rank was 460, and her Amazon.co.uk was a staggering 24! She can now say her book was an Amazon bestseller on the day of its release, and she didn't have to buy a single copy of her own book, or ask anyone else to.

Category Bestseller Rankings

And anyway, where you rank in your book's categories is far more fun, and a hell of a lot more straightforward. You'll see these in the same place as your sales rank, although they'll only appear there if you're towards the top.

Will I ever forget the joyous day I saw *Mousetrapped*'s Kindle edition go to #1 in Kindle Store –> Books –> Non-fiction –> Travel –> United States –> Regions –> South –> South Atlantic? (I knew I'd made it then, let me tell you.) But here's the thing: that makes my book an Amazon bestseller, even if the category is so hilariously specific I'd never recall it from memory.

And look at my ranks in this screenshot, which was taken at precisely 5.32 p.m. on Sunday 20th March 2011. I'm #1 in good old South Atlantic, #2 in Orlando and #3 in Disney World. And South Atlantic is just for Kindle books, but the other two are taking into account *all books*. Pretty sweet, eh? And yet my sales rank is #3,489, or not exactly setting the world on fire.

The moral of the story: don't worry too much about your sales rank. And DON'T buy copies of your own book.

KDP Select

When I first released this book, KDP didn't exist. A few months ago, hundreds of self-published authors were singing its praises. More recently, they've been keen to avoid it. Today we can only wonder: *where are we with KDP Select?*

First of all, what *is* KDP Select? Basically it's a programme run by Amazon that:

- Compensates you for borrows from the Kindle Owner's Lending Library (KOLL)
- Enables you to promote your book as free for up to 5 days out of every 90.

Translated into Stuff We Care About speak, this means:

- You make a little bit more money, because you're getting paid when someone borrows your book
- You get oodles of free advertising because when your book is free, thousands of people seem to automatically download it
- You get the benefits of increased reviews, higher sale ranks, etc. from the free downloads/new readers.

Before we go any further, I want to make something clear: it allows you to promote your book *as* free. This means your book will be advertised as free—sold for nothing—for the days you enrol in the KDP Select promotion. It does not mean anything else, and it *especially* doesn't mean that Amazon will promote your book *for* free while it sells at normal price.

What's the catch? Well, there are a few:

- To enrol in KDP Select, your book *cannot* be available in digital format *anywhere* else. No Smashwords, no Barnes and Noble, no iBooks—not even a PDF that's free to download from your blog. (Paperback editions being available elsewhere are fine.) They must be exclusive to Amazon for the full 90 days of the minimum enrolment period, even if you withdraw it before the 90 days are up. If they're not and Amazon finds out, they are entitled to withhold any money you've earned under the KDP Select programme, and might even freeze your KDP account.

- Anecdotal evidence suggests that most people who download free books do it just because they're free. They might never read them—there's no incentive to, they were freebies—and if they do, they mightn't finish them, and even if they do, they might not bother reviewing them. The flip-side to this is that they *do* read and review them, but then hate them and give them one-star reviews. Why? Because why read the blurb, other reviews, etc. before downloading a free book? When it's free, there's no need to check if it's suitable for me.

- In terms of helping your sales ranks, etc. one free download is rumoured to be equal to about 0.1 paid sale in Amazon's eyes, at the moment. This means that when your book goes back to paid, the "bump" in its sale rank will be minimal.

- The compensation for borrows comes out of a shared fund. At the time of writing, this has been $600,000 for the last few months. So if 500,000 books are borrowed in July and each was borrowed once, each borrow earns the author around $1.20. The bad news about this is that the more titles enrolled in KDP Select and the more those titles are borrowed, the less each author's individual compensation, and the compensation might be less than the retail price of your book.

You may be wondering why, with all this bad news, I'm even mentioning KDP Select. The truth is I still like it. I still think it can help self-published authors, *if* they use it wisely and *if* they start seeing it for what—for all—that it is: free publicity.

When To Use KDP Select

Something happens when you set your book to free. It's like magic: one minute you've had 10 downloads all month, the next you've had 100 downloads in the last ten minutes. Setting your book to free is like lighting the fuse on a firework: all you need do is stand well back and watch it soar. But there's no point in lighting that firework unless we're having a party. Otherwise it's just an expensive waste. And that's how you should think of KDP: something to bring out for special occasions, and only when you're prepared to get the most out of it.

I think there are three great times to use KDP Select:

- **To launch your book**. If KDP Select had been around when I'd released *Mousetrapped*, I definitely would've used it. What other way can a no-name author without a shred of credibility to her name get thousands of people to notice her book, and hundreds of people to read it? No way I can think of that doesn't require the spending of lots of cash. Now I know what your reaction will be to this: *why would I give it away for free first? Shouldn't I let everyone who'll buy it* buy *it before I do that?* Think about it: how many people do you know for sure are going to buy your book as soon as it comes out? I'm guessing the answer is a number that will be entirely dwarfed by the figure you're likely to score on free downloads. On balance, the reviews, increased awareness, visibility, etc. you'll get from KDP Select will be worth a *lot* more to you. If a lot of people are guaranteed to buy your book when it comes out, you could do the sneaky KDP Select: set your book to free for a few days before you've told a single soul, least of all any of your first readers, that it's out. I'm on the fence about the fairness of this though—you should be rewarding your supporters, not tricking them into paying for something you're offering to others for free.

- **To launch your next book**. Imagine now, if you will, a slot machine making that winning *ding-ding-ding* sound, because the best way to use KDP Select is when the book you want to sell *isn't* the one KDP Selected. Let's say you've written a series, and the second title is about to come out. So to give it a little boost, you set the first title to free for five days with KDP Select. Now it truly is free advertising for your second book, because anyone who downloads the first for free and likes it can skip merrily along and pay for the next instalment.

- **To bring your book back to life**. Back in KDP Select's early days, there were lots of blog posts about it with names like "How KDP Select Saved My Book." You know the way in *ER* and *Grey's Anatomy* they get those human jump-lead thingies to shock people's tickers back to life? Well, KDP Select can be those jump-lead thingies for your book. If it's not selling very well anyway, what have you got to lose by setting it to free for a few days? Nothing. You only have everything to gain.

You don't have to use all of your five free days at once, but I recommend that you do. Each day's downloads will snowball, hopefully pushing you high onto the "Free" bestseller lists. You can't really achieve much in just one or two days of free; the best results come from using them all up together.

As for which *days*, I'd recommend going Thursday to Monday inclusive. Thursday is apparently the biggest day for e-book sales—why? I don't have a clue—and of course more books are sold on the weekends than weekdays, as Kindle owners are at home looking for books to spend their leisure time with.

A word of warning: removing your books for sale from Smashwords and all their Premium Catalogue channels is *not* easy. It can take weeks, and many, many e-mails before the books disappear entirely, and you can only enrol them in KDP Select once all trace of them have disappeared from everywhere else. If I was back at the start of my self-publishing experience again, I'd go exclusively with Amazon for the first three months of my book's life, doing a free promotion right out of the gate, and then only *after* that would I upload to Smashwords. It's what I plan to do with my next book, except that since it won't be my first one, the book I set to free will be a previously released title.

How To Use KDP Select

You can enrol any book of yours in KDP Select from your Bookshelf on KDP Select, or by checking the box next to the book's title and then selecting Action –> Enrol in KDP Select. To pick your free days, select "Manage Promotions" from the same menu.

Before you set your book to free, make sure that your listing *and* your book are both ready for it. Cast a critical eye over your product description, about the author, etc. and see if there is any room for improvement. Have you recently got a glowing review that might sway a few minds? Well, now is the time to add it in. Think about what's about to happen: thousands of eyes are about to land on your listing for the very first time. If you had just launched a website and were airing a primetime television commercial tomorrow evening, wouldn't you devote some time to checking that your website was ready for a few million visitors first? Your Amazon listing is no different, and neither is your book. Double-check it's as perfect as possible. Maybe even have another read through to see if you can spot any errors that have thus far avoided detection. Trust me when I say that people who get your book for free will expect far more perfection of it than those who hand over money for it. If there's as much as an *apostrophe* in the wrong place, you'll soon know all about it.

It's also a good idea to maximise the benefits of your free run by arranging some cross promotion for the first day it goes back to paid. Perhaps you could line this up with the beginning of your blog tour, or a Twitter contest you've organised, or maybe even try some paid-for advertising for forty-eight hours after your book goes back to paid. This way, the sales rank improvement hangover gets a few vodka shots and next thing you know, it's drunk again.

Or something.

I would also recommend that you *uncheck* the box for automatic re-enrol in the KDP Select program. Unless you've got further book releases planned in the near future, you'll only want to run your book through KDP Select's 90 days once. If you've checked automatic re-enrol (and I believe that's the default setting), you might well forget to uncheck it again before the next 90 days come around. Instead, I'd recommend that you take your success and build on it by going for full distribution, i.e. making your book available through all possible sales channels.

Affiliate Programmes

If you're going to be putting links to your book's online listings into your blog and tweets and onto your Facebook walls, you may as well earn commission on them from the sites in question. As I said in the section about monetising your blog, you'd have to sell a *lot* of books to earn even the price of one, but you have a greater chance of earning it off your own book than anyone else's (because there'll be more click-throughs). Sign up here:

- Amazon Associates: **affiliate-program.amazon.com**
- Smashwords Affiliates: **www.smashwords.com/about/affiliate**
- The Book Depository Affiliates: **affiliates.bookdepository.com/affiliates.**

Turning The Wheel

Haven't we been busy bees, eh? We decided to self-publish, we self-published, expertly built an online platform, used it to spread feverish anticipation about our book (or at least, got people to go, "Hmm. *Interesting...*"), launched our book like a moonrocket and maximised our Amazon presence so that anyone who makes it all the way to our listing will be so overcome with conviction that they'll not only buy our book, but *multiple* copies of it.

Or maybe just the one.

Maybe only a few copies a day, but still. Copies are being downloaded in exchange for cash. We are published authors, and people are reading our work. Hooray! But, um, what happens now?

The first three months after you release your book are a crucial time in which you have to work to ensure that your book doesn't disappear back into the abyss as quickly as it appeared from it. You won't be working as hard or as much as you did in the three months running up to publication, but you'll be working harder than you'll need to three months from now. Our main goal at this stage is to get Amazon to sell our books *for* us.

How does Amazon sell your book for you?

- By recommending it to their customers in e-mail shots
- By displaying it in features like "Customers Also Bought" and "You Might Also Be Interested In"
- By displaying it higher up search results.

There's no ethical way to *make* this happen, and it takes time for it to happen organically. For example, if you sold 20 copies of your book on Amazon today, that's an amoeba-like speck in Amazon's ocean. But if you sold 20 copies of your book every day for 90 days, you'd at least be visible to the naked eye. (Just bear with me here...) The sales data and mysterious Amazon algorithms have been laying down tracks for three months now, making connections between more and more customers and more and more books, and so the 20 you'll sell tomorrow will have a much more significant impact on your Amazon presence. Meanwhile, the reviews you've been collecting and the ones left by Amazon customers are telling both *other* Amazon customers and Amazon itself that not only is this book selling, but that it's selling because it's *good*.

Think of your Amazon presence like a watermill (without the grinding grain bit!): the water is the people you're sending Amazon's way, and the wheel represents sales of your books. The speed at which the mill is turning is how much help Amazon is giving your sales figures, how much work it's doing on your behalf. The more water you can direct at the wheel and the faster you can direct it there, the faster the wheel turns.

The key to this period in the life of your book is **consistency**. It doesn't matter if you only spend 30 minutes a day online or that you sell less than 10 books a day, so long as you're spending 30 minutes online and selling 10 books a day *every* day.

So what do you actually *do*?

Maintain A Workable Social Media Presence

Figure out how much time you can comfortably spend online a week—leaving plenty of time for sleeping, eating and writing your next book, of course—and then plan how you're going to use it.

Map out your **social media week**. Mine looks something like this:

- *Blog posts*: 1–3. Write them over the weekend with one eye on the television, try to keep them to less than 1,000 words—I'm a terror for overly long blog posts! — and then schedule them to post on Mondays, Wednesdays and Fridays, preferably. (To schedule a post, look to the right of the screen in the "New Post" window on WP; you'll see "Publish" and then a drop-down menu that starts with "immediately." Change to the date and time of your choosing and it'll post automatically at that time.) I try to have at least one that could spark a self-publishing-themed discussion of some sort, and I keep guest posts/advertising/news of events, etc. to a minimum. My blog is my main focus. Even if I'm extremely busy and drop everything else, I make sure that I update my blog. I think of it like my online "hub"; all roads — or URLs — lead to it. Downloading the free WP app to your smart phone will enable you to moderate and respond to comments on the go.

- *Twitter.* Back when *Mousetrapped* came out, I was on Twitter *all the time.* That was perhaps a tad unnecessary, but you do need to tweet often in the beginning, both to get used to using Twitter and to make some Twitter friends. But there are ways you can do this without developing a separation anxiety disorder whenever you're away from your phone. I use Twitter in three different ways. First, I use the **Buffer** App (www.bufferapp.com) to tweet interesting links. This makes up the majority of my tweeting. Whenever I find an interesting blog post or a share-worthy piece of news or a hilarious YouTube video that I think my followers will get a giggle out of, I add it to my Buffer Account. Then at times I've pre-specified on my Buffer Dashboard, these links get tweeted throughout the week until the tweets I've "buffered" run out. I do this Monday to Friday, and I make sure to spread them out to cover all time zones. This means that I can have a valuable Twitter presence without actually having to be there. Second, I downloaded the Twitter app to my smartphone so that in those time-to-kill moments — queuing, commercial breaks, bouts of insomnia — I can mark any tweets I want to respond to, retweet or investigate further later as "favourites" and come back to them later when I have more time. Third, I tweet-chat, meaning that I use Twitter to catch up with both real life and online friends.

- *Facebook.* The least demanding aspect of your social media platform will be your Facebook page. A few minutes a week should do it. Post an update about what you're up to (or if you're up to nothing much, post a link to one of your newest blog posts), or perhaps ask a question ("What was your favourite chapter/character/scene in *My Book*?") and respond to any comments that your lovely Facebook fans have left for you.

- *Blog reading and commenting.* Don't forget to read other people's blogs and to leave comments when you feel you have something to add. This will keep you up to date with what's happening in the blogosphere, provide you with fodder for your Buffer account and hopefully make some new blog-friend connections too.

Continue To Produce Quality Content

It is of the utmost importance that while you're busy promoting your book, you don't neglect the blog readers, Twitter followers and Facebook fans that will *never* buy it. An empty shell of a blog that only exists so you can remind us that your book is just $2.99 is never going to work, neither as effective book promotion *nor* a blog. Your social media presence, like everything else in this operation, has to be *genuine*.

And no matter what happens you need to continue to produce quality content (i.e. blog posts, etc.) and do so regularly. Far more people are interested in my blog—and have found me by way of it—than my books, and by some significant margin. I need to keep them interested, because they might eventually buy my book or, if they're not at all interested in it, they might buy the next one. Even if they *never* buy a book, their support will still be a huge help to me when I'm trying to sell it to other people, and spread the word that it exists. Also, I love blogging. I really do. And knowing that thousands of people are reading it makes it even sweeter.

Your blog shouldn't just be about your book but you should use it to keep people updated of its progress. If someone posts a review of your book or mentions it on their blog, or if in the Real World you're written about in a newspaper or interviewed on the radio, or if you hit a big sales milestone like 100, 500 or 1,000 copies, put it on your blog. Either post about it or add it to your "News" page.

Don't be concerned that it'll read like, "Look at me! Look what I've done!" Remember: this is *your* blog. It's all about you by default.

You may also have collected readers purely because they're interested in your self-publishing adventure and want to see how it's going for you. Let them know.

Shooting For The Moon
(Or Why You Shouldn't Just Listen to Me)

When it comes to ideas for ways we can attract new readers and keep the ones we have entertained, self-published authors tend to look to other self-published authors for ideas. This is fine, but you shouldn't *only* look to them. The bestselling authors in the world are all traditionally published — and yes, that includes our old friend *50 Shades* — so why not look to them too?

Here are some ideas I've, um, borrowed from some of my favourite traditionally published authors:

Michael Connelly's Photo Submission/Review Contest

Michael Connelly is my favourite author and I am glued to his website and Facebook page for updates. A few books ago — it may have been *The Brass Verdict* — his webmaster asked readers to send in photos of themselves reading his book. If you did, you got your picture on his website under a section called "Look Who's Reading [BOOK TITLE]" and if you were one of the first 1,000 people to do it, you got sent an exclusive little book about how he created his two main characters, Harry Bosch and Mickey Haller, that wasn't available to buy. When *Mousetrapped* came out, I invited readers to do the same thing with "Look Who's Reading *Mousetrapped*". I didn't reward them with anything but I *did* get some great content to add to my Facebook page.

Karin Slaughter's Newsletter

You may know Karin Slaughter as the author of gripping and occasionally gory thrillers like *Faithless*, *Fallen* and *Broken*, but did you know she has the funniest newsletter around? You know how it is: you find a new author you like, you sign up for their newsletter because you think you're going to want to hear from them, but then whenever it lands in your inbox you yawn and click Delete. Well, trust me when I say you won't be doing this with Slaughter's. They. Are. HILARIOUS. And she writes them in plain text! They don't even have any bells, whistles or fancy HTML. Sign up on her website to receive them so you can learn how it *should* be done. Then you can use MailChimp's wizard to design a simple newsletter template to send your own.

Miranda Dickinson's Video Blog

Miranda Dickinson is the author of bestsellers *Fairytale of New York* and *Welcome to My World*. This year, in the lead up to the publication of her third novel, *It Started With a Kiss*, she kept a video blog/diary of the entire process: from writing the first draft of the book right through to publication, launch, etc. We're all fascinated with how other writers write, so to see a successful author at work is incentive enough to watch these videos, but you also can't help but keep tuning in to see what excitement is coming up next. (And of course, you ultimately want to buy the book whose birth you witnessed too.) Another idea: Miranda's e-book edition of *It Started With a Kiss* contains "bonus features" like deleted scenes and commentary! Intriguing.

Ali McNamara's Breakfast with Ali

Ali McNamara is the author of *From Notting Hill... With Love Actually* and she (or someone clever she knows) has had a great idea to help publicize her new book, *Breakfast at Darcy's.* "Breakfast with Ali" is a challenge: Ali must eat something different for breakfast every day for 30 days—and blog about it, of course. I think it's great fun and something different. Plus, it's the kind of thing a self-publisher could easily replicate.

Paid-for Advertising

As I write this my books have been on sale for over two years and I have yet to spend as much as a penny on advertising. But then, it really took the best part of a year for my first book to start selling well. If you don't have the time but you do have the cash, then maybe paying for some well-placed and targeted advertising is the solution for you. I'm considering doing it with my next book, just to give it a little launch-time boost.

Before you do anything, decide on an advertising budget. This should be equal to or less than a figure you wouldn't mind chucking down the toilet in cash right now, because there's a chance spending it on advertising might sell as many books as doing that (i.e. none at all). I would be very slow to spend any more on $500 on my entire advertising budget, and I'd try to keep it to more like $300.

Where can you advertise your book? I think there's only three viable possibilities for the self-published author:

1. **Kindle Nation Daily** (www.kindlenationaldaily.com) is a website, e-mail update and Facebook page for Kindle owners that promises to deliver "all things Kindle, every day". They offer a number of sponsorship options for self-published authors who want to get their books in front of Kindle-owning eyes, ranging from a One-Day Sponsorship Kindle National Daily Free Book Alert ($139.99) which makes you and your book the sole sponsor of KND's popular "free book" post—note, your book isn't the free book they're talking about, so it doesn't have to be free—to a service that tells KDN users when your book *is* free for just $29.99. You might opt for one of the more expensive sponsorship deals during

your launch week or even on launch day, or use the free book highlighter service to bump up your free downloads when using KDP Select.

2. **Book blogs.** Many book bloggers take banner advertisements that run across the top of their homepage and/or sidebar adverts for books that run in the, er, sidebar. Depending on the popularity of the book blog, the prices for these can range from suspiciously reasonable to terrifyingly expensive. However if you've written a crime novel and you find a popular book blogger who only reads and reviews crime, then you know that money spent on advertising there will be money *well* spent, because everyone who sees it will be a reader of books like yours. Spend some time looking for suitable blogs or sites and read them for a while before you make your final decision. Maybe target the book blogs you've already sent review copies to. If the price is high, ask for evidence of value for money, i.e. hit statistics, follower numbers, etc. This is something I'd do after the initial push, maybe a month or six weeks after you've released your book.

3. **Targeted advertising.** You might already be familiar with Facebook ads, that let you specify *exactly* the kinds of people you want to see your ads and then take a charge out of a specified budget each time they show it to them. For example, I could tell Facebook that I want fans of Bill Bryson who also list "travel" and "reading" as hobbies to see an ad for my book *Backpacked*, and I want to set a budget of $100. They start flashing my book cover in the sidebar of travelling and reading Bill Bryson fans, and they do it until my $100 runs out. Facebook ads are *super* easy to design and you can pay for *impressions* (it appears on the page) or *clicks* (um... when someone clicks). Just look for the "create an ad" link the next time you're logged into Facebook. The good news is that Goodreads has now started running a similar scheme, and over there, it's even better because we know there's a great chance that everyone who sees our ad will already love reading *and* sharing reviews with their friends. Because the amounts here don't have to be astronomical, this is perhaps a strategy you could repeat, i.e. once a quarter, you spend $50 on Facebook advertising and $50 on Goodreads.

Watch For Opportunities

Keep an eye out online for ways you can promote your book. Come across a fabulous new book blog? E-mail the owner to see if they'd like a copy of your book. See that one of your blogger friends is looking for guest posts to put on her blog? Offer to write one about your self-publishing experiences. From time to time you even see tweets from journalists looking to speak to self-publishers about their experiences for an article on the subject. Volunteer!

Be Nice

Thank everyone. Respond to reader e-mails (the non-crazy ones, anyway). Be generous. Return favours. At all times, *be nice*.

Wait

One of the most important things you can learn to do as a self-published author is to *wait*. Your blog won't wake up in the morning with 2,000 followers, and you won't become a #1 bestseller overnight. These things take *time*. Remember, for almost a year my book was selling around 100 copies a month. I was frustrated, but I held on. Then over the 2010 Christmas period, something magical happened: my book sold 1,000 copies in 30 days. Since then, sales have never gone anywhere near that original 100 again. So even if you feel like you're doing a lot of work and getting nowhere, don't stress. And whatever you do, don't give up. Just *wait*.

What NOT To Do

I could write a whole other book on what not to do to promote your book, but as we're already up to way over 100,000 words, I'm going to keep it short and sweet here. Kindly refrain from doing any of these things, okay? Thanks.

Promote Your Book Offline

I've worked with a number of self-published authors who have been traditionally published in the past, and the number one mistake I see them making is trying to promote their self-published work in the same way their publishers did their traditionally published work. They hire publicists, hand over wads of cash in exchange for polished press releases and badger newspaper editors, radio show producers and even TV stations in the hope that news of their book will get a mention in print or on air.

No, no, no, no, NO.

Just *no.*

When you self-publish, your book is either predominantly or only for sale online. Therefore advertising offline is a *complete* waste of time, and a very expensive one.

I wouldn't even bother pursuing offline attention, such as reviews and interviews in newspapers. If it comes to you, great. By all means take advantage of it.

But I wouldn't spend too much time chasing it, because if you're not in bookshops, it's worthless to you.

If I hear about a traditionally published book on the radio or see an ad for it on TV or in print, I might think to myself, Oh, that looks interesting. But I need to see that book again, on the shelves of a bookshop, to be reminded and nudged into purchasing it. With self-published books, there is no such reminder.

As for public relations people and publicists, no one can sell your book like you can, and they can't sell self-published books at *all.* They don't know how. They can only model their efforts on what publishing houses do and hope for the best. What self-publishing success do you know of that came via a PR company, eh? There aren't any. John Locke, the first self-published author to sell 1,000,000 Kindle books, famously spent a small fortune on the traditional promotional efforts he believed would help sell his book (newspaper and TV advertisements, press releases, even ads in movie theatres) and *none* of them worked. It was just a gigantic waste of time and money. So instead he turned to blogging, Twitter and building a mailing list of fans—all of which are free to do, I might add— and the rest is history.

In my experience, newspapers and radio shows only come calling when your book is *already* a success, because that's a story. "Author publishes own book" is not.

Hire Someone To "Do" Your Social Media

Again, no one can sell your book like you can, which is the first reason you shouldn't hire someone else to do your online promotion for you.

The second is that the best blogs, Twitter accounts and Facebook presences make a direct connection with their readers, followers and fans, and this is impossible to achieve if there's a "social media guru" between you and them. It's like paying someone else to give your friend a hug.

Thirdly, it's stupid. Social media isn't rocket science. You don't need any special training or experience to do it and you only need to be pointed in the direction of the people who do it well to do it well yourself. Books like these can get you set up with the basics and offer you little tips and tricks, but there's no major skill involved. So why waste money paying somebody who pretends there is? Not only can you do it yourself, but the results will be infinitely better if you do.

Let Your Friends Defend Your Honour

A few months ago a friend of mine self-published a book and submitted it to a very popular book blogger for review. I've been reading this book blogger's posts longer than I've known my friend's plans to self-publish; it's one of my favourite book review sites. It's not anything fancy: the blogger just reads the books, tells us what's they're about and then gives us a verdict out of ten based on how much she liked it. Sometimes I totally disagree with her, but she's always fair, and when she has to criticise she'll always add an apologetic "this just wasn't my kind of thing" or "remember, this is just my opinion". In other words, she's a balanced, professional book blogger.

Who didn't particularly like my friend's book. She didn't *not* like it; she was on the fence. She gave it six out of ten and amongst plenty of praise for the writing, humour and descriptions, said that she didn't like the main character and didn't find her actions believable.

My friend was momentarily upset that the review wasn't glowing, but she wasn't devastated. She knew — as I did — that not *all* reviews can be glowing, and that this was just one book blogger's opinion, and that in the scheme of things, not that many people would even read it. She sent the blogger an e-mail expressing her disappointment that she didn't like it more, but also thanking her for taking the time to review it and promising to keep her on the review copy list for her next book. The blogger replied with a thank you and said there was a lot about the book she *did* like and that she'd love to receive a copy of the new book. In other words: perfect author behaviour.

But *friends* of my friends didn't take it as well. One of them took it upon herself to leave a comment on the review refuting everything the blogger had criticised, and not in a polite way. She also referred to the author in such a way that it was clear to everyone that the two were personal friends. The blogger responded, defending herself, and the defending friend left another comment, this one much nastier and full of insults, including a line about how the blogger was probably just a failed writer herself who was so jealous of everyone else's success that she couldn't write positive reviews. The situation snowballed out of control and within hours, people in my Twitter stream were posting links to the exchange saying things like, "How NOT to respond to a review... Yikes!"

It was embarrassing. I don't actually think my author friend appreciated just *how* embarrassing, or how badly it reflected on her. I think she thought that because she wasn't the one commenting it was okay, but of course anyone with half a brain would conclude that she was friends with the person who *was*.

Clearly, my friend's friend thought she was doing something good. She thought she was defending her friend's honour, and letting everyone who read the review know that, actually, the book was good. But all she was doing was turning people off ever reading my friend's book, this one or the ones she releases in the future. She was making my friend look like a complete amateur who didn't know how to behave in public.

So rein in your friends. Explain to them that the internet never forgets, and that the only way to respond to a negative review is not to. The same goes for any other "favours" they might think to do for you: sending e-mails about your book to everyone they know, writing suspiciously glowing Amazon reviews, tweeting links to your website every 30 seconds. All they'll be doing is making *you* look bad.

Release Multiple Books Simultaneously

There's a school of thought that says don't do anything to promote your book until you have several books to promote. The idea is that if you manage to find a reader and convince them to buy one of your books, there are another two or three or more for them to buy immediately afterwards, thus converting the effort of promoting one book into the sale of several.

Seems like a good idea, right?

It's not. At least *I* don't think it is. In fact, I completely disagree with it. I believe you need to release your books one at a time with space in between, and market, promote and sell them that way too. Here's why.

We've talked already about the science of book-selling. Let's say now that getting me to buy your book involves at least three steps. You need to:

1. Tell me about it
2. Pique my interest
3. Give me a reason (i.e. make me care enough) to buy it.

Let me give you a real-life example of how this 1–2–3 process led me to buy a self-published e-book. One day I was reading a blog post about how some self-publishers had been adding things like "For Fans of Dan Brown" to their e-book titles and how Amazon had now moved to crack down on their clever (and a bit cheeky!) use of their system. The post mentioned two UK self-publishers, Louise Voss and Mark Edwards, who had done this to great effect with their e-book *Catch Your Death*. So that's how I found out the book existed — through a blog post. My interest was piqued when I read that the thriller was partly set at the Cold Research

Unit in Salisbury, because anything that involves viruses is a winner for me. (In another life I wanted to be a virologist.) So I went to look it up on Amazon, where a combination of what I already knew, the synopsis and the pair's writing credentials gave me reason enough to buy it. And so, because Mark and Louise had a good book that was the kind of thing I liked to read (it was well reviewed and they've since signed a huge deal with HarperCollins in the UK), and they'd designed a convincing Amazon listing, the only real work they had to do was inform me of their book's existence, and it's this that marketing multiple books simultaneously — or waiting until you have multiple books to market — cripples.

You want to create as many worthwhile opportunities as possible to inform new readers that your book exists, without boring the arses off the readers who are already along for the ride, i.e. your blog readers, Twitter followers, Facebook fans, newsletter recipients, etc. The way to do this is to squeeze every last bit of Interesting Juice out of each book, and then give everyone a chance to recover before you go at it again with your next title.

Take *Mousetrapped*. I started building anticipation about that book approximately three months before I released it. Here's some of the things I did:

- I blogged about my decision to self-publish it
- I blogged about the logistics of self-publishing it
- I shared my cover design process and other milestones such as the finished blurb
- I made two book trailers (see the Videos page)
- I offered copies to book bloggers
- I was interviewed by book bloggers and other sites
- I wrote guest posts for other blogs
- I had "#MousetrappedMondays" on Twitter where I made a thing of containing my self-promotion to 3–5 tweets every Monday in the lead up to its release, and then I released the book on the final #MousetrappedMonday, 29 March 2010
- I posted photos of my first proof copy, my first box of books, my bookstore launch, etc.
- I set up a Facebook page, asked friends to like it, and posted updates about the book on the wall
- I gave away copies on my blog
- I tweeted links to all of the above.

And in these ways, I told people that *Mousetrapped* existed, and I managed to get some of those people to buy it when it came out, to recommend it to friends and family and to mention it on their own online homes. And here is the key: when *Backpacked* came out more than a year later, I was able to do all those things again and more besides. Why? Because I now had a completely different title that generated new material for me to blog about, etc. and because enough time had passed for (i) the people who had been around since the beginning to forgive all my *Mousetrapped* talk and (ii) a whole new audience to turn to face my way, i.e. new Twitter followers, new friends of my Facebook fans, new blog readers of my blog friends, etc. Enough time had passed for me to reach loads of new people using the same methods as I had before – and to do it without pissing people off.

What if I had released all of my books at the same time? I would only ever have reached that first, small group. My original readers. The ones who came on board at the beginning. Now maybe they would've been loyal enough to buy all of my books, but what then? I can't continue to churn out post after tweet after post about the same old stuff, so I can't blog about my books. No one likes "My book is on Amazon. Buy it!" tweets, so that's out too. And what are all my lovely fans going to do after they've read all my books? What now?

I know the temptation to get the next book out there right now is overwhelming, especially if it's already written and ready to go. If someone sends you an e-mail saying "Just read *Your First Book* – loved it!!! When is the next one out? Can't wait to read it!" there's a reptilian part of your brain that considers going to KDP right that minute to upload the book, just so you don't lose that sale. Because that's The Big Fear, isn't it? That that reader will have forgotten all about you by the time your next book comes out. Well, guess what? I have to wait a year between books for *all* of my favourite writers – because that's the speed at which the publishing world works – and I manage it just fine. I never forget about them. Instead, I wait anxiously for their new books to come out. The waiting makes the reading sweeter. I've spent 364 days of every year waiting for a new Michael Connelly novel for almost half my life, and somehow I manage. I also buy every single one of his books. And if I do forget? Amazon reminds me in my recommendations whenever I visit the site. Sometimes they even e-mail me too. If that fails, I still have his Facebook fan page and newsletter to remind me of it.

You have to look at this in the long term. Yes, the person who e-mailed you might not buy your next book because by the time it comes out six months from now, they'll have forgotten about it. But the people who will find out about you for the first time when you put a full launch effort into your next title is a far greater number. As I've already said, organic growth is always better. You promote this first book well, you focus entirely on the one title, and hopefully you carry a lot of the readers you gain with you on to the next book. You repeat the process in a few month's time, and now you're carrying forward the readers from the first and second books, and they all read both of them. And so on and on. I think those readers, thanks to the longer relationship they'll have with you, will be a lot more likely to stick around in the long term that someone you managed to sell three 99c books to and then never interacted with again.

One of the people I follow on Twitter released three different books in rapid succession (I'd say, all within the same month) a while back. They were all quite different titles, and he'd never released anything before. He didn't blog really, so Twitter was his main online home. At the time of the release, there was a lot of Twitter talk about it, but that soon dropped off, like a rock dropping off the edge of a cliff, once the third book had been released. Since then? Nothing. Nada. Not a word. There's nothing new to report, and he's nice enough not to use his tweets for advertisements, so now he's stuck. And so are his sales. If he'd spread out those releases, he might be heading into the summer now with a brand new book to promote – and so, new things to tweet about (like how he came to have his cover design, what a headache e-book formatting is, what he's doing different this time around, etc.) – and I'd be willing to bet that he'd definitely get more sales. He has more Twitter followers now than he did when he released those books, and I – and all his other followers – are likely to have more people around us too, and so if I retweeted one of his book links, his audience would be much larger now than it was then. So, he should have waited. He should have spread out the release dates of his books.

What I'm basically trying to say is this:

- Each title release creates a wealth of material you can use to promote your book
- Putting this material online is one of the ways people find out that your book exists
- Informing people that your book exists is the first step in getting them to buy it
- You can't constantly use your online platform to promote your book, and it's not much fun to do that anyways
- Different people are following you and your followers than will be in six months' or a year's time
- The only way to maximize (i) how much material you get out of each book and (ii) the new people who see that material is to spread out your books
- What you sacrifice in I-just-finished-the-first-I'll-buy-the-next-one sales, you'll more than make up for with new, more loyal readers in the long term.

Forget Your Manners

Some self-published authors seem to be stricken with a mutant strain of highly resistant Entitlement Syndrome. Symptoms include: thinking that everyone is just *dying* to read their book; sending book reviewers e-mails like "My book *needs* to be read"; sending e-mails to *everyone* saying something similar; being controversial about publishing just for the sake of it; more than occasionally using words and phrases like "gatekeepers", "The Big Six", "revolution", "tenant farming", "Stockholm Syndrome" and "indie" while also not knowing what they're on about; offering self-publishing advice at a price when their own sales are in the three-digits, pronouncing the death of (i) print books, (ii) bookshops and (iii) the evil corporate entities who man the gates between our dreams and reality; responding to negative reviews with a tone that says "*You* don't know what you're talking about"; never commenting on someone else's blog without at least *three* hyperlinks to places where their own book is on sale, and a really serious, not-at-all-casual mention of their book in said comment, e.g. "I know what you mean about KDP Select. When I was promoting my 3,103 5* reviewed steampunk dystopian love story, *All This and a Bag of Android Cats*, I found that...". At the time of diagnosis over 90% of sufferers are given less than three months to continue selling books, and some are warned that they are only moments away from a catastrophic career implosion. There's no known cure—although swift smacks upside the head have been known to be effective in temporarily alleviating the symptoms—leaving only one sure-fire method of protection against this devastating syndrome: *abstinence*.

The Role Of Luck

One thing that we can be certain plays a role in whether a book ends up on the bestseller list or in the remainder pile is *luck*. Now while I don't subscribe to the notion that we make our own luck, I *do* think you can position yourself so that you're first in the queue to receive some of it. The best way to explain this—and everything else I've been talking about—is to share with you what's happened to me.

I released *Mousetrapped* in March 2010. Sales steadily ticked over for the first six months of its life, but the proceeds were barely keeping me in coffee grounds, let alone ink cartridges.

By September 1st I'd sold the grand total of 531 copies, or an average of 88 copies per month. I was happy with this because that was almost exactly my goal: 100 copies in a month, 500 in six months, 1,000 in a year. I'd been chronicling my self-printing adventures, as I called them, on my blog, and had promised readers a breakdown of my royalties and sales figures after six months, so I posted them.

These posts brought a lot of traffic to my blog, and as a result my sales kicked up a notch. In September, October and November 2010, I sold 184, 174 and 180 copies respectively. My sales had more than doubled, but the growth was all in e-books. With me getting to keep over $2 from every $2.99 e-book sold, I wasn't complaining.

In the meantime, something happened in the real world: I was invited to speak about how I used social media to sell my book at a self-publishing conference in Dublin. How did this happen? Back in January when I was preparing to self-publish my book, I got chatting to a woman called Vanessa on Twitter. Vanessa, it turned out, was the owner of a company that ran writers' workshops and offers services like manuscript critique. A lot of the other Irish writers I was talking to on Twitter knew her as well, and I went along to one of the workshops to meet up with them all. When I found out Vanessa was organising a self-publishing conference, I decided to attend and booked a place. I thought it would be a great learning and networking opportunity. Then, a couple of weeks before the conference, a problem with a keynote speaker arose. Vanessa, knowing about my self-publishing story and knowing that I was going to be attending anyway, asked me if I would fill in. I was only too happy to, and (luckily!) it went really well. Not only that, but I was quoted in an article in *The Sunday Independent* newspaper the week before the conference, which talked about the self-publishing success of the conference's keynote speakers.

Next: Christmas happened. Santa must have brought lots of people new Kindles, because my e-book sales suddenly spiked. I'd sold 180 copies in November but in December, I sold 422 — and hit 1,000 copies sold, four months ahead of schedule. But then something even crazier happened: in January, I sold nearly a thousand copies. Now every month for three months, I'd sold double what I'd sold the month before.

One day I sat down at my desk, went to WordPress and wrote a blog post basically saying "What the hell just happened to my e-book sales?" I included some charts and told everybody how, between Christmas Eve and the end of January, I'd sold more than a thousand copies of my book — having taken *eight months* to sell the thousand before that.

This post proved popular and Eoin Purcell, the editor of the Irish Publishing News website, asked if he could repost it on IPN. I said yes, and he did. *The Bookseller*, the biggest publishing trade publication on this side of the pond, put a link to the post in their morning briefing e-mail. This increased my blog traffic but other than that, I didn't think too much more about it.

Three days later an e-mail arrived in my inbox with an e-mail address ending in "sunday-times.ie." It was an enquiry from a writer for the Irish edition of *The Sunday Times* newspaper expressing interest in writing a piece about my e-book success. He'd seen my post on IPN. *The Sunday Times?!?!* I couldn't say yes quick enough. The story was about how, having been rejected by traditional publishing based on the non-existence of a market for my book, I'd turned to self-publishing, which provided me with access to a global market and used outlets like social media to get people interested in my writing as opposed to the book. I was so excited the day the story came out, thinking that surely, it couldn't get better than this. But the following week there were e-mails from no fewer than *five* different radio shows asking me to come on and talk about my self-publishing success story. One of them was the most listened to weekend radio show in Ireland, with over 400,000 listeners. Big-name traditionally published authors (or their publicists!) would kill to get on the show, but somehow, I'd been invited onto it.

This was all in February 2011, and it bumped up my sales another few notches. But luck hasn't abandoned me yet. In February of this year (2012) I was asked to deliver Faber & Faber's first ever self-publishing course at their Faber Academy. This was a big gig—Faber had their reputation to uphold, and they were already taking a chance offering a self-publishing course where they were better known for literary courses like writing novels, short stories and poetry. They needed a self-publisher who (a) could speak in public, (b) wasn't one of the "down with the gatekeepers!" brigade but was actually quite sensible about self-publishing and (c) had had some success. The course was being organised by a friend I'd made on Twitter and when he mentioned the course to a friend *he'd* made on Twitter, she suggested that I'd be a perfect fit—because she was also my editor and had seen me speak back at the self-publishing conference the year before.

As I write this I've just been in a national newspaper in Ireland, am about to appear in the *Sunday Times* again and was on a national radio show last week talking about how to self-publish. (I have to admit, I probably have *50 Shades* to thank for all that work!) I also have three speaking engagements booked for September: one through my old friend Vanessa, one because someone googled "Irish self-publisher" and got me, and one through my appearance at Faber Academy. And all the while, my books continue to sell.

Now you can read that and say to yourself, "She was just *really* lucky." I *have* been lucky; I don't deny that. But in all those things I've just described, the luck accounted for only about 5% of the reason why things happened. I had control over the other 95%, and you do too. You can be ready for luck. You can point it your way. You can *make luck your only variable.*

Selling Books

My e-book sales took off by themselves, without any help from the press coverage or appearances. (The proof: most of them were in the US and in the UK. All my press, with the sole exception of a mention of my blog in *Writers' Magazine*, has been here in Ireland.) I did it through producing a good book with an attractive cover, maximising my Amazon listings, behaving professionally at all times, blogging, tweeting and using Facebook.

Becoming The Story

People are interested in my success because it has a few interesting angles. I went to work to Disney World, I successfully self-published a book that got rejected by traditional publishing, even though I've successfully self-published I'm still pursing traditional publication and I managed to promote my book for free. These are all more interesting stories than the one about me writing a book and self-publishing it. Find yourself an angle and then push it.

Doing Things Well

If someone is thinking about writing an article about self-publishing and your name comes up, that's not luck, It's your hard work paying off. You've been recognised as a good example. And if this person then goes to your blog and sees it laid out like the website of a professional writer, they know you're the person to help them with their research. If they see some multi-coloured widgets and a book cover that looks like crap, they'll find someone else. Similarly, because I was successful at my first speaking engagement, I got another one. And so on and so on. When I'm invited on to a radio show, I always arrive prepared and do everything I can to give a good interview. Then, the next time someone is thinking of using me as a subject, they know they can rely on me to deliver the goods.

Saying "Yes"

When Vanessa asked me to talk at the self-publishing conference, I said yes without even thinking, despite the fact that the last time I'd spoken in public was more than ten years before and during a debating class in school. I had no idea what I would say or how I would say it, and on the day I just noted some reminders to myself on a legal pad, got up and told my story. Not all speaking engagements pay but most do, and some are worth doing even if they don't pay, purely because of how much they'll raise your profile and the people you might meet there. If you can, say yes. You can't even *imagine* what opportunities may arise.

Networking

I always used to imagine networking as going to yuppie-filled events where you have to wear name-tags and shamelessly swap business cards with the other yuppies, and therefore something I could never bring myself to do. But what I've learned in the last year is that just using social media is networking. (The movie was called *The Social Network*, wasn't it?!) It's chatting to people at writing and book-related events you go to. It's just being friendly. It's offering to help people out with something, like an article they're writing or a giveaway they're trying to organise, or sending out complimentary copies of your book. Do you know how many of the opportunities I've got have come, directly or indirectly, out of me using Twitter? I'll tell you: *all of them*. (Although, I *do* recommend you get yourself some snazzy business cards!)

And finally, throughout all this I'm still doing what I've always done — blogging, tweeting, using Facebook — and I will always continue to do it. I always remind myself that among my blog readers is at least one person who bought and read my book a year ago, when it came out, and who doesn't need to hear anything else about it when they come to my blog. They want new content and if they don't get it, I'll lose them. Moreover, you never know who that new content will bring to your blog, and what opportunity they'll bring to you.

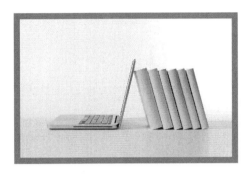

PART 6:
Being A
Self-Published Author

Sales Reporting And Payment

How do you know if someone has bought your book? How do you know when they bought it and from where? And why hasn't CreateSpace sent you that $2.05 they owe you from the copy of your book that your grandmother bought yesterday morning?

CreateSpace

Whenever you log on to CreateSpace and see your Member Dashboard, the number of copies your book has sold to date this month will be displayed next to its title. This updates not far off real time, in my experience, but only for Amazon.com and eStore sales. If you sell a book through any retailer in your expanded distribution channel (i.e. any retailer that isn't an Amazon site) it can take weeks to show up in your reports. Infuriatingly, you won't be able to see when or where those sales occurred — only that they have.

You can also run reports to look at your sales data from a specific period or overall. You can run these reports by title or sales channel, or you can run a report showing your payment history.

CreateSpace pay royalties 30 days after the end of the calendar month during which you earned those royalties, e.g. you get paid for sales that occurred in January at the end of February. Depending on your location this payment will be made via direct deposit or by cheque.

Since CreateSpace started selling in Europe as well, they now pay in three different currencies: dollars, British pounds and euro. The minimum payment threshold is $100/£100/€100. If you don't meet this threshold, your royalties will be carried over to the next month. All payments are sent with remittance advices.

Remember, when you're running sales reports that unless you provide tax information, the amount you get paid will be that less 30%.

Amazon KDP

You can see your monthly sales to date by logging on to Amazon KDP, clicking "Reports" at the top of the screen and then "Month-to-date Unit Sales." There's a separate tab for the Amazon.com, Amazon.co.uk, Amazon.de etc. Kindle stores. It's been my experience that these update in almost real time.

You might also see refunds listed in your sales reports. Don't get too upset about them — it's incredibly easy to accidentally download a Kindle book, especially on the Kindle itself, and this is normally why customers request refunds. I think the most I had was five in a month of eight hundred or so sales in total, so it's not a cause for concern.

If your title is enrolled in KDP Select, you'll also see "Borrows" and "Free" (books downloaded during your free promotion days) columns.

You can also access the last six weeks' worth of sales and royalties, which is a feature I've never understood considering payment periods are only ever a month long. (So seeing royalties from a six week period is just needlessly confusing.) You can also generate MS Excel reports for previous months, which are available after the 15th of that month.

You will receive three different sets of payments from KDP: the Amazon.com royalties will arrive by US dollar cheque (or direct deposit if you live in the States), the Amazon.co.uk royalties will arrive by British pound cheque and the other European Amazon stores will arrive in a euro cheque. Depending on your location, you might be eligible to receive direct deposits. For instance, I live in Ireland and receive dollar and pound cheques, but I get my European Kindle sales that occur in euro directly deposited into my account.

Payments are made 60 days after the end of the calendar month in which the royalties were earned, so at the end of February I got paid for what I'd sold in December.

KDP has minimum royalty thresholds too, such as:

- $10/£10/€10 for Electronic Funds Transfers (EFT)
- $100/£100/€100 for cheques.

If you don't make these thresholds, your royalties will carry over to the next payment period. All payments are sent with remittance advices.

Smashwords

Bet you were reading that and thinking, "Hey, this is all pretty straightforward. I sell books, I can check how many I've sold at any time and then the nice people pay me my share every month, and they even send cheques with very favourable exchange rates right to my door. Simples!"

Well here comes Smashwords, and they're about to ruin all of our fun. *And* mess up our otherwise pristine accounting system.

When you log on to Smashwords and see your dashboard, you'll see "Books Sold" at the top of one of the columns and a number underneath it. You'll also see the phrase "Total Books Sold" in the left-hand sidebar and next to it, the same number that appeared in the column.

But both those numbers are lies of omission, because they only refer to *books you sold on Smashwords.com.*

For months I thought that all I'd got out of the very painful experience of uploading my e-book to Smashwords (remember those 1,300 pages?) were nine sales. *Nine.* Until one evening I logged in and noticed that in the left-hand sidebar was a link called "Sales and Payment History." Curious, I clicked it, and discovered an Aladdin's Cave of sales I'd made that I knew nothing about, sales from the likes of Apple (iBooks), Barnes and Noble and Sony.

So forget what you see on the Dashboard, and go straight to Sales and Payment History. Here you'll see a summary of your sales listed on the left-hand side, and underneath that how much money Smashwords has collected on your behalf but not yet paid you. Underneath that again is how much they've paid you in the past.

In the last year, I have failed to find any rhyme or reason as to when Smashwords updates its third-party sales data, other than that they take absolutely *ages.* And even when they've reported your sales, they take another few months to pay you for them. But they only pay once a quarter (and by PayPal, hooray!) so there's no point getting your knickers in a twist over it. It's just annoying, especially when CreateSpace and KDP have spoiled us so. Although when the sales *do* come in, they're always a nice surprise.

The good news is that you can see how up to date your sales are, and how up to date your payments are. It softens the blow. *Slightly.* Exempt from all this are sales from Smashwords.com themselves, which are updated in real time along with their royalties.

Smashwords will pay you whatever balance is owing within 40 days of the close of each quarter, although normally it's more like 30 days. Their quarters are:

- Q1: January-March (paid at end of April-ish)
- Q2: April-June (paid at end of July-ish)
- Q3: July-September (paid at end of October-ish)
- Q4: October-December (paid at end of January-ish).

They also have a minimum payment threshold of $10 for PayPal payments.

Well, Hello There Peter Paranoia! Welcome Back

Kindly refrain from doing silly things like sending registered letters to Smashwords HQ threatening them with legal action because your friend told you that they bought your book from Barnes and Noble last Tuesday and even though you've waited patiently for *four whole days* you still haven't even been notified of this sale, much less paid for it, and if they don't hand over that $1.83 right this minute you'll have no choice but to instruct your lawyer to initiate proceedings.

Each of the services we're dealing with here clearly state on their websites that sales data is NOT reported in real time (although CreateSpace and KDP do an excellent job of reporting in *almost* real time). They are crystal clear about when they pay. They are not stealing your money, or hiding your sales. Chillax.

Keeping Accounts

You are now essentially running your own business and, unfortunately, that comes with a *lot* of paperwork. Your responsibilities will vary depending on where in the world you live, but most of us will have to file a tax return of some sort that tells our government:

- how much we earned from our books
- how much we had to spend to earn that money
- how much tax we owe on the difference.

In order to tell them those figures, we need to know them ourselves. This is why keeping organised and accurate accounts is *so* important. Back in 2010 I wasn't even thinking about this but let me tell you that after having to go back and do it, I'll never make the same mistake again. Here's a very simple system that I use for my own income and expenditure:

Create An Income/Expenditure Spreadsheet

Open a new Excel document and create four columns: number (format: *text*), date (format: *date*), description (format: *text*) and amount (format: *currency to two decimal points*). Now merge the top row of each of those four columns and label it "Income". Copy and paste so you have an identical set of columns immediately after them, and label those ones "Expenditure".

When you receive, for instance, a royalty payment, enter it in the first available space in the Income columns, making it the next available number ("10") and recording the date it was received, where it came from ("CreateSpace-July") and the amount it was for. Then take a red pen—I only use Sharpies—and write the number on the physical item (in this case the remittance advice) as well.

So let's say I bought some ink cartridges, and this was the tenth thing I had spent money on during my self-publishing operation thus far. I'd write "10" on the receipt in red, and enter the date I bought the cartridges, the word "ink cartridges" and the amount on the receipt in the corresponding row on my spreadsheet.

Make An "Accounts" E-mail Folder

All e-mail programs, be they web-based or on your computer, allow you to create folders. Create one now for your accounts. Then whenever you book a flight to travel to a speaking engagement, order a proof copy or purchase supplies online, you can send the confirmation e-mail directly into this folder where it'll stay safe until you have a chance to print it out.

Try to keep your Income/Expenditure spreadsheet up to date as things happen, as opposed to waiting until the items are printed out. This way it'll be in chronological order at the end of the year.

Buy Yourself Some Office Supplies

Is there anything more exciting than stationery shopping? If there is, I've yet to discover it. And there's nothing better than having a Staples spree when you actually *need* the stationery or office supplies in question. (Me needing the stationery I'm buying is *quite* the rare occurrence.) So go forth and purchase yourself an accordion file—one of those document holders with five or six separate compartments, ideally with a flap that closes with a snappy clasp—and a sturdy ring binder with some flashy dividers.

Label the divisions something like Royalty Statements, Other Income, Bills, Receipts, Tax Documents and anything else you think you might need. This is where we're going to store all our paperwork until we prepare our accounts at the end of the year; it's easy to throw a receipt or a remittance advice in here when we're in a rush, and we know it'll be safe there until we need it.

What's A Business Expense?

As a general rule, your taxable income will be your income minus your business expenses, and evidence of those are the most important documents you'll keep on file. It's up to you to decide—and maybe, to prove—what's a business expense, but here are some of mine to give you an idea:

- Anything directly linked with self-publishing my books: cover design, editing/proofreading services, proof copies, stock, etc.
- For a while I rented a "hot desk" in a shared office; that was decidedly a business expense
- My phone bill

- Business cards
- Membership fees of any professional body, e.g. The Society of Authors
- Postage, including postage on contest/giveaway prizes
- My WordPress personalised domain upgrade
- A new computer and word-processing software
- Office supplies
- Travel to/from speaking engagements, associated accommodation and food expenses
- If you work from home, you could feasibly add in *some* of your energy bills.

End of Year Accounts

If you manage to stay organised until the end of the year, you should find yourself with an up-to-date Income/Expenditure spreadsheet and all the relevant documents, if not yet printed out then ready and waiting for you to do so.

Then all you need to do is file them sequentially in your fancy ring binder, along with a print-out of your tallied spreadsheet. I also like to print out bank statements so I can see how much the British pound cheque for x was in my own currency. And that's it: you should be all set for your accountant or, if you're feeling patient, tallying your tax obligations yourself. Good luck!

US Tax Withholdings

Disclaimer: This is __NOT__ intended to be legal advice, and shouldn't be taken as such. Please refer to the instructions on the website of the self-publishing service in question for information specific to your country and your government's revenue agency for information specific to your situation.

CreateSpace, Amazon KDP and Smashwords are all based in the United States. For this reason, if they are helping you generate revenue they must, by law, ensure that you are paying income tax on that revenue and that you are paying it to the government of the United States. In practice this means they withhold 30% of emergency tax from all your royalty payments.

If you *live* in the United States, you can skip the rest of this bit because you already have the Mighty Social Security Number. You give it to the companies you're using along with a postal address, and they pay you. We're all *very* jealous.

If you *don't*, however, you'll have to apply for a sort of special Social Security Number that will enable you, depending on where you do live, to get all of your earnings from the companies in question and pay any due tax on them to your own government.

Note: earnings from European Amazons and Amazon.co.uk are not subject to withholding.

I recently saw someone on Twitter throwing poisonous darts Smashwords's way because of this "bureaucracy." Look, sunshine: Smashwords and their pals are not doing this because they get their kicks from rolling us around in red tape. They are doing it because *it is the law*. If you don't like it, I have a solution for you: DON'T SELF-PUBLISH YOUR BOOK.

You have three options when it comes to this tax situation:

The Easy Option

Do nothing. If you don't submit any US tax information, your earnings will be deducted 30%. The good news is that you don't have to do anything, but of course the bad news is you won't be getting paid all the money you earn. The worse news is that you'll have to pay more tax to your own government on the money you do receive, so you're effectively subjecting yourself to double taxation.

On the, um, plus side (?), you don't have to actually *do* anything.

If for example you live in the UK and the majority of your sales seem to be taking place on the Amazon.co.uk site, then maybe you don't mind paying 30% on your meagre US earnings.

If you choose this option, once a year—usually in February or March—the companies that have been withholding 30% of your earnings will send you a Form 1042-S: Foreign Person's US Source Income Subject to Withholding for your records. This will show the amount withheld in total for the previous calendar year.

The Difficult Option

If your country has a tax treaty with the United States, you may be eligible for a reduced rate of withheld tax or, potentially, eligible to have none of it withheld at all. But you need to jump through a few hoops first.

Start with applying to the United States' Internal Revenue Service (IRS) for an Individual Tax Identification Number (ITIN). To do this you'll need:

- A notarised copy of your passport
- A W-7 form
- A letter from Smashwords, Amazon KDP or CreateSpace to prove that you have a valid reason for applying for an ITIN. This can be requested from CreateSpace by e-mail; Smashwords have a link on their Payee Information page. (You need to have accrued at least $10 in royalties before you can ask Smashwords for one of these letters.) You only need a letter from ONE of these outlets.

You can get a W-7 form from here: **www.irs.gov/pub/irs-pdf/iw7.pdf**. You can get more information about completing the form here: **www.irs.gov/pub/irs-pdf/fw7.pdf**. When you have all your documentation together, mail everything to the address on the form.

Alternatively if you live near a US Embassy, you can take your documentation there. They will notarize a copy of your passport for you.

Then you'll be assigned your very own ITIN, which you'll receive in the mail. Now you need to complete a W8-BEN form, otherwise known as the mouthful Certificate of Foreign Status of Beneficial Owner for United States Tax Withholding, and send one to each of the three companies: CreateSpace, Amazon KDP and Smashwords.

You can get a W8-BEN form from here: **www.irs.gov/pub/irs-pdf/fw8ben.pdf**. You can get more information about completing the form here: **www.irs.gov/pub/irs-pdf/iw8ben.pdf**.

Check the individual websites for the mailing address to which you need to send them to.

I started this process back in April of last year (2011) and after three failed attempts, finally received my ITIN eight months later. I couldn't have done it without the advice of self-published bestselling author Sally Clements, who has kindly agreed to share her advice here.

Please note again that this is <u>NOT</u> intended to be legal advice, and shouldn't be taken as such. Please refer to the instructions on the website of the self-publishing service in question for information specific to your country and your government's revenue agency for information specific to your situation. What follows is intended as a guideline <u>only</u>.

"A first look at the W-7 form and its documentation can strike fear into the heart of the bravest author. So here's a step by step look at how I filled mine in, and received my ITIN. I was lucky to have the help of my publisher, The Wild Rose Press, and Canadian author Bronwyn Storm (**www.bronwynstorm.com**) in filling mine out. I'm based in Ireland, so do take that into account if you're applying from a different country.

The W-7 is filled in online.

Open up a blank W-7 from here: **www.irs.gov/pub/irs-pdf/iw7.pdf**

And the 'how to complete a W-7' instructions from here: **http://www.irs.gov/pub/irs-pdf/iw7.pdf**

And the online document which details tax treaty article numbers: **http://www.irs.gov/businesses/international/article/0,,id=96739,00.html#I**

First, read through the instructions file. Then leave it open or print it out to refer to while completing the W-7.

Here's how I completed it, starting at the top:

- Reason for submitting a W-7. You are a non-resident alien, so check "a"
- Check "h". Beside "h" list your exception. Authors are exception 1d. So put in here, *1(d) – Royalty income*
- After that, list your treaty county (in my case, "*Ireland*") and the treaty article number
- The treaty article number is found in this link, **http://www.irs.gov/businesses/international/article/0,,id=96739,00.html#I**
- And in the case of Ireland, is 12.

Now into the body of the form. It is important that no lines are left blank. I suggest filling this out carefully, with the instructions page open or printed off next to you, just to make sure you don't forget anything.

- Name
- Name at birth if different
- Applicant's mailing address. (Remember if you don't have a ZIP code, put "nozip")
- Foreign address if different from above. (If you don't enter an address in here, make sure to add N/A in all of these boxes, the form will be sent back if any line is left empty.)
- Birth information.

Now for the section on 'other information':

- 6a is your country or countries of citizenship
- 6b is your foreign tax ID number. I put my Irish tax number in here
- 6c is your U.S. Visa (if you have one)

- 6d I sent a notarized copy of my passport that I got from the American Embassy in Dublin. In order to get it, you have to make an appointment and attend with the completed W-7, money to pay for the notarized copy, a completed W-8 form and a copy of the letter from your publisher/Amazon/Smashwords, confirming that you need a W-7. Tick passport in this box, and fill in the relevant details. Remember to put N/A in any boxes that you aren't completing
- 6e is for visiting professors and students. I entered No
- 6f is therefore N/A
- 6g is therefore N/A.

Finally, the last section deals with signatures. I was the applicant, so signed, dated and added phone number. I put N/A in all the boxes pertaining to 'delegate'.

When you take your passport to receive a notarized copy, the official will scan and make sure that your W-7 and other documents are correct. Do please double-check that you have all relevant documentation by reading through the W-7 instructions before setting out.

Nine weeks later, I received my ITIN."

Thank you, Sally! You can find out more about Sally and her books on her blog, **http://sallyclements.blogspot.com**. Now a word of warning: I mentioned I had three failed attempts. The first time it was because I sent it to the wrong address. I was using an out-of-date form, and the address on it wasn't the correct one. Check online instead. The second time, my notarized copy was missing an apostille. What the fudge is that, you ask? I didn't know either. It's basically a stamp from your consulate saying that it's really a notarised copy of your passport. Shouldn't the notary bit satisfy that? You would think so, but this is the IRS we're talking about. I also live some distance from my nearest US Embassy, so I completed the entire process by mail. I'm guessing that's why I was waiting so much longer for my ITIN than Sally was waiting for hers.

Once you have your ITIN, fill in a W8 form for each of your companies (CreateSpace, Amazon KDP and Smashwords). Make sure you use the "Reference" line of the form to identify yourself to the company in question, i.e.:

- For CreateSpace, enter your Member ID which can be found on your Dashboard
- For Amazon KDP, enter your Publisher Number which can be found in the bottom right-hand corner of your Account Details page

- For Smashwords, enter the e-mail address associated with your account.

Now up until the beginning of this year, when CreateSpace et al received your W8 forms, they'd refund you all the tax they'd withheld to date. Unfortunately this no longer happens; any withheld money goes straight to the IRS. You'll start getting 100% royalty cheques instead of 70% immediately, but if you want the rest of that money back, you'll have to apply for the IRS to it. Or you could use **TaxBack.com**. They will prepare your tax return for you, deal with the IRS on your behalf and ensure that you get all the refunds you're entitled to for either a small flat fee or a percentage of your refund. I've used them myself and I can highly recommend them.

The Suspiciously Easy Option

Technically you are an individual who is earning income through the US, and so *technically* you should apply for an ITIN. But there is another, simpler way: applying for an Employer Identification Number, or EIN. I think strictly-speaking this is for self-publishers who ignored my advice and set up their own publishing companies, but I will tell you that I know people without publishing companies who have EINs and then you can make of that what you will.

Self-publisher **David Gaughran** got an EIN, and he shared his experience on my blog a few months back. The process basically consists of:

- Calling the IRS at +1 267 941 1099
- Telling them you're applying for an EIN for a foreign entity and, if they ask, that you're a business owner
- If they ask for a SS-4, saying you were told you don't need that and, if they persist, hanging up, calling back and trying your luck with someone else
- Giving them your personal details
- Telling them that, yes, it's for compliance with withholding
- Telling them that, yes, it's for e-books
- Having a pen to write down your EIN. Which you just got. Yes, *over the phone*. In *minutes*. With not a notarised document in sight.

Hence the *suspiciously* bit. Look, here's what I'd do. If you've started the ITIN process, continue it. If not, try to get an EIN. If you don't, apply for an ITIN instead. But do it as *soon* as you start earning royalties.

The Easy Option That Costs Money

Taxback.com also offer ITIN and EIN services, if you don't mind paying someone else to take care of this particular headache for you.

Updating And Unpublishing Books

Chances are you'll need to update or make changes to your paperback and e-books at some stage in the future. This may be immediately after you release it (because you didn't check that proof properly, did you?) or months or even a year later, when you're about to release your second book and you want to put a teaser chapter at the end of your paperback.

Can you do this? Yes. *How* do you do this? Well, I'll tell you.

Updating Your CreateSpace Paperback

Go to the Project Homepage of the title you want to change and click "Interior." You should see a button that either says "Change" or "Unlock." Click it. Upload a new PDF file with your desired changes and then go through the tail end of your publishing process again: submit for processing, order a proof copy and then check and approve the proof. While all this is going on, your book will be on "hold" and will probably become unavailable on Amazon.com. If you do it quickly that's all that'll happen (because the other retailers can take up to 8 weeks to update), but leave it long enough and the others will go the same way.

In all likelihood there will be a delay between you updating your book and customers receiving the updated edition when they purchase your book. This shouldn't be more than 8 weeks.

You have another option, which I've just done myself and do NOT recommend: release a new, separate edition. This is like a nightmare in a teacup, and leads to all sorts of crazy complicated Amazon problems. Technically you should do this if the first edition of your book varies from the second (because remember, we're supposed to use a new ISBN for each new edition) but honestly, I wouldn't even bother. It's way too much trouble.

Updating Your E-Books

This is even easier: make your changes and upload new MS Word files. Simples! Make sure you are replacing the file in your existing edition and NOT creating a new edition from scratch, which will only lead to confusion.

When you upload a new edition of your e-book, anyone who has purchased an older edition can download the newest one, but future purchasers will only have access to the newest file.

Deleting Your Book

Hopefully you'll never want to do this, but you *can* delete your titles. Amazon, however, won't delete the listings (because they want to keep them active in case anyone has second-hand editions to sell, etc.) and so you'll forever be a ghost on there, showing "Available from these sellers." Spooky...

When It Doesn't Work

If your book doesn't sell or sells for a while and then drops off the radar, then you potentially have one or more of the following problems:

Your Book Looks Like a Pile of Poo

It doesn't matter if you've written the next *Cloud Atlas*, *Room* or *The Time Traveller's Wife*. If the cover looks like something your cat threw up and then another cat threw up on, it's not going to sell.

Think of all the hard work you have to do just to get me headed to your Amazon listing with an idea that, hey, I might actually buy that book. But then I get there and see a cover that assures me you're a self-publisher, putting a huge question mark over whether or not your book is any good. (Call this unfair all you want; it's *reality*.) And if I can tell you've self-published just by the quality of your cover, i.e. how much it looks like one of those crappy Cover Creator templates, then I can also tell that you haven't self-published very well and my money will stay in my pocket.

Same goes for clicking your "Look Inside" on Amazon and seeing that the first line of your book is at the top of page 1, and it says "Chapter One." I'm not looking for perfection here, but I am looking for a sense of what a book is supposed to be like, i.e. *professionalism*. I want a quality product in exchange for my money and if you can't give me that, I'm not going to give you my money.

The biggest tragedy here is that some really good self-published books don't get read because their covers are rubbish or their listings don't have the right information or the author's blog is a mess. Writing a good book is the hardest part. How would you feel if, having mastered that, everything else you did—or didn't bother to do—let you down? What a wasted opportunity.

And please, spare me the "people aren't giving my book a chance!" excuse. No, really. *Please.* Your job is not to convince people to give your book a charitable chance. Your job is to convince people that they want to read it.

You Haven't Worked Hard Enough

Self-publishing is a business, and you need to treat it as such. You are selling a product, even if your ultimate goal is not financial. To become a successful self-publisher you need to consider yourself an entrepreneur.

If you were talking to someone who is single-handedly starting up their own business, what kind of things would you expect them to say? I would be surprised if they didn't tell me they'd worked all the hours that were in the day to get their business up and running, sacrificed time with friends and family, and focused all of their energies on one thing: achieving success. Does this sound like a description of you getting your book to sell?

While you were writing the book, you were a writer. You could live *la vie boheme,* hang out in Parisian-style cafes smoking Marlboro Reds and talk about how you'd spend your last euro on a book instead of food because art nourishes you more. (Or, if you're me, spend much of the day in your PJs dreaming about hanging out in Parisian cafes drinking tiny espressos.) This was allowed because you were a writer: a creative, head-in-the-clouds type. But once you turned your scribbles into a book, slapped a price tag on it and encouraged/begged people to buy it, you got into business. You became that entrepreneur.

I'm continually amazed at stories of self-publishers who lob their book up on Amazon, set up a static website and then sit back and relax, expecting the readers to come to them. A website is not a shop window; people will *never* happen upon it unless you send them there.

As for self-publishers who refuse to send out review copies or will only offer PDFs because they "can't afford" it, well, I have a special place reserved on my People Who Have Annoyed Me list for *you.* If you didn't have any money at all, would you still open a restaurant or try to bring a new product to the market? No. Of course not. And as I've shown in this book, the money you do have to spend isn't that much at all, especially if you're creative (which, as a writer, I'm assuming you are!). But you *do* have to spend it.

E-books are exploding now, and the self-publishers who got in on the act are reaping the rewards. As I type this, the magical interweb is whispering about a mega-selling e-book author in the US who is poised to sign her name to a *seven-figure book deal* by the end of this week. Reading these stories, it's easy to come to the conclusion that uploading an e-book to Amazon guarantees sales and success, but this isn't true. It's never true. If you ever read a story like this, I'd encourage you to ignore the sensationalist headlines, find the author's blog and see what *they* have to say about the reason for their success. It's always a variation on the same thing: *lots of hard work.*

If you want to treat self-publishing your book as a hobby, feel free. Just don't expect me to pay for what this hobby produces.

You Haven't Worked Hard for Long Enough

You have to give this thing at least a year. Self-publishing is not a sprint, but a marathon. You're not going to sell every single copy you'll ever sell in the first week, and you can't expect to sit back and relax after just a month.

Self-publishing expert Aaron Shepard says that a POD book takes a year to reach its full potential. Now while I think e-books skew this a bit, it's still essentially true. It's certainly been my experience that after almost a year of slogging away and having good results, everything came together and suddenly became *great.*

This has a lot to do with Amazon, I believe, where as I've already said, sales lead to more sales. Imagine a year's worth of purchases, recommendations, appearances in "Customers Also Bought", reviews, etc. etc. Every day your book is getting more and more primed to sell. Just hang in there.

You Haven't Done It Right

Somewhere along the way, you've ignored something I recommended. This won't work if you do everything except instead of a blog, you just create a website. Or you do everything but you price your e-book $9.99. Or you do everything except put your book on Amazon's Kindle store because you don't like the company.

These are the most common areas, I think, where self-publishers make mistakes:

- **Pricing.** They price their work too high—it needs to be priced to sell
- **Cover.** I think we've already covered that—no pun intended!
- **Delusions of grandeur.** Symptoms include saying things like, "I know if someone just gives my book a chance, they'll love it" and embarrassingly gushing, ahem, *reviews,* that compare it to Hemingway, Orwell, etc. Also known as Coming Across As a Jerk No One Wants to See Succeed Syndrome.

Your Book Isn't Good

Maybe your book just isn't any good. No one wants to hear this, but sometimes that is the case. If you've followed my advice and got some positive feedback from unbiased, professional sources, then this shouldn't be the case. But if you haven't and you've self-published after your sister who, like, reads a book a *week* said she "enjoyed" it, then it might well be.

Failed self-publishers sometimes say things like:

- I know the book is good; it just doesn't have a very wide appeal
- Its market is very niche
- It's very different to your book, so I can't do what you did
- People won't give self-published books a chance
- I can't explain what it's like in a few sentences; people need to read the whole book.

But these are all *excuses*, and poor ones at that.

- If your book doesn't have appeal why does it exist? Are you a *Selling Houses* fan, by any chance?
- *Mousetrapped* was super-niche; all the agents and publishers I sent it to confirmed that for me. But I found a way around it by getting people interested in reading more of my writing as opposed to me writing about a specific topic.
- When you promote your book online, sell your paperbacks from Amazon and publish e-books, you are effectively selling to the whole world. So if you can't find an audience, your readers must be on another celestial body.
- There is nothing in this book that can't be applied to any type of book, so save me the whole my-book-is-a-novel-yours-is-non-fiction crap. All the big selling e-book authors write fiction, so you're going to have to come up with a better excuse than that, I'm afraid.
- If people aren't giving your book a chance [eye roll], that's your fault. Remember: our job is to convince them that they want to read it, not do us a favour by picking it up out of charity.
- If you can't write a moderately-decent blurb for your own book, then I have my doubts about you being able to write a moderately-decent book.

And if you want to claim that the kind of people who would want to read your book don't use the internet, fine, but then why did you publish in a way that only makes your book available online?

Thousands if not millions of excellent books enter the book world every month, and some of them disappear again without trace. I'm not saying that your book isn't selling just because it isn't good, nor am I saying that if your book is good it will definitely sell. There will always be the bestseller and the title discounted on the remainder pile, and no one can say exactly why this is. But if your book isn't selling, ask yourself could it be down to one of the reasons I've just outlined — because, if it *is* one of them, then you might be able to do something about it.

And That's All, Folks

And that, my friends, is that. I hope I've helped you self-publish and sell your book, kept you mildly entertained for however long it took you to read this book or, at the very least, persuaded you not to ask Amazon — and therefore, me — for a refund.

If you've read this book all in one go and before you've even finished *writing* your book, I'm sure it sounds like an awful lot of work. But most of it is *fun*, and when someone sends you a message saying how much they've enjoyed your book, or you get a cheque for money your writing earned, or you get called *a writer*, it all feels worth it. And I don't want to get all dramatic and emotional now, mere sentences before the end, but doing this could even change your life.

It's changed mine.

I'll leave you with the five biggest lessons I've learned since I self-published my book:

1. Everything takes much longer than you think it's going to take
2. You can't correct your own book
3. Never, ever, EVER use tabs to indent your paragraphs
4. All the hard work is worth it — eventually!
5. No matter what happens, hang in there for at least a year.

And if you were wondering what you do once a year has passed, well...

Then you release another book, and do it all over again.

Good luck!

(You can do this.)

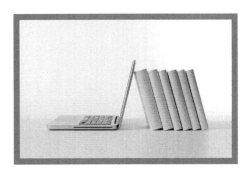

Some Useful Stuff

Useful Links

Social Media

www.wordpress.com
www.blogger.com
www.twitter.com
www.facebook.com

Print On Demand Services

www.createspace.com
www.lulu.com

E-book Self-Publishing

kdp.amazon.com
www.smashwords.com

Manuscript Assessment & Editorial Services

www.inkwellwriters.ie
www.bubblecow.co.uk
www.writing.ie

Financial Services

www.paypal.com
www.xe.com (currency converter)
www.taxback.com

Photo Stock Websites

www.istockphoto.com
www.shutterstock.com
www.corbisimages.com

Cover Design Services

www.designforwriters.com
Contact: Andrew, who does my covers

Video Sharing

www.youtube.com
www.vimeo.com

Author Profiles

www.goodreads.com
authorcentral.amazon.com
authorcentral.amazon.co.uk

Printing Services

www.vistaprint.com

E-book Reading Applications

www.adobe.com/products/digitaleditions
www.amazon.com/gp/kindle/pc/download
www.amazon.com/gp/kindle/mac/download

Miscellaneous

www.xtranormal.com (type-to-animate video site)
www.random.org (random number generator)
www.theselfpublishingreview.wordpress.com (review site)
www.google.com/reader (Google Reader)
www.mailchimp.com (mailing list and newsletters)
www.kindleboards.com (Kindle forums)
www.ebookpartnership.com (e-book conversion)
www.bufferapp.com (scheduling tweets application)

Me

www.catherineryanhoward.com
www.twitter.com/cathryanhoward
www.facebook.com/mousetrappedbook

Books I Recommend

Even though some of these books are not about self-publishing or even writing with self-publishing in mind, I have found them extremely useful.

Writing the Book

How Not To Write a Novel: 200 Mistakes to Avoid At All Costs if You Ever Want to Get Published, Howard Mittelmark and Sandra Newman, Penguin, 2009

Story: Structure, Substance, Style and the Prinicples of Screenwriting, Robert McKee, Methuen Publishing, 1999

Nail Your Novel: Why Writers Abandon Books and How You Can Draft, Fix and Finish With Confidence, Roz Morris, Kindle Media, 2010

Promoting the Book

Aiming at Amazon, Aaron Shepard, Shepard Publications, 2007

Wannabe a Writer We've Heard Of?, Jane Wenham Jones, Accent Press, 2010

Tweet Right: The Sensible Person's Guide to Twitter, Nicola Morgan, Crabbit Publishing, 2012

The Writing Life

On Writing: A Memoir of the Craft, Stephen King, New English Library, 2001

The Forest for the Trees: An Editor's Advice to Writers, Betsy Lerner, Riverhead Books, 2010

Other Self-Publishing Guides

The Naked Author: A Guide to Self-publishing, Alison Baverstock, Bloomsbury, 2011

Not a Gold Rush: The Taleist Self-Publishing Survey, Dave Cornford and Steven Lewis, Amazon Digital Services, 2012

Shameless Promotion of
My Other Self-Publishing Book

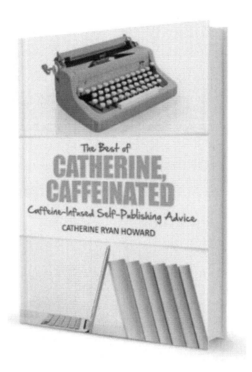

Coffee addict and bestselling self-published author Catherine Ryan Howard has been blogging about her adventures in self-publishing (or self-printing, as she likes to call it) on her popular blog, Catherine, Caffeinated, since November 2009.

Now all of her caffeine-infused advice, information, tips and tricks—all 120,000 words of it—have been compiled in this e-book title. Learn everything Catherine did in the order she learned it, or use the category listings to navigate the posts by specific topic.

The ideal companion to any self-publishing/printing adventure,
***The Best of Catherine, Caffeinated* is best enjoyed with the highly**
caffeinated beverage of your choice.

Just 99c on the Kindle Store

About the Author

CATHERINE RYAN HOWARD is a writer, blogger and coffee enthusiast from Cork, and one of Ireland's most successful self-published authors.

Catherine self-published her first book, a travel memoir called *Mousetrapped: A Year and A Bit in Orlando, Florida*, in March 2010, after her book about Space Shuttle launches, humidity-challenged hair, Bruce Willis, the Ebola virus and an Irish girl working in Walt Disney World failed to find a publisher. Starting from scratch and using only social media, Catherine has managed to shift over 12,000 copies of *Mousetrapped* to date, and gone on to release two other full-length books: *Backpacked: A Reluctant Trip Across Central America* and *Self-Printed: The Sane Person's Guide to Self-Publishing*. She is also the author of *More Mousetrapped: A Little Bit More From That Year and A Bit* and *The Best of Catherine, Caffeinated: Caffeine-Infused Self-Publishing Advice*. Her next book, *Travelled: 10 Tales About Not Staying At Home*, is scheduled for release towards the end of 2012.

Her success story has been featured in the likes of the *Irish Independent*, *Sunday Times* and *Irish Examiner* newspapers, and Catherine has been interviewed on numerous radio shows including Arts Extra on BBC Radio Ulster and The Marian Finucane Show on RTE Radio 1. She also delivered Faber Academy's first ever self-publishing course at Faber & Faber, London, in February 2012 and continues to be a guest tutor there.

Before writing full-time, Catherine worked as an administrator in the Netherlands, a campsite courier in France and a front desk agent in a hotel in Walt Disney World, Florida. She dreams of becoming a NASA astronaut when she grows up. (She's 30.)

She currently divides her time between the desk and the sofa.

www.catherineryanhoward.com

Acknowledgements

Thank you to Andrew Brown, Alison Baverstock, Averill Buchanan, Sally Clements, Joel Friedlander, David Gaughran, Lena Goldfinch, Michael Harling, Diana Horner, Katie Mack, Nicola Morgan, Roz Morris, Vanessa O'Loughlin, David Wright, the lovely people who read my blog, books and tweets, and my Nespresso machine which was pulling double-duty during the updating of this book.

And thank YOU for reading.

Now kindly go tell everyone you've ever met in your life about this book.

(Joke!)

(Sort of…)